Discrimination in International Investment Arbitration

OXFORD INTERNATIONAL ARBITRATION SERIES

Series Editor: Loukas Mistelis

The aim of this series is to publish works of quality and originality on specific issues in international commercial and investment arbitration. The series aims to provide a forum for the exploration of important emerging issues and those issues not adequately dealt with in leading works. It should be of interest to both practitioners and scholarly lawyers.

Discrimination in International Investment Arbitration

MICHAIL RISVAS

Lecturer in Law, University of Southampton, Law School

OXFORD
UNIVERSITY PRESS

OXFORD
UNIVERSITY PRESS

Great Clarendon Street, Oxford, OX2 6DP,
United Kingdom

Oxford University Press is a department of the University of Oxford.
It furthers the University's objective of excellence in research, scholarship,
and education by publishing worldwide. Oxford is a registered trade mark of
Oxford University Press in the UK and in certain other countries

First Edition published in 2023

Published in the United States of America by Oxford University Press
198 Madison Avenue, New York, NY 10016, United States of America

British Library Cataloguing in Publication Data
Data available

Library of Congress Control Number: 2023943280

ISBN 978–0–19–285726–2

DOI: 10.1093/law-iic/9780192857262.001.0001

Printed and bound by
CPI Group (UK) Ltd, Croydon, CR0 4YY

General Editor's Preface

This series of monographs is dedicated to specific issues in international arbitration law and practice and gives authors the opportunity and the challenge of a more in-depth treatment than is possible in leading generalist works. It also provides an international forum for the profound exploration of important practical and theoretical matters and will further the development of arbitration as a self-luminous academic discipline and major international legal practice area.

This twenty-fourth title in the series is a monograph by an experienced academic and practitioner. It provides a profound analysis of the scholarship and the case law of investment treaty arbitral tribunals on *non-discrimination obligations* contained in international investment agreements: more specifically, National Treatment, Most-Favoured-Nation (MFN), non-impairment clauses, and, finally, the non-discrimination components of Fair and Equitable Treatment (FET) and expropriation. Dr Risvas demonstrated that 'there is no jurisprudence constante in relation to key legal questions, ranging from the content of the applicable legal test and the meaning of each step of the legal test to procedural questions regarding the burden and standard of proof, as well as the standard of review' in relation to non-discrimination obligations. He offers, in this monograph 'a comprehensive and systematic analytical and normative framework of what is perhaps one of the most … complex [and] … chaotic areas of international investment law, covering both substantive as well as procedural and evidentiary questions'.

Over the last fifteen year there is already a significant amount of writing on the topic.[1] However, there is no consensus, let alone clarity, as to what constitutes discrimination and what is the relevant legal test to establish discrimination in investment arbitration cases. While likeness and less favourable treatment are clearly considered undisputed conditions and criteria for establishing discrimination (notwithstanding the different approaches by tribunal depending on industry sector, regulatory framework, and issues of treaty interpretation), there is no similar consensus in respect of intent to discriminate or the relation of the conditions with regulatory policy objectives of the State adopting measures which may be deemed discriminatory. Ultimately, the

[1] See, eg, N DiMascio and J Pauwelyn, 'Nondiscrimination in Trade and Investment Treaties: Worlds Apart or Two Sides of the Same Coin?' (2008) 102 American Journal of International Law 48; F Baetens, 'Discrimination on the basis of Nationality: Determining Likeness in Human Rights and Investment Law' in SW Schill (ed), *International Investment Law and Comparative Public Law* (OUP 2010) 279–315; F Ortino, 'Non-Discriminatory Treatment in Investment Disputes' in P-M Dupuy, E-U Petersmann, and F Francioni (eds), *Human Rights in International Investment Law and Arbitration* (OUP 2009) 344–366; AD Mitchell, D Heaton, and C Henckels, *Non-Discrimination and the Role of Regulatory Purpose in International Trade and Investment Law* (Edward Elgar 2016); A Reinisch and C Schreuer, *International Protection of Investments: The Substantive Standards* (CUP 2020), Chs 4–6.

two options are either a case-by-case assessment or a more objective standard where intent and policy objectives would not have any impact on determining whether discrimination exists or not. Dr Risvas sheds light on the approaches adopted by various arbitral tribunals and provides much needed clarity. He also explores the different non-discrimination obligations provided for in international investment agreements. He argues that national treatment, MFN, non-discrimination under the FET standard, and expropriation 'all fall within the same paradigm of discrimination'.

The book, following a substantive introduction, is organized in three substantive chapters and one concluding chapter.

Chapter 2 provides the paradigms of discrimination in US, EU, and human rights anti-discrimination law: disparate treatment and disparate impact discrimination and put forward the argument that discrimination obligations in international investment law inevitably fall within the disparate treatment paradigm. It also examines the relationship between different non-discrimination obligations contained in international investment agreements.

Chapter 3 is dedicated to the legal test for establishing violations of the different non-discrimination obligations contained in international investment agreements with particular focus on likeness and less favourable treatment. It also discusses the concept of 'discrimination "because of" a protected ground, discriminatory intent and public policy justifications'.

Finally, Chapter 4 explores evidentiary matters, the allocation of the burden of proof, the standard of review, and the standard of proof. Chapter 5 provide concluding remarks.

This is a comprehensive and significant work on non-discrimination in the law and practice of investment arbitration. It is thorough and focused in its scope, research, and analysis, classically conceived and written as a monograph. It is also easily accessible and authoritative at the same time and provides a useful tool for arbitration practitioners and scholars alike.

Loukas Mistelis
Virginia Water
23 July 2023

Acknowledgements

'Our words are the children of many people'.[1] And indeed many people have helped me in this relatively long writing journey. The idea for this book can be traced back to my doctoral dissertation which I completed at the University of Oxford under the supervision of Professor Dan Sarooshi KC. Dan combines rare intelligence and even rarer kindness and has been very supportive during, as well as after, my DPhil. I am particularly grateful to the Academy of Athens, and, in particular, to Professor Emmanuel Roucounas for awarding me the scholarship for postgraduate studies in public international law, as well as the Faculty of Law and Balliol College of the University of Oxford for the Volterra Fietta scholarship for public international law and other smaller grants during my Oxford years. I would also like to thank the examiners of the initial and final versions of my doctoral dissertation: Professor Andrew Lang (at the time at the London School of Economics, and now at the University of Edinburg), Professor Catherine Redgwell (at the time Chichele Professor of Public International Law at Oxford), Professor Martins Paparinskis (at the time at Oxford, and now at University College London), and Dr Martin Dawidowicz (at the time at Oxford, and now at the University of Uppsala). I am also indebted to other Oxford faculty members and, in particular, to Professors Dapo Akande and Liz Fisher.

Many thanks are also owned to Professor Stephan Schill (University of Amsterdam), who has been supportive for several years now. I am also grateful to all my colleagues at the University of Southampton for their support and in particular the current and previous Head of School, Professors Werner Scholtz, Brenda Hannigan, Harry Annison, and, in particular, Professor Emily Reid and Dr Megan Pearson (who read large parts of the book manuscript).

At Oxford, I was supported by a network of friends and fellow international law students whom I should thank: Dr Antonios Kouroutakis (also later a colleague at IE University in Spain), Dr Kosmas Kaprinis, Dr Vasiliki Brisimi, Dr Maria Ioannidou, Dr Julian Nowag, Dimitrios Katsikis, Dr Velimir Živković, Dr Ryan Manton (also later a colleague at Three Crowns), Dr Anna Begemann, and Dr Gregory Messenger. At IE University I would also like to thank Professor Marco De Benito.

In Paris, initially at Freshfields and later at Three Crowns, I was fortunate to meet Dr Georgios Petrochilos KC, to whom I am grateful because he trusted me with my first real job in international arbitration and offered me tough but invaluable training. In addition to Georgios, working in international arbitration I met wonderful people, including Anastasia Davis Bondarenko, Antonios Vassiloconstantakis, Stavros

[1] G Seferis, translated by E Keely and P Sherrard, *George Seferis: Collected Poems* (Princeton University Press 1967) 409 ('Είναι παιδιά πολλών ανθρώπων τα λόγια μας').

Michalopoulos, Athina Papaefstratiou-Fouchard, Gisele Stephens-Chu, Leon Firios, Louis-Alexis Bret, Ben Prewett, Mark Wassouf, and Dr Tariq Baloch. Special thanks are also owned to my three French friends and colleagues who made me feel welcome and less of a foreigner when I arrived in Paris: Charles Bouttier, Yann Dehaudt-Delville, and Alexandre Meyniel.

At the University of Athens, where I completed my first degree in law I was influenced and/or supported by several professors. Special thanks are owned to Professors Andreas Chelmis, Maria Gavouneli, Fay Pazartzis, Philippos Spyropoulos, Nikos Alivizatos, Christos Mylonopoulos, and the late Stavros Tsakyrakis. Dr Anastasios Gourgourinis, who—although he joined the Law Faculty after I graduated—has been a true friend for more than a decade now. I would also like to thank Professor Stelios Stamatopoulos of the University of Thrace. I should also thank the friends whom I met at the University of Athens, including Dr Michail Dekastros (with whom I worked together Three Crowns in Paris and who has always been there for me in good and bad times), Demosthenes Tsoukalas, Dr Orestis Omran, Dr Stavros Pantazopoulos, Dr Stavros Makris, Dr Andriani Kalintiri, and Dr Eirini Kikarea (among others).

I would like to thank Oxford University Press, its delegates and dedicated staff as well as the Oxford International Arbitration series editor, Professor Loukas Mistelis, and the five anonymous reviewers of the book proposal and manuscript.

Special mention needs to be made of my four-year old daughter, Alexandra, as this book is one of the many reasons she spent less time than she should with her father. I would also like to thank her mother (and my ex-wife), Eugénie, for being an exceptional mother to her.

Finally, I am grateful for their support to my sister, Constantina, and, above all else, my parents, Aleka and Nikos, and my aunt, Vasiliki. I dedicate this book to them.

Any errors or omissions are solely my responsibility.

The text is, as far as possible, current as of April 2023.

London, 18 April 2023

Contents

Table of Cases

INTERNATIONAL COURTS

COURT OF JUSTICE OF THE EUROPEAN UNION

EUROPEAN COURT OF HUMAN RIGHTS

INTER-AMERICAN COURT OF HUMAN RIGHTS

INTERNATIONAL COURT OF JUSTICE

PERMANENT COURT OF INTERNATIONAL JUSTICE

UN HUMAN RIGHTS COMMITTEE

INTERNATIONAL TRIBUNALS

International Criminal Tribunal for the Former Yugoslavia

INTERNATIONAL ARBITRAL TRIBUNALS

ICC (INTERNATIONAL CHAMBER OF COMMERCE)

ICSID (INTERNATIONAL CENTRE FOR SETTLEMENT OF INVESTMENT DISPUTES) (including ICSID Additional Facility)

IUSCT (IRAN-UNITED STATES CLAIMS TRIBUNAL)

ITLOS (INTERNATIONAL TRIBUNAL FOR THE LAW OF THE SEA)

LCIA (LONDON COURT OF INTERNATIONAL ARBITRATION)

PCA (PERMANENT COURT OF ARBITRATION)

SCC (STOCKHOLM CHAMBER OF COMMERCE)

UNCITRAL (UNITED NATIONS COMMISSION ON INTERNATIONAL TRADE LAW)

UNITED NATIONS RIAA AWARDS

OTHER TRIBUNAL DECISIONS

WORLD TRADE ORGANIZATION

APPELLATE BODY

NATIONAL JURISDICTIONS

Canada

France

Germany

United Kingdom

United States

Table of Legislation

TREATIES AND CONVENTIONS

DRAFT CONVENTIONS

INTERNATIONAL AND REGIONAL TRADE AGREEMENTS

EUROPEAN UNION

Treaties and Agreements

Directives

Regulations

NATIONAL JURISDICTIONS

RULES OF PROCEDURE

ARBITRAL RULES

Abbreviations

AB	Appellate Body
ACHR	American Convention on Human Rights
AfCFTA	African Continental Free Trade Area
AJIL	American Journal of International Law
ALI	American Law Institute
ASIL	American Society of International Law
BIT	Bilateral Investment Treaty
CETA	Comprehensive Economic and Trade Agreement
CPTPP	Comprehensive and Progressive Agreement for Trans-Pacific Partnership
CUP	Cambridge University Press
DCS	Directly Competitive or Substitutable
DR–CAFTA	Dominican Republic–Central America Free Trade Agreement
ECHR	European Convention on Human Rights
ECtHR	European Court of Human Rights
EJIL	European Journal of International Law
EU	European Union
FCN	Friendship, Commerce and Navigation
FDI	foreign direct investment
FET	fair and equitable treatment
GATT	General Agreement on Tariffs and Trade
GC	Grand Chamber
IACHR	Inter-American Court of Human Rights
ICCPR	International Covenant on Civil and Political Rights
ICJ	International Court of Justice
ICLQ	International and Comparative Law Quarterly
ICSID	International Centre for the Settlement of Investment Disputes
IISD	International Institute for Sustainable Development
ILC	International Law Commission
ILM	International Legal Materials
ILR	International Law Reports
ITLOS	International Tribunal for the Law of the Sea
IUSCT	Iran–United States Claims Tribunal
JIEL	Journal of International Economic Law
JWIT	Journal of World Investment and Trade
LCIA	London Court of International Arbitration
LGDJ	Librairie générale de droit et de jurisprudence
MFN	Most Favoured Nation
MLR	Modern Law Review
NAFTA	North American Free Trade Agreement
OECD	Organisation for Economic Co-operation and Development
OUP	Oxford University Press

PCA	Permanent Court of Arbitration
PCIJ	Permanent Court of International Justice
RGDIP	Revue Générale de Droit International Public
RIAA	Reports of International Arbitral Awards
SCC	Stockholm Chamber of Commerce
SCM	Subsidies and Countervailing Measures
SPS	Sanitary and Phytosanitary
TBT	Technical Barriers to Trade
TCA	Trade and Cooperation Agreement
TFEU	Treaty on the Functioning of the European Union
UCLA	University of California, Los Angeles
UNCITRAL	United Nations Commission on International Trade Law
USCMA	United States–Mexico–Canada Agreement
VAT	Value Added Tax
VCLT	Vienna Convention on the Law of the Treaties
WTO	World Trade Organization

Note on Citations

This book follows the Oxford University Standard for the Citation of Legal Authorities (OSCOLA). Awards and decisions of arbitral tribunals, unless otherwise stated, can be found at <https://www.italaw.com/>, <https://icsid.worldbank.org/en/>, <or https://legal.un.org/riaa/>. All the WTO or GATT reports and materials can be found at the WTO website (<https://www.wto.org/>). All reports of GATT Panel and WTO Panels and the Appellate Body are cited using the official short title used by the WTO. All decisions of the International Court of Justice and the Permanent Court of Justice as well as the parties' pleadings can be found at <https://www.icj-cij.org/>, decisions of the Court of Justice of the European Union at <https://curia.europa.eu/jcms/jcms/j_6/en/>, judgments of the European Court of Human Rights at <https://hudoc.echr.coe.int/sites/eng/Pages/search.aspx>, and decision of the Iran–US Claims Tribunal at <https://iusct.com/>.

Internal references and emphasis in quotations are omitted unless otherwise indicated.

The author acted as counsel for the Claimants in *Marfin Investment Group Holdings SA and others v Republic of Cyprus*, ICSID Case No ARB/13/27, which is discussed in this book.

Note on Citations

1
Introduction

> Now the judge restores equality: if we represent the matter by a line divided into two unequal parts, he takes away from the greater segment that portion by which it exceeds one-half of the whole line, and adds it to the lesser segment. When the whole has been divided into two halves, people then say that they 'have their own', having got what is equal. This is indeed the origin of the word dikaion (just): it means dicha (in half), as if one were to pronounce it dichaion; and a dikast (judge) is a dichast (halver).
>
> Aristotle[*]

1.1 Setting the Scene

The Hague, 1931–1932. Following a Polish request to the League of Nations High Commissioner, the Permanent Court of International Justice (PCIJ), the predecessor of the International Court of Justice (ICJ), was called upon to decide, inter alia, 'the exact interpretation of Article 104(5) of the Treaty of Versailles'.[1] Article 104(5) contained a non-discrimination clause stipulating that:

> The Principal Allied and Associated Powers undertake to negotiate a Treaty between the Polish Government and the Free City of Danzig, which shall come into force at the same time as the establishment of the said Free City, with the following objects:
>
> ...

[*] ('ὁ δὲ δικαστὴς ἐπανισοῖ, καὶ ὥσπερ γραμμῆς εἰς ἄνισα τετμημένης, ᾧ τὸ μεῖζον τμῆμα τῆς ἡμισείας ὑπερέχει, τοῦτ' ἀφεῖλε καὶ τῷ ἐλάττονι τμήματι προσέθηκεν. ὅταν δὲ δίχα διαιρεθῇ τὸ ὅλον, τότε φασὶν ἔχειν τὸ αὑτοῦ ὅταν λάβωσι τὸ ἴσον. τὸ δ' ἴσον μέσον ἐστὶ τῆς μείζονος καὶ ἐλάττονος κατὰ τὴν ἀριθμητικὴν ἀναλογίαν. διὰ τοῦτο καὶ ὀνομάζεται δίκαιον, ὅτι δίχα ἐστίν, ὥσπερ ἂν εἴ τις εἴποι δίχαιον, καὶ ὁ δικαστὴς διχαστής.') Aristole, *Nichomachean Ethics*, 1132a9-10. English Translation available at <http://www.perseus.tufts.edu/hopper/text?doc=Perseus%3Atext%3A1999.01.0054%3Abekker+page%3D1132a>.

[1] *Treatment of Polish Nationals and Other Persons of Polish Origin or Speech in the Danzig Territory (Advisory Opinion, 4 February 1932)*, PCIJ Rep series A/B No 44, 5. For a historical and legal background in relation to the Free City of Danzig, see K Parlett, 'The PCIJ's Opinion in *Jurisdiction of the Courts of Danz*ig. Individual Rights under Treaties' (2008) 10 Journal of History of International Law 119, 123–129 and JK Bleimaier, 'The Legal Status of the Free City of Danzig 1920–1939: Lessons to be Derived from the Experiences of a Non-State Entity in the International Community' (1989) 2 Hague Yearbook of International Law 69. In a similar historical context see *Questions relating to Settlers of German Origin in Poland (Advisory Opinion, 10 September 1923)*, PCIJ Rep. series B, No 6, 19–20, 35–38.

5. To provide against any discrimination within the Free City of Danzig to the detriment of citizens of Poland and other persons of Polish origin or speech.[2]

The PCIJ observed that the 'the text does not say between whom no discrimination is to be made'.[3] For the majority, the starting point was that '[t]he prohibition against discrimination can best be understood in the light of the circumstances which led to the creation of Danzig as a Free City'.[4] In that vein, '[i]t is precisely because of their Polish character that discrimination against Polish nationals and other persons of Polish origin or speech is prohibited at Danzig'.[5] On the contrary, Judges Guerrero, Rostworowski, Fromageot, and Urrutia issued a dissenting opinion holding the view that nothing in Article 104(5) 'require[d] proof that the discrimination is based on an intention to cause prejudice to the Poles'[6] and emphasized that the prohibition of discrimination was not limited 'based upon the Polish character of those against whom it is practiced'.[7] The dissenting judges were of the view that accepting such interpretation would result in guaranteeing equal treatment of Polish nationals in Danzig only in relation to foreigners residing in Danzig and not Danzig nationals.[8]

Three years later, the PCIJ was confronted with another case revolving around discrimination. In *Oscar Chin*, the Court was called to interpret the equal treatment clause contained in Article I of the Saint-Germain Convention providing that:

> [t]he Signatory Powers undertake to maintain between their respective nationals and those of States, Members of the League of Nations, which may adhere to the present Convention a complete commercial equality in the territories under their authority within the area defined by Article 1 of the General Act of Berlin of February 26, 1885, set out in the Annex hereto but subject to the reservation specified in the final paragraph of that Article.[9]

[2] Article 104(5), Treaty of Versailles (signed 28 June 1919, entered into force 10 January 1920) 225 CTS 188.

[3] *Treatment of Polish Nationals and Other Persons of Polish Origin or Speech in the Danzig Territory (Advisory Opinion, 4 February 1932)*, PCIJ Rep series A/B No 44, 29.

[4] ibid, 27.

[5] ibid, 28; the majority also highlighted that 'the injunction "to provide against any discrimination to the detriment of" these persons is of general application, in so far as such discrimination is made on account of Polish citizenship, origin or speech', ibid.

[6] *Dissenting Opinion of Judges José Gustavo Guerrero, Count Michał Cezary Rostworowski, Henri Fromageot and Francisco José Urrutia Olano, Treatment of Polish Nationals and Other Persons of Polish Origin or Speech in the Danzig Territory (Advisory Opinion, 4 February 1932)*, PCIJ Rep series A/B No 44, 47.

[7] ibid.

[8] ibid ('It will be readily perceived that, if this were so, a measure which placed the Polish nationals at Danzig in a position of inferiority to the nationals of Danzig would not constitute discrimination such as is forbidden by the Treaty, provided only that it was declared applicable to all persons of other than Danzig nationality').

[9] The Convention of Saint-German revisited the General Act of the Berlin Conference (1884–1885) and the General Act and Declaration of Brussels (1890); Convention revising the General Act of Berlin, 26 February 1885, and the General Act and Declaration of Brussels, 2 July 1890, signed at Saint-Germain-en-Laye (singed 10 September 1919, entered into force 31 July 1920) 8 LNTS 25; General Act of the Conference of Berlin Concerning the Congo (26 February 1885) (1909) 3 AJIL Supplement 7; General Act of the Brussels Conference Relating to the African Slave Trade (signed 2 July 1890, entered into force 31 August 1891) 173 CTS 293. The interpretation of that clause proved difficult for the Court. The President of the PCIJ wrote to the absent Judge Kellogg that '[t]he Drafting Committee had a good deal of difficulty with the preparation of the Judgment', O Spiermann, *International Legal Argument in the Permanent Court of International Justice* (CUP 2005) 365. See also M Craven, 'Between Law and History: the Berlin Conference of 1884–1885 and the Logic of Free Trade' (2015) 3 London

After the Great Crash of 1929, the Belgian Congo and in particular its fluvial transportation sector (which was of vital importance to the Colony's economy) run into severe financial difficulties. In 1931, Belgium decided to intervene and provided support to State-controlled companies, including the shipping company *Union Nationale des Transports Fluviaux* (*Unatra*), but not to private (Belgian or foreign) companies, such as the transport enterprise of a British national, Oscar Chinn. Britain exercised diplomatic protection on behalf of him and the case was brought before the PCIJ. One of the key questions was whether Belgium's support to Unatra was incompatible with the 'complete commercial equality' guaranteed by the Saint-Germain Convention. At least implicitly, the majority did recognize that the economic crisis was to be taken into account.[10] The majority concluded that under the equal treatment clause of the Saint-Germain Convention:

> [t]he form of discrimination which is forbidden is therefore *discrimination based upon nationality and involving differential treatment by reason of their nationality* as between persons belonging to different national groups.[11]

The PCIJ dismissed the discrimination claim finding that 'the treatment accorded to Unatra was based on the special position of that Company, as a Company under the supervision of the Belgian Government' and '[t]hese measures, as decreed, would have been inapplicable to concerns not under government supervision, whether of Belgian or foreign nationality'.[12] In other words, no discriminatory intent was found:

> [e]ven supposing that Unatra took advantage of the temporary lowering of its rates to endeavour to concentrate in its hands the business of its competitors, *it cannot be inferred, especially having regard to the circumstances already mentioned, that this was the motive and aim of the action of the Belgian Government.*[13]

The decision was adopted with six votes to five. In particular, Judges Altamira, Anzilotti, van Eysinga, and President Hurst took issue with the majority's approach on discrimination.[14] President Hurst categorically stated that 'it is not necessary to show that the

Review of International Law 31. See also E Roucounas, *A Landscape of Contemporary Theories of International Law* (Brill Nijhoff 2019) 435–438.

[10] *The Oscar Chinn case (United Kingdom v Belgium), Judgment*, PCIJ Series A/B No 63, 88; see also ibid: '[f]avourable business conditions and good-will are transient circumstances, subject to inevitable changes; the interests of transport undertakings may well have suffered as a result of the general trade depression and the measures taken to combat it'. Paparinskis also notes that 'the more lax approach was possibly influenced by the Great Depression', M Paparinskis, *The International Minimum Standard and Fair and Equitable Treatment* (OUP 2013) 29.

[11] *The Oscar Chinn case (United Kingdom v Belgium)*, Judgment, PCIJ Series A/B No 63, 87 (emphasis added).

[12] ibid.

[13] ibid, 86 (emphasis added). See also T Weiler, 'Saving Oscar Chin: Non-Discrimination in International Investment Law' in T Weiler (ed), *International Investment Law and Arbitration: Leading Cases from the ICSID, NAFTA, Bilateral Treaties and Customary International Law* (Cameron May 2005) 557–595.

[14] *Separate Opinion of Judge Walther Schücking, The Oscar Chinn case (United Kingdom v Belgium), Judgment*, PCIJ Series A/B No 63, 148–149, agreeing with the Separate Opinion of Judge van Eysinga.

discrimination was based on nationality, in the sense that the differentiation was made because the persons possessed a particular nationality'.[15] In his dissenting opinion Judge Altamira focused on *impact* rather discriminatory *intent*. He emphasized that Article I of the Saint-Germain Convention was 'certainly tantamount to a prohibition of any discrimination' and that, although Belgium enjoyed regulatory freedom,

> this freedom, though very wide, cannot be exercised beyond the point where it would entail infringement of the equality accorded to such nationals in their commercial activities. This point would be reached as soon as the measure taken by the Belgian Government *affected* fundamentally the commercial activities which foreigners are entitled to engage in the Congo under the same basic conditions as Belgian nationals.[16]

Judge van Eysinga also found a violation of equal treatment focusing on the detrimental effect of the measures.[17]

The world has changed drastically since the 1930s, but to the international economic law *connoisseurs*, the issues that divided the PCIJ are strikingly similar to those that investment treaty tribunals are currently struggling with.[18] The same is true in relation to the interpretation of non-discrimination obligations in the World Trade Organization (WTO),[19] which will not be examined in this book. Whether non-discrimination

[15] *The Oscar Chinn case (United Kingdom v Belgium)*, Judgment, PCIJ Series A/B No 63, Dissenting Opinion of Sir Cecil James Barrington Hurst, 128.

[16] *The Oscar Chinn case (United Kingdom v Belgium)*, Judgment, PCIJ Series A/B No 63, Dissenting Opinion of Judge Altamira, 92–93 (emphasis added).

[17] *The Oscar Chinn case (United Kingdom v Belgium)*, Judgment, PCIJ Series A/B No 63, Separate Opinion of Judge van Eysinga, 139; 'the inequality of treatment created by the Belgian Government's measure of June 20th, 1931, in favour of Unatra and to the detriment of the only other enterprise in the Congo which exclusively transported the goods of others, namely, Mr. Chinn's business, is in conflict with the international obligations of the Belgian Government towards the United Kingdom'.

[18] In *Norwegian Loans* before the ICJ, Norway argued that 'discrimination was justified because it was based on good-will'. However, Judge Reed in his dissent categorically rejected the argument that 'international law considers that discrimination, if based on either good-will or ill-will, ceases in some mysterious manner to be discriminatory': *Certain Norwegian Loans (France v Norway)* Judgment, Dissenting Opinion of Judge Reed [1957] ICJ Rep 79, 88–89. The tribunal in *Feldman v Mexico* accurately observed that '[d]espite its deceptively simple language, the interpretative hurdles for Article 1102 [of the NAFTA providing for National Treatment] are several', *Marvin Roy Feldman Karpa v United Mexican States*, ICSID Case No ARB(AF)/99/1, Award, 16 December 2002, para 166.

[19] See eg AB, *EC—Bananas III*, para 216 ('a determination of whether there has been a violation of Article III:4 does not require a separate consideration of whether a measure "afford[s] protection to domestic production"'); AB, *Korea—Various Measures on Beef*, para 137 ('[a] formal difference in treatment between imported and like domestic products is thus neither necessary, nor sufficient, to show a violation of Article III:4. Whether or not imported products are treated "less favourably" than like domestic products should be assessed instead by examining whether a measure modifies the conditions of competition in the relevant market to the detriment of imported products'); AB, *Thailand—Cigarettes (Philippines)*, para 128 ('what is relevant is whether such regulatory differences distort the conditions of competition to the detriment of imported products. If so, then the differential treatment will amount to treatment that is "less favourable" within the meaning of Article III:4') and para 134; Panel, *US—Tuna (Mexico) II (Article 21.5—Mexico)*, para 7.479; citing AB, *EC—Seal Products*, para 5.117 ('for the purposes of an analysis under Article III:4, a panel is not required to examine whether the detrimental impact of a measure on competitive opportunities for like imported products stems exclusively from a legitimate regulatory distinction'). Cf AB, *Dominican Republic—Cigarettes*, para 96 ('the existence of a detrimental effect on a given imported product resulting from a measure does not necessarily imply that this measure accords less favourable treatment to imports if the detrimental effect is explained by factors or circumstances unrelated to the foreign origin of the product'); Panel, *EC—Approval and Marketing of Biotech Products*, para 7.2514. See also WJ Davey and KE Maskus, '*Thailand-Cigarettes (Philippines)*: A More Serious Role for the 'Less Favourable Treatment' Standard of Article III:4' (2013) 12 World Trade Review 163, 175; M Ming Du, 'The Rise of the National Regulatory Autonomy in the GATT/WTO Regime' (2011) 14 JIEL 639. The adoption of an impact-based discrimination paradigm was one of the points of criticisms levelled against the WTO Appellate Body by the US, which has led to a

clauses contained in investment treaties prohibit (i) any measure having adverse effects on foreign investors or (ii) only measures (which can be shown to be) enacted on the basis of the investors' nationality (or another impermissible characteristic such as religion or race) has divided arbitral tribunals.[20]

Discrimination cases are difficult cases,[21] partly due to the fact that legal clauses prohibiting discrimination are conceptually linked with the idea of equality.[22] According

diplomatic deadlock and the institution's paralysis; United States Trade Representative, *Report on the Appellate Body of the World Trade Organization* (February 2020), 90:

> [o]ne of the key principles of the WTO agreements is the requirement that Members not discriminate against trade from other Members. This fundamental principle, reflected in the national treatment and most-favored nation obligations, was not intended to prevent Members from pursuing their legitimate policy objectives.
>
> The Appellate Body, however, has found a measure to be discriminatory (and therefore not consistent with WTO rules) based solely on evidence that the measure may impact imports from one Member more than those of another, even though converting a non-discrimination inquiry into a detrimental impact test renders almost any origin-neutral measure vulnerable to challenge in WTO dispute settlement. It is much more difficult to pursue legitimate public policy measures under the legal standard the Appellate Body has invented than under the standards to which Members actually agreed. In addition, the Appellate Body's approach would have WTO adjudicators second-guess Members' legislatures and serve as the ultimate arbiters of a range of important legislative questions, which is not a role that WTO Members assigned to them under the WTO agreements.

See also J Pauwelyn, 'WTO Dispute Settlement Post 2019: What to Expect?' (2019) 22 JIEL 297; BM Hoekman and PC Mavroidis, 'To AB or Not to AB? Dispute Settlement in WTO Reform' (2020) 23 JIEL 1; S Lester, B Mercurio, and A Davies, *World Trade Law: Text, Materials and Commentary* (3rd edn, Hart 2018) 281–284.

[20] See Chapter 3.

[21] This can be also attributed to the nature of international trade. As Adam Smith noted, the efforts of international trade negotiators do not 'belong so much to the science of a legislator, whose deliberations ought to be governed by general principles which are always the same, as to the skill of that insidious and crafty animal, vulgarly called a statesman or politician whose councils are directed by the momentary fluctuations of affairs', A Smith, *An Inquiry into the Nature and Causes of The Wealth of the Nations, Vol 2* (Clarendon Press 1869) 41.

[22] <IBT>*Case concerning rights of nationals of the United States of America in Morocco, Judgment (France v US)* [1952] ICJ Rep 176</IBT>, 182: 'the intention of the most-favoured-nation clauses was to establish and to maintain at all times fundamental equality without discrimination among all of the countries concerned'. The ICJ rejected the US argument that 'the most favoured-nation clauses in treaties made with countries like Morocco should be regarded as a form of drafting by reference rather than as a method for the establishment and maintenance of equality of treatment without discrimination amongst the various countries concerned': ibid, 191. RC Snyder, 'The Most Favored Nation Clause and Recent Trade Practices' (1940) 55 Political Science Quarterly 77, 77 ([MFN] 'embodies the principle of equality of treatment in international economic relation'); G Schwarzenberger, 'Most Favoured Nation in British State Practice' (1945) 22 BYIL 96 99 (MFN's 'main function consists in forming an agency of equality'); D Sarooshi, 'The Move from Institutions: The Case of the World Trade Organization' (2006) 100 ASIL Proceeding 298, 299 ('the two nondiscrimination principles of Most Favored Nation Treatment and National Treatment are in substance a reflection of the application of the value of equality-that governments should ensure that like cases are treated equally'); T Cottier and M Oesch, 'Direct and Indirect Discrimination in WTO and EU Law' in SE Gaines, B Egelund Olsen, and K Engsig Sørensen (eds), *Liberalising Trade in the EU and the WTO: A Legal Comparison* (CUP 2012) 141–175, 142. See also *Plama Consortium Limited v Republic of Bulgaria*, ICSID Case No ARB/03/24, Award, 27 August 2008, para 184: 'with regard to discrimination, it corresponds to the negative formulation of the principle of equality of treatment. It entails like persons being treated in a different manner in similar circumstances without reasonable or justifiable grounds.' In like manner, GATT and WTO Panels also repeatedly ruled that the term 'less favourable treatment' is to 'be found throughout the General Agreement and later Agreements negotiated in the GATT framework as an expression of the underlying principle of equality of treatment of imported products as compared to the treatment given either to other foreign products, under the most favoured nation standard, or to domestic products, under the national treatment standard of Article III', GATT Panel, *US—Section 337 Tariff Act*, para 5.11; Panel, *Japan—Film*, para 10.379; Panel, *US—COOL*, para 7.232; see also AB, *EC—Bananas III*, para 190 ('[t]he essence of the non-discrimination obligations is that like products should be treated *equally*, irrespective of their origin') (emphasis added). See also *Parkerings-Compagniet AS v Republic of Lithuania*, ICSID Case No ARB/05/8 Award, 11 September 2007, para 367 ('national treatment, most favoured-nation-treatment or non-discrimination at large, will in effect bar discrimination against foreign nationals investing in the country concerned'); *Vladimir Berschader and Moise Berschader v The Russian Federation*, SCC Case No 080/2004, Separate Opinion by Todd Weiler, 21 April 2006, para 20 ('the MFN standard is a tried-and-true expression of the international economic law principle of non-discrimination');

to the famous Aristotelian definition, equality consists of *treating like cases alike*.[23] The concept of equality is highly abstract and, therefore, enjoys quasi-universal acceptance, as people tend to agree on abstract concepts, but disagree on how these concepts are to be applied in concrete situations.[24] Very few would take issue with the value of equality in principle; however, what equality entails for specific cases is highly contested.[25] This is the case with non-discrimination in international investment law. Even scholars who are highly critically of the investment treaty arbitration regime and argue in favour of restricting the scope of substantive standards of protection recognize that non-discrimination is essential for investors' protection.[26] As Sharpston, an Advocate General of the EU Court of Justice, has stated, the 'classic formulation of the principle of equality, such as Aristotle's "treat like cases alike" [,] leaves open the crucial question

Metalpar SA and Buen Aire SA v Argentine Republic, ICSID Case No ARB/03/5, Award, 6 June 2008, para 162 ('[t]reating different categories of subjects differently is not unequal treatment. The principle of equality only applies between equal subjects, not between unequal subjects'), also quoted in *RREEF Infrastructure (GP) Limited and RREEF Pan-European Infrastructure Two Lux Sàrl v Kingdom of Spain*, ICSID Case No ARB/13/30, Decision on Responsibility and on the Principles of Quantum, 30 November 2018, para 431; see also *Mohammad Ammar Al-Bahloul v Republic of Tajikistan*, Partial Award on Jurisdiction and Liability, SCC Case No V064/2008, 2 September 2009, para 271; *Tza Yap Shum v Republic of Peru*, ICSID Case ARB/07/6, Decision on Jurisdiction and Competence, 19 June 2009, para 195; *Telefónica SA v The Argentine Republic*, ICSID Case No ARB/03/2025, Decision of the Tribunal on Objections to Jurisdiction, 25 May 2006, para 98; *National Grid Plc v Argentine Republic*, UNCITRAL Decision on Jurisdiction, 20 June 2006, para 92; *Daimler Financial Services AG v Argentine Republic*, ICSID Case No ARB/05/1, Award 22 August 2012, para 242. See also ILC, Final Report of the Study Group on the Most-Favoured Nation Clause (2015) II(2) Yearbook of International Commission ('ILC 2015 MFN Report'), para 75: 'the purpose of a "right" in the context of MFN and national treatment is to ensure that an investor has equality of competitive opportunities with other foreign investors or with nationals as the case may be'.

[23] Aristotle, *Nicomachean Ethics*, 1131a10-b15; *Politics*, III 9, 1280 a8-15, III 12, 1282b18-23. See also Case C-279/93, *Finanzampt Koln-Altstadt v Schumacker* [1995] ECR I-225, para 30: '[i]t is also settled law that discrimination can arise only through the application of different rules to comparable situations or the application of the same rule to different situations'. In public international law, equality is similarly formulated: 'discrimination may in general be said to arise where those who are in all material respects the same are treated differently, or where those who are in material respects different are treated in the same way', R Jennings and A Watts, *Oppenheim's International Law, Volume 1 Peace* (9th edn, OUP 1992) 378; *Minority Schools in Albania (Advisory Opinion, 6 April 1935)* PCIJ Rep Series A/B, No 64, 19 ('Equality in law precludes discrimination of any kind; whereas equality in fact may involve the necessity of different treatment in order to attain a result which establishes an equilibrium between different situations'); see also *Dissenting Opinion of Judge Tanaka, South West Africa case (Ethiopia v South Africa, Liberia v South Africa) (Second Phase)* [1966] ICJ Rep 6, 306 ('to treat unequal matters differently according to their inequality is not only permitted but required'); see also N Tzouvala, *Capitalism as Civilisation: A History of International Law* (CUP 2020) 149–158. See also EW Vierdag, *The Concept of Discrimination in International Law, with Special References to Human Rights* (Martinus Nijhoff 1973) 61.

[24] It is telling that although the UN Charter does not refer to human rights with the notable exception of Article 1(3) which does list as one of the purposes of the organization '[t]o achieve international co-operation in solving international problems of an economic, social, cultural, or humanitarian character, and in promoting and encouraging respect for human rights and for fundamental freedoms for all without distinction as to race, sex, language, or religion'. Charter of the United Nations (adopted 26 June 1945, entered into force 24 October 1945) 1 UNTS 16, Art 1(3); W Schabas, *The European Convention on Human Rights: A Commentary* (OUP 2015) 555.

[25] S Besson, *The Morality of Conflict: Reasonable Disagreement and the Law* (Hart 2005) 156; T Cottier, 'Towards a Five Storey House' in C Joerges and E-U Petersmann (eds), *Constitutionalism, Multilevel Trade Governance and International Economic Law* (Hart 2011) 495–531, 523. See also R Dworkin, *Sovereign Virtue, the Theory and Practice of Equality* (Harvard University Press 2000) 2; ('"Equality" is a contested concept. People who praise it or disparage it disagree about what they are praising or disparaging. The correct account of equality is itself a difficult philosophical issue'). See also A Sen, *Inequality Reexamined* (OUP 1995) 13 ('every normative theory of social arrangement that has at all stood the test of time seems to demand equality of something—something that is regarded as particularly important in that theory'). See also FA Hayek, *The Constitution of Liberty* (Routledge 2006) 77: '[w]e do not object to equality as such. It merely happens to be the case that a demand for equality is the professed motive of most of those who desire to impose upon society a preconceived pattern of distribution'.

[26] See eg D Schneiderman, *Constitutionalizing Economic Globalization: Investment Rules and Democracy's Promise* (CUP 2008) 230–237.

of which aspects should be considered relevant to equal treatment and which should not'.[27] Thus, '[t]his formulation of equality requires us to identify those characteristics that are relevant for determining whether actors are "situated equally". In other words, '[t]he nondiscrimination provisions' textual ambiguity makes purposive interpretation inevitable'.[28] Hence, 'an additional set of value choices and rules would be needed to implement a norm of equal treatment'.[29] The choice of the primary value to be used as the criterion to determine relations of equality is linked with the general institutional framework of the community[30] and is itself value-dependent. Yet, this is circular, and this is why the value preferred is what Castoriadis calls a 'proto-value'.[31] Unsurprisingly, the concept of equality has come under attack as being an 'empty concept', tautological and circular.[32] All legal terms necessitate interpretative choices,[33] but 'the discretionary

[27] Opinion of AG Sharpston, Case C-427/06 *Birgit Bartsch v Bosch und Siemens Hausgeräte (BSH) Altersfürsorge GmbH*, 22 May 2008, para 44. '"Equality" necessarily implies the existence of some extraneous criterion by reference to which the content is to be determined', *Dissenting Opinion by Sir Cecil Hurst, Count Michał Cezary Rostworowski and Demetre Negulesco, Minority Schools in Albania (Advisory Opinion, 6 April 1935)* PCIJ Rep Series A/B, No 64, 25. For a good example cf the Panel's and the AB's approach in the *Tariff Preferences* case. The Panel held that 'the term "non-discriminatory" in footnote 3 [of the Enabling Clause] requires that identical tariff preferences under GSP [(Generalised Scheme of Preferences)] schemes be provided to all developing countries without differentiation, except for the implementation of a priori limitations', Panel, *EC—Tariff Preferences*, para 7.161. The AB reversed the Panel's decision:

> the term 'non-discriminatory' in footnote 3 does not prohibit developed-country Members from granting different tariffs to products originating in different GSP beneficiaries, provided that such differential tariff treatment meets the remaining conditions in the Enabling Clause. In granting such differential tariff treatment, however, preference-granting countries are required, by virtue of the term 'non-discriminatory', to ensure that identical treatment is available to all similarly-situated GSP beneficiaries, that is, to all GSP beneficiaries that have the 'development, financial and trade needs' to which the treatment in question is intended to respond.

AB, *EC—Tariff Preferences*, para 173. See also Y Qin, 'Defining Nondiscrimination under the law of the World Trade Organization' (2005) 23 Boston University International Law Journal 215, 297 ('[t]he analysis of the case EC-Preferences has shown how different norms and values could guide the tribunals to reach different conclusions on the basis for determining similarly-situated countries'); L Bartels and C Häberli, 'Binding Tariff Preferences for Developing Countries under article II GATT' (2010) 13 JIEL 969; PM Gerhart and AS Kella, 'Power and Preferences: Developing Countries and the Role of the WTO Appellate Body' 30 North Carolina Journal of International Law and Commercial Regulation 515; E Kessie, 'The Legal Status of Special and Differential Treatment Provisions under the WTO Agreements' in G Bermann and PC Mavroidis (eds), *WTO Law and Developing Countries* (CUP 2007) 12–35; AD Mitchell, 'A Legal Principle of Special and Differential Treatment for WTO Disputes' (2006) 5 World Trade Review 445.

[28] O Suttle, *Distributive Justice and World Trade Law: A Political Theory of International Trade Regulation* (CUP 2018) 189.

[29] D Tarullo, 'Logic, Myth, and the International Economic Order' (1985) 26 Harvard International Law Journal 533, 540. Aristotle himself was aware that multiple conceptions of justice exist: 'All are agreed that justice in distributions must be based on desert of some sort, although they do not all mean the same sort of desert; democrats make the criterion free birth; those of oligarchical sympathies wealth, or in other cases birth; upholders of aristocracy make it virtue', Aristotle, *Nichomachean Ethics*, 1131a8.

[30] P Raynaud, 'Le juge, la loi, le droit: de Platon à Aristote' in O Cayla and M-F Renoux-Zagamé (eds), *L'office de juge: part de souveraineté ou puissance nulle* (Bruylant, LGDJ 2001) 5–16, 15.

[31] C Castoriadis (translated by A Arato), 'From Marx to Aristotle, from Aristotle to Us' (1978) 45 Social Research 667, 708–709.

[32] P Westen, 'The Empty Idea of Equality' (1982) 95 Harvard Law Review 537; see also L Alexander, 'What Makes Wrongful Discrimination Wrong? Biases, Preferences, Stereotypes, and Proxies' (1992) University of Pennsylvania Law Review 149, 191. D Locke, 'The Trivializability of Universalizability' (1968) 77 The Philosophical Review 25, 25. Nevertheless, this attack on equality has proved controversial and generated persuasive rebuttals: for a critique of Westen's theory see J Waldron, 'The Substance of Equality' (1991) 89 Michigan Law Review 1350; cf S Guest, 'The Role of Moral Equality in Legal Argument' in F Du Bois (ed), *The Practice of Integrity: Reflections on Ronald Dworkin and South African Law* (Juta and Co Ltd 2005) 18–43, 23.

[33] On that point both positivist and critical legal approaches converge, see M Koskenniemi, *From Apology to Utopia: The Structure of the International Legal Argument* (CUP 2005) 341 ('[t]he one thing that unites Kelsen and McDougal, the rule and the policy- approach, is their insistence on the indeterminate, subjective, political

zone of a court or tribunal is likely to increase with factors such as the breadth and vagueness of the treaty norms'.[34] Interpreting non-discrimination entails wide discretion for the adjudicator.[35] Given the conceptual link with equality, the same key interpretative questions which divided the PCIJ and divide investment treaty tribunals exist (and have existed for a long time) in other legal fields, including domestic law. This is perhaps one of the reasons that certain States, such as China, were traditional reluctant to include National Treatment clauses in their investment treaties.[36]

character of interpretation. They, as Richard Falk for example, criticize disguising the arbitrariness of interpretation under the fictions of textual clarity or juristic method. They propose that interpretation be conducted openly by reference to important values'); H Kelsen (translated by M Knight), Pure Theory of Law (University of California Press 1967) 349 ('every law-applying act is only partly determined by law and partly undetermined'); HLA Hart, *The Concept of Law* (Clarendon Press 1961) 132; MS McDougal, 'International Law, Power and Policy' (1953) 82 RCADI 133; MS McDougal, 'Law as a Process of Decision: A Policy-Oriented Approach to Legal Study' (1956) 1 Natural Law Forum 53; MW Reisman, 'The View from the New Haven School of International Law' (1992) 86 ASIL Proceedings 118; R Higgins, 'Policy Considerations and the International Judicial Process' (1968) 17 ICLQ 58; D Kennedy, 'Theses about International Law Discourse' (1980) 23 German Yearbook of International Law 353; E McWhinney, *Judicial Settlement of International Disputes. Jurisdiction, Justiciability and Law-Making on the Contemporary International Court* (Martinus Nijhoff 1991); H Lauterpacht, *The Development of International Law by the International Court* (Stevens and Sons 1958) 75; Y Shany, 'No Longer a Weak Department of Power? Reflections on the Emergence of a New International Judiciary' (2009) 20 EJIL 73; A von Bogdandy and I Venzke, 'Beyond Dispute: International Judicial Institutions as Lawmakers' (2011) 12 German Law Journal 971; A von Bogdandy and I Venzke, 'In Whose Name? An Investigation of International Courts' Public Authority and Its Democratic Justification' (2012) 23 EJIL 7; I Venzke, *How Interpretation Makes International Law: On Semantic Change and Normative Twists* (OUP 2012); J Scott and SP Sturm, 'Courts as Catalysts: Rethinking the Judicial Role in New Governance' (2007) 13 Columbia Journal of European Law 565. For an insightful empirical analysis of the profile(s) of arbitrators in investment treaty arbitration, see S Puig, 'Social Capital in the Arbitration Market' (2014) 25 EJIL 387; S Puig and A Strezhnev, 'The David Effect and ISDS' (2017) 28 EJIL 731.

[34] A Roberts, 'Power and Persuasion in Investment Treaty Interpretation: The Dual Role of States' (2010) AJIL 179, 187.

[35] 'The ambiguity of concepts like . . . discrimination gives them [arbitrators] a wide authority in virtually any field of public law', G Van Harten, *Investment Treaty Arbitration and Public Law* (OUP 2006) 93; J Cornides, 'Three case studies on "Anti-Discrimination"' (2012) 23 EJIL 517, 542. See also J Basdevant, 'L'affaire des pêcheries des côtes septentrionales de l'Atlantique entre *Etats-Unis d'Amerique et Grande-Bretagne*' (1912) RGDIP 421, 540 ('la question de la méthode d'interprétation des clauses d'égalité ne peut être considérée comme tranchée définitivement en droit international positif'). Kelsen argued that 'the use by a constitutional tribunal of general vague equitable principles, such as justice or equality, would encroach upon legislative competence. Such an event would, it can be supposed, have been thought a government of judges by Kelsen', M Davis, 'A Government of Judges: An Historical Re-View' (1987) 35 American Journal of Comparative Law 559, 565; Kelsen (n 33) 241 (emphasis added); cf E Lambert, *Le Gouvernement des Juges et la lute contre la Législation Sociale aux États-Unis* (Marcel Giard 1921); H Kelsen, 'La gurantie juridictionelle de la Constitution' (1928) 45 Revue du droit public 197. In the US context, Sunstein and others have demonstrated through empirical research that 'in areas involving . . . discrimination, for example, splits between Democratic and Republican appointees seem to have become especially dramatic', C Sunstein, D Schkade, and LM Ellman, *Are Judges Political?: An Empirical Analysis of the Federal Judiciary* (Brookings Institution 2006) 87. See also F Zarbiyev, 'On the Judge Centredness of the International Legal Self'(2021) 32 EJIL 1139 and P Webb, *International Judicial Integration and Fragmentation* (OUP 2013).

[36] Approximately half of the Chinese BITs do not contain a National Treatment provision, and 'earlier Chinese BITs do not offer any NT protection', W Shan, N Gallagher, and S Zhang, 'National Treatment for Foreign Investment in China: A Changing Landscape' (2012) 27 ICSID Review 120, 133. On China's investment treaty policy and practice see Y Li and C Bian, 'China's Stance on Investor-State Dispute Settlement: Evolution, Challenges, and Reform Options' (2020) 67 Netherlands International Law Review 503; T Cohen and D Schneiderman, 'The Political Economy of Chinese Bilateral Investment Treaty Policy' (2017) 5 Chinese Journal of Comparative Law 110; LE Trakman, 'Geopolitics, China, and Investor-State Arbitration' in L Toohey, CB Picker, and J Greenacre (eds), *China in the International Economic Order: New Directions and Changing Paradigms* (CUP 2015) 268–292; G Wang, *International Investment Law: A Chinese Perspective* (Routledge 2014); W Shan and N Gallagher, *Chinese Investment Treaties: Policies and Practice* (OUP 2009); SW Schill, 'Tearing Down the Great Wall: The New Generation Investment Treaties of the People's Republic of China' (2007) 15 Cardozo Journal of International and Comparative Law 73.

1.2 Scope, Methodology, and Contribution of this Book

Having established both the importance and the complexity of non-discrimination clauses in international economic law, this section sets out in greater details the scope of the analysis contained in this book and its methodological approach (Section 1.2.1), as well as the original contribution which this book aspires to make in the relevant scholarship (Section 1.2.2).

1.2.1 Scope and Methodology

Certain aspects of the principle of non-discrimination in international economic law may reflect obligations under customary law[37] (even *jus cogens*[38]) or form part

[37] Regarding the principle of equal treatment of bondholders in debt restructuring, see eg M Waibel, *Sovereign Defaults before International Courts and Tribunals* (CUP 2011) 68–87 and 151–152; cf the approach of the majority and the minority in the *Young Loan Arbitration* (1980) 19 ILM 1358; LC Buchheit and JS Pam, 'The Pari Passu Clause in Sovereign Debt Instruments' (2003) 53 Emory Law Journal 869; see also *Biloune and Marine Drive Complex Ltd v Ghana Investments Centre and the Government of Ghana*, Award on Jurisdiction and Liability, 27 October 1989, 95 ILR 183, 203: 'Long-established customary international law requires that a State accord foreign nationals within its territory a standard of treatment no less than that prescribed by international law. Moreover, contemporary international law recognizes that all individuals, regardless of nationality, are entitled to fundamental human rights (which, in the view of the Tribunal, include property as well as personal rights), which no government may violate. Nevertheless, it does not follow that this Tribunal is competent to pass upon every type of departure from the minimum standard to which foreign nationals are entitled, or that this Tribunal is authorized to deal with allegations of violations of fundamental human rights.' See also JB Moore, *Digest of International Law, Vol 2* (Government Printing Office 1906) 57 ('Citizens of the United States in Colombia are exempted from paying any tax from which the subjects or citizens of another power are exempt, both by the "favored nation" clause of our treaty of 1846 with Colombia, and by the general principle of the law of nations which justifies this Government in insisting that there shall be no undue discrimination against citizens of the United States wherever they may be resident', Mr Bayard, Secretary of State, to Mr Walker, chargé at Bogota, 28 April 1888). See also the excellent analysis in Paparinskis (n 10) 41–46, 78, and 99–100. See also MS McDougal, HD Lasswell, and L-C Chen, 'The Protection of Aliens from Discrimination and World Public Order: Responsibility of States Conjoined with Human Rights' (1976) 70 AJIL 432. As an ICSID tribunal put it: '[c]ustomary international law imposes two limitations on the power to tax. Taxes may not be discriminatory and they may not be confiscatory', *Burlington Resources Inc v Republic of Ecuador, ICSID Case No ARB/08/5 (formerly Burlington Resources Inc and others v Republic of Ecuador and Empresa Estatal Petróleos del Ecuador (PetroEcuador))*, Decision on Liability, 14 December 2012, para 393. See also AE Gildemeister, 'Burlington Resources, Inc v Republic of Ecuador, How Much is Too Much: When is Taxation Tantamount to Expropriation?' (2014) 29 ICSID Review 315.

[38] See International Law Commission, Draft articles on Responsibility of States for Internationally Wrongful Acts with commentaries (2001) II Yearbook of the International Law Commission 31, 87: 'Those peremptory norms that are clearly accepted and recognized include the prohibitions of aggression, genocide, slavery, racial discrimination, crimes against humanity and torture, and the right to self-determination.' Cf *Bernhard von Pezold and Others v Republic of Zimbabwe*, ICSID Case No ARB/10/15, Award, 28 July 2015, para 738:

> The Tribunal notes that the prohibition of racial discrimination is an obligation *erga omnes* as confirmed by the ICJ in Barcelona Traction … Yet it is still arguable as to whether this obligation has evolved to the level of jus cogens due to the many exceptions to and permissible derogations from it.' The Inter-American Court of Human Rights (IACHR) also considers that the principle of equality before the law, equal protection before the law and non-discrimination belongs to jus cogens, because the whole legal structure of national and international public order rests on it and it is a fundamental principle that permeates all laws. Nowadays, no legal act that is in conflict with this fundamental principle is acceptable, and discriminatory treatment of any person, owing to gender, race, color, language, religion or belief, political or other opinion, national, ethnic or social origin, nationality, age, economic situation, property, civil status, birth, or any other status is unacceptable. This principle (equality and non-discrimination) forms part of general international law. At the existing stage of the development

of international public policy.[39] However, this book primarily focuses on non-discrimination obligations contained in international investment treaties.[40] This is in line with the orthodox position in international law that, as a general rule, and in the absence of specific treaty commitments,[41] States are free to discriminate between foreign investors or between foreign and domestic investors.[42] This is despite the prevalent view (at least since the First World War and in particular the Second World War) that non-discrimination in the realm of international economic relations is closely connected with international cooperation and peace.[43] Given that non-discrimination

of international law, the fundamental principle of equality and non-discrimination has entered the realm of *jus cogens*.

IACHR *(Advisory Opinion, OC-18/03), Requested by the United Mexican States, Juridical Condition and Rights of Undocumented Migrants*, 17 September 2003, para 101 (emphasis removed). See also G Ténékidès, 'L'action des Nations unies contre la discrimination raciale' (1980) 168 RCADI 269.

[39] For example in relation to the principle of equality between creditors in insolvency proceedings, F Mantilla-Serrano, 'International Arbitration and Insolvency Proceedings' (1995) 11 Arbitration International 51, 70.

[40] Cf *RREEF Infrastructure (GP) Limited and RREEF Pan-European Infrastructure Two Lux Sàrl v Kingdom of Spain*, ICSID Case No ARB/13/30, Decision on Responsibility and on the Principles of Quantum, 30 November 2018, para 428: '[t]he Tribunal considers that FET encompasses the principle of non-discrimination and it will analyse it as such for purposes of this case. However, had the ECT not contained an express provision on FET or protecting investors against non-discrimination, this principle would still be applicable on the basis of customary international law'.

[41] On the relationship between non-discrimination and stabilization clauses see *Aguaytia Energy, LLC v Republic of Peru*, ICSID Case No ARB/06/13, Award, 11 December 2008, para 96. The clause in question (quoted in ibid, para 85) provided that 'Stability of the right to non-discrimination, as provided for in item c), article 10, of Legislative Decree 662, which implies that the STATE or neither one of its bodies, notwithstanding these may include entities or companies from the Central Government, Regional or Local Governments, may apply a differentiated treatment to AGUAYTIA by reason of its nationality, the sectors or types of economic activity it shall develop, or the geographical location of the firm in which it invests, and neither as far as the matters herein below specified'.

[42] *Eastern Extension, Australasia and China Telegraph Company, Ltd (Great Britain) v United States* (1923) 6 RIAA 112, 117: 'It is perfectly legitimate for a Government, in the absence of any special agreement to the contrary, to afford to subjects of any particular Government treatment which is refused to the subjects of other Governments, or to reserve to its own subjects treatment which is not afforded to foreigners. Some political motive, some service rendered, some traditional bond of friendship, some reciprocal treatment in the past or in the present, may furnish the ground for discrimination.' See also *Alex Genin Eastern Credit Limited Inc. and AS Baltoil v the Republic of Estonia*, Award, ICSID Case No ARB/99/2, 25 June 2001, para 368 ('[c]ustomary international law does not, however, require that a state treat all aliens (and alien property) equally, or that it treat aliens as favourably as nationals'); *Asian Agricultural Products Ltd (AAPL) v Sri Lanka*, ICSID Case No ARB/87/3, Dissenting Opinion of Samuel Asante, 27 June 1990, (1991) 6 ICSID Review 574, 584 (1991) 30 ILM 580, 642 ('[i]t bears emphasis that national and most-favoured-nation treatment does not derive from customary law'); Jennings and Watts (n 23) 376M Paparinskis, 'MFN Clauses and International Dispute Settlement: Moving beyond Maffezini and Plama?' (2011) 26 ICSID Review 14, 17; A Newcombe and L Paradell, *Law and Practice of Investment Treaties* (Kluwer Law International 2009) 149. On discrimination in the context of FET or expropriation and customary law, see Chapter 3. See also *The United States of America on Behalf of George W Hopkins v The United Mexican States* (Docket No 39) (1927) 21 AJIL 160, 166–167, (1926) 4 RIAA 41, 47 ('There is no ground to object that this amounts to a discrimination by a nation against its own citizens in favor of aliens. It is not a question of discrimination but a question of difference in their respective rights and remedies. The citizens of a nation may enjoy many rights which are withheld from aliens, and, conversely, under international law aliens may enjoy rights and remedies which the nation does not accord to its own citizens').

[43] After the First World War, one of the Fourteen Points proclaimed by President Wilson was the 'removal, so far as possible, of all economic barriers and the establishment of an equality of trade conditions among all the nations consenting to the peace and associating themselves for its maintenance'. According President Franklin Delano Roosevelt's Secretary of State (1933–1944), Cordell Hull, 'enduring peace and the welfare of nations are indissolubly connected with friendliness, fairness, equality and the maximum practicable degree of freedom in international trade', C Hull, *Economic Barriers to Peace* (Woodrow Wilson Foundation 1937) 14; in other words Hull's view was that 'unhampered trade dovetailed with peace; high tariffs, trade barriers, and unfair economic competition with war' JE Spero and JA Hart, *The Politics of International Economic Relations* (Wadsworth Publishing 2010) 3. Before the Second World War, 'the foremost proponent and practitioner of discriminatory trade restrictions was Nazi Germany, which regarded the principle of the most-favoured-nation treatment as a particularly

obligations are primarily a matter of treaty law in international investment law, this book focuses on how arbitral tribunals interpret these treaty obligations. In other words, this book is about the interpretation of international investment treaties,[44] rather than the interpretation of customary international law,[45] although some references to customary international obligations of States in relation to foreign investments will be made. This book examines five key non-discrimination obligations contained in international investment treaties: National Treatment, Most Favoured Nation (MFN) Treatment, the non-discrimination aspect of Fair and Equitable Treatment (FET), the prohibition against arbitrary and/or discriminatory measures (commonly referred to as 'non-impairment' clauses), and non-discrimination in the context of direct or indirect expropriation. When analysing the relevant case law, each of these five non-discrimination obligations will be examined in separate sections.

There are three areas of study that, despite their significant theoretical and practical importance, are outside the scope of this book: non-discrimination in relation to questions regarding (i) jurisdiction, (ii) quantum of compensation that successful claimants are entitled to receive, and (iii) the constitution of arbitral tribunals. In other words, this book focuses on the (potential) liability of States for violating treaty commitments not to discriminate against foreign investors. The first question which is outside the scope of this book is whether MFN clauses apply to dispute resolution provisions by allowing foreign investors to use MFN clauses contained in the applicable investment treaty to rely on more favourable dispute resolution provisions contained in investment treaties concluded between the Host States and third States, that is, States other than the investors' Home States.[46] This book does not deal with this thorny question as it

vicious offshoot of a discredited *liberalismus*. It utilized all kinds of trade controls to make the German economy self-sufficient and provide it with the implements for war', ILC, First Report on the Most-Favoured-Nation Clause (1969) 2 Yearbook of the International Law Commission 157, 163; M Risvas, 'Non-discrimination and the Protection of Foreign Investments in the Context of an Armed Conflict' in K Fach Gómez, A Gourgourinis, and C Titi (eds), *International Investment Law and the Law of Armed Conflict European Yearbook of International Economic Law: special issue* (Springer 2019) 199–215, 208; H Grant Cohen, 'Nations and Markets' (2020) 23 JIEL 793, 800–801.

[44] On the interpretation of investment treaties, in particular in the light of the Vienna Convention on the Law of Treaties (adopted 23 May 1969, entered into force 27 January 1980) 1155 UNTS 331; see also K Magraw, 'Investor-State Disputes and the Rise of Recourse to State Party Pleadings As Subsequent Agreements or Subsequent Practice under the Vienna Convention on the Law of Treaties' (2015) 30 ICSID Review 142; Roberts (n 34); E Shirlow and M Waibel, 'A Sliding Scale Approach to *Travaux* in Treaty Interpretation: The Case of Investment Treaties' BYIL (forthcoming).

[45] On the interpretation of customary international law see M Lando, 'Identification as the Process to Determine the Content of Customary International Law' (2022) 42 Oxford Journal of Legal Studies 1040; P Merkouris, J Kammerhofer, and N Arajärvi (eds), *The Theory, Practice, and Interpretation of Customary International Law* (CUP 2022).

[46] See generally SW Schill, 'Allocating Adjudicatory Authority: Most-Favoured-Nation Clauses as a Basis of Jurisdiction—A Reply to Zachary Douglas' (2011) 2 Journal of International Dispute Settlement 353; Z Douglas, 'The MFN Clause in Investment Arbitration: Treaty Interpretation Off the Rails' (2011) 2 Journal of International Dispute Settlement 97; J Maupin, 'MFN-Based Jurisdiction in Investor–State Arbitration: Is There Any Hope for a Consistent Approach?' (2011) 14 Journal of International Economic Law 157; M Paparinskis, 'MFN Clauses and International Dispute Settlement: Moving beyond Maffezini and Plama' (2011) 26 ICSID Review 14; TH Cheng and R Trisotto 'Urbaser SA and others v Argentine Republic and Teinver SA and others v Argentine Republic, A Workaround to the Most-Favoured-Nation Clause Dispute' (2014) 29 ICSID Review 289; I Uchkunova and O Temnikov, 'Toss out the Baby and Put the Water to Bed: On MFN Clauses and the Significance of Treaty Interpretation' (2015) 30 ICSID Review 414; FO Vicuña, 'Reports of [Maffezini's] demise have been greatly exaggerated' (2012) 3 Journal of International Dispute Settlement 299; Y Radi, 'The Application of the

has been already extensively, if not exhaustively, debated in international investment treaty case law and scholarship.[47] The second question not examined in this book concerns the calculation of compensation for breaches of non-discrimination obligations in international investment treaty arbitration. Remedies in international investment treaty arbitration take usually (but not always) the form of monetary compensation.[48] With few exceptions concerning mostly damages resulting from armed conflict and other similar situations, most investment treaties contain provisions regarding compensation only in cases of lawful expropriation.[49] There are few cases dealing with the calculation of damages to be awarded for breaches of non-discrimination obligations. As Walde and Sabahi observed:

> [t]he calculation of due compensation for expropriation is, in spite of debates, relatively well established. There is, however, little precedent and even less theoretical analysis of how financial compensation should be assessed for breaches of non-expropriation standards of treatment in investment treaties, such as in particular national treatment and fair and equitable treatment. So far, tribunals have tended to gravitate, for understandable reasons, towards analogy with either the expropriation standard or the breach of contract standard.[50]

As the topic has not been fully explored in the scholarship, it constitutes a fertile area of future research. Finally, this book will not examine discrimination in the context of arbitral appointments, a topic which is increasingly on the agenda of the international arbitration community.[51]

On methodology, this book heavily focuses on the case law of investment tribunals, aiming to distil the legal propositions in relation to discrimination, without dwelling too much on the specific facts of each case. This methodological choice is linked to the

Most-Favoured-Nation Clause to the Dispute Settlement Provisions of Bilateral Investment Treaties: Domesticating the "Trojan Horse'" (2007)18 EJIL 757; see R Radović, 'Between Rights and Remedies: The Access to Investment Treaty Arbitration as a Substantive Right of Foreign Investors' (2019) 10 Journal of International Dispute Settlement 42; MS Abdel Wahab, 'Itisaluna and Others v Iraq: The OIC Agreement Conundrum: Consent to ICSID Arbitration and the MFN Clauses Saga' (2021) 36 ICSID Review 1; Y Banifatemi, 'The Emerging Jurisprudence on the Most-Favoured-Nation Treatment in Investment Arbitration' in A Bjorklund, I Laird, and S Ripinsky (eds), *Investment Treaty Law: Current Issues III* (BIICL 2009) 241–273, 250.

[47] References to key cases and scholarship on the matter can be found in Chapter 3 of this book.

[48] See D Sarooshi and M Risvas, 'Foundational Concept—State Responsibility' in K Nadakavukaren Schefer and T Cottier (eds), *Elgar Encyclopedia of International Economic Law* (forthcoming).

[49] J Bonnitcha and S Brewin, 'Compensation under Investment Treaties' IISD (November 2020) 8, available at <https://www.iisd.org/system/files/publications/compensation-treaties-best-practicies-en.pdf>; see also E Aisbett and J Bonnitcha 'A Pareto-Improving Compensation Rule for Investment Treaties' (2021) 24 JIEL 181.

[50] TW Wälde and B Sabahi, 'Compensation, Damages, and Valuation' in P Muchlinski, F Ortino, and C Schreuer (eds), *The Oxford Handbook of International Investment Law* (OUP 2008) 1052–1119, 1082–1083. On the calculation of damages in investment treaty arbitration see the two classic monographs on the subject: I Marboe, *Calculation of Compensation and Damages in International Investment Law* (2nd edn, OUP 2017); B Sabahi, *Compensation and Restitution in Investor–State Arbitration: Principles and Practice* (OUP 2011).

[51] U Sharma, 'The Invisible Stigmatisation of Female Practitioners in International Arbitration' (2021) 17 International Journal of Law in Context 371; HA Kadouf and UA Oseni, 'The Discrimination Conundrum in the Appointment of Arbitrators in International Arbitration' (2012) 29 Journal of International Arbitration 519. See also *Jivraj v Hashwani* [2011] UKSC 40.

fact that, unlike common law systems, public international law in general and international investment law in particular do not follow a system of legally binding precedent,[52] although it is undeniable that investment treaty tribunals engage in some form of law-making.[53] Article 59 of the ICJ Statute is categorical: '[t]he decision of the Court has no binding force except between the parties and in respect of that particular case'.[54] As Schreuer and Weiniger observe, while '[i]n actual fact, tribunals in investment disputes, including ICSID [(International Centre for Settlement of Investment Disputes)] tribunals, rely on previous decisions of other tribunals whenever they can', '[a]t the same time, it is also well established that the doctrine of precedent, in the sense known in the common law, does not apply in international adjudication'.[55] The relatively flexibility in relation to precedent is also evidenced by the fact that even annulled arbitral awards are cited by arbitral tribunals.[56] (The term 'case law' in this book is used liberally, not having the narrow, technical meaning that it has in common law systems.)

1.2.2 The Contribution of this Book

The contribution that this book makes to the existing literature is three-fold.

First, this is the first book to analyse in a systematic and comprehensive manner all the main non-discrimination obligations contained in investment treaties: National Treatment, MFN Treatment, the non-discrimination aspect of FET, 'non-impairment' clauses, and non-discrimination in the context of expropriation. Non-discrimination

[52] See G Kaufmann-Kohler, 'Arbitral Precedent: Dream, Necessity or Excuse?: The 2006 Freshfields Lecture' (2007) 23 Arbitration International 357; J Paulsson, 'The Role of Precedent in Investment Treaty Arbitration' in K Yannaca-Small (ed), *Arbitration Under International Investment Agreements: A Guide to the Key Issues* (2nd edn, OUP 2018) 81–100; cf the excellent trilogy R Bhala, 'The Myth About Stare Decisis and International Trade Law (Part One of a Trilogy)' (1999) 14 American University International Law Review 845; R Bhala, 'The Precedent Setters: De Facto Stare Decisis in WTO Adjudication (Part Two of a Trilogy)' (1999–2000) 9 Journal of Transnational Law and Policy 1; R Bhala, 'The Power of the Past: Towards De Jure Stare Decisis in WTO Adjudication (Part Three of a Trilogy)' (2001) 33 George Washington International Law Review 873; J Commission, 'Precedent in Investment Treaty Arbitration—A Citation Analysis of a Developing Jurisprudence' (2007) 2 Journal of International Arbitration 129.

[53] SW Schill, 'System-Building in Investment Treaty Arbitration and Lawmaking' (2011) 12 German Law Journal 1083, 1086; see also M Mitsi, *The Decision-making Process of Investor-State Arbitration Tribunals* (Kluwer Law International 2019). *Sanum Investments Limited v Lao People's Democratic Republic*, UNCITRAL, PCA Case No 2013-13, Award on Jurisdiction, 13 December 2013, para 349 ('it is not difficult for the parties to a dispute to find prior decisions in support of their conflicting positions. The Tribunal is not obliged to follow any particular prior decision but it cannot ignore the arguments of the Parties and the decisions they have used to support them').

[54] Statute of the International Court of Justice, Article 59. See also Article 38(1), ibid:

1. The Court, whose function is to decide in accordance with international law such disputes as are submitted to it, shall apply:
   a. international conventions, whether general or particular, establishing rules expressly recognized by the contesting states;
   b. international custom, as evidence of a general practice accepted as law;
   c. the general principles of law recognized by civilized nations;
   d. subject to the provisions of Article 59, judicial decisions and the teachings of the most highly qualified publicists of the various nations, as subsidiary means for the determination of rules of law.

[55] C Schreuer and M Weiniger, 'A Doctrine of Precedent?' in P Muchlinski, F Ortino, and C Schreuer (eds), *The Oxford Handbook of International Investment Law* (OUP 2008) 1188–1206, 1189. See also E De Brabandere, *Investment Treaty Arbitration as Public International Law: Procedural Aspects and Implications* (CUP 2014) 94–95.

[56] M Csernus, 'Is There Life After Death?: The Persuasive Value of Annulled Investment Awards' (2022) 23 Journal of International Dispute Settlement 393, 412.

obligations in international investment law are of fundamental importance. This is especially true in relation to the National Treatment aspect[57] (guaranteeing 'inland parity'[58]) as well as the MFN aspect[59] (guaranteeing 'foreign parity'[60]) of the principle of non-discrimination. As a result, this book fills an important gap in international investment law scholarship.[61] Despite the plethora of arbitral awards rendered by tribunals constituted on the basis of investment treaties and the relatively rich case law on non-discrimination, as two leading authors and arbitrators observed in 2020:

> [t]he jurisprudence of investment tribunals on national treatment remains in a developing status. Many aspects are not yet clearly established. Especially, questions relating to the relevant comparators and to the existence and scope of justifications on grounds of public interest need further elaboration.[62]

Schill makes similar observations:

> [t]he precise scope of non-discrimination provisions has so far not been settled in treaty practice or arbitral jurisprudence. Similar to non-discrimination provisions in international trade law or domestic constitutional law, they pose problems relating to their proper interpretation, in particular regarding the standard of comparison (the

[57] 'Article 1102 [of NAFTA] embodies a principle of fundamental importance, both in international trade law and the international law of investment, that of non-discrimination', *Corn Products International Inc v United Mexican States*, ICSID Case No ARB(AF)/04/1, Decision on Responsibility, 15 January 2008, para 109; UNCTAD Series on issues in international investment agreements, *National Treatment* (UN, NY and Geneva 1999) 1 ('[t]he national treatment standard is perhaps the single most important standard of treatment enshrined in international investment agreements'); A Bjorklund, 'The National Treatment Obligation' in K Yannaca-Small, *Arbitration Under International Investment Agreements: A Guide to the Key Issues* (2nd edn, OUP 2018) 532–561, 561 ('the national treatment obligation is at the core of the international investment regime'). See also B Sabahi, N Rubins, and D Wallace, Jr, *Investor-State Arbitration* (2nd edn, OUP 2019), Chapter 17 ('Discrimination: National Treatment, Most-Favored Nation Treatment, and Discriminatory Impairment'). Already in the era of Friendship Commerce and Navigations (FCN) treaties, the progenitor of BITs, national treatment was a "cardinal objective" of the FCN treaties', KJ Vandevelde, *The First Bilateral Investment Treaties U.S. Postwar Friendship, Commerce, and Navigation Treaties* (OUP 2017) 431. On the link between National Treatment and domestic developments policy and goals (in particular in the African context) see D Npoanlari Dagbanja, *The Investment Treaty Regime and Public Interest Regulation in Africa* (OUP 2022) 13.

[58] Schwarzenberger (n 22), 119.

[59] This is also the case, perhaps even more so, in the World Trade Organization (in particular regarding the MFN principle); the WTO Appellate Body described the MFN under Article 1 of the General Agreement on Tariffs and Trade (GATT) as the 'cornerstone of GATT', AB, Canada—*Autos*, para 69, and 'one of the pillars of the WTO trading system', AB, *EC—Tariff Preferences*, para 101; see also Panel, *Colombia—Ports of Entry* para 7.320; Panel, *US—Anti-dumping and Countervailing Duties (China)*, para 14.165. The WTO Appellate Body also noted that '[f]or more than fifty years, the obligation to provide most-favoured-nation treatment in Article I of the GATT 1994 has been both central and essential to assuring the success of a global rules-based system for trade in goods', AB, *US—Section 211 Appropriations Act*, para 297. This was also true during the (first) period of globalization in the long 19th century (1815–1914). In the 1870s the Earl of Granville, British Foreign Secretary remarked, in a letter to the British Minister in Washington, that 'the most-favoured-nation clause has now become the most valuable part of our system of commercial treaties and exists between nearly all nations of the earth', K Hyder (Hasan), *Equality of Treatment and Trade Discrimination in International Law* (Springer 1968) 23–24; V Heiskanen, 'The Regulatory Philosophy of International Trade Law' (2004) 38 JWT 1, 2; Schwarzenberger (n 22) 97.

[60] Schwarzenberger (n 22) 119.

[61] For a powerful overview of the scholarship on international investment law see SW Schill, 'W(h)ither Fragmentation? On the Literature and Sociology of International Investment Law' (2011) 22 EJIL 875.

[62] A Reinisch and C Schreuer, *International Protection of Investments: The Substantive Standards* (CUP 2020) 679.

tertium comparationis) and the admissibility of, and possible justifications for, differentiations between different groups of investors.[63]

Recent challenges arising out of the regulatory response of States to the Covid-19 pandemic,[64] new technology,[65] or Russia's and the West's actions in relation to the war in Ukraine[66] further highlight the practical importance of an in-depth study of non-discrimination obligations in international investment law. This monograph is also the first book to examine non-discrimination in international investment treaty arbitration in conjunction with the concept and function of discrimination in other legal regimes, such as US, EU, and human rights anti-discrimination practice.[67] Although comparative analyses of human rights and international investment treaty[68] and, more broadly, international economic law,[69] have been attempted, there is no book examining non-discrimination in international investment treaty arbitration taking into account domestic and international human rights practice in relation to non-discrimination.

Second, this is the first monograph to explore the relationship between the different non-discrimination obligations contained in international investment treaties. Investment tribunals have noted that the case law to date has failed to disentangle different investment protection standards,[70] a matter of significant practical importance.

[63] SW Schill, *The Multilateralization of International Investment Law* (CUP 2009) 77.

[64] G Stephens-Chu, 'Discrimination Claims by Foreign Investors in the Aftermath of the COVID-19 Pandemic' in Y Levashova and P Accaoui Lorfing (eds), *Balancing the Protection of Foreign Investors and States Responses in the Post-Pandemic World* (Kluwer Law International 2022) 171–189; T Sharmin and E Laryea, 'Australian COVID-19 Measures and its International Investment Obligations' (2022) 21 Journal of International Trade Law and Policy 182; N Lavranos and A Mazlom, 'The Investment Treaty Implications of Covid-19 Responses by States' (2021) 6 European Investment Law and Arbitration Review Online 1; FI Paddeu and K Parlett, 'COVID-19 and Investment Treaty Claims' Kluwer Arbitration Blog (30 March 2020), available at <http://arbitrationblog.kluwerarbitration.com/2020/03/30/covid-19-and-investment-treaty-claims/>

[65] Q Zhang and A Mitchell, 'Data Localization and the National Treatment Obligation in International Investment Treaties' (2022) 21 WTR 391.

[66] J Zrilič, 'Are We in for a New Wave of Investment Arbitrations?: Russia's Measures Against Foreign Investors and Investment Treaty Implications' VerfBlog (21 March 2022), available at <https://verfassungsblog.de/are-we-in-for-a-new-wave-of-investment-arbitrations/>

[67] See Chapter 2.

[68] See DA Desierto, *Public Policy in International Economic Law: The ICESCR in Trade, Finance, and Investment* (OUP 2015); F Baetens, 'Discrimination on the basis of Nationality: Determining Likeness in Human Rights and Investment Law' in SW Schill (ed), *International Investment Law and Comparative Public Law* (OUP 2010) 279–315; DA Desierto, 'Shifting Sands in the International Economic System: "Arbitrage" In International Economic Law And International Human Rights' (2018) 49 Georgetown Journal of International Law 1019; E Castellarin, 'Le principe de non-discrimination' in W Ben Hamida and F Coulée (eds), *Convergences et contradictions du droit des investissements et des droits de l'homme: une approche contentieuse* (Pedone 2017) 171–196.

[69] E-U Petersmann, 'The WTO Constitution and Human Rights' (2000) 3 JIEL 19; P Alston, 'Resisting the Merger and Acquisition of Human Rights by Trade Law: A Reply to Petersmann' (2002) 13 EJIL 815; R Howse, 'Human Rights in the WTO: Whose Rights, What Humanity? Comment on Petersmann' (2002) 13 EJIL 651; E-U Petersmann, 'Human Rights, International Economic Law and Constitutional Justice: A Rejoinder' (2008) 19 EJIL 955; T Cottier, J Pauwelyn, and E Bürgi (eds), *Human Rights and International Trade* (OUP 2005); A Lang, 'Re- thinking Trade and Human Rights' (2007) 15 Tulane Journal of International and Comparative Law 335; ATF Lang, 'Reflecting on "Linkage": Cognitive and Institutional Change in the International Trading System' (2007) 70 MLR 523; P-M Dupuy, E-U Petersmann, and F Francioni (eds), *Human Rights in International Investment Law and Arbitration* (OUP 2009). See also JE Alvarez, *Boundaries of Investment Arbitration: The Use of Trade and European Human Rights Law in Investor-State Disputes* (JurisNet 2018) and S Steininger, 'What's Human Rights Got To Do With It? An Empirical Analysis of Human Rights References in Investment Arbitration' (2018) 31 Leiden Journal of International Law 33. See also E-U Petersmann, *Transforming World Trade and Investment Law for Sustainable Development* (OUP 2022), in particular Chapter 6.

[70] *Mobil Exploration and Development Inc Suc Argentina and Mobil Argentina SA v Argentine Republic*, ICSID Case No ARB/04/16, Decision on Jurisdiction and Liability, 10 April 2013, para 810 ('The Tribunal finds that that

This book argues that National Treatment, MFN, the prohibition against arbitrary and/or discriminatory measures, discrimination under the FET standard, and expropriation, all fall within the same paradigm of discrimination ('disparate treatment' or 'direct' discrimination). As will be explained in Chapters 2 and 3, this means that to succeed in a discrimination claim an investor must establish a link between the adverse consequence of a particular measure and a protected characteristic of the foreign investor suffering such consequence. The primary difference is that in a National Treatment and MFN Treatment analysis, less favourable treatment must be linked to the *nationality* of the investor, while in clauses prohibiting arbitrary and/or discriminatory measures, FET, and expropriation, the measures constituting less favourable treatment must be linked to the *nationality or another protected characteristic* of the investor.[71] Another reason why the question regarding the application (or non-application) of MFN clause to dispute settlement matters is not examined in this book is that viewing non-discrimination obligations in international investment treaty arbitration as form of 'disparate treatment' discrimination does not seem to offer a conclusive answer in that question.

Third, this book contributes to the doctrine and theory of international investment law by developing a normative argument in relation to both substantive and evidentiary matters. In that regard, the main argument of this book is that non-discrimination obligations in investment treaty arbitration fall within the 'disparate treatment' discrimination paradigm, which means that it is the claimant (the foreign investor) which must prove that the less favourable treatment it receives compared to another investor (in like circumstances) is because of its nationality or another characteristic (which constitutes an impermissible ground for differentiation, eg race, ethnicity, or religion). In practical terms, a measure giving rise to less favourable treatment of the foreign investor is discriminatory in the absence of a valid, legitimate (and non-discriminatory) policy objective pursued by the State when enacting and implementing the measure(s). This book also examines the evidentiary difficulties that investors face in establishing discrimination, and in particular the imposition of a robust procedural duty of both parties to cooperate and produce the relevant evidence which they possess, or have access to, and the acceptance of circumstantial evidence.[72] This book rejects arguments

ICSID case-law generates some confusion and overlap between these different standards of protection found in most BITs'); *El Paso Energy International Company v The Argentine Republic*, ICSID Case No ARB/03/15, Award, 31 October 2011, para 226: 'ICSID case-law has developed in a way that generates some confusion and overlap between these different standards of protection found in most BITs. In view of this situation, which is not conducive to security of the legal framework and predictability of its application to foreign investments, the Tribunal will endeavour to clarify as much as possible the scope of the different standards of protection, for it is convinced that they should not be used indifferently one for the other.'

[71] In relation to National Treatment and MFN, Mitchell, Heaton and Henckels reach the same conclusion: 'applying national treatment and most favoured nation treatment provisions in light of a treaty's object and purpose will almost inevitably require a decision-maker to consider regulatory purpose', AD Mitchell, D Heaton, and C Henckels, *Non-Discrimination and the Role of Regulatory Purpose in International Trade and Investment Law* (Edward Elgar 2016) 97.

[72] To borrow the words of the US Supreme Court, '[p]roof of discriminatory motive is critical, although it can in some situations be inferred from the mere fact of differences in treatment', *Teamsters v United States*, 431 US 324, 335 fn 15 (1977).

calling for the reversal of the burden of proof (from the foreign investor to the Host State) in line with the position of the majority of arbitral awards. Nonetheless it places emphasis on the other approaches capable of addressing the evidentiary challenges that proof of discrimination gives rise to, thereby contributing towards a more balanced discrimination test in investment treaty arbitration.[73] The normative arguments of this book in relation to evidentiary matters in relation to non-discrimination in international investment treaty arbitration also draw from the relevant case law of different courts and tribunals.

There are two normative considerations underpinning the thesis advanced in this book. First, it is submitted that this argument strikes the right balance between on the one hand the need to protect foreign investors and investments against discrimination, and on the other, States' right to regulate by exercising discretion in selecting the most appropriate policy solutions. Second, the arguments in relation to key procedural and evidentiary matters regarding discrimination (burden of proof, standard of proof, and standard of review) reflect, and are informed by, the principle of equality of parties in international arbitral proceedings. This principle is reflected in different arbitration rules. For example, Article 17(1) of the United Nations Commission on International Trade Law (UNICTRAL) Arbitration Rules provides that '[s]ubject to these Rules, the arbitral tribunal may conduct the arbitration in such manner as it considers appropriate, provided that the parties are treated with equality and that at an appropriate stage of the proceedings each party is given a reasonable opportunity of presenting its case'.[74]

This book is structured as follows. Chapter 2 first sets out the two paradigms of discrimination in US, EU, and international human rights anti-discrimination law: disparate treatment and disparate impact discrimination (Section 2.1). This section explores the concepts of disparate treatment and disparate impact discrimination (Section 2.1.1), sets out the key differences between disparate treatment discrimination and disparate impact discrimination (Section 2.1.2), and, finally, examines the role of circumstantial evidence and adverse inferences in proving disparate treatment or direct discrimination (Section 2.1.3). Section 2.2 argues that discrimination obligations in international investment law fall within the disparate treatment paradigm and Section 2.3 explores the relationship between different non-discrimination obligations contained in investment treaties. Chapter 3 discusses the legal test for establishing violations of the different non-discrimination obligations contained in investment treaties, examines likeness (Section 3.1), less favourable treatment (Section 3.2), while Section 3.3 explores the notions of discrimination 'because of' a protected ground, discriminatory intent and public policy justifications. Each section is further divided into two

[73] J Paulsson, Denial of Justice in International Law (CUP, Cambridge 2005) 14: '[w]hatever the rosy rhetoric about the equality of treatment of nationals and foreigners, the very fact of being foreign creates an inequality. The foreigner's obvious handicap—his lack of citizenship—is usually compounded by vulnerabilities with respect to many types of influence: political, social, cultural'.

[74] 2010 UNICTRAL Arbitration Rules and 2021 UNCITRAL Arbitration Rules, Article 17(1). See also Chapter 4.

subsections. The first subsection of each section (Sections 3.1.1, 3.2.1, and 3.3.1) presents the relevant case law, separately for each of the five aspects of non-discrimination (National Treatment (Sections 3.1.1.1, 3.2.1.1, and 3.3.1.1), MFN (Sections 3.1.1.2, 3.2.1.2, and 3.3.1.2), non-impairment clauses (Sections 3.1.1.3, 3.2.1.3, and 3.3.1.3), FET (Sections 3.1.1.4, 3.2.1.4, and 3.3.1.4), and expropriation (Sections 3.1.1.5, 3.2.1.5, 3.3.1.5)). The second subsection of each section presents the normative suggestions of this book (Sections 3.1.2, 3.2.2, and 3.3.2). Chapter 4 focuses on evidentiary matters. The first section of that chapter (Section 4.1) deals with the allocation of the burden of proof, Section 4.2 discusses the standard of review, and Section 4.3 analyses the standard of proof. Like the previous chapter, each of these sections of Chapter 4 is divided into two parts. The first part is descriptive setting out the relevant case law (Sections 4.1.1, 4.2.1, and 4.3.1 and 4.3.1), while the second part is normative, offering this book's normative suggestions in relation to these key evidentiary questions (Sections 4.1.2, 4.2.2, and 4.3.2). Section 4.1.2.1 explores the principle *actori incumbit probatio*, and Section 4.1.2.2 examines the role of the parties' duty to cooperate in the production of evidence and the tribunals' power to draw adverse inferences in alleviating the evidentiary difficulties which investors are facing in trying to establish discrimination, and, in particular, link less favourable treatment with a protected characteristic. Chapter 5 concludes.

2

The Nature of Non-discrimination Obligations Contained in International Investment Treaties

Chapter 2 contains the theoretical framework of the analysis of non-discrimination obligations in international investment law presented in this book. Section 2.1 traverses US, EU, and international human rights anti-discrimination law and sets out the two main paradigms of discrimination: 'disparate treatment' discrimination and 'disparate impact' discrimination. Section 2.1.1 provides a basic introduction to these two forms of discrimination, Section 2.1.2 delves into their differences, and Section 2.1.3 analyses the role of circumstantial evidence and adverse inferences in proving disparate treatment or direct discrimination. The purpose of this section is not to embark on a comprehensive comparative analysis of anti-discrimination law and practice; rather, this section explores how different domestic and international courts have dealt with discrimination-related questions, with the view of drawing helpful insights for the interpretation of non-discrimination provisions in international investment law. Section 2.2 makes the argument that all non-discrimination obligations contained in investment treaties fall within the disparate treatment discrimination paradigm and explains the implications of such classification. Finally, Section 2.3 explores the relationship between the different non-discrimination obligations in international investment treaty arbitration. Section 2.3.1 focuses on the relationship between National Treatment and most favoured nations (MFN) on the one hand, and clauses prohibiting arbitrary and/or discriminatory measures (non-impairment clauses) on the other. Sections 2.3.2 and 2.3.3 discuss the relationship between discrimination and fair and equitable treatment (FET) and discrimination and expropriation respectively.

2.1 Two Paradigms of Discrimination: Disparate Treatment (or Direct) Discrimination and Disparate Impact (or Indirect) Discrimination

2.1.1 Disparate Treatment (or Direct) Discrimination and Disparate Impact (or Indirect) Discrimination

For every concept, numerous different conceptions exist.[1] Discrimination is no different. This chapter explains that by examining discrimination case law in national, transnational, and international legal systems (such as the US, the EU, the UK, the European Convention on Human Rights (ECHR),[2] and the American Convention on Human Rights (ACHR)[3,4]), two main paradigms of discrimination emerge: (i) disparate treatment or direct discrimination, and (ii) disparate impact or indirect discrimination.[5] The distinction between disparate treatment and disparate impact discrimination is well entrenched.[6] In some jurisdictions this distinction is explicitly set out in the relevant legislation and many courts consider the two forms of discrimination mutually exclusive.[7] According to Khaitan '[a]ll jurisdictions, with the possible exception of Canada, make a distinction between these forms of discrimination'.[8] However, the distinction has been criticized by various scholars who propose a unified non-discrimination test to promote substantive equality,[9] and, in any event, is not always

[1] On the concept/conception distinction see HLA Hart, *The Concept of Law* (The Clarendon Press 1961) 155–159; J Rawls, *Theory of Justice* (rev edn, Harvard University Press 1999) 4–5; R Dworkin, *Taking Rights Seriously* (Harvard University Press 1977) 134–136.

[2] Convention for the Protection of Human Rights and Fundamental Freedoms (adopted 4 November 1950, entered into force 3 September 1953) 213 UNTS 222.

[3] American Convention on Human Rights (adopted 22 November 1969, entered into force 18 July 1978) 1144 UNTS 123.

[4] Naturally, the universe of the adjudication of discrimination claims is even broader, see eg A Trebilock, 'Approaches to Discrimination Claims: A Comparison of the Administrative Tribunals of the Asian Development Bank and the Inter-American Development Bank Group' (2022) 12 Asian Journal of International Law 216.

[5] For an overview of the different US and the EU anti-discrimination regimes, see also G de Búrca, 'The Trajectories of European and American Antidiscrimination Law' (2012) 60 American Journal of Comparative Law 1. On EU gender equality policies see I Bego, *Gender Equality Policy in the European Union: A Fast Track to Parity for the New Member States* (Palgrave Macmillan 2015); on the historical development of EU discrimination law, S Burri, 'EU Anti-discrimination Law: Historical Development and Main Concepts' in Y Li and J Goldschmidt (eds), *Taking Employment Discrimination Seriously: Chinese and European Perspectives* (Martinus Nijhoff 2009) 209–238. On equality and non-discrimination in EU law, R Lang, *Complex Equality and the Court of Justice of the European Union; Reconciling Diversity and Harmonisation* (Brill Nijhoff 2018). For a comparison between EU and ECHR law on non-discrimination see C Nikolaidis, *The Right to Equality in European Human Rights Law* (Routledge 2015). For a comparison between US and ECHR, see C Nikolaidis, 'Unravelling the Knot of Equality and Privacy in the European Court of Human Rights and the US Supreme Court: From Isonomia to Isotimia' (2018) 18 Human Rights Law Review 719.

[6] K Linos, 'Path Dependence in Discrimination Law: Employment Cases in the United States and the European Union' (2010) 35 Yale Journal of International Law 115, 119.

[7] *R (on the application of E) v Governing Body of JFS* [2009] UKSC 15, para 57; *Raytheon Co v Hernandez* 540 US 44, 53 (2003); *Ricci v DeStefano*, 557 US 557.

[8] T Khaitan, *A Theory of Discrimination Law* (OUP 2015) 160.

[9] S Fredman, *Discrimination Law* (2nd edn, OUP 2011); BJ Flagg, '"Was Blind, but Now I See": White Race Consciousness and the Requirement of Discriminatory Intent' (1993) 91 Michigan Law Review 953, 960; R Post, 'Prejudicial Appearances: The Logic of American Antidiscrimination Law' (2000) 88 California Law Review 1, 39.

clear cut, especially across different legal systems, raising important philosophical questions. As Campbell and Smith explain:

> [d]espite the fact that the Equality Act—and equivalent statutes in many other jurisdictions—set out different tests for direct and indirect discrimination, there is considerable disagreement about how the distinction between these two forms of discrimination should be understood.[10]

The *JFS* case which divided the UK Supreme Court is a case in point, with the majority (Lord Phillips, Lady Hale, Lord Mance, Lord Clarke, and Lord Kerr) holding that the school had *directly* discriminated on grounds of race and two of the minority (Lord Hope and Lord Walker) holding that this was a case of *indirect* discrimination.[11]

The US Supreme Court has explained the difference between the tests under disparate treatment and disparate impact discrimination in the following manner:

> [l]iability in a disparate-treatment case 'depends on whether the protected trait ... *actually motivated* the employer's decision.' By contrast, disparate-impact claims 'involve employment practices that are facially neutral in their treatment of different groups but that in fact fall more harshly on one group than another *and* cannot be justified by business necessity.'[12]

The Equal Protection Clause of the US Constitution does not prohibit disparate impact discrimination, as the Supreme Court held in *Washington v Davis*.[13] By contrast, disparate impact discrimination is prohibited under Title VII of the Civil Rights Act, an act was passed by the Congress in 1964 in the context of the US civil rights movement, constituting the catalyst in US anti-discrimination law.[14] This was established

[10] C Campbell and D Smith, 'Distinguishing Between Direct and Indirect Discrimination' (2023) 86 MLR 307, 308. See also N Bamforth, 'Approaching the Indirect-Direct Discrimination Distinction: Concepts, Justifications and Policies' in H Collins and T Khaitan (eds), *Foundations of Indirect Discrimination Law* (Hart 2018) 57–82. See also S Atrey, 'Structural Racism and Race Discrimination' (2021) 74 Current Legal Problems 1; S Atrey, *Intersectional Discrimination* (OUP 2018); I Solanke, *Discrimination as Stigma: A Theory of Anti-discrimination Law* (Hart 2017).

[11] *R (on the application of E) v Governing Body of JFS and the Admissions Appeal Panel of JFS* [2009] UKSC 15; see also M Connolly, *The Judiciary, Discrimination Law and Statutory Interpretation: Easy Cases Making Bad Law* (Routledge 2018) 101–102; M Pearson, 'Religious Discrimination and the "Hierarchy of Rights": Non-existent, Appropriate or Problematic?' (2016) 16 International Journal of Discrimination and the Law 37.

[12] *Raytheon Co v Hernandez*, 540 US 44 (2003), 52 citing *Teamsters v United States*, 431 US 324 (1977) (emphasis added).

[13] *Washington v Davis*, 426 US 229, 239 (1976) ('The central purpose of the Equal Protection Clause of the Fourteenth Amendment is the prevention of official conduct discriminating on the basis of race. It is also true that the Due Process Clause of the Fifth Amendment contains an equal protection component prohibiting the United States from invidiously discriminating between individuals or groups. *Bolling v Sharpe*, 347 US 497 (1954). But our cases have not embraced the proposition that a law or other official act, without regard to whether it reflects a racially discriminatory purpose, is unconstitutional solely because it has a racially disproportionate impact.').

[14] Between 1964 and 1990 the number of discrimination cases before US Courts grew exponentially. For a statistical analysis, see JJ Donohue III and P Siegelman, 'The Changing Nature of Employment Discrimination Litigation' (1991) 43 Stanford Law Review 983. On the relationship between the Equal Protection Clause of the US Constitution and disparate impact discrimination see RA Primus, 'Equal Protection and Disparate Impact: Round Three' (2003) 117 Harvard Law Review 494.

by the Supreme Court in *Griggs v Duke Power Co* case[15] in 1971—a decision which has been described as the most important discrimination case since *Brown*.[16] As Justice O'Connor observed in another case, 'the necessary premise of the disparate impact approach is that some employment practices, *adopted without a deliberately discriminatory motive, may in operation be functionally equivalent to intentional discrimination*'.[17]

A similar distinction between disparate treatment and disparate impact discrimination exists in European non-discrimination law, which is inspired from, and developed much later than, US law.[18] In the landmark *Jenkins* case, decided in 1981, the Court of Justice of the European Union (CJEU) essentially adopted discrimination test based on impact.[19] *Griggs v Duke Power Co* was explicitly referred to in the claimant's submissions[20] and the opinion of the Advocate General.[21] The CJEU's approach in relation to indirect discrimination was later codified in secondary EU legislation. However,

[15] *Griggs v Duke Power Co*, 401 US 424 (1971).

[16] L Carlson, *Comparative Discrimination Law* (Brill 2017) 50; *Brown v Board of Education*, 347 US 483 (1954); *Griggs v Duke Power Co*, 401 US 424 (1971).

[17] *Watson v Fort Worth Bank & Trust*, 487 US 977, 987 (1988) (emphasis added). See also *Teamsters v United States*, 431 US 324, 335 fn 15 (1977) ('Proof of discriminatory motive, we have held, is not required under a disparate impact theory'). See also JR Bent, 'The Telltale Sign of Discrimination: Probabilities, Information Asymmetries, and the Systemic Disparate Treatment Theory' (2011) 44 University of Michigan Journal of Law Reform 807.

[18] See I Tourkochoriti, 'Jenkins v. Kingsgate and the Migration of the US Disparate Impact Doctrine in EU Law' in F Nicola and B Davies (eds), *EU Law Stories: Contextual and Critical Histories of European Jurisprudence* (CUP 2017) 418–445; D Sabbagh, 'La discrimination sur le lieu de travail: éléments pour une comparaison transatlantique' (2019) 102 Droit et Société 321; G de Búrca, 'The Trajectories of European and American Antidiscrimination Law' (2012) 60 American Journal of Comparative Law 1, 4; G Quinn and E Flynn, 'Transatlantic Borrowings: The Past and Future of EU Non-Discrimination Law and Policy on the Ground of Disability' (2012) 60 American Journal of Comparative Law 23; B De Witte, 'New Institutions for Promoting Equality in Europe: Legal Transfers, National Bricolage and European Governance' (2012) 60 American Journal of Comparative Law 49; JC Suk, 'From Antidiscrimination to Equality: Stereotypes and the Life Cycle in the United States and Europe' (2012) 60 American Journal of Comparative Law 75; Linos (n 6) 137. This is also the case with UK anti-discrimination law, C McCrudden, 'A Common Law of Human Rights?: Transnational Judicial Conversations on Constitutional Rights' (2000) 20 Oxford Journal of Legal Studies 499, 501.

[19] Case C-96/80, *JP Jenkins v Kingsgate (Clothing Productions) Ltd* [1981] ECR 911, para 13. In 1986 the CJEU held that there was discrimination in cases of an undertaking that 'excludes part-time employees from its occupational pension scheme' and 'that exclusion affects a far greater number of women than men unless the undertaking shows that the exclusion is based on objectively justified factors unrelated to any discrimination on grounds of sex.' Case C-170/84, *Bilka-Kaufhaus GmbH v Weber von Hartz*, 13 May 1986, para 31.

[20] Case C-96/80, *JP Jenkins v Kingsgate (Clothing Productions) Ltd* [1981] ECR 911, 916: 'Mrs Jenkins also refers to the principle enunciated by the Supreme Court of the United States in *Griggs v Duke Power Co* 401 US 424 (1971), according to which what must be prohibited are not merely practices which are intended to discriminate, but equally those which are discriminatory in their effect, irrespective of the intentions of their authors.' ibid, 917: 'If a condition or requirement which must be met in order to obtain equal pay for equal work operates so as to exclude women and cannot be shown to have a manifest relationship to the services involved, the application of such a condition or requirement must be considered to be contrary to the principle of equal pay. That is in application of the principle or "adverse impact" enunciated by the Supreme Court of the United States (in *Griggs v Duke Power Co*) and by the British Parliament in Section 1 (1) (b) of the Sex Discrimination Act.'

[21] Case 96/80, *JP Jenkins v Kingsgate (Clothing Productions) Ltd*, Opinion of Advocate General Warner, 28 January 1981, [1981] ECR 911, 936–937:

> As has been observed more than once, the Supreme Court of the United States and this Court often find themselves confronted with similar problems. Although of course the provisions of the United States Civil Rights Act of 1964 that were in question in the Griggs case were worded differently from Article 119 of the Treaty, their essential purpose was the same, except in so far as the provision in question in the Griggs case was about racial discrimination, not sex discrimination. Indeed in *Dothard v Rawlinson* (1977) 433 US 321 the Supreme Court applied similar reasoning to sex discrimination. I draw considerable comfort from finding that my conclusion accords with the conclusions of that court in those cases.

Tourkochoriti describes the 'story of Jenkins [as] a stark example of the migration of legal ideas', I Tourkochoriti, '*Jenkins v. Kingsgate* and the Migration of the US Disparate Impact Doctrine in EU Law' in F Nicola

there are also differences regarding the understanding of disparate impact (or indirect discrimination) between the United States and the European Union. For example, as Linos explains:

> [t]he U.S. Supreme Court insisted that plaintiffs must identify with substantial specificity the causal link between the employer practice and the harmful practice and the harmful effect. In contract, the ECJ effectively held that statistics alone sufficed to establish disparate impact.[22]

The terms equivalent to 'disparate treatment' and 'disparate impact' discrimination in EU law are 'direct' and 'indirect' discrimination.[23] In EU Directives focusing on specific aspects of discrimination,[24] 'direct discrimination' is similarly defined.[25] For example, Directive 2000/43 defines direct discrimination in the following manner: 'direct discrimination shall be taken to occur where one person is treated less favourably than

and B Davies (eds), *EU Law Stories: Contextual and Critical Histories of European Jurisprudence* (CUP 2017) 418–445, 418.

[22] Linos (n 6) 118. See also *Essop and others v Home Office (UK Border Agency)*; *Naeem v Secretary of State for Justice* [2017] UKSC 27, para 33: '[i]n order to succeed in an indirect discrimination claim, it is not necessary to establish the reason for the particular disadvantage to which the group is put. The essential element is a causal connection between the [provision, criterion or practice] and the disadvantage suffered, not only by the group, but also by the individual. This may be easier to prove if the reason for the group disadvantage is known but that is a matter of fact, not law'.

[23] As Linos explains, '[t]wo separate theories, disparate treatment and disparate impact, have been available to employees alleging discrimination in both the United States and the European Union. Disparate treatment theory challenges intentional discrimination. Disparate impact theory challenges employer practices that appear neutral, but have the effect of harming minority groups. The EU analog to disparate treatment is direct discrimination, and the EU analog to disparate impact is indirect discrimination'. Linos (n 6) 117. See also M Möschel, 'The Strasbourg Court and Indirect Race Discrimination: Going Beyond the Education Domain' (2017) 80 MLR 110, 123 ('where direct discrimination and the principle of formal equality "only" prohibits the different treatment of similar situations on the basis of a prohibited ground, indirect discrimination goes further by prohibiting the similar treatment of different situations when certain seemingly neutral provisions, measures or practices have a negative impact on certain groups').

[24] Council Directive 2000/43/EC of 29 June 2000 implementing the principle of equal treatment between persons irrespective of racial or ethnic origin; Council Directive 2000/78/EC of 27 November 2000 establishing a general framework for equal treatment in employment and occupation; Directive 2006/54/EC of 5 July 2006 on the implementation of the principle of equal opportunities and equal treatment of men and women in matters of employment and occupation; Council Directive 2004/113/EC of 13 December 2004 implementing the principle of equal treatment between men and women in the access to and supply of goods and services.

[25] These EU Directives are not the only source of non-discrimination obligations in EU law. The principle of equality is reflected in several provisions of primary EU law (such as Articles 28, 40(2), 45, 46, 49, 50, and 110 of the TFEU) and the EU Charter of Fundamental Rights also contains non-discrimination obligations: Article 20 and Article 21. Non-discrimination is also recognized as general principle of the EU legal order; see Case C-245/81, *Edeka Zentrale AG v Federal Republic of Germany* [1982] ECR 2745, para 11: 'the prohibition of discrimination contained in the second subparagraph of Article 40 (3) of the Treaty [Article 40(2) of the TFEU] is merely a specific enunciation of the general principle of equality which is one of the fundamental principles of Community law'. See also Case C-356/12, *Wolfgang Glatzel v Freistaat Bayern*, 20 May 2014, para 43 ('[t]he principle of equal treatment is a general principle of EU law, enshrined in Article 20 of the Charter, of which the principle of non-discrimination laid down in Article 21(1) of the Charter is a particular expression'); Case C-535/03, *Unitymark and North Sea Fishermen's Organisation* [2006] ECR I-2689, para 53; Case C-245/81, *Edeka Zentrale AG v Federal Republic of Germany* [1982] ECR 2745, para 11; *Seda Kücükdeveci v Swedex GmbH & Co KG*, 19 January 2010, para 27; see also T Cottier and M Oesch, 'Direct and Indirect Discrimination in WTO and EU Law' in SE Gaines, B Egelund Olsen, and K Engsig Sørensen (eds), *Liberalising Trade in the EU and the WTO: A Legal Comparison* (CUP 2012) 141–175, 151. See also M Brillat, *Le principe de non discrimination à l'épreuve des droits européens* (LGDJ 2015).

another is, has been or would be treated in a comparable situation *on grounds of* racial or ethnic origin'.[26] In the same Directive indirect discrimination is defined as follows:

> indirect discrimination shall be taken to occur where an apparently neutral provision, criterion or practice would put persons of a racial or ethnic origin at a particular disadvantage compared with other persons, unless that provision, criterion or practice is objectively justified by a legitimate aim and the means of achieving that aim are appropriate and necessary.[27]

Directives 2000/78, 2006/54, and 2004/113 contain similar definitions for direct and indirect discrimination.[28] In the UK, the 2010 Equality Act (designed to replace and unify different non-discrimination-related pieces of legislation[29]) adopts the same distinction between direct and indirect discrimination[30] and provides the following definition for the former: '[a] person (A) discriminates against another (B) if, *because of* a protected characteristic, A treats B less favourably than A treats or would treat others.'[31] By contrast, '[i]ndirect discrimination (or "disparate impact" as it is called in the United States) involves an apparently neutral practice or policy which puts persons belonging to a protected group at a particular disadvantage'.[32] Under Section 19 of the UK 2010 Equality Act, 'indirect discrimination' is defined as follows:

> (1) A person (A) discriminates against another (B) if A applies to B a provision, criterion or practice which is discriminatory in relation to a relevant protected characteristic of B's.
> (2) For the purposes of subsection (1), a provision, criterion or practice is discriminatory in relation to a relevant protected characteristic of B's if—
> (a) A applies, or would apply, it to persons with whom B does not share the characteristic,
> (b) it puts, or would put, persons with whom B shares the characteristic at a particular disadvantage when compared with persons with whom B does not share it,
> (c) it puts, or would put, B at that disadvantage, and
> (d) A cannot show it to be a proportionate means of achieving a legitimate aim.[33]

[26] Directive 2000/43/EC, Article 2(2)(a) (emphasis added).
[27] Directive 2000/43/EC, Article 2(2)(b).
[28] Directive 2000/78/EC, Articles 2(a) and 2(b); Directive 2006/54/EC, Articles 2(1)(a) and 2(1)(b); Directive 2004/113, Articles 2(a) and 2(b).
[29] Pearson (n 11) 38. The Acts replaced were the Equal Pay Act 1970, the Sex Discrimination Act 1975, and the Race Relations Act 1976.
[30] 2010 Equality Act, Sections 13 and 19.
[31] 2010 Equality Act, Section 13(1) (emphasis added).
[32] Khaitan (n 8) 73.
[33] Equality Act, Sections 19(1) and 19(2).

Section 19(3) of the Equality Act includes a list of the 'relevant protected characteristics' (age, disability, gender reassignment, marriage and civil partnership, race, religion or belief, sex, and sexual orientation).[34]

Disparate impact (or indirect) discrimination ultimately found its way in international human rights law,[35] partly under the influence of EU law on the jurisprudence of the European Court of Human Rights (ECtHR).[36] The ECtHR recognized that a disproportionate adverse impact of a measure on certain group(s) amounts to discrimination.[37] In the words of the ECtHR, 'a difference in treatment may take the form of disproportionately prejudicial effects of a general policy or measure which, though couched in neutral terms, discriminates against a group' and 'may amount to "indirect

[34] ibid, Section 19(3).

[35] For an overview of the universe of non-discrimination provisions in different international human rights instruments, see M Mwakagali, *International Human Rights Law and Discrimination Protections: A Comparison of Regional and National Responses* (Brill 2018); Lord Lester of Herne Hill, 'Non-Discrimination in International Human Rights Law' in Commonwealth Secretariat (ed), *Developing Human Rights Jurisprudence Volume 6: Sixth Judicial Colloquium on the Domestic Application of International Human Rights Norms* (The Commonwealth Secretariat 1995) 9–30. For a comparison between the international human rights and international investment treaty arbitration regimes see eg Y Radi (ed), *Research Handbook on Human Rights and Investment* (Edward Elgar 2018).

[36] G de Búrca, 'The Trajectories of European and American Antidiscrimination Law' (2012) 60 American Journal of Comparative Law 1, 4; *DH and Others v Czech Republic*, Application No 57325/00, 13 November 2007, paras 85–91; *Stec and others v United Kingdom*, Application Nos 65731/01 and 65900/01, 12 April 2006, para 58. Until the adoption of the 12th Additional Protocol, the ECHR did not contain an autonomous and general obligation of discrimination. Article 1 of the 12th Additional Protocol to the ECHR provides that:

1. The enjoyment of any right set forth by law shall be secured without discrimination on any ground such as sex, race, colour, language, religion, political or other opinion, national or social origin, association with a national minority, property, birth or other status.

2. No one shall be discriminated against by any public authority on any ground such as those mentioned in paragraph 1.

Protocol No 12 to the Convention for the Protection of Human Rights and Fundamental Freedoms (adopted 4 November 2000, entered into force 01 April 2005) ETS No 177, Article 1. Article 14 of the ECHR guarantees '[t]he enjoyment of the rights and freedoms set forth in this Convention' 'without discrimination on any ground such as sex, race, colour, language, religion, political or other opinion, national or social origin, association with a national minority, property, birth or other status.' See also *Biao v Denmark* [GC], Application No 38590/10, 24 May 2016, para 89 (emphasis added); *Carson and others v United Kingdom* [GC], Application No 42184/05, 16 March 2010, para 61; *DH and Others v Czech Republic* [GC], Application No 57325/00, 13 November 2007, para 175; *Burden v United Kingdom* [GC], Application No 13378/05, 29 April 2008, para 60. See also OM Arnardóttir, *Equality and Non-Discrimination under the European Convention on Human Rights* (Martinus Nijhoff 2002).

[37] See eg *Hugh Jordan v United Kingdom*, Application No 24746/94, 4 May 2001, para 154 ('Where a general policy or measure has disproportionately prejudicial effects on a particular group, it is not excluded that this may be considered as discriminatory notwithstanding that it is not specifically aimed or directed at that group'). See also *DH and Others v Czech Republic*, Application No 57325/00, 13 November 2007, para 175 ('discrimination means treating differently, without an objective and reasonable justification, persons in relevantly similar situations'); *Willis v The United Kingdom*, Application No 36042/97, para 48; *Okpisz v Germany*, Application No 59140/00, para 33 ('a difference of treatment is discriminatory for the purposes of Article 14 of the Convention if it "has no objective and reasonable justification", that is if it does not pursue a "legitimate aim" or if there is not a "reasonable relationship of proportionality between the means employed and the aim sought to be realised"'); *Lithgow and others v The United Kingdom*, Application Nos 9006/80, 9262/81, 9263/81, 9265/81, 9266/81, 9313/81, 9405/81, 8 July 1986, para 177. Likewise, in the *Perreux* case, it was recognized that once the claimant establishes a prima facie of discrimination it is up to respondent to prove that such discrimination was justified. CE, 30 October 2009, *Mme Perreux*. See also C Charpy, 'The *Conseil d'État* Abandons Its *Cohn Bendit* Case-Law; *Conseil d'Etat*, 30 October 2009, *Mme Perreux*' (2010) 6 European Constitutional Law Review 123, 134: 'According to the supreme administrative court, it is first up to the petitioner who complains of having been discriminated against to substantiate the complaint. Subsequently, it is up to the defendant to advance exonerating facts.' See also CE, 10 January 2011, *Mme A*. The case is famous because the Conseil d'État overruled its prior decision and held that individuals could invoke rights provided for in EU Directives as a ground for annulling administrative decisions CE, 30 October 2009, *Perreux*; P Craig and G de Búrca, *The Evolution of EU Law* (2nd edn, OUP 2011) 348. See also E Castellarin, 'Le principe de non-discrimination' in W Ben Hamida and F Coulé (eds), *Convergences et contradictions du droit des investissements et des droits de l'homme: une approche contentieuse* (Pedone 2017) 171–196.

discrimination", which does not necessarily require a discriminatory intent'.[38] In the landmark case of *DH and others v Czech Republic*, the ECtHR held that:

> [w]here it has been shown that legislation produces such a discriminatory effect, the Grand Chamber considers that, as with cases concerning employment or the provision of services ... it is not necessary in cases in the educational sphere to prove any discriminatory intent on the part of the relevant authorities.[39]

The UN Human Rights Committee in interpreting Article 26 UN International Covenant on Civil and Political Rights (ICCPR) prohibiting discrimination[40] clarified that 'the intent of the legislature is not alone dispositive in determining a breach of Article 26 of the Covenant. A politically motivated differentiation is unlikely to be compatible with article 26. *But an act which is not politically motivated may still contravene article 26 if its effects are discriminatory*'.[41] In another case, the Human Rights Committee held that 'a violation of article 26 can also result from the discriminatory effect of a rule or measure that is neutral at face value or without intent to discriminate', provided that 'the detrimental effects of a rule or decision exclusively or disproportionally affect persons having a particular race, colour, sex, language, religion, political or other opinion, national or social origin, property, birth or other status' and 'rules or decisions with such an impact ... [are not] based on objective and reasonable grounds'.[42] As the International Court of Justice (ICJ) noted in the *Qatar v UAE* case, the International Convention on the Elimination of All Forms of Racial Discrimination (CERD), 'prohibits all forms and manifestations of racial discrimination, *whether arising from the purpose of a given restriction or from its effect*'.[43]

[38] *Biao v Denmark* [GC], Application No 38590/10, 24 May 2016, para 103; *DH and Others v Czech Republic* [GC], Application No 57325/00, 13 November 2007, para 175; *Hugh Jordan v United Kingdom*, Application No 24746/94, 4 August 2001, para 154 ('Where a general policy or measure has disproportionately prejudicial effects on a particular group, it is not excluded that this may be considered as discriminatory, notwithstanding that it is not specifically aimed or directed at that group').

[39] *DH and others v Czech Republic* [GC], Application No 57325/00, 13 November 2007, para 194 (internal references omitted). See also *Zarb Adami v Malta*, Application No 17209/02, 20 June 2006, para 82 ('it has not been shown that the difference in treatment pursued a legitimate aim and that there was a reasonable relationship of proportionality between the means employed and the aim sought to be realised').

[40] International Covenant on Civil and Political Rights (adopted 16 December 1966, entered into force 23 March 1976) 999 UNTS 171 Article 26: 'All persons are equal before the law and are entitled without any discrimination to the equal protection of the law. In this respect, the law shall prohibit any discrimination and guarantee to all persons equal and effective protection against discrimination on any ground such as race, colour, sex, language, religion, political or other opinion, national or social origin, property, birth or other status.' See also UN Human Rights Committee, *CCPR General Comment No 18: Non-discrimination*, 10 November 1989, para 7: 'While these conventions deal only with cases of discrimination on specific grounds, the Committee believes that the term "discrimination" as used in the Covenant should be understood to imply any distinction, exclusion, restriction or preference which is based on any ground such as race, colour, sex, language, religion, political or other opinion, national or social origin, property, birth or other status, and which has the purpose or effect of nullifying or impairing the recognition, enjoyment or exercise by all persons, on an equal footing, of all rights and freedoms.'

[41] *Simunek, Hastings, Tuzilova and Prochazka v Czech Republic*, Communication No 516/1992, UN Doc CCPR/C/54/D/516/1992, 31 July 1995, para 11.7 (emphasis added).

[42] *Rupert Althammer v Austria*, Communication No 998/2001, UN Doc CCPR/C/78/D/998/2001, 8 August 2003, para 10.2.

[43] *Application of the International Convention on the Elimination of All Forms of Racial Discrimination (Qatar v United Arab Emirates)*, Preliminary Objections, Judgment, [2021] ICJ Rep 71, 109, para 112 (emphasis added); see also ibid: '[i]n the Court's view, the various measures of which Qatar complains do not, *either by their purpose or by*

Although de jure discrimination (ie discrimination based on measures which explicitly adopt as the basis for different treatment a protected characteristic) constitutes perhaps the most stereotypical form of disparate treatment or direct discrimination, the latter should not be equated with de jure discrimination. As Campbell and Smith argue:

> Direct discrimination ... arises where D treats C adversely and treats C's possession of a protected characteristic as a factor in favour of according the adverse treatment to C. By contrast, indirect discrimination occurs where D does not treat C's possession of a protected characteristic as a factor in favour of according C adverse treatment but, nevertheless, acts in a way that disproportionately disadvantages members of a group to which C belongs (a group that is marked out by its members' possession of a protected characteristic) and, by doing so, disadvantages C. This way of understanding the distinction ... has significant advantages over both the facial neutrality approach and the suggestion that direct discrimination is intentional whereas indirect discrimination is not. In particular, it better captures the moral differences between different types of discriminatory act. As such, it explains why the law might want to distinguish between direct and indirect discrimination in the first place.[44]

As a result, a distinction must be made between (i) de jure discrimination, ie discrimination which expressly uses a protected ground as the basis for granting less favourable treatment (involving measures which discriminate 'on their face') and (ii) disparate treatment or direct discrimination. The overlap between the two, although common and significant, is not complete. The two categories are conceptually distinct. In other words, in the US (and, at least to some extent in the EU and UK) although most of the cases of disparate treatment (or direct discrimination) would involve measures explicitly adopting as the basis for different treatment the protected ground, this is not always (and does not always need to be) the case. The touchstone for classifying a particular form of discrimination as disparate treatment (or direct) discrimination is not whether the protected ground is expressly mentioned as the relevant criterion for granting less favourable treatment, but whether there is a connection between the protected ground and less favourable treatment.

The philosophical foundation of disparate treatment discrimination is not clear. As Benjamin Eidelson explains in his monograph on the philosophy of non-discrimination:

their effect, give rise to racial discrimination against Qataris as a distinct social group on the basis of their national origin' (emphasis added).

[44] Campbell and Smith (n 10) 330; see also ibid, 313–318. See also F Ortino, 'Non-Discriminatory Treatment in Investment Disputes' in P-M Dupuy, E-U Petersmann, and F Francioni (eds), *Human Rights in International Investment Law and Arbitration* (OUP 2009) 344–366. An infamous example of intentional but inherent discrimination was the creation of the 'independent' Bantustan States during the apartheid era, which was a mechanism by which the Government of South Africa attempted to replace race as the formal basis of discrimination against black South African with citizenship, M Milanovic, *Extraterritorial Application of Human Rights Treaties: Law, Principles, Policy* (OUP 2011) 80; J Crawford, *The Creation of States in International Law* (2nd edn, OUP 2006) 338–348; see also M Jackson, 'The Definition of Apartheid in Customary International Law and the International Convention on the Elimination of All Forms of Racial Discrimination' (2022) 71 ICLQ 831.

> [u]nder American, British, and European law, indirect discrimination is essentially conduct that imposes disproportionate burdens on some class of people and fails some special standard of justification. This category, I will suggest, encompasses two very different kinds of acts. The first type of act is indeed discrimination, but is not in any irreducible sense indirect ... The second type of act, by contrast, is not merely a kind of ordinary or direct discrimination. But I will suggest that it is not best thought of as discrimination at all. Rather, prohibitions on such cases of 'indirect discrimination' are best seen as redistributive programs to expand access to opportunity, akin in many respects to a moderate but compulsory practice of positive discrimination or affirmative action.[45]

Therefore, to the extent that disparate impact discrimination is not concerned with distributive goals, 'the legal notion of indirect discrimination is not the name of a *kind* of discrimination, but rather a convenient legal fiction that empowers us to hold defendants liable for what is, in the end, ordinary (but second-order) discrimination'.[46] In that vein, discrimination based on impact presupposes the historical existence of direct, intent-based discrimination.[47] Depending on what the purpose of impact-based discrimination is considered to be, its function could be seen as either 'corrective' or

[45] B Eidelson, *Discrimination and Disrespect* (OUP 2015) 39.

[46] ibid, 46. Eidelson defines 'second-order discrimination' as follows: '[f]ormally, a person commits second-order discrimination on the basis of P when she discriminates on the basis of P in adopting a rule or decision to discriminate on the basis of Q in some other dimension of treatment. Second-order discrimination on the basis of P is thus a special case of ordinary discrimination on the basis of P; it is discrimination on the basis of P in a particular kind of dimension of treatment.' ibid, 41. The analysis of Holmes (adopting this conception of indirect discrimination) is also illuminating:

> But like principles forbidding direct discrimination, principles forbidding indirect discrimination merely forbid discrimination on certain grounds. Formally, that is all they have to them. What they do is expand the relevant range of grounds. A ground which would not otherwise be a forbidden ground of discrimination (say, physical strength) becomes a forbidden ground of dis- crimination because it bears a certain relationship to the prohibited ground of distinction (sex). It is not a hybrid action-regarding and non-action regarding principle because the second part—the part that concerns itself with the disproportionate impact on a certain group—is not qualifying the principle but deter- mining its application. It specifies the conditions under which a ground of discrimination that would otherwise not be forbidden becomes an extra forbid- den ground of discrimination. The discrimination counts as indirect discrimination on grounds of sex because it is discrimination on grounds of physical strength (which in turn bears a certain relationship to sex) ... There are no non-action-regarding anti-discrimination principles and there are no anti-discrimination principles in which variable x (the ground on which the action is performed) is omitted. It is merely that some- times the ground is directly forbidden (sex) and sometimes it is indirectly forbid- den (physical strength).

E Holmes, 'Anti-Discrimination Rights Without Equality' (2005) 68 Modern Law Review 175, 184. This is also the view adopted by Gardner, see eg J Gardner, 'Liberals and Unlawful Discrimination' (1989) 9 Oxford Journal of Legal Studies 1.

[47] See eg K Lippert-Rasmussen, *Born Free and Equal? A Philosophical Inquiry into the Nature of Discrimination* (OUP 2014) 7 ('indirect discrimination is asymmetrically parasitic on direct discrimination in that the former requires the (past) presence of the latter, but not the other way round'); J Gardner, 'On the Grounds of her Sex(uality)' (1998) 18 Oxford Journal of Legal Studies 167, 182:

> There are various moral arguments, for example, for attending to the discriminatory side-effects of some decisions as well as the discriminatory grounds on which they were reached. These arguments supply the foundation for the secondary paradigm of indirect discrimination (or "disparate impact" discrimination) found in today's more sophisticated antidiscrimination statutes. For example: prohibitions on direct discrimination alone typically do rather little to expand the options of those who have been directly discriminated against in the past, when the world has been so comprehensively organized around their absence.

For a criticism of this conceptualization see O Doyle, 'Direct Discrimination, Indirect Discrimination and Autonomy' (2007) 27 Oxford Journal of Legal Studies 537. See also WK Murray, 'Discriminatory Taint' (2022) 135 Harvard Law Review 1192; I Solanke, *Discrimination as Stigma: A Theory of Anti-discrimination Law* (Hart 2017).

'redistributive'. The former seeks to remedy the evidentiary difficulties of proving discriminatory intent; the latter is not concerned with effectively precluding intentional discrimination in cases in which is impossible to prove intent, but with achieving egalitarian goals.[48] It is perhaps the adoption of the 'corrective' conception that led certain judges and scholars to question the distinction between the two forms of discrimination suggesting a unified test.[49] At the same time, the 'redistributive' dimension of disparate impact discrimination led to criticism as an 'affirmative action' programme.[50] The choice of what is the ultimate purpose of prohibiting measures having a disparate impact is a normative choice, which can only be made on policy grounds.[51] As accurately observed, although '[i]ndirect discrimination has a solid foothold in our thinking about discrimination', 'it is unclear what exactly indirect discrimination amounts to'.[52] This uncertainty relates to the purpose of disparate impact discrimination.[53] Whether its purpose is (i) to address evidentiary difficulties in proving discriminatory intent or

[48] T Khaitan and S Steel, 'Wrongs, Group Disadvantage and the Legitimacy of Indirect Discrimination Law' in H Collins and T Khaitan, *Foundations of Indirect Discrimination Law* (Hart 2018) 197–221, 197.

[49] See *British Columbia (Public Service Employee Relations Commission) v British Columbia Government Service Employees' Union* [1999] 3 SCR 3, para 27: 'The distinction between a standard that is discriminatory on its face and a neutral standard that is discriminatory in its effect is difficult to justify, simply because there are few cases that can be so neatly characterized'; S Fredman, 'Direct and Indirect Discrimination: Is There Still a Divide' in H Collins and T Khaitan (eds), *Foundations of Indirect Discrimination Law* (Hart 2018) 31–55, 55 ('courts in the US and the UK have found it difficult to draw a bright line distinction between direct and indirect discrimination'). See also G Rutherglen, 'Disparate Impact, Discrimination, and the Essentially Contested Concept of Equality' 74 Fordham Law Review 2313, 2330:

> Liability has actually been imposed usually only when there is some reason to believe that the employer has engaged in intentional discrimination . . . Liability for disparate impact under Title VII, whatever the hopes of its advocates, has never strayed very far from liability for intentional discrimination. Claims of disparate impact, although doctrinally distinct from claims of intentional discrimination, remain bound by the same limiting principles embedded in the overlapping consensus.

McLachlan J suggested a unified test according to which a prima facie discriminatory measure is justified only if the standard was adopted 'for a purpose rationally connected to the performance of the job', 'in an honest and good faith belief that it was necessary to the fulfilment of that legitimate work-related purpose', and 'is reasonably necessary to the accomplishment of that legitimate work-related purpose', *British Columbia (Public Service Employee Relations Commission) v British Columbia Government Service Employees' Union* [1999] 3 SCR 3, para 54. Flagg (n 9) 993 ('The constitutional challenger bears the burden of persuasion on the question of the existence of racially disparate effects. Once disparate impact is proven, the burden of production shifts to government to articulate the purposes behind the challenged rule of decision').

[50] See eg *Ricci v DeStefano*, 557 US 557, 595–596 (2009) (Scalia J, concurring); J Fishkin, *Bottlenecks: An New Theory of Equal Opportunity* (OUP 2014) 246 ('In recent years, disparate impact law has come under intense fire from those, most prominently Justice Antonin Scalia, who view it essentially as an affirmative action program—as a means of redistributing opportunities from one group to another that is in tension with the constitutional guarantee of equal protection of the laws').

[51] Primus (n 14) 536. See also T Khaitan and S Steel, 'Wrongs, Group Disadvantage and the Legitimacy of Indirect Discrimination Law' in H Collins and T Khaitan (eds), *Foundations of Indirect Discrimination Law* (Hart 2018) 197–221, 221 (arguing that '[i]ndirect discrimination liability draws upon both corrective and distributive justice requirements').

[52] Lippert-Rasmussen (n 47) 73.

[53] For a criticism of the disparate impact theory see M Selmi, 'Was the Disparate Impact Theory a Mistake?' (2006) 53 UCLA Law Review 701, 767–768:

> The central mistake behind the disparate impact theory was a belief that the law could do the work of social change when, in fact, much of the battle to remedy discrimination was lost when we moved away from the focus on intent. Rather than a new theory of discrimination, what was needed was a more expansive definition of intent—one that would have highlighted the reality that discrimination was a present experience rather than one of the distant past.

In *Griggs* the starting basis of the Supreme Court's analysis was that 'Congress directed the thrust of the [Civil Rights] Act to the consequences of employment practices, not simply the motivation', *Griggs v Duke Power Co*, 401 US 424 (1971).

(ii) to combat and eliminate embedded racism and, more generally, structural discrimination in the society is a matter of debate.[54]

2.1.2 Key Differences between Disparate Treatment Discrimination and Disparate Impact Discrimination

Broadly speaking, and despite the various approaches that different jurisdictions adopt, there are four main differences between disparate treatment (or direct) discrimination and disparate impact (or indirect) discrimination.[55] The first difference between the two forms of discrimination is that disparate treatment discrimination requires discriminatory intent or a connection between the protected ground and less favourable treatment. As Khaitan explains in disparate treatment or direct discrimination, less favourable treatment is accorded:

> 'on the ground of' a protected characteristic (such as race, sex, religion) or, sometimes, a combination of such characteristics (to deal with intersectional or multiple ground discrimination faced by, say, black women) ... the treatment must be 'on the ground of' (or 'because of', 'based on', 'for a reason related to') a protected characteristic. Some causal connection between the protected ground and the treatment in question is required. Opinions diverge on whether this is an objective standard or a subjective one.[56]

In US law, disparate treatment discrimination is understood as intentional discrimination.[57] While the US Supreme Court noted ' "[d]isparate treatment" is the most easily understood type of discrimination',[58] there is nothing easy or straightforward in understanding disparate treatment discrimination as intentional discrimination. As Huq accurately observes:

> [b]ut what does it mean to say that an official action is motivated by a 'discriminatory intent'? And how can litigants in practice prove up an allegation of improper motivation? These simple questions turn out to have complex answers. For the federal judiciary has not homed in upon a single definition of discriminatory intent. Nor has

[54] See Primus (n 14) 518–536; PL Perry, 'Two Faces of Disparate Impact Discrimination' (1991) 59 Fordham Law Review 523, 570–574; R Belton, 'The Dismantling of the Griggs Disparate Impact Theory and the Future of Title VII: The Need for a Third Reconstruction' (1990) 8 Yale Law and Policy Review 223, 224–225.

[55] As Craig and de Búrca observe, '[t]he legal meaning of the term is nonetheless more complex than might initially be thought ... The characterization of a case as involving direct or indirect discrimination can be difficult. The broader the definition of direct discrimination, the greater the potential overlap there is with indirect discrimination, as exemplified by the CHEZ case. The dividing line can also be contestable and controversial.' P Craig and G de Búrca, *EU Law: Text, Cases, and Materials* (7th edn, OUP 2020)1002.

[56] Khaitan (n 8) 69.

[57] See *Watson v Fort Worth Bank & Trust*, 487 US 977 (1988), 986 ('the Court has consistently used disparate treatment theory, in which proof of intent to discriminate is required'); *Washington v Davis* 426 US 229 (1976) 240. See also *Texas Department of Community Affairs v Burdine* 450 US 248 (1981).

[58] *Teamsters v United States*, 431 US 324, 335 fn 15 (1977).

it developed a consistent approach to the evidentiary tools through which discriminatory intent is substantiated.[59]

In the EU and the UK, direct discrimination cases (the analogous concept of disparate treatment discrimination) are understood differently. Courts reject the relevance of intent and instead adopt an objective 'but-for' test.[60] This is clearly shown in *R v Birmingham City Council, ex p Equal Opportunities Commission*. In that case the House of Lords unanimously agreed with Lord Goff that:

> [t]here is discrimination under the statute if there is less favourable treatment on the ground of sex, in other words if the relevant girl or girls would have received the same treatment as the boys but for their sex. *The intention or motive of the defendant to discriminate*, though it may be relevant so far as remedies are concerned … *is not a necessary condition of liability; it is perfectly possible to envisage cases where the defendant had no such motive, and yet did in fact discriminate on the ground of sex.*[61]

Direct discrimination in EU law includes not only cases in which the measure in question was adopted explicitly on the basis of a protected characteristic but also situations 'where one person is treated less favourably than another is, has been or would be treated in a comparable situation' and that 'underlying unequal treatment is *directly linked* to' an impermissible characteristic.[62] In earlier case law there was a tendency in EU jurisprudence to conflate 'direct discrimination' with de jure discrimination, ie discrimination which was 'overt' and explicit, and 'indirect discrimination' with de facto

[59] AZ Huq, 'What Is Discriminatory Intent' (2018) 103 Cornell Law Review 1211, 1215.

[60] E Ellis and P Watson, *EU Anti-discrimination Law* (2nd edn, OUP 2012) 167:

> [W]hether the alleged discrimination is direct or indirect, all that is required to establish causation is that 'but for' belonging to the protected category, the victim would not have sustained the disadvantage alleged. For this purpose, it is unnecessary to prove any particular motive or intention on the part of the respondent.

See also ibid, 165. S Fredman, 'Direct and Indirect Discrimination: Is There Still a Divide?' in H Collins and T Khaitan (eds), *Foundations of Indirect Discrimination Law* (Hart 2018) 31–55, 36 ('it is now settled law that the motive of the perpetrator is irrelevant. Rather, UK courts have established a "but for" test, which founds liability on the simple causative assessment that "but for" the applicant's protected characteristic, she would not have been treated less favourably. Instead of intention, the key factor distinguishing direct and indirect discrimination has been held to be the possibility of justification'). On the emergence of the 'but-for' test in the UK, see eg Connolly (n 11) 91–97.

[61] *R v Birmingham City Council, ex p Equal Opportunities Commission* [1989] AC 1155, 1194 (emphasis added); this approach was also followed by the majority of the House of Lords in *James v Eastleigh Borough Council* [1990] 2 AC 751. However, Lord Phillips, found the 'but-for' test 'not helpful', and, instead, it is 'better simply to ask what were the facts that the discriminator considered to be determinative when making the relevant decision', *R (on the application of E) v JFS Governing Body* [2009] UKSC 15, para 16; see also ibid, para 13 ('In the phrase "grounds for discrimination", the word "grounds" is ambiguous. It can mean the motive for taking the decision or the factual criteria applied by the discriminator in reaching his decision. In the context of the 1976 Act "grounds" has the latter meaning.').

[62] See also n 46; Case C-499/08, *Ingeniørforeningen i Danmark v Region Syddanmark* [2010] ECR I-9343, Opinion of the Advocate General Juliane Kokott, para 26; this approach was adopted by the Court, see Case C-499/08, *Ingeniørforeningen i Danmark v Region Syddanmark* [2010] ECR I-09343, paras 19–24; see also Case C-177/88, *Elisabeth Johanna Pacifica Dekker v Stichting Vormingscentrum voor Jong Volwassenen (VJV-Centrum) Plus* [1990] ECR I-03941 para 17 ('the reply to the question whether the refusal to employ a woman constitutes direct or indirect discrimination depends on the reason for that refusal. If that reason is to be found in the fact that the person concerned is pregnant, then the decision is directly linked to the sex of the candidate').

discrimination, ie discrimination which was 'disguised', the result of measures which do not explicitly differentiate persons on the basis of an impermissible characteristic.[63] However, as Ellis and Watson explain:

> [t]his early attempt to explain the difference between direct and indirect discrimination was confusing; direct discrimination is here linked with overt conduct, while indirect discrimination is linked with disguise. Yet, notionally at least, either sort of discrimination can be either overt or disguised; and, in practice, it is more often direct discrimination which is disguised by its perpetrator, whilst indirect discrimination is frequently quite overt.[64]

Subsequent case law seems to 'confirm that direct discrimination could be both overt and covert'.[65] Broadening the scope of direct discrimination even further, the CJEU held that direct discrimination in EU law also includes discrimination by association.[66]

The second difference is that disparate treatment discrimination concerns the comparison of the treatment received by individuals, while disparate impact discrimination is based on a comparison between groups.[67]

The third difference between the two types of discrimination is that justifications can be used as a defence in disparate impact or indirect discrimination cases, while this is not normally the case in disparate treatment discrimination. At the same time, while in both US and EU a much broader set of justifications is available in disparate impact (or indirect) discrimination (unlike in disparate treatment or direct discrimination), in the EU 'the very decisions that conflated the two doctrines allowed for broad defenses formerly confined to disparate impact to be introduced in disparate treatment jurisprudence'.[68]

[63] See Case C-43/75, *Gabrielle Defrenne v Société anonyme belge de navigation aérienne Sabena* [1976] ECR 455, para 18.

[64] Ellis and Watson (n 60) 144. See Case C-69/80, *Worringham v Lloyds Bank Ltd* [1981] ECR 767.

[65] Ellis and Watson (n 60) 145.

[66] Case C-303/06, *S Coleman v Attridge Law and Steve Law* [2008] ECR I–5603. For a criticism see M Connolly, 'The Myth of Associative Discrimination and the Court of Justice's Great Vanishing: Part 2' (2021) 72 Northern Ireland Legal Quarterly 510; M Connolly, 'The "Associative" Discrimination Fiction: Part 2' (2021) 72 Northern Ireland Legal Quarterly 29.

[67] Khaitan (n 8) 74–75.

[68] Linos (n 6) 119–120. This is perhaps because the role of justifications in determining discrimination is well entrenched in EU law more generally, see Case C-356/12, *Wolfgang Glatzel v Freistaat Bayern*, 20 May 2014, para 43 ('[a] difference in treatment is justified if it is based on an objective and reasonable criterion, that is, if the difference relates to a legally permitted aim pursued by the legislation in question, and it is proportionate to the aim pursued by the treatment'); Case C-127/07, *Société Arcelor Atlantique et Lorraine and Others v Premier ministre, Ministre de l'Écologie et du Développement durable, Ministre de l'Économie, des Finances et de l'Industrie*, 16 December 2008, paras 25 and 26: 'A breach of the principle of equal treatment as a result of different treatment presumes that the situations concerned are comparable, having regard to all the elements which characterize them. The elements which characterize different situations, and hence their comparability, must in particular be determined and assessed in the light of the subject-matter and purpose of the Community act which makes the distinction in question. The principles and objectives of the field to which the act relates must also be taken into account'. See also Case 114/76, *Bela-Mühle Josef Bergmann KG v Grows-Farm GmbH & Co KG* [1977] ECR 1211, para 7 and Case C-122/95, *Germany v Council* [1998] ECR I-973, paras 68 and 71. Such reversal of the burden of proof in discrimination cases has led some to challenge the constitutionality of this allocation of the burden of proof as contrary to fair trial guarantees in the Czech Republic but the Supreme Court rejected the challenge, M Selucká, M Grochová, and J Komendová, 'Czech Republic' in M Mercat-Bruns, DB Oppenheimer, and C Sartorius (eds), *Comparative Perspectives on the Enforcement and Effectiveness of Antidiscrimination Law* (Springer 2018) 153–173, 166.

In disparate treatment discrimination cases proving (directly or indirectly) discriminatory intent or a link with a protected characteristic and different treatment is part of the claimant's positive case. In disparate impact discrimination, 'the respondent's opportunity to explain the requirement comes in the form of the justification defence, which the court will scrutinise to determine whether it is a proportionate means of achieving a legitimate aim.'[69] This is expressly provided in the very definition of indirect discrimination under the relevant EU Directives,[70] which codify the case law of the CJEU.[71] As Lady Hale held, '[t]he main difference between them is that direct discrimination cannot be justified. Indirect discrimination can be justified if it is a proportionate means of achieving a legitimate aim.'[72] In other words, the absence of a justification is a separate and key step of the legal test for establishing disparate impact discrimination.[73]

The fourth difference is that in disparate treatment discrimination the burden of proof is allocated to (and remains with) the claimant; it never shifts. As explained above, in the US to succeed in a disparate treatment discrimination claim, the claimant must first prove a prima facie intentional discrimination on behalf of the employer. In particular, the claimant must prove that the employer was motivated in his or her decision by the employee's race or another protected characteristic.[74] Once a prima facie case for discrimination has been made, 'the burden then must shift to the employer to articulate (rather than prove[75]) some legitimate, non-discriminatory reason for the employee's rejection.'[76] It is the burden of production that shifts and not the burden of persuasion;[77]

[69] S Fredman, 'The Reason Why: Unravelling Indirect Discrimination' (2016) 45 Industrial Law Journal 349, 349. See also *Homer v Chief Constable of West Yorkshire Police* [2012] UKSC 15 para 19 (per Lady Hale): '[a] provision, criterion or practice is justified if the employer can show that it is a proportionate means of achieving a legitimate aim. The range of aims which can justify indirect discrimination on any ground is wider than the aims which can, in the case of age discrimination, justify direct discrimination.'

[70] See Section 2.1.1.

[71] M Connolly, *Equality, Discrimination, and the Law* (Routledge 2022) 84. Case C-170/84, *Bilka-Kaufhaus GmbH v Karin Weber von Hartz* [1984] ECR 1607, para 36.

[72] *R (on the application of E) v JFS Governing Body* [2009] UKSC 15, para 57 (Lady Hale).

[73] Fredman (n 9) 154 ('indirect discrimination ... is formulated in different ways, but broadly speaking has three elements: equal treatment; a disproportionately exclusionary impact on those sharing a protected characteristic; and the absence of an acceptable justification'). As Fredman argues, 'the point of indirect discrimination is precisely that there is no disparate treatment on the basis of a characteristic peculiar to a protected characteristic', S Fredman, 'The Reason Why: Unravelling Indirect Discrimination' (2016) 45 Industrial Law Journal 231, 242.

[74] For doing so on a prima facie basis, the claimant must show '(i) that he belongs to a racial minority; (ii) that he applied and was qualified for a job for which the employer was seeking applicants; (iii) that, despite his qualifications, he was rejected; and (iv) that, after his rejection, the position remained open and the employer continued to seek applicants from persons of complainant's qualifications', *McDonnell Douglas Corp v Green*, 411 US 792 (1973). It is thus clear that '[t]he burden of establishing a prima facie case of disparate treatment is not onerous. The plaintiff must prove by a preponderance of the evidence that she applied for an available position for which she was qualified, but was rejected under circumstances which give rise to an inference of unlawful discrimination', ibid (emphasis added).

[75] 'The defendant need only articulate—but need not prove—the existence of a non-discriminatory reason', *Fisher v Vassar College*, 70 F.3d 1420, 1433 (2nd Cir 1995), affirmed en banc, 114F.3d 1332 (1997), certiorari denied, 118 S Ct 851 (1998).

[76] *McDonnell Douglas Corp v Green*, 411 US 792 (1973), 802. English law in that respect is an outlier: 'there may well be a defect in our law of discrimination. In contrast to the law in many countries, where English law forbids direct discrimination it provides no defence of justification', *R (on the application of E) v Governing Body of JFS* [2009] UKSC 15, para 9.

[77] However, in both direct and indirect discrimination, EU law provides for a reversal of the burden of persuasion:

> Member States shall take such measures as are necessary, in accordance with their national judicial systems, to ensure that, when persons who consider themselves wronged because the principle of equal

'[t]he ultimate burden of persuading the trier of fact that the defendant intentionally discriminated against the plaintiff remains at all times with the plaintiff'.[78] At that stage, the claimant may adduce evidence to demonstrate that the legitimate reason invoked by respondent was 'in fact, pretext'.[79] Therefore, the claimant 'may succeed in this either directly by persuading the court that a discriminatory reason more likely motivated the employer or indirectly by showing that the employer's proffered explanation is unworthy of credence'.[80] The UK Supreme Court also made clear in *Royal Mail Group Ltd v Efobi* that in disparate treatment discrimination cases, and despite the changes in the wording of the relevant legislative provisions, the burden of proof remains with the claimant.[81] The UK Supreme Court emphatically clarified that, although adverse inferences can be drawn in non-discrimination cases when the Respondent fails to produce relevant evidence,[82] this power cannot be exercised lightly and '[w]here it is said that an adverse inference ought to have been drawn from a particular matter—here the absence of evidence from the decision-makers—the first step must be to identify the precise inference(s) which allegedly should have been drawn'.[83] By contrast, in disparate impact or indirect discrimination the respondent bears burden of proof in relation to justifications, once less favourable treatment is established.[84]

> treatment has not been applied to them establish, before a court or other competent authority, facts from which it may be presumed that there has been direct or indirect discrimination, it shall be for the respondent to prove that there has been no breach of the principle of equal treatment.

Directive 2000/43, Article 8(1). See also the effectively the same provision in Directive 2000/78, Article 10(1); Directive 2006/54/EC, Article 10; Directive 2004/113, Article 19(1). See also Case C-83/14, *CHEZ Razpredelenie Bulgaria AD v Komisia za zashtita ot diskriminatsia* EU:C:2015:480, paras 77 and 78; Case C-415/10, *Galina Meister v Speech Design Carrier Systems GmbH* [2012] ECR I-217, para 40; Case C-303/06, *S Coleman v Attridge Law and Steve Law* [2008] ECRI-5603, para 54. See also Ellis and Watson (n 60) 157–163.

[78] *Texas Department of Community Affairs v Burdine*, 450 US 248, 253 (1981); *Reeves v Sanderson Plumbing Products, Inc*, 530 US 133, 153 (2000): 'The ultimate question in every employment discrimination case involving a claim of disparate treatment is whether the plaintiff was the victim of intentional discrimination'. *Hazen Paper Co v Biggins*, 507 US 604, 610 (1993): 'a disparate treatment claim cannot succeed unless the employee's protected trait actually played a role in that process and had a determinative influence on the outcome.' According to Justice O'Connor, 'there are significant differences between shifting the burden of persuasion to the employer in a case resting purely on statistical proof, as in the disparate impact setting, and shifting the burden of persuasion in a case like this one, where an employee has demonstrated by direct evidence that an illegitimate factor played a substantial role in a particular employment decision' *Price Waterhouse v Hopkins*, 490 US 228, 275 (1989) (Justice O'Connor, concurring opinion).

[79] *McDonnell Douglas Corp v Green*, 411 US 792, 804 (1973).

[80] *Texas Department of Community Affairs v Burdine*, 450 US 248, 256 (1981).

[81] *Royal Mail Group Ltd v Efobi* [2021] UKSC 33, para 37: 'in placing upon the claimant the burden of proving facts from which the tribunal could conclude (in the absence of any other explanation) that there was discrimination, the tribunal did not make an error of law'.

[82] ibid, paras 39–47.

[83] ibid, para 43.

[84] In *Wards Cove Packing Co, Inc v Atonio*, a 5:4 decision the Supreme Court required the claimant to establish that the statistical difference in treatment was the result of the measure in question *Wards Cove Packing Co, Inc v Atonio*, 490 US 642 (1989). It was in response to this and other Supreme Court decisions that Congress enacted the 1991 Civil Rights Act, which confirmed that the burden of justifying the decision causing disparate impact lies with the respondent. The 1991 amendment provided that disparate impact discrimination is established when 'a complaining party demonstrates that a respondent uses a particular employment practice that causes a disparate impact on the basis of race, color, religion, sex, or national origin and the respondent fails to demonstrate that the challenged practice is job related for the position in question and consistent with business necessity' 42 USC s 2000e-2(k)(1)(A)(i). See also Linos (n 6) 118. See also DC Malamud, 'Values, Symbols, and Facts in the Affirmative Action Debate' (1997) 95 Michigan Law Review 1668, 1694; YNA Pappoe, 'The Shortcomings of Title VII for the Black Female Plaintiff' (2019) 22 University of Pennsylvania Journal of Law and Social Change 1, 6.

2.1.3 The Role of Circumstantial Evidence and Adverse Inferences in Proving Disparate Treatment or Direct Discrimination

In the United States, the challenges of proving discriminatory intent in the context of disparate treatment claims are (at least partly) addressed by accepting circumstantial evidence and drawing adverse inferences. According to the US Supreme Court:

> [t]he employer simply treats some people less favorably than others *because of* their race, color, religion, sex, or national origin. Proof of discriminatory motive is critical, although it can in some situations be inferred from the mere fact of differences in treatment.[85]

In *St Mary's Honor Center v Hicks* the US Supreme Court required the claimant to prove not only that the reason invoked by respondent was a pretext but also 'both that the reason was false, and that discrimination was the real reason'.[86] In 2010 the Supreme Court clarified that for doing so the claimant can rely on indirect evidence.[87] In that framework of analysis, 'the court should review the record as a whole'[88] and '[p]roof that the defendant's explanation is unworthy of credence is simply one form of circumstantial evidence that is probative of intentional discrimination, and it may be quite persuasive'.[89] A complication arises in cases in which the respondent has a mixed motive, ie when the relevant decision is partly motivated by discriminatory intent and other non-discriminatory reasons. In 1989 in *Price Waterhouse v Hopkins* the Supreme Court held that 'once a plaintiff in a Title VII case shows that gender played a motivating part in an employment decision, the defendant may avoid a finding of liability only by proving that it would have made the same decision even if it had not allowed gender to play such a role'.[90] Partly in response to *Price Waterhouse v Hopkins* (and other Supreme Court

[85] *Teamsters v United States*, 431 US 324, 335 fn 15 (1977) (emphasis added); see also *Hazen Paper Co v Biggins*, 507 US 604, 609 (1993). For a critique of the behavioural theories underpinning intent and whether disparate treatment discrimination should include decisions based on unconscious bias, see L Hamilton Krieger and ST Fisker, 'Behavioral Realism in Employment Discrimination Law: Implicit Bias and Disparate Treatment' (2006) 94 California Law Review 997.

[86] *St Mary's Honor Center v Hicks*, 509 US 502, 515 (1993). For a criticism see eg MS Brodin, 'The Demise of Circumstantial Proof in Employment Discrimination Litigation: St. Mary's Honor Center v. Hicks, Pretext, and the "Personality" Excuse' (1997) 18 Berkeley Journal Employment and Labor Law 183; WR Corbett, 'The "Fall" of Summers, the Rise of "Pretext Plus", and the Escalating Subordination of Federal Employment Discrimination Law to Employment at Will: Lessons from McKennon and Hicks' (1996) 30 Georgia Law Review 305; DA Calloway, 'St. Mary's Honor Center v. Hicks: Questioning the Basic Assumption' (1994) 26 Connecticut Law Review 997; DC Malamud, 'The Last Minuet: Disparate Treatment After Hicks' (1995) 93 Michigan Law Review 2229; MA Schuman, 'The Politics of Presumption: St. Mary's Honor Center v. Hicks and the Burdens of Proof in Employment Discrimination Cases (1993) 9 St John's Journal of Legal Commentary 67; M Selmi, 'Proving Intentional Discrimination: The Reality of Supreme Court Rhetoric' (1997) 86 Georgetown Law Journal 279.

[87] *Reeves v Sanderson Plumbing Products, Inc*, 530 US 133, 135 (2000).

[88] ibid.

[89] ibid, 147.

[90] *Price Waterhouse v Hopkins*, 490 US 228, 244–245 (1989). For a personal account of the case see A Hopkins, '*Price Waterhouse v. Hopkins*: a personal account of a sexual discrimination plaintiff' (2005) 22 Hofstra Labor and Employment Law Journal 357.

decisions[91]), limiting the claimant's ability to prove discrimination, Congress passed the 1991 Civil Rights Act, amending the 1964 Civil Rights Act.[92] On the issue of mixed intent, the 1991 Act provided that 'an unlawful employment practice is established when the complaining party demonstrates that race, color, religion, sex, or national origin was *a motivating factor* for any employment practice, even though other factors also motivated the practice'.[93] However, this is extremely difficulty because:

> [p]roving any form of causation is difficult for disparate treatment plaintiffs. Causation occurs in the mind of the decisionmaker / defendant. And most of the relevant evidence tends to be under the control of the defendant. This lack of access to evidence makes proving any type of causation difficult, and therefore makes burden-shifting normatively desirable . . . What this means is that, to prove but-for causation, a plaintiff essentially has to prove a negative: the absence of any other independently sufficient cause. However difficult this may be in the physical world of torts, where there are a limited number of observable causes for an event, it tends to be extremely difficult in antidiscrimination law, where decision makers may have any number of reasons for a decision, none of which are observable and any of which might be independently sufficient to reach the decision.[94]

In 2003 the Supreme Court clarified that 'direct evidence of discrimination is not required in mixed-motive cases'[95] and explained that '[c]ircumstantial evidence is not only sufficient, but may also be more certain, satisfying and persuasive than direct evidence'.[96] Essentially, allowing indirect evidence to prove discriminatory intent counterbalances the inherent difficulty in doing so.[97] In cases in which the respondent was found to engage in a widespread de facto case of racial segregation over a long period of time, the Supreme Court held that that respondent needed to prove not only the existence of valid regulatory reason behind the measure but the absence of discriminatory intent.[98]

[91] *Library of Congress v Shaw*, 478 US 310 (1986); *Patterson v McLean Credit Union*, 491 US 164 (1989); *Wards Cove Packing Co, Inc v Atonio*, 490 US 642 (1989) (discussed below); *Martin v Wilks*, 490 US 755 (1989); *Lorance v AT&T Technologies, Inc*, 490 US 900 (1989); *EEOC v Arabian American Oil Co (Aramco)*, 499 US 244 (1991); *West Virginia University Hospitals, Inc v Casey*, 499 US 83 (1991); see also DR Livingston, 'The Civil Rights Act Of 1991 and EEOC Enforcement' (1993) 23 Stetson Law Review 53, 54–55.

[92] BC Mizer, 'Toward a Motivating Factor Test for Individual Disparate Treatment Claims' (2001) 100 Michigan Law Review 234, 238.

[93] 42 US Code s 2000e–2(m) (emphasis added).

[94] MJ Katz, 'Gross Disunity' (2010) 114 Penn State Law Review 857, 881–882.

[95] *Desert Palace, Inc v Costa*, 539 US 90, 101–102 (2003); Primus (n 14) 499.

[96] *Desert Palace, Inc v Costa*, 539 US 90, 100 (2003).

[97] MJ Zimmer, 'A Chain of Inferences Proving Discrimination' (2008) 79 University of Colorado Law Review 1243, 1295. See also D Chin and J Golinsky, 'Employment Discrimination: Moving Beyond McDonnell Douglas: A Simplified Method for Assessing Evidence in Discrimination Cases' (1998) 64 Brooklyn Law Review 659, 674. In disparate treatment cases evidentiary difficulties also stem from the fact that the analysis concerns one or very few individuals: '[e]mployment decisions that affect only one or a few persons present especially difficult problems of proof', JR Lindgren and others, *The Law of Sex Discrimination* (4th edn, Wadsworth 2011) 89. See also Flagg (n 9) 993.

[98] *Keyes v School District No 1*, 413 US 189, 208–211 (1973).

In the EU context, as explained above,[99] the connection between the protected ground and less favourable treatment is an objective one and, in both direct and indirect discrimination the burden of persuasion remains with the claimant, while the burden of production shifted to the respondent after the claimant establishes 'facts from which it may be presumed that there has been direct or indirect discrimination'.[100] To establish such presumption, the case law of the CJEU confirms the failure or refusal to provide salient information by the respondent is a relevant consideration.[101] In *CHEZ*, the CJEU held that the domestic courts of the EU Member States must:

> take account of all the circumstances surrounding the practice at issue, in order to determine whether there is sufficient evidence for a finding that the facts from which it may be presumed that there has been direct discrimination on grounds of ethnic origin have been established, and to ensure that a refusal of disclosure by the respondent, here CHEZ RB, in the context of establishing such facts is not liable to compromise the achievement of the objectives pursued by Directive 2000/43.[102]

The ECtHR adopts a rather inquisitorial (or investigatory) as opposed to adversarial model in relation to evidence.[103] As Arnardóttir explains:

> [i]n investigatory proceedings, however, both parties have a duty to cooperate with the Court in establishing the facts and disregard of that duty may result in the Court drawing adverse inferences. This again decreases the practical importance of the difference between the two types of proceedings. The European Court of Human Rights follows the investigatory model of proceedings in the sense of an active role in fact-finding.[104]

[99] See Section 2.1.1.

[100] Directives 2000/43, Article 8(1); Directive 2000/78, Article 10(1); Directive 2006/54, Article 19(1); Directive 2004/113, Article 9(1).

[101] Case C-415/10, *Galina Meister v Speech Design Carrier Systems GmbH*, [2012] ECR I-217, para 42: 'Therefore, it is for the referring court to ensure that the refusal of disclosure by Speech Design, in the context of establishing facts from which it may be presumed that there has been direct or indirect discrimination against Ms Meister, is not liable to compromise the achievement of the objectives pursued by Directives 2000/43, 2000/78 and 2006/54. It must, in particular, take account of all the circumstances of the main proceedings, in order to determine whether there is sufficient evidence for a finding that the facts from which it may be presumed that there has been such discrimination have been established.'

[102] Case C-83/14, *CHEZ Razpredelenie Bulgaria AD v Komisia za zashtita ot diskriminatsia* EU:C:2015:480, para 80. See also F Benoît-Rohmer, 'Lessons from the Recent Case Law of the EU Court of Justice on the Principle of Non-discrimination' in L S Rossi and F Casolari (eds), *The Principle of Equality in EU Law* (Springer 2017) 151–166, 163.

[103] *Case of Ireland v The United Kingdom*, Application No 5310/71, 18 January 1978, para 160: '[i]n order to satisfy itself as to the existence or not in Northern Ireland of practices contrary to Article 3 (art. 3), the Court will not rely on the concept that the burden of proof is borne by one or other of the two Governments concerned. In the cases referred to it, the Court examines all the material before it, whether originating from the Commission, the Parties or other sources, and, if necessary, obtains material proprio motu'. See also *Case of Georgia v Russia (I)* [GC], Application No 13255/07, 3 July 2014, para 95, in which it stressed: '[i]n establishing the existence of an administrative practice, the Court will not rely on the concept that the burden of proof is borne by one or other of the two Governments concerned, but will rather study all the material before it, from whatever source it originates'.

[104] OM Arnardóttir, *Equality and Non-Discrimination under the European Convention on Human Rights* (Martinus Nijhoff 2002) 69.

The approach of the ECtHR in relation to evidentiary issues and the allocation of the burden of proof in discrimination cases while not agnostic to asymmetry of information. However, in *Nachova v Bulgaria*:

> '[t]he Grand Chamber reiterates that in certain circumstances, where the events lie wholly, or in large part, within the exclusive knowledge of the authorities, as in the case of the death of a person within their control in custody, the burden of proof may be regarded as resting on the authorities to provide a satisfactory and convincing explanation of, in particular, the causes of the detained person's death.... The Grand Chamber cannot exclude the possibility that in certain cases of alleged discrimination it may require the respondent Government to disprove an arguable allegation of discrimination and—if they fail to do so—find a violation of Article 14 of the Convention on that basis. However, where it is alleged—as here—that a violent act was motivated by racial prejudice, such an approach would amount to requiring the respondent Government to prove the absence of a particular subjective attitude on the part of the person concerned.[105]

Therefore, the ECtHR concluded that 'the alleged failure of the authorities to carry out an effective investigation into the supposedly racist motive for the killing' does not 'shift the burden of proof to the Government with regard to the alleged violation of Article 14 of the Convention taken in conjunction with the substantive aspect of Article 2'.[106] In indirect discrimination cases, the ECtHR explicitly recognized that reversing the burden of persuasion and requiring the respondent State to produce evidence in relation to justification for less favourable treatment is necessitated by asymmetry of information.[107]

[105] *Nachova and others v Bulgaria* [GC], Application Nos 43577/98 and 43579/98, 6 July 2005, para 157. See also, ibid, para 157: 'While in the legal systems of many countries proof of the discriminatory effect of a policy or decision will dispense with the need to prove intent in respect of alleged discrimination in employment or the provision of services, that approach is difficult to transpose to a case where it is alleged that an act of violence was racially motivated.'

[106] ibid.

[107] In *DH and others v Czech Republic*, the ECtHR held:

> [w]here an applicant alleging indirect discrimination thus establishes a rebuttable presumption that the effect of a measure or practice is discriminatory, the burden then shifts to the respondent State, which must show that the difference in treatment is not discriminatory. Regard being had in particular to the specificity of the facts and the nature of the allegations made in this type of case, it would be extremely difficult in practice for applicants to prove indirect discrimination without such a shift in the burden of proof.

DH and others v Czech Republic [GC], Application No 57325/00, 13 November 2007, paras 187–189; see also ibid, para 186 ('to guarantee those concerned the effective protection of their rights, less strict evidential rules should apply in cases of alleged indirect discrimination'); in the same case, the Court observed 'to guarantee those concerned the effective protection of their rights, less strict evidential rules should apply in cases of alleged indirect discrimination', ibid, para 186. Regarding refugee status determinations and the need for flexibility see *J K and others v Sweden*, Application No 59166/12, 23 August 2016, paras 91–99.

2.2 Non-discrimination in Investment Treaty Arbitration as a Form of Disparate Treatment (or Direct) Discrimination

This section argues that it is well-established—and clearly reflected in the relevant case law, State practice and scholarship—that National Treatment and MFN clauses only prohibit less favourable treatment, ie discrimination, because of, or, on the basis of the investors' nationality. Likewise, non-impairment clauses, FET, and the non-discrimination obligation in the context of expropriation prohibit discrimination because of any protected characteristic (including, but not limited to, nationality). But what does discrimination 'because of' or 'on the basis of' national origin (or another protected ground) mean in international investment treaty arbitration? This book argues that the answer to that question lies in viewing non-discrimination obligations in international investment law as a form of disparate treatment (or direct) discrimination. The previous sections explored the two paradigms of discrimination ('disparate treatment' discrimination and 'disparate impact discrimination') which originated in US anti-discrimination legislation and practice in the second half of the twentieth century, and were transplanted in other jurisdictions, including international and supranational ones, such as the EU and the ECHR. This section argues that, *without being identical*, in the light of the different legal, institutional, cultural, and political contexts, all non-discrimination obligations contained in investment treaties are closer to the 'disparate treatment' or direct discrimination paradigm (than to 'disparate impact' or indirect discrimination paradigm). This understanding of non-discrimination in international investment treaty arbitration has four important practical implications. First, the comparison to establish discrimination is always between individual investors (and not groups). Second, discrimination cannot be established merely by proving the existence of less favourable treatment accorded by the Host State to the foreign investor. For foreign investors to succeed in discrimination claims in investment treaty arbitration their less favourable treatment must be connected to their foreign nationality or another impermissible basis for differentiation such as their race, religion, or ethnicity. Such connection, this book argues, is intrinsically (and logically) linked to the absence of a legitimate, non-discriminatory, public policy objective pursued by the State in enacting and implementing the measure(s) resulting in less favourable treatment.[108] Third, the burden of proving discrimination (including the connection between the less favourable treatment of the foreign investor and the impermissible ground for differentiation) falls squarely on the investor. The evidentiary challenges for investors, and ways to address them, are analysed in Chapter 4. Fourth, like in disparate or direct discrimination, there is no separate step which would allow the Respondent to rely on justifications (as in disparate impact or indirect discrimination), unless the treaty contains a general exception clause.

[108] See Chapter 3, Section 3.3 below.

There are several reasons for understanding and interpreting non-discrimination obligations under investment treaties as 'disparate treatment' or 'direct' discrimination obligations. Although not always properly articulated or explained, with some exceptions,[109] arbitral tribunals, States (either in their submissions or treaty drafting) and scholars endorse this conception. This is clearer in relation to National Treatment clauses, as they have received comparatively more attention in investment treaty arbitral practice and scholarship. Several tribunals have emphasized that National Treatment prohibits discrimination on the basis or *because of nationality*. The tribunal in *ADM v Mexico* clarified that '[t]he national treatment obligation under Article 1102 [of NAFTA providing for National Treatment] is an application of the general prohibition of *discrimination based on nationality*'.[110] In *Total v Argentina* the tribunal held that 'the purpose [of National Treatment] is to ascertain whether the protected investments have been treated worse without any justification, *specifically because of their foreign nationality*'.[111] In *Cargill v Mexico* the tribunal concluded that 'the discrimination was based on nationality both in intent and effect'[112] and in *Loewen v USA* the tribunal held that 'Article 1102 [of NAFTA] is direct only to nationality-based discrimination and that it proscribes only demonstrable and significant indications of bias and prejudice on the basis of nationality, of a nature and consequence likely to have affected the outcome of the trial'.[113] The tribunals in *SD Myers v Canada* and *Pope & Talbot v Canada* moved away from an impact-based discrimination paradigm and cited a document prepared by the Organisation for Economic Co-operation and Development (OECD) which provided that:

> [m]ore general considerations, such as the policy objectives of Member countries, could be taken into account to define the circumstances in which comparison between foreign-controlled and domestic enterprises is permissible inasmuch as those objectives are not contrary to the principle of National Treatment. In any case, *the key* to determining whether a discriminatory measure applied to foreign-controlled enterprises constitutes an exception to National Treatment *is to ascertain whether the discrimination is motivated, at least in part, by the fact that the enterprises concerned are under foreign control.*[114]

[109] See Chapter 3, Section 3.3.1 below.

[110] *Archer Daniels Midland Company and Tate & Lyle Ingredients Americas, Inc v United Mexican States*, ICSID Case No ARB(AF)/04/5, Award, 21 November 2007, para 193 (emphasis added).

[111] *Total SA v Argentine Republic*, ICSID Case No ARB/04/01, Decision on Liability, 27 December 2010, para 344 (emphasis added); see also ibid, para 213: 'different treatment between foreign and national investors who are similarly situated or in like circumstances must be nationality-driven. Accordingly, a foreign investor who is challenging measures of general application as de facto discriminatory under Article 4 of the BIT has to show a *prima facie* case of nationality-based discrimination'.

[112] *Cargill Inc v United Mexican States*, ICSID Case No ARB(AF)/05/2, Award, 18 September 2009, para 220.

[113] *The Loewen Group Inc and Loewen v United States*, Award, ICSID Case No ARB(AF)/98/3, 25 June 2003, para 139.

[114] OECD, *National Treatment for Foreign-Controlled Enterprises* (OECD Publications 1993) 22 (emphasis added); *S D Myers, Inc v Government of Canada*, UNCITRAL, Partial Award, 13 November 2000, para 248; *Pope & Talbot Inc v Government of Canada*, UNCITRAL, Award on the Merits of Phase 2, 10 April 2001, para 78.

In *Tecmed v Mexico*, the tribunal rejected the National Treatment claim because:

> [t]he Claimant has failed to furnish convincing or sufficient evidence to prove, at least prima facie, that the Claimant's investment received, under similar circumstances, less favorable treatment than that afforded to nationals of the State receiving the investment or of a third State, or that said investment was subject to discriminatory treatment *upon the basis of considerations relative to nationality or origin of the investment or the investor.*[115]

In *Champion Trading v Egypt*, the need to establish a link between discrimination and foreign nationality was also emphasized:

> [t]he non-discrimination principle is found in Art. II (2)(a) of the BIT [the Egypt–US bilateral investment treaty (BIT)], which prohibits discrimination *based on nationality* and requires the State to treat equally investments that are in like situations.
>
> The purpose of Art. II (2)(a) is to promote foreign investment and *to guarantee the foreign investor that his investment will not because of his foreign nationality be accorded a treatment less favourable* than that accorded to others in like situations.[116]

In *Methanex v USA*, the tribunal held that '[i]n order to sustain its claim under Article 1102(3) [of NAFTA], Methanex must demonstrate, cumulatively, that *California intended to favour domestic investors by discriminating against foreign investors* and that Methanex and the domestic investor supposedly being favored by California are in like circumstances'.[117] In *Casinos Austria v Argentina*, the tribunal also clarified that National Treatment 'prohibits nationality-based discriminations between foreign investors and their investments, on the one hand, and national investors and their investments, on the other'.[118] In *Festorino v Poland*, the tribunal framed the discrimination test as follows:

[115] *Técnicas Medioambientales Tecmed, SA v United Mexican States*, ICSID Case No ARB (AF)/00/2, Award, 29 May 2003, para 181 (emphasis added).

[116] *Champion Trading Company and Ameritrade International, Inc v Arab Republic of Egypt*, Award ICSID Case No ARB/02/9, 27 October 2006, paras 125 and 126 (emphasis added). See also ibid, para 156: '[s]ince the Arbitral Tribunal came to the conclusion that the companies were not in a like situation, it does not need to analyze the other requirements which prohibit *discrimination on the grounds of nationality*' (emphasis added).

[117] *Methanex Corporation v the United States of America*, UNCITRAL, Final Award of the Tribunal on Jurisdiction and Merits, 3 August 2005, Part IV, Chapter B, para 12 (emphasis added). See also *Merrill & Ring Forestry LP v Government of Canada*, ICSID Case No UNCT/07/1, ICSID Administrated, Award, 31 March 2010, para 94. As Bjorklund explains, '[e]ven if a tribunal determines that the foreign entity is in like circumstances with the more favourably treated domestic entity, however, it must also examine whether the host state had legitimate, non-nationality-based reasons for according the two entities different treatment', A Bjorklund, 'The National Treatment Obligation' in K Yannaca-Small (ed), *Arbitration Under International Investment Agreements: A Guide to the Key Issues* (2nd edn, OUP 2018) 532–561, 532.

[118] *Casinos Austria International GmbH and Casinos Austria Aktiengesellschaft v Argentine Republic*, ICSID Case No ARB/14/32, Decision on Jurisdiction, 29 June 2018, para 249; see also ibid, para 250: 'The purpose of non-discrimination provisions is to ensure equal treatment as a precondition for fair competition at any given moment in time, not to freeze market regulation over time.'

> [t]o find that these facts demonstrate actionable discrimination, the Tribunal would have to be in possession of significantly more evidence proving (i) that the Claimants and PGNiG were afforded noticeably different treatment in proceedings similar enough to be compared; and (ii) that *such a discrepancy was nationality-based and not the result of some other confounding variable unrelated to nationality.*[119]

In *Resolute Forest v Canada* the parties disagreed precisely about this.[120] Claimant argued that to establish a breach of National Treatment under the North American Free Trade Agreement (NAFTA) showing likeness and less favourable treatment was sufficient; in other words, it was not necessary to demonstrate that discrimination was linked to the foreign investor's nationality.[121] According to the Claimant, 'it is not required to demonstrate discriminatory intent nor show nationality-based discrimination'[122] as '[h]ad the NAFTA Parties wanted to limit the scope of the prohibited conduct in Article 1102(3) to nationality-based discrimination, they could have chosen to add the criterion 'by reason of nationality' in Article 1102(3) as they did in Article 1102(4)'.[123] However, the Claimant also accepted that there is no violation of National Treatment if the State can prove that the measure resulting in less favourable treatment was unrelated to the investor's foreign nationality and had a reasonable nexus to public policy objectives.[124] Canada emphasized that National Treatment prohibits nationality-based discrimination and 'the burden does not shift to the Respondent once a presumptive violation has been shown, as the Claimant suggests'.[125] The tribunal unequivocally sided with Canada:

> the affirmed and widely recognized aim of NAFTA Article 1102 is to prevent nationality-based discrimination. This aim has been consistently affirmed for many years by the three NAFTA parties, including in the current case. Numerous NAFTA Chapter 11 tribunals have also interpreted and applied Article 1102 as such. It should be stressed, however, that a claimant does not have to provide proof positive of discriminatory intent to prevail in a claim under Article 1102. This is agreed to by the

[119] *Festorino Invest Limited and others v Republic of Poland*, SCC Case No 2018/098, Award, 30 June 2021, para 747 (emphasis added). See also ibid, para 669 (regarding Respondent's criticism of Claimant's confused and overlapping discrimination claims). See also *Adel A Hamadi Al Tamimi v Sultanate of Oman*, ICSID Case No ARB/11/33 Award, 3 November 2015, para 467 ('[t]here is no evidence, furthermore, that the Claimant was treated in a particular manner because of his nationality').

[120] *Resolute Forest Products Inc v Government of Canada*, PCA Case No 2016-13, Award, 25 July 2022; cf ibid, Separate Opinion of Dean Cass, paras 86–124.

[121] See *Resolute Forest Products Inc v Government of Canada*, PCA Case No 2016-13, Award, 25 July 2022, para 466.

[122] ibid, para 468.

[123] Quoted in ibid, Separate Opinion of Dean Cass, para 90.

[124] *Resolute Forest Products Inc v Government of Canada*, PCA Case No 2016-13, Award, 25 July 2022, para 501 ('The Claimant contends that, having met each element of the UPS test, the burden shifts to Canada to justify its discrimination of Resolute and its investments by showing that nationality was not a factor in the adoption of the measures and that the measures do not undermine the NAFTA objectives, the two conditions listed in *Pope & Talbot* […], i.e., that the measures have a reasonable nexus to government policies that (i) do not distinguish on their face or de facto between foreign-owned and domestic companies and (ii) do not otherwise unduly undermine the investment liberalising objectives of NAFTA').

[125] ibid, para 504.

> Parties to this case as well as by the United States and Mexico. As held by past tribunals, in some cases, short of a smoking-gun, such proof of discriminatory intent may be impossible to provide. That being said, *nationality*-based discrimination is still at the heart of NAFTA Article 1102 (including its paragraph 3).[126]

However, as explained in the separate opinion of Dean Cass the parties' disagreement was more about the allocation of the burden of proof[127] and less about whether National Treatment prohibits nationality-based discrimination.[128]

Tribunals adopt the same conception of non-discrimination (ie falling within the 'disparate treatment' paradigm) in relation to other non-discrimination obligations as well. For example, regarding MFN, in *MNSS v Montenegro* the tribunal held that '[t]he breach of this standard requires proof that investments in like circumstances have been discriminated *on the basis of their nationality*'.[129] Another tribunal interpreting a non-impairment clause held that '[u]sually, the discrimination is based on the nationality of the foreign investor'.[130] As the tribunal held in *Crystallex v Venezuela* (in the context of discrimination under FET and expropriation) to 'show discrimination the investor must prove that it was subjected to different treatment in similar circumstances without reasonable *justification, typically on the basis of its nationality or similar character*'.[131] In *Oxus v Uzbekistan*, the tribunal did hold that 'the standard of discrimination refers *primarily* to a discrimination based on nationality'.[132] Expropriation is no

[126] *Resolute Forest Products Inc v Government of Canada*, PCA Case No 2016-13, Award, 25 July 2022, para 546 (emphasis in the original).

[127] See Chapter 4.

[128] *Resolute Forest Products Inc v Government of Canada*, PCA Case No 2016-13, Separate Opinion of Dean Cass, 25 July 2022, paras 95 and 96:

> The Tribunal's Award characterizes the Claimant as merely arguing that no nationality-based reason is required for its case in chief—what a claimant must show in order to shift the evidentiary burden to a respondent. I do not believe that this sufficiently captures the strength of the position advocated by the Claimant.
>
> Unlike the Tribunal's Award, I read the Claimant's submissions in this case as stating the stronger proposition that under Article 1102(3) no nationality-based reason for less favourable treatment is necessary to recover against the State. In other words, the Claimant's position is that: (i) it is not necessary for a claimant stating a claim under Article 1102(3) to show nationality-based treatment as a part of its case, and (ii) a demonstration by a respondent that there were other reasons for disparate treatment and no nationality-based treatment would not overcome a showing of less favourable treatment.

[129] *MNSS BV and Recupero Credito Acciaio NV v Montenegro*, ICSID Case No ARB(AF)/12/8, Award, 4 May 2016, para 358.

[130] *Venezuela US, SRL v Bolivarian Republic of Venezuela*, PCA Case No 2013–34, Partial Award on Jurisdiction and Liability, 5 February 2021, para 223.

[131] *Crystallex International Corporation v Bolivarian Republic of Venezuela*, ICSID Case No ARB(AF)/11/2, Award, 4 April 2016, para 715 (emphasis added).

[132] *Oxus Gold Plc v Republic of Uzbekistan*, UNCITRAL, Final Award, 17 December 2015, para 794 (emphasis added). The tribunal interpreted Article 2(2) of the Agreement between the Government of the United Kingdom of Great Britain and Northern Ireland and the Government of the Republic of Uzbekistan for the Promotion and Protection of Investments (signed 24 November 1993, entered into force 24 November 1993) (UK–Uzbekistan BIT), a provision combining FET, non-impairment, full protection and security, and umbrella clauses which provided that 'Investments of nationals or companies of each Contracting Party shall at all times be accorded fair and equitable treatment and shall enjoy full protection and security in the territory of the other Contracting Party. Neither Contracting Party shall in any way impair by unreasonable or discriminatory measures the management, maintenance, use, enjoyment or disposal of investments in its territory of nationals or companies of the other

different; discrimination in the context of expropriation is prohibited only if, and to the extent, any differences regarding which property has been expropriated are linked to investors' nationality or another impermissible ground.[133] In *Methanex v USA*, the tribunal distinguished between 'intentional discrimination' (which could give rise to an expropriation claim) and 'non-discriminatory regulation for a public purpose' (which could not):

> [i]n the Tribunal's view, Methanex is correct that an intentionally discriminatory regulation against a foreign investor fulfils a key requirement for establishing expropriation. But as a matter of general international law, a non-discriminatory regulation for a public purpose, which is enacted in accordance with due process and, which affects, inter alios, a foreign investor or investment is not deemed expropriatory and compensable unless specific commitments had been given by the regulating government to the then putative foreign investor contemplating investment that the government would refrain from such regulation.[134]

A study by the United Nations Conference on Trade and Development (UNCTAD) explains that '[a]n expropriation that targets a foreign investor is not discriminatory per se: the expropriation must be based on, linked to or taken for reasons of, the investor's nationality'.[135] According to the 2012 edition of *Brownlie's Principles of Public International Law*, '[t]he test of discrimination is the intention of the government: the fact that only aliens are affected may be incidental, and, if the taking is based on economic and social policies, it is not directed against particular groups simply because they own the property involved'.[136] Likewise, Collins explains that '[t]he relevant test for the breach of the National Treatment standard is whether the alleged discrimination is effectively based upon nationality rather than some other policy reason'.[137] However, targeting foreign investors' property on the basis of characteristics other than nationality (such as race as in *Von Pezold v Zimbabwe*[138]) also constitutes discrimination.

In addition to the jurisprudence of arbitral tribunals, the understanding of non-discrimination as a form of 'disparate treatment' discrimination is clearly reflected

Contracting Party. Each Contracting Party shall observe any obligation it may have entered into with regard to investments of nationals or companies of the other Contracting Party.'

[133] Cf A Reinisch, 'Expropriation' in P Muchlinski, F Ortino, and C Schreuer (eds), *The Oxford Handbook of International Investment Law* (OUP 2008) 407–458, 451: 'discriminatory intent or effect only serves as a subsidiary or additional element evidencing indirect expropriation. As such it must be distinguished from other discriminatory state measures contrary to investment standards, such as most-favoured-nation or national treatment, which are usually contained in BITs and other investment agreements'.

[134] *Methanex Corporation v the United States of America*, UNCITRAL, Final Award of the Tribunal on Jurisdiction and Merits, 3 August 2005, Part IV, Chapter D, para 7.

[135] UNCTAD, *Expropriation: UNCTAD Series on Issues in International Investment Agreements II* (UN 2012) 34.

[136] JR Crawford, *Browlie's Principles of Public International Law* (8th edn, OUP 2012) 625, fn 114.

[137] D Collins, *An Introduction to International Investment Law* (CUP 2023)116.

[138] *Bernhard von Pezold and others v Republic of Zimbabwe*, ICSID Case No ARB/10/15, Award, 28 July 2015, para 501 ('As regards to the criterion of non-discrimination in the Swiss BIT's expropriation provision, the evidence supports a conclusion that the Claimants were targeted as a result of their skin colour and, hence, the taking was discriminatory in breach of the Swiss BIT'). Cf *RosInvestCo UK Ltd v The Russian Federation*, SCC Case No V079/2005, Final Award, 12 September 2010, para 555 ('The [Russia–UK BIT] uses the term in Article 2(2)

in State practice. States usually emphasize in their submissions that the measures resulting in less favourable treatment are prohibited only if are motivated by the nationality of the investors.[139] Recent treaty drafting unequivocally points to the same direction. The new generation of investment treaties or model BITs, such as the new generation BIT between Brazil and India[140] and Canada's 2021 Model BIT,[141] support the view that differences in treatment, even if detrimental to foreign investors, do not give rise to breach of non-discrimination obligations on their own, especially if they are the result of legitimate, good faith state regulation in the public interest. For example,

regarding discriminatory measures and in Article 5(1) regarding discriminatory expropriations. In the view of the Tribunal, in both provisions, the term focuses on a discrimination between nationals and foreigners').

[139] N DiMascio and J Pauwelyn, 'Nondiscrimination in Trade and Investment Treaties: Worlds Apart or Two Sides of the Same Coin?' (2008) 102 AJIL 48, 77. Regarding Article 1102 of the NAFTA this is not invariably the case and some States did not raise such an argument, T Weiler, *The Interpretation of International Investment Law, Equality, Discrimination and Minimum in Historical Context* (Martinus Nijhoff 2013) 436. 'As Canada previously argued, a national treatment violation must be founded upon a finding of discrimination based on a foreign investor's nationality. This position has been unanimously supported by the United States and Mexico. Specifically, the United States agrees that "[a] claimant must establish that the measure, whether in law or in fact, treats foreign investors or investments less favorably than domestic investors or investments on the basis of nationality." By failing to require proof of nationality-based discriminatory treatment, the *Bilcon* tribunal erred in its interpretation of Article 1102. This Tribunal should not do the same, and instead, should follow the mandate given to it by the NAFTA Parties, and reaffirmed in the NAFTA Parties submissions here, by limiting its analysis with respect to Article 1102 to whether the Claimant has proven *nationality-based* discrimination. Any differing or broader interpretation put forward by the Claimant must be rejected.' *Mesa Power Group, LLC v Government of Canada*, UNCITRAL, PCA Case No 2012-17, Government of Canada, Response to 1128 Submissions, 26 June 2015, para 16 (emphasis in the original). 'The purpose of Article 1102 is to protect against *nationality-based* discrimination. Article 1102 is not intended to prohibit all differential treatment among investors and investments, but to ensure that the NAFTA Parties do not treat investors in like circumstances differently based on their NAFTA-Party nationality. A claimant must establish that the measure, whether in law or in fact, treats foreign investors or investments less favorably than domestic investors or investments on the basis of nationality. All three NAFTA Parties agree on this point. The Parties' common, concordant, and consistent position constitutes the authentic interpretation of Article 1102 and, under the Vienna Convention on the Law of Treaties, "shall be taken into account, together with the context".' *Mesa Power Group, LLC v Government of Canada*, UNCITRAL, PCA Case No 2012–17, Second Submission of the United States of America, 12 June 2015, para 3 (emphasis in the original). Cf ibid, para 2, fn 3 ('The requirement to show discrimination on the basis of nationality under Article 1102 does not require a showing of discriminatory intent'). 'Article 1102 is intended to prevent discrimination on the basis on nationality. Mexico agrees that the NAFTA Parties are unanimously of the view that a national treatment violation requires a finding of discrimination based on a foreign investor's nationality.' *Mesa Power Group, LLC v Government of Canada*, UNCITRAL, PCA Case No 2012-17, Second Submission of Mexico pursuant to NAFTA Article 1128, 12 June 2015, para 4. These submissions were made in the context of the *Mesa Power v Canada* arbitration. However, the tribunal did not examine the National Treatment obligation because 'the FIT [(Feed-In Tariff)] Program constitutes procurement by the Government of Ontario under Article 1108(7)(a) of the NAFTA', *Mesa Power Group, LLC v Government of Canada*, UNCITRAL, PCA Case No 2012-17, Award, 24 March 2016, para 465. See also *Gramercy Funds Management LLC and Gramercy Peru Holdings LLC v Peru*, ICSID Case No UNCT/18/2, Submission of the United States of America, 21 June 2019, para 50 and *Vento Motorcycles, Inc v United Mexican States*, ICSID Case No ARB(AF)/17/3, Submission of the United States of America, 23 August 2019, para 4: National Treatment 'is not intended to prohibit all differential treatment among investors or investments. Rather, it is designed only to ensure that the Parties do not treat entities that are "in like circumstances" differently based on nationality' but '[a] claimant is not required to establish discriminatory intent'.

[140] Investment Cooperation and Facilitation Treaty between the Federative Republic of Brazil and the Republic of India (signed 25 January 2020, not yet into force), Article 5.3: 'For greater certainty, this Article shall not be interpreted as obliging the Parties to compensate for inherent competitive disadvantages which result from the foreign character of the investors and their investments.' On new trends in treaty drafting W Alschner, *Investment Arbitration and State-Driven Reform: New Treaties, Old Outcomes Investment Arbitration and State-Driven Reform: New Treaties, Old Outcomes* (OUP 2022), Chapters 7 and 8.

[141] Canada's 2021 Model BIT also makes clear that National Treatment obligations 'prohibit discrimination based on nationality. A difference in treatment accorded to an investor or covered investment and a Party's own investors or investments of its own investors does not, in and of itself, establish discrimination based on nationality', Canada's 2021 Foreign Investment Promotion and Protection Agreement (FIPA) Model, Article 5(5); ibid, Article 6(5): 'Paragraphs 1 and 2 prohibit discrimination based on nationality. A difference in treatment accorded to an

Canada's 2021 Model BIT makes clear that the MFN obligation 'prohibit[s] discrimination based on nationality. A difference in treatment accorded to an investor or covered investment and a non-Party's investors or investments of a non-Party's investors does not, in and of itself, establish discrimination based on nationality'.[142] Another example is the Comprehensive and Progressive Agreement for Trans-Pacific Partnership (CPTPP) Drafters' Note on Interpretation of 'In Like Circumstances' Under Article 9.4 (National Treatment) and Article 9.5 (Most-Favoured-Nation Treatment) (CPTPP Drafters' Note):

> Articles 9.4 [National Treatment] and 9.5 [MFN] do not prohibit all measures that result in differential treatment. Rather, they seek to ensure that foreign investors or their investments are not treated less favourably on the basis of their nationality.[143]

This view is also shared by different scholars. According to Bjorklund, '[t]he case law accords with the position that the less favourable treatment [in National Treatment] must be motivated, at least inferentially, by nationality-based discrimination'.[144] Essentially, as Ortino observes, National Treatment in international economic law 'rests on the prohibition of using nationality or origin (of the product or investor) as the explicit or implicit regulatory criterion'.[145] Likewise, DiMascio and Pauwelyn observe in their seminal article on non-discrimination that (after *Pope and Talbot v Canada*)'[e]very subsequent major investment decision has agreed that the national treatment test's objective is to ferret out discrimination based upon nationality, though some tribunals have disagreed about the method of accomplishing that result'.[146] Collins explains that the purpose of National Treatment in international investment law is to protect 'individual investors from targeted attacks by host States'.[147] In her monograph on MFN, Crépet Daigremont accurately observes that MFN clauses do not prohibit less favourable treatment of similarly situated investors, unless the different treatment depends on the origin of the foreign investor or investment.[148]

investor or covered investment and a non-Party's investors or investments of a non-Party's investors does not, in and of itself, establish discrimination based on nationality.'

142 Canada's 2021 Foreign Investment Promotion and Protection Agreement (FIPA) Model, Article 6(5).

143 CPTPP Drafters' Note, para 2.

144 Bjorklund (n 117) 532–561, 539. See also B Sabahi and others, *Investor-State Arbitration* (2nd edn, OUP 2019), Chapter 17 ('Discrimination: National Treatment, Most-Favored Nation Treatment, and Discriminatory Impairment').

145 F Ortino, 'From "Non-discrimination" to "Reasonableness": A Paradigm Shift in International Economic Law' (Jean Monnet Working Paper 2005), available at <http://ssrn.com/ abstract=922524>, 10. See also M Herdegen, *Principles of International Economic Law* (2nd edn, OUP 2016) 450: '[t]he obligation of national treatment also protects investors against de jure as well as de facto discriminations based on nationality. In practice, most of the discriminatory measures relate to a de facto discrimination.'

146 DiMascio and Pauwelyn (n 139) 72; see also ibid, 76 ('tribunals have had to decide who carries the burden of proving that less favourable treatment *is based upon the investment's nationality*') (emphasis added).

147 D Collins, 'National treatment in emerging market investment treaties' in A Kamperman Sanders (ed), *The Principle of National Treatment in International Economic Law: Trade, Investment and Intellectual Property* (Edward Elgar 2014) 161–182, 165

148 C Crépet Daigremont, *La Clause de la Nation la Plus Favorisée* (Pedone 2015) 240 (emphasis in the original): 'tout ce qui est similaire et traité différement n'est pas nécessairement prohibé; tout ce qui est similaire et traité différemment selon l'origine *est prohibé*'.

The idea that in the realm of the protection of foreign investments less favourable treatment is prohibited only if it is accorded on the basis of the investors' nationality or another non-legitimate basis has deep historical roots.[149] The *ELSI* case was a rare occasion in which the ICJ interpreted the prohibition against arbitrary and discriminatory measures under the Friendship, Commerce and Navigation (FCN) treaty between US and Italy—a form of treaty which is considered as the progenitor of modern BITs.[150] The Court rejected the discrimination claim on the basis that 'there is no sufficient evidence before the Chamber to support the suggestion that *there was a plan to favour* IRI at the expense of ELSI.'[151] Article 1 of the 1967 OECD Convention on the Protection of Foreign Property states that:

> Each party shall at all times ensure fair and equitable treatment to the property of the nationals of the other Parties. It shall accord within its territory the most constant protection and security to such property and shall not in any way impair the management, maintenance, use, enjoyment or disposal thereof by unreasonable or discriminatory measures. The fact that certain nationals of any State are accorded treatment more favourable than that provided for in this Convention shall not be regarded as discriminatory against nationals of a Party by reason only of the fact that such treatment is not accorded to the latter.[152]

[149] See eg JB Moore, *Digest of International Law, Vol 6* (Government Printing Office 1906) 282 (Mr Gresham, Secretary of State to Mr Morse, 31 May 1893) 192 MS Dom Let 184: '"Nothing short of convincing evidence" that an American citizen "is the victim of intentional discrimination, partiality, or other injustice on the part of the court in which the prosecution is pending, could justify diplomatic intervention in his behalf"' (emphasis added). See also *Brewer, Moller & Co Case* (1903) 10 RIAA 423, 423 ('If it were shown that this tax was specially levied upon Germans owning warehouses, because they were Germans, or that for any other reason they were unlawfully classified, the allegation might need further consideration; but it so clearly appears that the tax is a general one, and that the classification is made upon a basis of the values of property, that it excludes any such inference'). See also the *Gilga* case before the Mixed Arbitral Tribunal for Upper Silesia, quoted in ML Milanov, in H Ruiz Fabri, and M Erpelding (eds), *The Mixed Arbitral Tribunals, 1919–1939: An Experiment in the International Adjudication of Private Rights* (Nomos 2023) 197–241, 231:

> If, therefore, nationals have to be dismissed for economic reasons, the dismissal may also extend under the same conditions to persons possessing the right of residence because they are not entitled to privileged treatment. But neither should they be less well treated. In their case, as in the case of nationals, there must therefore be examined without regard to nationality whether, taking into account a social and family conditions, there are actual reasons important enough to justify their dismissal.... the only reason for the dismissal of the complainant was his nationality.

See also G Kaeckenbeeck, *The International Experiment of Upper Silesia* (OUP 1942) 199.

[150] On FCN treaties see KJ Vandevelde, *The First Bilateral Investment Treaties U.S. Postwar Friendship, Commerce, and Navigation Treaties* (OUP 2017); JF Coyle, 'The Treaty of Friendship, Commerce and Navigation in the Modem Era' (2012) 51 Colombia Journal of Transnational Law 302; H Walker Jr, 'Modern Treaties of Friendship, Commerce and Navigation' (1958) 42 Minnesota Law Review 1491. See also A Wang, *The Interpretation and Application of the Most-Favored-Nation Clause in Investment Arbitration* (Brill Nijhoff 2022), Chapter 2. In *Certain Iranian Assets* the Court exercised judicial economy in relation to the discrimination claim, *Certain Iranian* Assets *(Islamic Republic of Iran v USA)* Judgment, 30 March 2023, para 158: '[s]ince the Court has concluded that the measures adopted by the United States are "unreasonable", it is not necessary to examine separately whether they are "discriminatory"'.

[151] *Elettronica Sicula SpA (ELSI) (USA v Italy)* (Judgment) [1989] ICJ Rep 15, 71–72 para 122 (emphasis added).

[152] 1967 Draft Convention on the Protection of Foreign Property, Article 1. See also Article 1 of the Abs-Shawcross Draft Convention on Investment Abroad: 'Each Party shall at all times ensure fair and equitable treatment to the property of the nationals of the other Parties. Such property shall be accorded the most constant protection and security within the territories of the other Parties and the management, use and enjoyment thereof shall not in any way be impaired by unreasonable or discriminatory measures.' See also AA Fatouros, 'An International Code to Protect Private Investment-Proposals and Perspectives (1961) 14 The University of Toronto Law Journal 77; G Schwarzenberger, 'The Abs-Shawcross Draft Convention on Investments Abroad: A Critical Commentary' (1961) 14 Current Legal Problems 213; CL Lim, J Ho, and M Paparinskis, *International Investment Law and Arbitration: Commentary, Awards and other Materials* (2nd edn, CUP 2021) 64; Y Chernykh, 'The Gust of

According to the notes and comments of Article 1, '[t]he essence of discrimination ... is differentiation introduced in the treatment of property as a result of the measures in question, which is not justified by legitimate considerations'.[153]

Further, adopting a 'disparate impact' discrimination (rather than 'disparate treatment' discrimination) paradigm in international investment law avoids casting the net too wide and strikes a fair balance between market objectives and State regulatory policies.[154] The purpose of National Treatment is to discipline protectionism, and a broader construction of National Treatment clauses would render other non-contingent treaty standards (and in particular FET) meaningless or of limited practical importance.[155] Even authors who reject the consideration of intent as part of the discrimination test, recognize that this might lead to unreasonable results.[156] The tribunal in *Feldman* offers an insightful analysis on the rationale for examining the 'motives' behind Host State's actions in National Treatment claims:

> if the motives for the government's actions should not be examined, there is effectively no way for the Claimant or this Tribunal to make the subjective determination that the discriminatory action of the government is a result of the Claimant's nationality, again in the absence of credible evidence from the Respondent of a different motivation. If Article 1102 [of NAFTA] violations are limited to those where there is explicit (presumably *de jure*) discrimination against foreigners, e.g., through a law that treats foreign investors and domestic investors differently, it would greatly limit the effectiveness of the national treatment concept in protecting foreign investors.[157]

Therefore, if the (less favourable) treatment accorded to the foreign investor is linked with a legitimate public policy objective, rather than motivated by the investor's

Wind: The Unknown Role of Sir Elihu Lauterpacht in the Drafting of the Abs-Shawcross Draft Convention' in SW Schill, CJ Tams, and R Hofmann (eds), *International Investment Law and History* (Edward Elgar 2018) 241–285.

153 1967 Draft Convention on the Protection of Foreign Property, Article 1 Notes and Comments, para 8(d).

154 See S Cho and J Kurtz, 'Convergence and Divergence in International Economic Law and Politics' (2018) 29 EJIL 169, 192.

155 Bjorklund (n 117) 532–561, 540: 'The argument that any disparate impact, no matter how small, can sustain a national treatment claim fails for historical as well as textual reasons. First, it does not comport with the general understanding that the purpose of the national treatment obligation is to discourage protectionism. Secondly, this interpretation is also inconsistent with the existence in most treaties of non-contingent obligations.'

156 See eg F Baetens, 'Discrimination on the basis of Nationality: Determining Likeness in Human Rights and Investment Law' in SW Schill (ed), *International Investment Law and Comparative Public Law* (OUP 2010) 279–316, 280: '[t]his chapter does not advocate the adoption of an intent requirement for the establishment of a non-discrimination breach but tribunals should assess whether a finding of discrimination might lead to the manifestly unreasonable result of outlawing a measure which has the mere coincidental effect of mostly affecting foreigners'.

157 *Marvin Roy Feldman Karpa v United Mexican States*, ICSID Case No ARB(AF)/99/1, Award, 16 December 2002, para 183. Mexico challenged the tribunal's approach before Canadian Courts (as Canada was the seat of the arbitration) but without success. The *United Mexican States v Marvin Roy Feldman Karpa* 74 OR 3d 180 (2005), para 58: 'Mexico was not required at the hearing to produce information it did not wish to produce. It decided, however, to produce certain taxpayer information. That information failed to satisfy the tribunal which, in turn, led the tribunal to conclude that if Mexico had evidence that a domestic taxpayer had "been treated in a manner equivalent to the claimant ... [it] would have provided that evidence." In my view, the tribunal was entitled to come to such a conclusion'.

nationality, there is no violation. The same rationale applies in relation to other non-discrimination obligations in international investment law.

Finally, the absence of general exceptions clauses in international investment treaties requires examination of whether a link between the less favourable treatment and a protected ground exist at the stage of establishing violations of non-discrimination standards. In *SD Myers v Canada*, the endorsement of that particular conception of discrimination was justified on the basis that, with some rare exceptions,[158] investment treaties do not contain general exception clauses, like Article XX of the World Trade Organization (WTO) General Agreement on Tariffs and Trade (GATT)[159] or Article XIV of the General Agreement on Trade in Services (GATS).[160,161] However, even in the context of WTO law leading international trade scholars have argued that the analysis on whether the States' measures were protectionist in the context of National Treatment should take place at the stage of determining violations of National Treatment and not at the stage of justifications under General Exceptions clauses.[162] Practically, the same measure that would be found in violation of National Treatment or MFN Treatment clauses contained in investment treaties without general exceptions provisions, would also fail to satisfy the requirement of the chapeau of general exceptions provisions.[163]

[158] See eg Energy Charter Treaty (ECT) (adopted 17 December 1994, entered into force 16 April 1998) 2080 UNTS 95, Article 24; Investment Agreement for the Common Market for Eastern and Southern Africa (COMESA) Common Investment Area (23 May 2007, not yet in force), Article 22; China-New Zealand Free Trade Agreement (signed 7 April 2008, entered into force 1 October 2008), Article 200; Agreement between Canada and the Republic of Peru for the Promotion and Protection of Investments (signed 14 November 2006, entered into force 20 June 2007), Article 10; Bilateral Investment Treaty between the Government of the Hashemite Kingdom of Jordan and the Government of the Republic of Singapore (signed 16 May 2004, entered into force 22 August 2005), Article 18; see also L Sabanogullari, *General Exceptions Clauses in International Investment Law: The Recalibration of Investment Agreements via WTO-Based Flexibilities* (Nomos 2018); B Legum and I Petculescu, 'GATT Article XX and International Investment Law' in R Echandi and P Sauvé (eds), *Prospects in International Investment Law and Policy* (CUP 2013) 340–362. See also S Spears, 'The Quest for Policy Space in a New Generation of International Investment Agreements' (2010) 13 JIEL 1037. See also AB, *China—Publications and Audiovisual Products*, para 223 ('WTO Members' regulatory requirements may be WTO consistent in one of two ways. First, they may simply not contravene any WTO obligation. Secondly, even if they contravene a WTO obligation, they may be justified under an applicable exception. The reference to "a manner consistent with the WTO Agreement" seems to us to encompass both types of WTO-consistency.')

[159] (Adopted 30 October 1947, not in force) 55 UNTS 194. The GATT 1947 was brought into force on a provisional basis by the Protocol of Provisional Application (adopted 30 October 1947, entered into force 1 January 1948) 55 UNTS 308. GATT 1994 (adopted 15 April 1994, entered into force 1 January 1995) 1867 UNTS 187 incorporates, by reference, GATT 1947.

[160] (Adopted 15 April 1994, entered into force 1 January) World Trade Organization, Annex 1B, 1869 UNTS 183.

[161] *SD Myers, Inc v Government of Canada*, UNCITRAL, Partial Award, 13 November 2000, para 246 ('[i]n the GATT context, a prima facie finding of discrimination in "like" cases often takes place within the overall GATT framework, which includes Article XX (General Exceptions). A finding of 'likeness' does not dispose of the case. It may set the stage for an inquiry into whether the different treatment of situations found to be "like" is justified by legitimate public policy measures that are pursued in a reasonable manner').

[162] See G Grossman, H Horn, and PC Mavroidis, 'National Treatment' in H Horn and PC Mavroidis (eds), *Legal and Economic Principles of World Trade Law* (CUP 2012) 205–353.

[163] GATT, Article XX, chapeau ('Subject to the requirement that such measures are not applied in a manner which would constitute a means of arbitrary or unjustifiable discrimination between countries where the same conditions prevail, or a disguised restriction on international trade, nothing in this Agreement shall be construed to prevent the adoption or enforcement by any contracting party of measures'). GATS, Article XIV, chapeau ('Subject to the requirement that such measures are not applied in a manner which would constitute a means of arbitrary or unjustifiable discrimination between countries where like conditions prevail, or a disguised restriction on trade in services, nothing in this Agreement shall be construed to prevent the adoption or enforcement by any Member of measures'). On the similarities between the requirement of Article XX of the GATT and FET under investment treaties see A Gourgourinis, 'Reviewing the Administration of Domestic Regulation in WTO and Investment Protection Law: The International Minimum Standard of Treatment of Aliens as "One Standard to Rule Them All"?' (2011) 8 Transnational Dispute Management 1.

As Newcombe observes '[i]n strict legal terms', 'general exceptions are unlikely to provide greater or lesser flexibility to regulators to regulate. General exceptions make explicit what is implicit in investment treaty obligations'.[164] According to the tribunal in *Bilcon v Canada*, '[t]he approach taken in Pope & Talbot, would seem to provide legally appropriate latitude for host states, even in the absence of an equivalent of Article XX of the GATT, to pursue reasonable and non-discriminatory domestic policy objectives through appropriate measures *even when there is an incidental and reasonably unavoidable burden on foreign enterprises*'.[165] While the absence of general exceptions clause might not alter the outcome of a particular case, it affects the analytical process for reaching that outcome. This has important evidentiary consequences, which will be addressed in detail in Chapter 4.

2.3 The Relationship between Different Non-discrimination Obligations Contained in Investment Treaties

Despite the fact that several hundred arbitral awards have been rendered post-1990,[166] after the 'Big Bang' explosion of investment treaties in the universe of international economic law,[167] one of the less clear areas of international investment law concerns the relationship of different non-discrimination standards contained in investment treaties. As recognized by the tribunal in *British Caribbean Bank v Belize*, there is an inevitable degree of overlap between the substantive standards of treatment in international investment law as 'each of the standards set out in the Treaty expresses a particular aspect of the overall objective of protection of investments' and '[t]heir potentially overlapping application reflects this complementarity'.[168] However, when and how the substantive obligations under investment treaties (and in particular non-discrimination

[164] A Newcombe, 'General Exceptions in International Investment Agreements in MC Cordonier Segger, M Gehring, and A Newcombe (eds), *Sustainable Development in World Investment Law* (Kluwer Law International 2011) 355–370, 369.

[165] *William Ralph Clayton and others v Government of Canada*, PCA Case No 2009–04, Award on Jurisdiction and Liability, 17 March 2015, para 723 (emphasis added).

[166] The first investment arbitration was *AAPL v Sri Lanka* with the tribunal rendering its award in 1990, *Asian Agricultural Products Ltd v Republic of Sri Lanka*, ICSID Case No ARB/87/3; Award, 27 June 1990. See also J Paulsson, 'Arbitration without Privity' (1995) 10 ICSID Review 232. On the 'pre-history' and history of investment treaty arbitration see D Schneiderman, *Investment Law's Alibis: Colonialism, Imperialism, Debt and Development* (CUP 2022); see also K Miles, *The Origins of International Investment Law: Empire, Environment and the Safeguarding of Capital* (CUP 2013); J Yackee, 'Investor-State Dispute Settlement at the Dawn of International Investment Law: France, Mauritania, and the Nationalization of the MIFERMA Iron Ore Operations' (2019) 59 American Journal of Legal History 71; JW Yackee, 'Expelling the "Sinister Vilgrain": Nationalization, Diplomacy, and Sugar in the People's Republic of Congo, 1970–1978' (2021) 44 French Historical Studies 119 (2021); JW Yackee, 'The First Investor-State Arbitration' (2016) 17 JWIT 40; T St John, *The Rise of Investor-State Arbitration: Politics, Law, and Unintended Consequences* (OUP 2018); J Hepburn and others, 'Investment Law before Arbitration' (2020) 23 JEIL 929.

[167] M Risvas, 'International Law as the Basis for Extending Arbitration Agreements concluded by States or State Entities to Non-Signatories' (2022) 71 ICLQ 183, 199.

[168] *British Caribbean Bank Ltd v Government of Belize*, PCA Case No 2010–18/BCB-BZ, Award, 19 December 2014, para 280. The tribunal also held that '[n]othing in the Treaty supports the Respondent's allegation that the Treaty standards are alternatives to each other, such that a violation of any one precludes a violation of another', ibid.

obligations) overlap is far from clear.[169] Building on the understanding of non-discrimination clauses in international investment law as forms of 'disparate treatment' discrimination,[170] this book offers for the first time a comprehensive analysis of the complex interplay between such clauses. Section 2.3.1 analyses the relationship between clauses prohibiting only nationality-based discrimination (National Treatment and MFN) on the one hand and non-impairment clauses on the other. Section 2.3.2 and Section 2.3.3 deal with the relationship between standalone non-discrimination obligations and non-discrimination aspects of the obligation to accord FET and the rules regarding expropriation respectively.

2.3.1 The Relationship between National Treatment and MFN on the One Hand and Clauses Prohibiting Arbitrary and/or Discriminatory Measures

Non-impairment clauses have given rise to complex questions regarding their relationship with other substantive treaty standards.[171] Whether the prohibition against arbitrary or discriminatory measures (which has a long history[172]) is contained in a separate treaty clause or is combined in the same provision with other substantive obligations (providing for Fair and Equitable Treatment and/or Full Protection and Security) does not seem to affect its interpretation.[173] As most non-impairment clauses prohibit arbitrary *or* (rather than 'and') discriminatory measures, these standards are not cumulative,[174] unless the specific investment treaty explicitly states so.[175] This means that a State can be found to have acted in an arbitrary but not discriminatory manner and vice versa.

[169] On the overlapping nature of investment standards see the analysis in F Ortino, *The Origin and Evolution of Investment Treaty Standards: Stability, Value, and Reasonableness* (OUP 2019) 111–113.

[170] See Section 2.1 above.

[171] V Heiskanen, 'Arbitrary and Unreasonable Measures' in A Reinisch (ed), *Standards of Investment Protection* (OUP 2008)87–110, 89.

[172] See A Reinisch and C Schreuer, *International Protection of Investments: The Substantive Standards* (CUP 2020) 817–819.

[173] U Kriebaum, 'Arbitrary/Unreasonable or Discriminatory Measures' in M Bungenberg and others (eds), *International Investment Law* (CH Beck, Hart, Nomos 2013) 790–806, 794–795. Cf C Titi, 'Full Protection and Security, Arbitrary or Discriminatory Treatment and the Invisible EU Model BIT' (2014) 15 JWIT 534, 550.

[174] Reinisch and Schreuer (n 172) 817; *Joseph Charles Lemire v Ukraine*, ICSID Case No ARB/06/18, Decision on Jurisdiction and Liability, 14 January 2010, para 260; *AES Summit Generation Limited and AES-Tisza Erömü Kft v Republic of Hungary*, ICSID Case No ARB/07/22, Award, 23 September 2010, para 10.3.2; *Dan Cake SA v Hungary*, ICSID Case No ARB/12/9, Decision on Jurisdiction and Liability, 24 August 2015, para 156. See also *Certain Iranian Assets (Islamic Republic of Iran v USA)* Judgment, 30 March 2023, para 145: '[t]he Court notes that the second clause uses a disjunctive "or", not a conjunctive "and", to prescribe protection against "unreasonable or discriminatory measures". In the case concerning *Elettronica Sicula S.p.A. (ELSI) (United States of America v. Italy)*, the Court conducted separate examinations as to whether the measures concerned were either "discriminatory" or "arbitrary" (see *Judgment, I.C.J. Reports 1989*, pp. 72–77, paras. 121–130). The Court considers that the terms "unreasonable" or "discriminatory" in the second clause of Article IV, paragraph 1, reflect two different standards against which the conduct of a State may be separately assessed.'

[175] *Ronald S Lauder v Czech Republic*, UNCITRAL, Final Award, 3 September 2001, para 219: 'The Arbitral Tribunal considers that a violation of Article II(2)(b) of the Treaty requires both an arbitrary and a discriminatory measure by the State. It first results from the plain wording of the provision, which uses the word "and" instead of the word "or" (although in that case the tribunal was mistaken as to the text of the BIT which used "or" and not "and"; Reinisch and Schreuer (n 172) 817; Kriebaum (n 173) 794).

As explained above, all non-discrimination obligations in investment treaties prohibit disparate treatment or direct discrimination.[176] Essentially, their difference revolves around the type of the protected ground, ie the characteristic which according to each provision constitutes an impermissible basis for granting different (less favourable) treatment. National Treatment and MFN clauses focus on nationality-based discrimination,[177] ie nationality is the protected ground, and, therefore, it is prohibited for States to make distinctions resulting in less favourable treatment on the basis of the foreign investors' nationality. Other non-discrimination standards prohibit less favourable treatment based not only on the investor's nationality but also on a broader set of impermissible grounds (eg race or religion).[178]

This view is reflected in the jurisprudence. In *Ulysseas v Ecuador*, the tribunal summarily rejected Respondent's argument that 'there is only one standard for discriminatory treatment, which is discrimination on the basis of nationality' in relation to the non-impairment clause in the US-Ecuador BIT.[179] In *National Grid v Argentina*, the tribunal held that the non-impairment clause contained in the UK–Argentina BIT 'does not limit discrimination to discrimination on the basis of nationality and may cover measures based on other grounds'.[180] It is therefore clear that there is a substantive overlap between MFN and National Treatment clauses on the one hand, and non-impairment clauses on the other. In *Cengiz v Libya* the tribunal dealt with claims on the basis of the Libya–Turkey BIT clause prohibiting unreasonable or discriminatory measures and the clause providing for National and MFN Treatment together, applying

[176] See Section 2.2 above.

[177] It seems that consensus exists that the legal test for establishing violations of National and MFN Treatment is the same, the only different being the domestic v foreign comparator; see eg *Mercer International Inc v Government of Canada*, ICSID Case No ARB(AF)/12/3, Award, 6 March 2018, para 7.10 ('[i]t is not in issue that the requirements for establishing a violation of NAFTA Article 1103 are the same as establishing a violation of NAFTA Article 1102, except that the applicable comparator, in like circumstances, is a foreign (non-Canadian) investor or investment'). On the economic analysis of the National Treatment and MFN obligations contained in investment treaties see AO Sykes, 'The Economic Structure of International Investment Agreements with Implications for Treaty Interpretation and Design' (2019) 113 AJIL 482, 510

[178] The relevant study by UNCTAD explains that while 'the national treatment and MFN standards deal with nationality-based discrimination, the non-discrimination requirement as part of the FET standard appears to prohibit discrimination in the sense of specific targeting of a foreign investor on other manifestly wrongful grounds such as gender, race or religious belief, or the types of conduct that amount to a "deliberate conspiracy [...] to destroy or frustrate the investment"', UNCTAD, *Fair and Equitable Treatment: UNCTAD Series on Issues in International Investment Agreements II* (UN 2012) 82; citing also *Glamis Gold, Ltd v The United States of America*, UNCITRAL, Award, 8 June 2009, para 542, fn 1087. See also Kriebaum (n 173) 798; Reinisch and Schreuer (n 172) 835. The ICJ in the *Qatar v UAE* case made clear that racial discrimination under the CERD, and in particular the term 'national origin' does not encompass 'current nationality', *Application of the International Convention on the Elimination of All Forms of Racial Discrimination (Qatar v United Arab Emirates)*, Preliminary Objections, Judgment, [2021] ICJ Rep 71, 106, para 105. See also C Briddick and C Costello, 'Introduction to the Symposium on Undoing Discriminatory Borders' (2021) 115 AJIL Unbound 328; ET Achiume, 'Digital Racial Borders (2021) 115 AJIL Unbound 333; C Costello and M Foster, 'Race Discrimination Effaced at the International Court of Justice' (2021) 115 AJIL Unbound 339; L Orgad, 'When Is Immigration Selection Discriminatory?' (2021) 115 AJIL Unbound 345; A Farahat, 'Discrimination Inside: Non-Discrimination as a Tool of Migrant Integration' (2021) 115 AJIL Unbound 350; C Briddick, 'When Does Migration Law Discriminate Against Women?' (2021) 115 AJIL Unbound 356; C Ó Cinnéide, 'Why Challenging Discrimination at Borders is Challenging (and Often Futile)' (2021) 115 AJIL Unbound 362.

[179] *Ulysseas, Inc v The Republic of Ecuador*, UNCITRAL, Final Award, 12 June 2012, paras 292 and 293; also relying on *Antoine Goetz et consorts v République du Burundi*, ICSID Case No ARB/95/3, 10 February 1999, para 121.

[180] *National Grid plc v The Argentine Republic*, UNCITRAL, Award, 3 November 2008, para 198.

the same legal test.[181] However, the prohibited grounds for differentiation in the case of non-impairment clauses is broader compared to those in National Treatment or MFN clauses. This practically means that a measure which is found to be in breach of National or MFN Treatment would necessarily violate the prohibition against arbitrary and/or discriminatory measures,[182] but not vice versa. In *Urbaser v Argentina*, interpreting the prohibition against 'discriminatory and unjustified measures' contained in Article III(1) of the Argentina–Spain BIT, the tribunal held that there is no 'additional requirement based on nationality. While it is correct to say that nationality is often a factor for testing whether a measure or decision qualifies as discrimination, as stated by Respondent, it does not appear as a criterion circumscribing the notion of "discriminatory measures" in Article III(1)'.[183]

2.3.2 Discrimination and Fair and Equitable Treatment

Unlike non-discrimination, which has a long history in international economic law,[184] FET is a relatively modern obligation.[185] Although rather laconic and abstract in their formulation,[186] FET clauses are of pivotal importance in international investment law, for both normative and practical reasons. According to Alvarez, FET obligations constitute the 'heart of the investment regime' being 'not only the most frequently invoked claim by investors', but 'also the most successful on their behalf'.[187] Clauses in investment treaties providing for non-discrimination are contingent standards; their violation depends on the outcome of a comparative exercise. By contrast, FET is an absolute, non-contingent standard; its breach does not depend upon a comparative examination.[188] As a result, the delineation between the scope of application of the FET standard on the one hand, and National Treatment and MFN obligations on the other,

[181] *Cengiz Insaat Sanayi ve Ticaret AS v Libya*, ICC Case No 21537/ZF/AYZ, Award, 7 November 2018, paras 522–543. See also *Alejandro Diego Díaz Gaspar v Republic of Costa Rica*, ICSID Case No ARB/19/13, Award, 29 June 2002 para 510.

[182] See eg *BG Group Plc v Republic of Argentina*, UNCITRAL, Award, 24 December 2007, para 355 ('the Tribunal accepts for the sake of its analysis, that a measure in breach of the national treatment or MFN standards of Article 3 of the BIT would unavoidably also be "discriminatory" in the sense of the second sentence of Article 2.2 of the BIT').

[183] *Urbaser SA and Consorcio de Aguas Bilbao Bizkaia, Bilbao Biskaia Ur Partzuergoa v The Argentine Republic*, ICSID Case No ARB/07/26, 8 December 2016, para 1082.

[184] See Chapter 1.

[185] Reinisch and Schreuer (n 172) 255; see also M Pinchis, 'The Ancestry of "Equitable Treatment" in Trade Lessons from the League of Nations during the Inter-War Period' (2014) 15 JWIT 13; M Paparinskis, *The International Minimum Standard and Fair and Equitable Treatment* (OUP 2013) 13–98.

[186] *Mondev International Ltd v United States of America*, ICSID Case No ARB(AF)/99/2, Award, 11 October 2002, para 118 ('[a] judgment of what is fair and equitable cannot be reached in the abstract; it must depend on the facts of the particular case').

[187] See V Zivkovic, 'Fair and Equitable Treatment between the International and National Rule of Law' (2019) 20 JWIT 513.

[188] See Reinisch and Schreuer (n 172) 346; M Jacob and SW Schill, 'Standards of Protection: Fair and Equitable Treatment: Content, Practice, Method' in M Bungenberg and others (eds), *International Investment Law* (CH Beck, Hart, Nomos 2013) 700–763, 702; P Dumberry, *The Fair and Equitable Treatment Standard: A Guide to NAFTA Case Law on Article 1105* (Kluwer Law International 2013) 27. See also E De Brabandere, 'Fair and Equitable Treatment and (Full) Protection and Security in African Investment Treaties Between Generality and Contextual Specificity' (2017) 18 JWIT 530.

appears to be more 'clear-cut'.[189] However, as Van Aaken and Kurtz explain, the case law is not always clear:

> the type of discrimination caught by [National Treatment] is purposeful protectionism, defined as a desire of a host state to protect a domestic actor vis-a-vis a competing foreign investor. There is then the question of what other forms of discrimination might be caught by the FET standard. Few arbitral awards have examined this in any detail, given the tendency to conflate [National Treatment] and the FET standard. One possibility is a type of hostile 'singling out' where the foreign investor is targeted for disadvantage by the host state simply because of their foreignness (rather than any desire to tilt the competitive scales in favor of a domestic actor). If this is to be the type [of] discrimination caught by the FET standard, there is little evidence of hostile singling out at play in the measures we have surveyed. To put it bluntly, we are dealing with classic protectionist measures, rather than any desire to harm or evict foreign actors, *per se*.[190]

As the tribunal in *Mobil v Argentina* noted, 'the distinction seems also difficult between arbitrary or discriminatory treatment and violation of the FET'.[191] In *OKO Pankki v Estonia*, the tribunal included the prohibition against targeted discrimination as a key component of the International Minimum Standard:

> [a]ccording to the minimum standard under customary international law, an investor is protected against the host state's fraud, bad faith, capricious and wilful discrimination or where the host state 'deprives an investor of acquired rights in a manner that leads to the unjust enrichment of the State'.[192]

In *OAO Tatneft v Ukraine*, the tribunal held that '[d]iscrimination is a ground for an additional claim concerning the breach of FET'.[193] The close connection between the

[189] Reinisch and Schreuer (n 172) 365.

[190] A van Aaken and J Kurtz, 'Prudence or Discrimination? Emergency Measures, the Global Financial Crisis and International Economic Law' 12 JIEL 859, 889. See also *Glamis Gold, Ltd v The United States of America*, UNCITRAL, Final Award, 8 June 2009, para 542, fn 1087: 'under the NAFTA, there are two types of discrimination: nationality-based discrimination and discrimination that is founded on the targeting of a particular investor or investment. The former falls under the purview of Article 1102 and Claimant does not argue this. Inasmuch as Claimant argues that it was discriminated against, this argument appears primarily in the discussion of Article 1110, in which Claimant asserts that the discriminatory nature of the California measures provides additional proof that the measures were not a bona fide exercise of State police power and thus a non-compensable regulation'.

[191] *Mobil Exploration and Development Inc Suc Argentina and Mobil Argentina SA v Argentine Republic*, ICSID Case No ARB/04/16, Decision on Jurisdiction and Liability, 10 April 2013, para 811. See also *Cavalum SGPS, SA v Kingdom of Spain*, ICSID Case No ARB/15/34, Decision on Jurisdiction, Liability and Directions on Quantum, 31 August 2020, para 410 ('[t]he obligation not to impair investments by unreasonable or discriminatory measures appears as a free-standing obligation in ECT Article 10(1), but there is no doubt that the FET standard contains the same obligation').

[192] *Oko Pankki Oyj, VTB Bank (Deutschland) AG and Sampo Bank Plc v The Republic of Estonia*, ICSID Case No ARB/04/6 (formerly *OKO Osuuspankkien Keskuspankki Oyj and others v Republic of Estonia*), Award, 19 November 2007, para 238. See also R Kläger, *'Fair and Equitable Treatment' in International Investment Law* (CUP 2011) 187; see also P Muchlinski, *Multinational Enterprises and the Law* (3rd edn, OUP 2021) 684 ('FET is case specific and requires a flexible approach, offering a general point of departure in formulating an argument that the foreign investor has not been well treated by discriminatory or other unfair measures').

[193] *OAO Tatneft v Ukraine*, PCA Case No 2008–8, Award on the Merits, 29 July 2014, para 408.

obligation to accord FET and the obligation to refrain from arbitrary or discriminatory measures led the tribunal the tribunal in *Unglaube v Costa Rica* to consider together cases dealing with FET and non-impairment clauses.[194]

Therefore, violations of the prohibition against discriminatory and/or arbitrary measures would normally entail a violation of the FET standard.[195] For example, in *Olin v Libya* the tribunal held that 'the FET standard encompasses an obligation not to discriminate'.[196] The opposite is not true.[197] According to the tribunal in *Arif v Moldova*, 'even though discrimination may also be considered an element of FET, the actions and omissions in breach of FET will not necessarily imply a breach with respect to non-discrimination'.[198] Likewise, in *Flemingo v Poland*, the tribunal made clear that

[194] *Marion Unglaube v Republic of Costa Rica*, ICSID Case No ARB/08/1, Award, 16 May 2012, para 263, fn 185 ('[w]hile this Award [in *Occidental v Ecuador*] dealt principally with the Fair and Equitable Treatment language of the Bilateral Investment Treaty, the factual and legal analysis was very close to that in *Nykomb* and *Saluka*').

[195] See eg *Oxus Gold Plc v Republic of Uzbekistan*, UNCITRAL, Final Award, 17 December 2015, para 785 and (n 132) and (n 200). See also *Ronald S Lauder v Czech Republic*, UNCITRAL, Final Award, 3 September 2001, paras 292–293; *CMS Gas Transmission Company v the Argentine Republic*, Award, ICSID Case No ARB/01/8, 12 May 2005, para 290 ('any measure that might involve arbitrariness or discrimination is in itself contrary to fair and equitable treatment'); *Rumeli Telekom AS v Republic of Kazakhstan*, ICSID Case No ARB/05/16, Award, 29 July 2008, para 680; *Parkerings-Compagniet AS v Republic of Lithuania*, ICSID Case No ARB/05/8, Award, 11 September 2007, para 280 ('The principle of *fair and equitable treatment* is violated where a host State's conduct is grossly unfair or discriminatory. Discrimination is a significant element in determining whether the standard of fair and equitable treatment has been breached'); *SAUR International v Argentine Republic*, ICSID Case No ARB/04/4, Decision on Jurisdiction and Liability, 6 June 2012, para 485; *RREEF Infrastructure (GP) Limited and RREEF Pan-European Infrastructure Two Lux Sàrl v Kingdom of Spain*, ICSID Case No ARB/13/30, Decision on Responsibility and on the Principles of Quantum, 30 November 2018, para 428 ('[t]he Tribunal considers that FET encompasses the principle of non-discrimination and it will analyse it as such for purposes of this case. However, had the ECT not contained an express provision on FET or protecting investors against non-discrimination, this principle would still be applicable on the basis of customary international law'); *Víctor Pey Casado and President Allende Foundation v Republic of Chile*, ICSID Case No ARB/98/2, Award, 8 May 2008, paras 670 and 672; *Mondev International Ltd v United States of America*, ICSID Case No ARB(AF)/99/2, Award, 11 October 2002, para 156; *Alejandro Diego Díaz Gaspar v Republic of Costa Rica*, ICSID Case No ARB/19/13, Award, 29 June 2002 para 507. See also CH Schreuer, 'Protection Against Arbitrary or Discriminatory Measures' in CA Rogers and RP Alford (eds), *The Future of Investment Arbitration* (OUP 2009) 183–198 ,189 ('[i]t is undeniable that the prohibition of arbitrary or discriminatory measures is related to that fair and equitable treatment standard'); S Vasciannie, 'The Fair and Equitable Treatment Standard in International Investment Law and Practice' (1999) 70 BYIL 99, 133: 'if there is discrimination on arbitrary grounds, or if the investment has been subject to arbitrary or capricious treatment by the host State, then the fair and equitable standard has been violated. This follows from the idea that fair and equitable treatment inherently precludes arbitrary and capricious actions against investors.' See also Weiler (n 139) 15–16. Cf *Mercer International Inc v Government of Canada*, ICSID Case No ARB(AF)/12/3, Award, 6 March 2018, para 7.51: 'So far as concerns the Claimant's claims of "discriminatory treatment" contrary to NAFTA Article 1105(1), the Tribunal's agrees with the non-disputing NAFTA Parties' submissions that such protections are addressed in NAFTA Articles 1102 and 1103, rather than NAFTA Article 1105(1).' The Tribunal in Glamis v USA referred to 'evident discrimination' as part of FET under Article 1105 of the NAFTA, *Glamis Gold, Ltd v The United States of America*, UNCITRAL, Final Award, 8 June 2009, para 828. It is unclear whether 'evident' implies a higher standard or refers to intentional (disparate treatment) discrimination, see also ibid, para 793 ('To begin, the Tribunal sees that, with respect to the Imperial Project and SB 22, there could be two possible forms of discrimination: (1) because Claimant is Canadian, and (2) regardless of nationality, because it is a class of one.')

[196] *Olin Holdings Limited v State of Libya*, ICC Case No 20355/MCP, Final Award, 25 May 2018, para 354.

[197] See Kläger (n 192) 285; see eg *Ronald S Lauder v Czech Republic*, UNCITRAL, Final Award, 3 September 2001, paras 214–303; *Alex Genin, Eastern Credit Limited, Inc and AS Baltoil v The Republic of Estonia*, ICSID Case No ARB/99/2, Award, 25 June 2001, paras 366–371; *Noble Ventures, Inc v Romania*, Award, ICSID Case No ARB/01/11, 12 October 2005, paras 175–180; *Azurix Corp v The Argentine Republic*, ICSID Case No ARB/01/12, Award, 14 July 2006, paras 385–393; *Siemens AG v Argentine Republic*, ICSID Case No ARB/02/8, Award, 6 February 2007, paras 289–309 and 310–321.

[198] *Mr Franck Charles Arif v Republic of Moldova*, Award, ICSID Case No ARB/11/23, 8 April 2013, para 515.

equal treatment per se does not automatically precludes violations of FET.[199] In *Oxus v Uzbekistan*, the tribunal held that under the applicable UK–Uzbekistan BIT:

> the duty to refrain from unreasonable or discriminatory measures as provided in Article 2(2) of the BIT are subsumed under the broader FET standard and that a behavior which is unreasonable or discriminatory in the sense of Article 2(2) would at the same time constitute a breach of the FET standard. This is not to say that both standards are fully equivalent, in particular … the FET standard may have a broader scope than the more specific duties to act in a reasonable and non-discriminatory way.[200]

In some cases, the parties agree that discrimination is one of the components of FET.[201] The close relationship between FET and discrimination is also explicitly acknowledged in more recent investment treaties (such as the Canada–European Union Comprehensive Economic and Trade Agreement (CETA)[202]) and model BITs (such as the 2019 Dutch Model BIT[203] and the 2021 Canada Model BIT[204]). As Vascienne aptly

[199] *Flemingo DutyFree Shop Private Limited v the Republic of Poland*, UNCITRAL, Award, 12 August 2016, para 531 ('Respondent is not correct when it argues that "fair and equitable treatment" boils down to treating foreign investors the same way as domestic and other foreign investors which also operated businesses at Chopin Airport. Equal treatment with domestic and other foreign entities is another specific standard, which is laid down in Article 4(1) of the Treaty: '[e]ach Contracting Party shall accord to investments of Investors of the other Contracting Party, treatment which shall not be less favourable than that accorded either to investments of its own investors or to investments of investors of any third state'. It is not because the host State would treat all investors—domestic as well as foreign—in the same way that such treatment could not be unfair or inequitable').

[200] *Oxus Gold plc v Republic of Uzbekistan*, UNCITRAL, Final Award, 17 December 2015, para 785; see also ibid, paras 319–323. See also Kläger (n 192) 291: 'Since decisions on either provision are often based on similar arguments of reasonableness, non-arbitrariness and non-discrimination, it seems at least improbable that arbitral tribunals draw differing conclusions in relation to an alleged non-discrimination when applying fair and equitable treatment or the duty to refrain from arbitrary and discriminatory measures in the same case.'

[201] See eg *Rumeli Telekom AS v Republic of Kazakhstan*, ICSID Case No ARB/05/16, Award, 29 July 2008, para 609.

[202] Comprehensive Economic and Trade Agreement (CETA) between Canada, of the one part, and the European Union and its Member States, of the other part (signed 30 October 2016), Article 8.10(2)(d): 'A Party breaches the obligation of fair and equitable treatment referenced in paragraph 1 if a measure or series of measures constitutes: … d) targeted discrimination on manifestly wrongful grounds, such as gender, race or religious belief'. See also the jointly released by the European Commission and Germany in 2022 'Draft Decision of the CETA Joint Committee' which provides that 'Article 8.10 shall be interpreted as follows':

> d) For greater certainty, a measure or series of measures constitute "targeted discrimination on manifestly wrongful grounds" in the meaning of Article 8.10.2(d) if
>
> - the measure or series of measures were patently not founded on reason or fact or were patently founded on illegitimate grounds such as prejudice or bias;
> - if a differential treatment based on gender, race or religious belief cannot be justified on the basis of objective and legitimate grounds, such as measures that are designed or applied to protect legitimate public welfare objectives, including health, the promotion of gender equality, environment (including climate protection) or safety.

[203] 2019 Dutch Model BIT, Article 9(2)(d): 'A Contracting Party breaches the aforementioned obligation of fair and equitable treatment where a measure or series of measures constitutes: … d) Direct or targeted indirect discrimination on wrongful grounds, such as gender, race, nationality, sexual orientation or religious belief'.

[204] 2021 Canada Model BIT, Article 8(1)(d): 'Each Party shall accord in its territory to a covered investment of the other Party and to an investor with respect to their covered investment treatment in accordance with the customary international law minimum standard of treatment of aliens. A Party breaches this obligation only if a measure constitutes: … d) targeted discrimination on manifestly wrongful grounds such as gender, race or religious beliefs'. On the relationship between FET and the International Minimum Standards of Treatment see the comprehensive analysis of Paparinskis (n 185).

observes in certain cases, non-discrimination will not 'necessarily satisfy the standard of fair and equitable treatment', while in other cases 'from the investor standpoint, national treatment may also be superior to fair and equitable treatment'.[205] According to Lim, Ho, and Paparinskis, 'arbitrary and discriminatory treatment' 'is perhaps the clearest example of a FET violation'.[206] At the same time, as another tribunal noted, '[w]hile, in certain cases, discriminatory treatment may give rise to a violation of fair and equitable treatment, in most cases discriminatory government actions are more properly judged against the requirements of national treatment and most- favoured nation treatment'.[207] Having found a breach of other treaty standards, usually regarding expropriation[208] or FET, tribunals exercise judicial economy in relation to the prohibition against arbitrary and/or discriminatory measures.

Finally, whether MFN clauses could be used to import FET clauses which do not exist in the basic investment treaty containing the MFN clause is a different question which is discussed in Chapter 3.[209]

2.3.3 Discrimination and Expropriation

The importance of protection against the risk of expropriation cannot be overstated and was indeed 'a principal motivating factor in the origin of the BITs'.[210] There is no general rule prohibiting discrimination in customary international economic law.[211] However, the requirement that an expropriation or nationalization must be non-discriminatory is well-entrenched in customary international law.[212] In 1964, the US Supreme Court

[205] Vasciannie (n 195) 7149. See also ibid, 133: '[i]n most cases, fair and equitable treatment stands independently of the most-favoured-nation and national treatment standards, and *vice versa*'. See also I Tudor, *The Fair and Equitable Treatment Standard in the International Law of Foreign Investment* (OUP 2007) 187–188.

[206] CL Lim, J Ho, and M Paparinskis, *International Investment Law and Arbitration: Commentary, Awards and other Materials* (2nd edn, CUP 2021) 335.

[207] *Alpha Projektholding GmbH v Ukraine*, ICSID Case No ARB/07/16, Award, 8 November 2010, para 419. See also FM Palombino, *Fair and Equitable Treatment and the Fabric of General Principles* (Asser Press 2018) 25–26 (arguing in favour of disentangling discrimination and FET). See also *El Paso Energy International Company v The Argentine Republic*, ICSID Case No ARB/03/15, Award, 31 October 2011, para 231 ('the Tribunal will examine first whether there is an indirect expropriation, second whether therbide is arbitrary or discriminatory treatment, third whether there is a violation of the FET, and fourth whether there is a breach of the FPS').

[208] *Bear Creek Mining Corporation v Republic of Peru*, ICSID Case No ARB/14/21, Award, 30 November 2017, para 553.

[209] See Chapter 3, Section 3.2.1.2.

[210] Vandevelde (n 150) 271; Ortino (n 169) 49.

[211] See Chapter 1, Section 1.2.1. However, 'the "non-discrimination" requirement is not extensively discussed in the literature or by international tribunals' N Rubins, T-N Papanastastiou, and NS Kinsella, *International Investment, Political Risk, and Dispute Resolution: A Practitioner's Guide* (2nd edn, OUP 2020) 196.

[212] *Affaire des biens britanniques au Maroc espagnol (Espagne c Royaume-Uni)* (1 May 1925) (1925) 2 RIAA 615, 647; *Norwegian shipowners' claims (Norway v United States)* (1922) 1 RIAA 307, 339; The sole arbitrator in LIAMCO emphasized that '[i]t is clear and undisputed that non-discrimination is a requisite for the validity of a lawful nationalisation. This is a rule well established in international theory and practice [reference omitted]. Therefore, a purely discriminatory nationalisation is illegal and wrongful', *Libyan American Oil Company (LIAMCO) v The Government of the Libyan Arab Republic* (12 April 1977) (1981) 20 ILM 1, 58–59; (1977) 62 ILR 140, 194. In *J S Pisani v the Turkish Government*, a case before the Anglo-Turkish Mixed Arbitral Tribunal, it was held that 'the Tribunal has to examine each expropriation separately in order to ascertain whether it was a bona fide one and whether it was or might have been applied indiscriminately to Turkish nationals as well as to foreigners', WH Hill, 'The Anglo-Turkish Mixed Arbitral Tribunal' (1935) 47 Juridical Review 241, 247. In discussing the *Emeric Kulin v Romania* (also known as the *Hungarian optants* case), concerning the implementation of the Romanian

held in the famous *Sabbatino* case that '[t]here are few if any issues of international law today on which the opinion seems to be so divided as the limitations on a state's power to expropriate the property of aliens'.[213] This extends to the role of the obligation of non-discrimination as well.[214] According to the Superior Court of Hamburg, '[a] nationalization which is directed specifically against foreigners is to be considered, however, discriminatory and thus an act which is not to be approved in accordance with the principles of public policy'.[215]

Two types of expropriation must be distinguished in international investment law: direct and indirect expropriation. According to UNCTAD:

agrarian reform in the interwar period, and the related expropriation of certain land belonging to Hungarian nationals, the Council of the League of Nations affirmed that '[t]here must be no inequality between Romanians and Hungarians, either in the terms of the Agrarian Law or in the way in which it is enforced', *Emeric Kulin v Romania* (10 January 1927), (1927) 7 Recueil des decisions des Tribunaux Arbitraux Mixtes institués par les traits de paix 138. The Council of the League of Nations, First Meeting, Forty-Seventh Session of the Council, 19 September 1927, (1927) 8 League of Nations Official Journal 1378, 1382. In the *Claim of the Standard Oil Company regarding certain Tankers* the tribunal stated that 'in application of a generally accepted principle, any person taking up residence or investing capital in a foreign country must assume the concomitant risks and must submit, under reservation of any measures of discrimination against him as a foreigner, to all the laws of that country', *The Deutsche Amerikanische Petroleum Gesellschaft oil tankers (USA, Reparation Commission)* (1926) 2 RIAA 777, 794; also *BP v Libya* (1974) 53 ILR 297 and *Aminoil v Kuwait* (1982) 21 ILM 976, 66 ILR 518, 585, para 87; J L Brierly, 'Règles générales du droit de la paix' (1936) 58 RCADI 1, 171; see also the UK's Memorial in *Anglo-Iranian Oil Co* where the following formulation is suggested:

> it is contrary to international law for a State to subject a concession, granted to a foreign company, to a measure of nationalization or expropriation, if such measure operates exclusively, or in a discriminatory manner, against the foreign company, and it is not shown by the expropriating Government that the measure was justified in order to protect the vital interests of the State-the desire of the State to realize greater profits from the concession not being, as a matter of international law, a sufficient ground to justify the expropriation.

Anglo-Iranian Oil Co, Section C—Memorial by the Government of the UK, 64, 100; A Newcombe and L Paradell, *Law and Practice of Investment Treaties: Standards of Treatment* (Kluwer Law International 2009) 373–374; Muchlinski (n 192) 676; S Friedman, *Expropriation in International Law* (Stevens & Sons Ltd 1953) 189–190; I Brownlie, *The System of the Law of Nations: State Responsibility* (OUP 1983) 81. However, non-discrimination is not explicitly mentioned in the 1962 UNGA Resolution on Permanent Sovereignty over Natural Resources, UNGA Res 1803 (XVII) (14 December 1962) 17 UN GAOR Supp (No 17) at 15/UN Doc A/5217 (1962). Oppenheim affirmed already in 1905 that 'every State is by the Law of Nations compelled to grant to foreigners equality before the law with its citizens as far as safety of person and property is concerned', L Oppenheim, *International Law: A Treatise* (Volume I, Peace, Longmans, Greens & Co 1905) 376. Hertz argues in the context of expropriation '[i]t does not matter whether the discrimination is open or veiled, if only there is evidence that in its effects the measure affects practically aliens alone', JH Hertz, 'Expropriation of Foreign Property' (1941) 35 AJIL 243, 249; see also AP Fachiri, 'Expropriation and International Law' (1925) 6 BYIL 159, 160–161, 171.

[213] *Banco Nacional de Cuba v Sabbatino*, 376 US 398, 428 (1964).

[214] On non-discrimination in the context of the Northern Rock nationalization see eg N Jansen Calamita, 'The British Bank Nationalizations: An International Law Perspective' (2009) 58 ICLQ 119, 123.

[215] *Sociedad Minera el Teniente SA v The Aktiengesellschaft Norddeutsche Attinerie (Chilean Copper case)*, Superior Court of Hamburg Docket No 80 0 4/73, Decision of 22 January 1973, (1973) 12 ILM 251, 276–278. See also RB Lillich, 'International Law and the Chilean Nationalizations: The Valuation of the Copper Companies' (1973) 7 International Lawyer 124; FO Vicuña, 'Some International Law Problems Posed by the Nationalization of the Copper Industry by Chile' (1973) 67 AJIL 711; GM Ingram, *Expropriation of U.S. Property in South America: Nationalization of Oil and Copper Companies in Peru, Bolivia and Chile* (Praeger 1974); TH Moran, *Multinational Corporations and the Politics of Dependence: Copper in Chile* (Princeton University Press 1974); EN Baklanoff, *Expropriation of U.S. Investments in Cuba, Mexico, and Chile* (Praeger 1975); I Seidl-Hohenveldern, 'Notes and Comments: Chilean Copper Nationalization Cases Before German Courts' (1975) 69 AJIL 110. The protests by the US against Romania in 1948 (which excluded from expropriatory measures Russian enterprises) and Cuba in 1960 (which targeted only companies of US interests) are another case in point: '[w]hile the United States' Government recognized the right of a sovereign power to expropriate property ... belonging to American nationals, the United States has likewise refused to recognize the validity of such expropriations in case where they are discriminatory by nature and effect', quoted in G White, *Nationalisation of Foreign Property* (Stevens and Sons Ltd 1961) 120.

> Direct expropriation means a mandatory legal transfer of the title to the property or its outright physical seizure ... Indirect expropriation involves total or near-total deprivation of an investment but without a formal transfer of title or outright seizure. The notion was recognized in international law long before the appearance of investment treaties.[216]

The categories of direct and indirect expropriation are mutually exclusive.[217] As the tribunal in *Telenor v Hungary* aptly observed '[n]owadays direct expropriation is the exception rather than the rule, as States prefer to avoid opprobrium and the loss of confidence of prospective investors by more oblique means'.[218] Although '[t]he basic rule seems to be that any measure of direct or indirect expropriation must be 'non-discriminatory', 'the precise scope of the non-discrimination obligation is unclear'.[219]

Conditions for lawful expropriation are substantially the same under customary international law and investment treaties.[220] According to the relevant UNCTAD study:

> [i]n order to be lawful, the exercise of this sovereign right requires, under international law, that the following conditions be met:
> (a) Property has to be taken for a public purpose;
> (b) On a non-discriminatory basis;
> (c) In accordance with due process of law;
> (d) Accompanied by compensation.[221]

The non-discrimination requirement in expropriation can be found in nearly every BIT.[222] The formulation of the clause slightly varies. BITs stipulate that the expropriation should be carried out 'in a non-discriminatory manner',[223] 'without discrimination',[224]

216 UNCTAD (n 135) 6–7. See also L Y Fortier and SL Drymer, 'Indirect Expropriation in the Law of International Investment: I Know It When I See It, or *Caveat Investor*' (2004) 19 ICSID Review 293; J Kammerhofer, *International Investment Law and Legal Theory: Expropriation and the Fragmentation of Sources* (CUP 2021).

217 *Enron Creditors Recovery Corporation (formerly Enron Corporation) and Ponderosa Assets, LP v Argentine Republic*, ICSID Case No ARB/01/3, Award, 22 May 2007, para 250.

218 *Telenor Mobile Communications AS v Republic of Hungary*, ICSID Case No ARB/04/15, Award, 13 September 2006, para 69.

219 Reinisch and Schreuer (n 172) 204.

220 MW Reisman and RD Sloane, 'Indirect Expropriation and its Valuation in the BIT Generation' (2004) 74 BYIL 115, 134. For a more sceptical approach on the customary nature of the obligation to provide compensation in case of expropriation see MC Porterfield, 'State Practice and the (Purported) Obligation under Customary International Law to Provide Compensation for Regulatory Expropriations' (2011) 37 North Carolina Journal of International Law 159.

221 UNCTAD (n 135) 1.

222 JW Salacuse, *The Law of Investment Treaties* (OUP 2010) 321; 'Most agreements include the same four requirements for a lawful expropriation, namely public purpose, non-discrimination, due process and payment of compensation', UNCTAD, *Bilateral Investment Treaties 1995–2006: Trends in Investment Rulemaking* (UN 2007)52; Article 6(b) 2012 US Model BIT.

223 Article 6(b) 2012 US Model BIT.

224 Article 4, Agreement between the People's Republic of China and the Portuguese Republic on the Encouragement and Reciprocal Protection of Investments (signed 9 December2005, entered into force 26 July 2008) (China–Portugal BIT).

'on-non-discriminatory basis',[225] or use other equivalent expressions.[226] These variations, however, are without legal significance.[227]

Non-discrimination is a necessary but not sufficient condition of lawful expropriation. In other words, the absence of non-discrimination does not render an unlawful expropriatory act lawful.[228] As the tribunal in *Pope and Talbot v Canada* held that Article 1110 of the NAFTA 'does cover non-discriminatory regulation that might be said to fall within an exercise of a state's so-called police powers'.[229] In the case of direct expropriation, the absence of discrimination per se does not preclude State's liability and its obligation to give compensation, although non-discrimination is crucial for the determination of *indirect* or *regulatory* expropriation.[230] Discrimination is indeed one of the indications supporting investors' arguments that their property has been expropriated.[231] In *WNC v Czech Republic*, the tribunal characterized the *Saluka* formula 'uncontroversial':

> [i]t is uncontroversial that 'States are not liable to pay compensation to a foreign investor when, in the normal exercise of their regulatory powers, they adopt in a

225 Article 1110 NAFTA; Article 14.8 and Annex 14-B USMCA; Article VI(1) ASEAN Investment Treaty.

226 See also Article 13(1)(b) ECT; A Reinisch, 'Is Expropriation Ripe for Codification? The Example of the Non-discrimination Requirement for Lawful Expropriations' in AK Bjorklund and A Reinisch (eds), *International Investment Law and Soft Law* (Edward Elgar 2012)271–304, 295; Salacuse (n 222) 321.

227 UNCTAD (n 135) 34.

228 *Certain German Interests in Polish Upper Silesia (Germany v Poland) (Merits)* PCIJ Series A, No 7, 4, 32–33; *Peter Pázmány University v the State of Czechoslovakia, Appeal from a Judgment of the Hungaro-Czechoslovak Mixed Arbitral Tribunal (Czechoslovakia v Hungary)*, PCIJ Series A/B, No 61, 208, 243.

229 *Pope & Talbot Inc v The Government of Canada*, UNCITRAL, Interim Award, 26 June 2000, para 96.

230 *Saluka Investments BV v The Czech Republic*, UNCITRAL, Partial Award, 17 March 2006, para 255. See also *Methanex Corporation v the United States of America*, UNCITRAL, Final Award of the Tribunal on Jurisdiction and Merits, 3 August 2005, Part IV, Chapter D, para 7; *Waste Management, Inc v United Mexican States*, ICSID Case No ARB(AF)/00/3, Award, 30 April 2004, para 144; and *Revere Copper and Brass, Inc v Overseas Private Investment Corp*, 56 ILR 258, 271, 17 ILM 1321, 1331; *Archer Daniels Midland Company and Tate & Lyle Ingredients Americas, Inc v United Mexican States*, ICSID Case No ARB(AF)/04/5, Award, 21 November 2007, para 250; *RosInvestCo UK Ltd v The Russian Federation*, SCC Case No V079/2005, Final Award, 12 September 2010, paras 449–454, 556, and 621–633; *Civilian Claims—Eritrea's Claims* 15, 16, 23 and 27–32, Partial Award (2004) 26 RIAA 195. See also *Marvin Roy Feldman Karpa v United Mexican States*, ICSID Case No ARB(AF)/99/1, Award, 16 December 2002, para 105 and *EnCana Corporation v Republic of Ecuador*, LCIA Case No UN3481, UNCITRAL, Award, 3 February 2006, para 173 citing the influential Restatement (Third) of Foreign Relations Law of the United States (1987), Section 712, comment g ('A state is not responsible for loss of property or for other economic disadvantage resulting from bona fide general taxation, regulation, forfeiture for crime, or other action of the kind that is commonly accepted as within the police power of states, if it is not discriminatory'). See also *Link-Trading Joint Stock Company v Department for Customs Control of the Republic of Moldova*, UNCITRAL, Final Award, 18 April 2002, paras 69–73. See generally J Paulsson, 'Indirect Expropriation in Investment Treaty Arbitrations' in J Paulsson and Z Douglas (eds), *Arbitrating Foreign Investment Disputes* (Kluwer Law International 2004) 145–158; LY Fortier and SL Drymer, 'Indirect Expropriation in the Law of International Investment: I know It When I See it, or *Caveat Investor*' (2004) 19 ICSID Review 293; R Higgins, 'The Taking of Property by the State: Recent Developments in International Law' (1982) 176 RCADI 259, 322–354; see also V Heiskanen, 'The Doctrine of Indirect Expropriation in Light of the Practice of the Iran-United States Claims Tribunal' (2007) 8 JWIT 215; AK Hoffmann, 'Indirect Expropriation' in A Reinisch (ed), *Standards of Investment Protection* (OUP 2008) 151–170; AM Daza-Clark, *International Investment Law and Water Resources Management: An Appraisal of Indirect Expropriation* (Brill Nijhoff 2017) 88–114.

231 *Fireman's Fund Insurance Co v United Mexican States*, ICSID Case No ARB(AF)/02/1, Award, 17 July 2006, paras 204-207. See also *Azurix Corp v The Argentine Republic*, ICSID Case No ARB/01/12, Award, 14 July 2006, para 312; Reinisch and Schreuer (n 172) 166; *Kuwait v Aminoil*, Award, 24 March 1982 (1982) 21 ILM 976 and *LIAMCO v Libya*, Arbitral Award, 12 April 1977 (1982) 62 ILR 140; see also D Khachvani, 'Compensation for Unlawful Expropriation: Targeting the Illegality' (2017) 32 ICSID Review 385, 402.

> non-discriminatory manner *bona fide* regulations that are aimed at the general welfare'.[232]

This is reflected in States' submissions to tribunals[233] as well as recent treaty drafting. For example, in the United States–Mexico–Canada Agreement (USMCA), which replaced NAFTA, the parties made clear that:

> [n]on-discriminatory regulatory actions by a Party that are designed and applied to protect legitimate public welfare objectives, such as health, safety and the environment, do not constitute indirect expropriations, except in rare circumstances.[234]

Likewise, CETA provides that:

> [f]or greater certainty, except in the rare circumstance when the impact of a measure or series of measures is so severe in light of its purpose that it appears manifestly excessive, non-discriminatory measures of a Party that are designed and applied to protect legitimate public welfare objectives, such as health, safety and the environment, do not constitute indirect expropriations.[235]

The US–Iran Claims Tribunal also held that 'State cannot guarantee the safety of an alien or of alien property. Responsibility is incurred only when police protection falls below a minimum standard of reasonableness', which is intrinsically linked to non-discrimination as '[o]rdinarily, the standard of police protection for foreign nationals is unreasonable if it is less than is provided generally for the State's nationals'.[236]

Findings regarding other obligations of non-discrimination might be relevant for determining whether discrimination occurred in the context of expropriation as well:

232 *WNC Factoring Limited v The Czech Republic*, PCA Case No 2014-34, Award, 27 February 2017, para 395 quoting *Saluka Investments BV v The Czech Republic*, UNCITRAL, Partial Award, 17 March 2006, para 255. See also *Marfin Investment Group Holdings SA and others v Republic of Cyprus*, ICSID Case No ARB/13/27, Award, 26 July 2018, para 826 ('the economic harm consequent to the non-discriminatory application of generally applicable regulations adopted in order to protect the public welfare do not constitute a compensable taking, provided that the measure was taken in good faith, complied with due process and was proportionate to the aim sought to be achieved').

233 See eg *Bear Creek Mining Corporation v Republic of Peru*, ICSID Case No ARB/14/21, Submission of Canada pursuant to Article 832 of the Canada-Peru Free Trade Agreement, 9 June 2016, para 6 ('[a] non-discriminatory measure that is designed to protect legitimate public welfare objectives does not constitute indirect expropriation except in rare circumstances where its impacts are so severe in the light of its purpose that it cannot be reasonably viewed as having been adopted and applied in good faith').

234 USMCA, Annex 14-B, para 3(b).

235 CETA, Annex 8-A, para 3.

236 *Emanuel Too v United States of America*, Award No 460–880-2 (29 December 1989) 23 IRAN–US CTR 378, 385–386.

> [w]ith regard to discrimination, the Tribunal similarly refers to its earlier findings on discrimination under FET which it considers relevant, *mutatis mutandis*, for its examination of the fulfilment of this particular requirement under expropriation.[237]

However, this does not mean that breaches of other treaty standards automatically lead to a determination that expropriation has occurred.[238]

[237] *Crystallex International Corporation v Bolivarian Republic of Venezuela*, ICSID Case No ARB(AF)/11/2, Award, 4 April 2016, para 715.

[238] *Vigotop Limited v Republic of Hungary*, ICSID Case No ARB/11/22, Award, 1 October 2014, para 310. According to the tribunal in *Corn Products International Inc v United Mexican States*, ICSID Case No ARB(AF)/04/1, Decision on Responsibility, 15 January 2008, para 90: 'it is necessary to bear in mind that there is a distinction between discriminatory treatment of the property of an investor (and, for that matter, unfair and inequitable treatment) and expropriation. It is not the case that, because a measure which affects property rights is discriminatory, it is therefore an expropriation (or something tantamount to an expropriation). Rather, if a measure is established to be an expropriation (or something tantamount thereto), it cannot then be justified if it is discriminatory'.

3

The Legal Test for Establishing Violations of Non-discrimination Obligations

Chapter 3 examines the case law of investment treaty tribunals in relation to different non-discrimination obligations and presents the normative arguments of this book. In the first and more descriptive part, the analysis is structured around three main questions. Section 3.1 and Section 3.2 focus on how investment treaty tribunals determine likeness and less favourable treatment respectively. Section 3.3 explores the link between less favourable treatment and a protected ground (such as the foreign investors' nationality) or what some tribunals view as discriminatory intent or legitimate public policy reasons. All three sections provide a descriptive analysis of the relevant case law and put forward normative arguments. Contrary to what is commonly the case in the relevant jurisprudence and scholarship, each non-discrimination obligation is examined separately, aiming towards greater analytical clarity. The National Treatment obligation is examined in Sections 3.1.1.1, 3.2.1.1, and 3.3.1.1. The Most Favoured Nation (MFN) obligation is discussed in Sections 3.1.1.2, 3.2.1.2, and 3.3.1.2. Non-impairment clauses are dealt with in Sections 3.1.1.3, 3.2.1.3, and 3.3.1.3 and non-discrimination under Fair and Equitable Treatment (FET) in Section 3.1.1.4, 3.2.1.4, and 3.3.1.4. Sections 3.1.1.5, 3.2.1.5, and 3.3.1.5 contain the analysis in relation to discrimination in the context of expropriation. Finally, having highlighted the inconsistencies of the case law, this book provides normative arguments in relation to each of the three key elements of the legal test for determining whether States discriminated against foreign investors (in Sections 3.1.2, 3.2.2, and 3.3.2).

3.1 Likeness

3.1.1 Case Law on Likeness

3.1.1.1 National Treatment

If the investor's claim does not fall within any applicable exception provided in the National Treatment clause contained in the relevant investment treaty,[1] the first component of the test for establishing violations of National Treatment (or other

[1] For one such example, see Article IV of the Agreement between the Government of Canada and the Government of the Arab Republic of Egypt for the Promotion and Protection of Investments (signed 13 November 1996, entered into force 3 November 1997) (Canada–Egypt BIT) providing that:

non-discrimination obligations) in international investment law is 'likeness', ie the determination of whether the foreign investor is in a similar situation or 'like circumstances' with domestic investors.[2] This is uncontroversial. Certain National Treatment clauses specify that the obligation is owed to foreign investors 'in like circumstances',[3] while such qualification is absent from other similar treaty provisions. In *Occidental v Ecuador*, the investor argued that the absence of the wording 'in like circumstances' in National Treatment clauses results in a less restrictive test, and, thus, being more favourable to the investor, can be imported through the MFN clause.[4] The tribunal did not address the issue. However, even in cases where likeness does not appear in the wording of the National Treatment clause, it is inherently part of the test.[5] According

1. Each Contracting Party shall grant to investments or returns of investors of the. other Contracting Party treatment no less favourable than that which, in like circumstances, it grants to investments or returns of its own investors with respect to the expansion, management, conduct, operation and sale or disposition of investments.
2. Subparagraph (3)(a) of Article II, paragraph (1) of this Article, and paragraphs (1) and (2) of Article V do not apply to:

...

d. the right of each Contracting Party to make or maintain exceptions within the sectors or matters listed in the Annex to this Agreement.

According to the Annex of the Canada–Egypt BIT:

> In accordance with Article IV, subparagraph 2(d), Canada reserves the right to make and maintain exceptions in the sectors or matters listed below:
>
> social services (i.e. public law enforcement; correctional services; income security or insurance; social security or insurance; social welfare; public education; public training; health and child care);
> services in any other sector;
> government securities - as described in SIC 8152;
> residency requirements for ownership of oceanfront land;
> measures implementing the Northwest Territories and the Yukon Oil and Gas Accords.

See also the tribunal's analysis in *Global Telecom Holding SAE v Canada*, ICSID Case No ARB/16/16, Award, 27 March 2020, paras 363–380; see also *Joseph Charles Lemire v Ukraine*, ICSID Case No ARB/06/18, Award, 28 March 2011, paras 46 and 47; *Ronald S Lauder v The Czech Republic*, UNCITRAL, Final Award, 3 September 2001, paras 218–220.

[2] R Dolzer, C Schreuer, and U Kriebaum, *Principles of International Investment Law* (3rd edn, OUP 2022) 254.

[3] The classic example is the North American Free Trade Agreement (NAFTA) (adopted 17 December 1992, entered into force 1 January 1994 (1993) 32 ILM 289), Article 1102, replaced by United States–Mexico–Canada Agreement (signed 30 November 2018, entered into forcel July 2020) (USMCA), Article 14.4(1). See also Dominican Republic–Central America Free Trade Agreement (CAFTA–DR) (adopted 5 August 2004, entered into force 1 March 2006), Article 10.3 (the parties to CAFTA–DR are Costa Rica, Dominican Republic, El Salvador, Guatemala, Honduras, Nicaragua, and the United States of America); Comprehensive Trade and Economic Agreement between Canada and the European Union (signed 30 October 2016, not yet to force) (CETA), Article 8.6(1) ('Each Party shall accord to an investor of the other Party and to a covered investment, treatment no less favourable than the treatment it accords, in like situations to its own investors and to their investments with respect to the establishment, acquisition, expansion, conduct, operation, management, maintenance, use, enjoyment and sale or disposal of their investments in its territory'); Free Trade Agreement between the United Kingdom of Great Britain and Northern Ireland and New Zealand (28 February 2022, entered into force 31 May 2023) (UK–New Zealand FTA), Article 14.6; Free Trade Agreement between the United Kingdom of Great Britain and Northern Ireland and Australia (17 December 2021, entered into force 31 May 2023) (UK–Australia FTA), Article 13.5;

[4] *Occidental Exploration and Production Company v* Ecuador, LCIA Case No UN 3467, Final Award, 1 July 2004, para 170; A Newcombe and L Paradell, *Law and Practice of Investment Treaties, Standards of Treatment* (Kluwer Law International 2009) 160.

[5] *Total SA v Argentine Republic*, ICSID Case No ARB/04/01, Decision on Liability, 27 December 2010, para 213 ('the Tribunal concludes that the absence of the term "like" in Article 4 of the BIT is not decisive since this element is inherent in an evaluation of discrimination'). See also *Consortium RFCC v Morocco*, ICSID Case No ARB/00/6, Award, 22 December 2003, para 53. National Treatment clauses in Chinese BITs do not contain references to 'like circumstances' unlike National Treatment clauses in investment chapters in Chinese FTAs. However, this difference does not translate into an actual conflict, see W Shan, N Gallagher, and S Zhang, 'National Treatment

to Diebold, 'a comparative element is inherent to the logic and structure of the non-discrimination principle in international economic law'.[6] Likewise, Weiler argued that 'the grantor will need to decide whether its [Treatment No Less Favourable] obligation should include an explicit reference to the "similar circumstances" caveat, or just leave it as implied. While this choice might change the aesthetic of a [Treatment No Less Favourable]-inspired clause, the functionality would likely unaffected.'[7]

The case law of investment treaty tribunals is, at best, unclear in relation to three key questions regarding 'likeness' in the context of discrimination, leading to 'unpredictable' outcomes.[8]

First, conflicting interpretations have been adopted on whether it is necessary to identify a specific comparator. In *Loewen v USA*, where the issue was the investor's treatment by a Mississippi Court, the tribunal dismissed the claim as 'their circumstances as litigants were very different' and there were no materials 'which enable such a comparison to be made'.[9]

Second, there is no settled approach in the relevant case law on how to determine likeness and different criteria have been used.[10] Several tribunals focus on the existence of a competitive relationship between domestic and foreign investors. In *Corn Products v Mexico*, 'the Tribunal [could not] escape the conclusion that the producers of like products which were directly competitive were in like circumstances as regards a measure designed expressly for the purpose of affecting that competition'.[11] In *Methanex v USA*, a case concerning a ban imposed by the State of California on the

for Foreign Investment in China: A Changing Landscape' (2012) 27 ICSID Review 120, 141; cf Chinese FTAs, eg the Free Trade Agreement between the Government of New Zealand and the Government of the People's Republic of China (signed 7 April 2008, entered into force 1 October 2008), Chapter 11, Articles 138 and 141. Article 138(1): 'Each Party shall accord to investments and activities associated with such investments, with respect to management, conduct, operation, maintenance, use, enjoyment or disposal, by the investors of the other Party treatment no less favourable than that accorded, in like circumstances, to the investments and associated activities by its own investors'. Article 141(3): 'Notwithstanding anything in paragraph 1, Article 138 shall not apply to any measure, which with respect to each Party, would not be within the scope of the national treatment obligations in any of that Party's existing bilateral investment treaties'.

[6] NF Diebold, 'Standards on Non-discrimination in International Economic Law' (2011) 60 ICLQ 831, 841.

[7] T Weiler, *The Interpretation of International Investment Law: Equality, Discrimination and Minimum Standards of Treatment in Historical Context* (Martinus Nijhoff 2013) 334.

[8] A Reinisch, 'National Treatment' in M Bungenberg, J Griebel, S Hobe and A Reinisch (eds), *International Investment Law* (C H Beck, Hart, Nomos 2013) 846–869, 859; *contra Consortium RFCC v Morocco*, ICSID Case No ARB/00/6, Award, 22 December 2003, para 53 ('Le contenu de cette disposition qui se rencontre systématiquement dans les traités de protection des investissements ne pose pas de problème d'interprétation particulier.').

[9] *The Loewen Group Inc and Loewen v United States*, Award, ICSID Case No ARB(AF)/98/3, 25 June 2003, para 140; see also J Paulsson, *Denial of Justice in International Law* (CUP 2005) 192 et seq. Cf *AES Summit Generation Limited and AES-Tisza Erömü Kft v Republic of Hungary*, ICSID Case No ARB/07/22, Award, 23 September 2010, para 10.3.53: 'Discrimination necessarily implies that the state benefited or harmed someone more in comparison with the generality. In this case, on the uncontradicted facts, the Tribunal finds that there has been no different treatment of AES Tisza in comparison with the other generators and, thus, that it was not the subject of discriminatory treatment'. See also *Antoine Goetz et consorts v République du Burundi*, ICSID Case No ARB/95/3, 10 February 1999, para 121 (on alleged discrimination in violation of Article 2 of the International Covenant on Economic, Social and Cultural Rights (adopted 16 December 1966, entered into force 3 January 1976) 993 UNTS 3).

[10] See generally Diebold (n 6); AD Mitchell, D Heaton, and C Henckels, *Non-Discrimination and the Role of Regulatory Purpose in International Trade and Investment Law* (Edward Elgar 2016) 64–96.

[11] *Corn Products International Inc v United Mexican States*, ICSID Case No ARB(AF)/04/1, Decision on Responsibility, 15 January 2008, paras 136; see also ibid, paras 120, 137–143.

methanol-based fuel-additive (Methyl Tert-Butyl Ether (MTBE)), the Claimant failed to convince the tribunal that domestic ethanol producers and foreign methanol producers were in competition and, consequently, in like circumstances.[12] Tribunals sometimes do not clearly distinguish between investors being in competition and belonging to the same sector. In *RDC v Guatemala*, the first arbitral award under the CAFTA–DR, the claimant argued that it was in like circumstances with domestic investors as 'both are competitors in the same economic sector since they have been competing to invest and operate the railroad and in leasing and developing the railroad's assets'.[13] The tribunal disagreed on the basis that 'the obvious difference in scale between the railroad for the exclusive exploitation of the sugar plantation of [the domestic investor] in the Dominican Republic and the railway operation of Claimant in Guatemala defeats the "like circumstances" argument'.[14] In *SD Myers v Canada*, one of the first North America Free Trade Agreement (NAFTA) cases (and the first investment treaty case to discuss the National Treatment obligation in detail[15]), the tribunal held that '[t]he concept of "like circumstances" invites an examination of whether a non-national investor complaining of less favourable treatment is in the same "sector" as the national investor' and clarified 'that the word "sector" has a wide connotation that includes the concepts of "economic sector" and "business sector"'.[16] Other tribunals confirmed this interpretation.[17] However, in *Champion Trading v Egypt* operating in the same sector was not per se sufficient to find that the companies were like.[18] In *Occidental v Ecuador*, the tribunal held that:

> 'in like situations' cannot be interpreted in the narrow sense advanced by Ecuador as the purpose of national treatment is to protect investors as compared to local

[12] *Methanex Corporation v the United States of America*, UNCITRAL, Final Award of the Tribunal on Jurisdiction and Merits, 3 August 2005, Part IV, Chapter B, paras 23–37. The tribunal also found that the WTO jurisprudence on likeness was not relevant.

[13] *Railroad Development Corporation v Republic of Guatemala*, Award, ICSID Case No ARB/07/23, 29 June 2012, para 153.

[14] ibid.

[15] J Kurtz, *The WTO and International Investment Law: Converging Systems* (CUP 2015) 95.

[16] *SD Myers, Inc v Government of Canada*, UNCITRAL, Partial Award, 13 November 2000, para 250; see also ibid, paras 250–254. According to a 1993 Organisation for Economic Co-operation and Development (OECD) analysis '[a]s regards the expression "in like situations", the comparison between foreign-controlled enterprises established in a Member country and domestic enterprises in that Member country is valid only if it is made between firms operating in the same sector', OECD, *National Treatment for Foreign-Controlled Enterprises* (OECD Publications 1993) 22. For that tribunal, as Kurtz explains, the existence of a competitive relationship that makes necessary the consideration of regulatory purpose for determining 'likeness', Kurtz (n 15) 123. See also Section 2.2 in Chapter 2.

[17] *Pope & Talbot Inc v Government of Canada*, UNCITRAL, Award on the Merits of Phase 2, 10 April 2001, para 78: 'as a first step, the treatment accorded a foreign owned investment protected by Article 1102(2) should be compared with that accorded domestic investments in the same business or economic sector'; *Archer Daniels Midland Company and Tate & Lyle Ingredients Americas, Inc v United Mexican States*, ICSID Case No ARB(AF)/04/5, Award, 21 November 2007, para 198: 'the domestic entities "in like circumstances" whose treatment should be compared are those firms operating in the same sector, which should be interpreted broadly to include the concepts of "economic sector" and "business sector"'.

[18] *Champion Trading Company and Ameritrade International, Inc v Arab Republic of Egypt*, Award ICSID Case No ARB/02/9, 27 October 2006, para 154 ('Although both kinds of companies operate in the same industry and are subject to same kind of rules, there is a significant difference between a company which opts to buy cotton from the Collection Centres at fixed prices and a company which opts to trade on the free market, whether or not the company is privately-owned or State-owned or whether the company is national or foreign').

> producers, and this cannot be done by addressing exclusively the sector in which that particular activity is undertaken.[19]

In *Merrill v Canada* it was held that 'it is not enough on occasions to undertake the comparison solely in the same sector of economic activity and it might be necessary, as in *Occidental, to consider whole sectors of the economy and business*'.[20] In *Levy v Peru*, the tribunal first observed that 'the banking sector is a sensitive area for any country' and that 'there are marked differences between the various banks operating in it'.[21] In rejecting the Claimant's submission, the tribunal held that belonging to the same financial sector and developing their activities in mutual competition[22] is not sufficient to determine likeness given that the benchmarks used were 'very general'.[23] The tribunal also noted a certain inconsistency in the Claimant's statement classifying the bank in question sometimes as a 'small bank' and sometimes as a systemic bank.[24] The dissenting arbitrator took issue with the majority's analysis, and, by relying on other investment cases,[25] emphasized that 'a higher or lower market share is irrelevant to set the relevant benchmark for comparison'.[26]

Other tribunals held that the 'same sector' or 'competitive relationship' criteria were not appropriate. Instead, they focused on whether the domestic and foreign investors fall under the same regulatory framework. According to one tribunal, 'the proper comparison is between investors which are subject to the same regulatory measures under the same jurisdictional authority'.[27] This criterion was also adopted in *Occidental v Ecuador* (and applied in a remarkably broad manner).[28] The tribunal compared Occidental not only to other oil exporters but also to exporters of other goods with regard to Value Added Tax (VAT) refunds. The tribunal noted that 'in like situations' cannot be interpreted in the narrow sense advanced by Ecuador as the purpose of National Treatment is to protect investors as compared to local producers, and this cannot be done by addressing exclusively the sector in which that particular activity is undertaken.[29]

[19] *Occidental Exploration and Production Company v Ecuador*, LCIA Case No UN 3467, Final Award, 1 July 2004, para 173.

[20] *Merrill & Ring Forestry LP v Government of Canada*, UNCITRAL, ICSID Administrated, Award, 31 March 2010, para 88 (emphasis added).

[21] *Renée Rose Levy De Levi v The Republic of Peru*, ICSID Case No ARB/10/17, Award, 26 February 2014, para 396.

[22] ibid, para 399.

[23] ibid, para 400.

[24] ibid.

[25] *Renée Rose Levy de Levi v Republic of Peru*, ICSID Case No ARB/10/17, Dissenting Opinion of Joaquín Morales Godoy, 26 February 2014, para 185; *International Thunderbird Gaming Corporation v United Mexican States*, UNCITRAL, Award, 26 January 2006, paras 175–183; *Corn Products International Inc v United Mexican States*, ICSID Case No ARB(AF)/04/1, Decision on Responsibility, 15 January 2008; *Tza Yap Shum v Republic of Peru*, ICSID Case ARB/07/6, Award, 7 June 2011, para 267.

[26] *Renée Rose Levy De Levi v The Republic of Peru*, ICSID Case No ARB/10/17, Dissenting Opinion of J Morales Godoy, 26 February 2014, para 185.

[27] *Merrill & Ring Forestry LP v Government of Canada*, UNCITRAL, ICSID Administrated, Award, 31 March 2010, para 89.

[28] See criticism in SD Franck, 'Occidental Exploration &Production Co. v. Republic of Ecuador. Final Award. London Court of International Arbitration Administered Case No. UN 3467' (2005) 99 AJIL 675, 679–680.

[29] *Occidental Exploration and Production Company v Ecuador*, LCIA Case No UN 3467, Final Award, 1 July 2004, para 173.

In *Grand River v USA* the tribunal held that the case law 'shows the identity of the legal regime(s) applicable to a claimant and its purported comparators to be a compelling factor in assessing whether like is indeed being compared to like for purposes of Articles 1102 and 1103'.[30] The same approach was followed in *Apotex v USA*.[31] This, together with policy considerations (regulatory likeness), was endorsed in the Comprehensive and Progressive Agreement for Trans-Pacific Partnership (CPTPP) Drafters' note.[32]

Finally, some tribunals take into account public policy considerations which motivate the measure(s) under examination in determining 'likeness'.[33] In *Pope and Talbot v Canada*, the tribunal rejected Canada's submission that differences in treatment should be on the basis of the foreign nationality of the investor in order to be 'less favourable', in favour of an alternative yet similar method of looking into discriminatory intent in the context of likeness.[34] The tribunal somewhat cryptically added that:

> [i]n one respect, this approach echoes the suggestion by Canada that Article 1102 prohibits treatment that discriminates on the basis of the foreign investment's nationality. The other NAFTA Parties have taken the same position. However, the Tribunal believes that the approach proposed by the NAFTA Parties would tend to excuse discrimination that is not facially directed at foreign owned investment.[35]

The unclear approach of the tribunal in *Pope and Talbot v Canada* in this regard led Weiler to argue that '[j]ust as a plain reading of the entirety of the *Pope & Talbot* Tribunal's award reveals the clarity of its opinion on the issue, so too does it quickly

[30] *Grand River Enterprises Six Nations, Ltd, et al v United States of America*, Award, UNCITRAL, 12 January 2011, para 167; *Merrill & Ring Forestry LP v Government of Canada*, UNCITRAL, ICSID Administrated, Award, 31 March 2010, para 94; see also *Windstream Energy LLC v Government of Canada*, PCA Case No 2013-22, Award, 27 September 2016, para 414 ('[u]nlike TransCanada and Samsung, the Claimant had a FIT Contract for offshore wind development, and indeed it was the only holder of such a contract').

[31] *Apotex Holdings Inc and Apotex Inc v United States of America*, ICSID Case No ARB(AF)/12/1, Award, 25 August 2014, para 8.43 ('It is common ground that all of the three domestic comparators proposed by the Claimants were in the same sector as the Claimants, sold like drug products to those sold by Apotex Inc., and were direct competitors in the US market. In these circumstances, in the Tribunal's view, the question of whether the Claimants and their investments were subject to the same legal regime or regulatory requirements (to those to which the identified US-comparators were subject) becomes an important potential differentiator.') See also, ibid, paras 8.40–8.57. See also *Gavrilovic and Gavrilovic doo v Republic of Croatia*, ICSID Case No ARB/12/39, Award, 26 July 2018, para 1193.

[32] CTPPT Drafters' Note, para 5: 'NAFTA tribunals have also accepted distinctions in treatment between investors or investments that are plausibly connected to legitimate public welfare objectives, and have given important weight to whether investors or investments are subject to like legal requirements.' See eg *Grand River Enterprises Six Nations Ltd, et al v United States of America*, UNCITRAL, Award, 12 January 2011, at paras 166–167; *GAMI Investments Inc v United Mexican States*, UNCITRAL, Award, 15 November 2004, paras 111–115; *Pope & Talbot Inc v Canada*, UNCITRAL, Award on the Merits of Phase 2, 10 April 2001, paras 78–79.

[33] This approach is similar to the approach of the CJEU in *Arcelor*, Case C-127/07, *Société Arcelor Atlantique et Lorraine and Others v Premier ministre, Ministre de l'Écologie et du Développement durable, Ministre de l'Économie, des Finances et de l'Industrie*, 16 December 2008, paras 34–38.

[34] *Pope & Talbot Inc v Government of Canada*, UNCITRAL, Award on the Merits of Phase 2, 10 April 2001, para 79 ('[a] formulation focusing on the like circumstances question, on the other hand, will require addressing any difference in treatment, demanding that it be justified by showing that it bears a reasonable relationship to rational policies not motivated by preference of domestic over foreign owned investments').

[35] *Pope & Talbot Inc v the Government of Canada*, UNCITRAL, Award on the Merits Phase 2, 10 April 2001, para 79. See eg *Parkerings-Compagniet AS v Republic of Lithuania*, ICSID Case No ARB/05/8, Award, 11 September 2007, para 370.

become manifest, upon reading of the text of NAFTA Article 1102, that there is no basis for supposing that less favourable treatment could be accorded under it, so long as nobody could prove that it was rendered discriminatorily, on the basis of nationality'.[36]

In *SD Myers v Canada*, another early Article 1102 NAFTA case in addition to the same sector analysis (discussed above), the tribunal held that '[t]he assessment of "like circumstances" must also take into account circumstances that would justify governmental regulations that treat them differently in order to protect the public interest'.[37] In *Corn Products v Mexico*, although the starting basis for determining likeness was the existence of a competitive relationship between the domestic and foreign investors,[38] the tribunal also took into account '[t]he purpose' of the tax measure in question which 'was avowedly to alter the terms of competition between them'[39]. In *Cargill v Poland* the tribunal concluded that there was 'no compelling economic or social reason justifying a determination that domestic sugar producers and the foreign isoglucose producer are not in like circumstances'.[40]

3.1.1.2 Most Favoured Nation Treatment

The analysis of many tribunals in relation to MFN mirrors the analysis of National Treatment *mutatis mutandis*.[41] This is expressly stated acknowledged by some tribunals. For example, in *Parkerings v Lithuania* the tribunal held that:

> Article IV of the Treaty is known as the standard of the '*Most-favoured-nation Treatment*'. *Most-favoured-nation clauses* (*MFN*) are by essence very similar to '*National Treatment*' clauses. They have similar conditions of application and basically afford indirect advantages to their beneficiaries, namely a treatment no less favourable than the one granted to third parties. Tribunals' analyses of the *National Treatment* standard will therefore also be useful to discuss the alleged violation of the *MFN* standard.[42]

In *Bayindir v* Pakistan the tribunal held that it:

> must thus review whether the Claimant has substantiated its allegation of breach of the MFN clause. For this purpose, it must start assessing the similarity of the situations

[36] Weiler (n 7) 438.

[37] *SD Myers, Inc v Government of Canada*, UNCITRAL, Partial Award, 13 November 2000, para 250.

[38] *Corn Products International Inc v United Mexican States*, ICSID Case No ARB(AF)/04/1, Decision on Responsibility, 15 January 2008, para 120.

[39] ibid. See also ibid, para 136 ('the present case concerns a measure the purpose of which was to affect the competition between the products produced by the foreign and domestic investors and to afford a considerable competitive advantage to the latter').

[40] *Cargill, Incorporated v Republic of Poland II*, UNCITRAL, Award, 5 March 2008, para 385; see also ibid, paras 332–333, and 339 ('the Tribunal reaches the conclusion that Cargill and domestic sugar producers are in like circumstances, subject to its reviewing whether a policy objective or public interest justifies a contrary conclusion').

[41] A Reinisch, and C Schreuer, *International Protection of Investments: The Substantive Standards* (CUP 2020) 726. See also C Crépet Daigremont, *La Clause de la Nation la Plus Favorisée* (Pedone 2015) 223–238.

[42] *Parkerings-Compagniet AS v Republic of Lithuania*, ICSID Case No ARB/05/8, 11 September 2007, Award, para 366; see also C McLachlan, L Shore, and M Weiniger, *International Investment Arbitration: Substantive Principles* (2nd edn, OUP 2017) 344.

> to be compared. As with national treatment, such similarity must be examined at the level of the contractual terms and circumstances.[43]

While it has been widely accepted that the qualification that the foreign investors to be compared must be 'in like circumstances' which appears in some, but not other, investment treaties does not play any role in the interpretation of National Treatment[44] and MFN clauses,[45] the position of the International Law Commission (ILC) in its 2015 report on MFN is more cautious:

> The practical importance of this issue is whether interpretations of agreements that contain the words 'in like circumstances' are relevant to the interpretation of agreements that do not contain such terminology. As noted below, there are dangers in adopting interpretations of one investment agreement as applicable automatically to other agreements, and this is even more so where the wording of the two agreements is different.[46]

3.1.1.3 Non-impairment Clauses

Likeness is also the starting point also in relation to non-impairment clauses.[47] However, the analysis of likeness (including the relevant criteria for its determination) is less extensive in claims based on non-impairment clauses compared to National Treatment.[48] In *Paushok v Mongolia* the tribunal emphasized that 'the sectors covered should relate to competitive and substitutable products',[49] also explicitly adopting a deferential approach by stating that '[i]t is not the role of the Tribunal to weigh the wisdom of legislation, but merely to assess whether such legislation breaches the Treaty'.[50] In *Nykomb v Latvia* the tribunal seems to consider the fact that the entities in question were subject to the same regulatory framework decisive for establishing likeness:

[43] *Bayindir Insaat Turizm Ticaret Ve Sanayi AS v Islamic Republic of Pakistan*, ICSID Case No ARB/03/29, Award, 27 August 2009, para 416.

[44] See Section 3.1.1.1.

[45] In *Parkerings v Lithuania* interpreting an MFN clause which did not include any reference to likeness, the tribunal held that '[t]he essential condition of the violation of a[n] MFN clause is the existence of a different treatment accorded to another foreign investor in a similar situation. Therefore, a comparison is necessary with an investor in like circumstances', *Parkerings-Compagniet AS v Republic of Lithuania*, ICSID Case No ARB/05/8, 11 September 2007, Award, para 369. See also *Consortium RFCC v Morocco*, ICSID Case No ARB/00/6, Award, 22 December 2003, para 53. For the issue in the context of National Treatment, see Section 3.1.1.1.

[46] ILC, Final Report of the Study Group on the Most-Favoured Nation Clause (2015) II(2) Yearbook of International Commission (ILC, '2015 MFN Report'), para 73.

[47] *Inversión y Gestión de Bienes, IGB, SL and IGB18 Las Rozas, SL v Kingdom of Spain*, ICSID Case No ARB/12/17, Award, 14 August 2015, para 193; see also CH Schreuer, 'Protection Against Arbitrary or Discriminatory Measures' in CA Rogers and RP Alford (eds), *The Future of Investment Arbitration* (OUP 2009) 193–194.

[48] See Section 3.1.1.1.

[49] *Sergei Paushok, CJSC Golden East Company and CJSC Vostokneftegaz Company v Government of Mongolia*, Award on Jurisdiction and Liability, UNCITRAL, 28 April 2011, para 315. For the purposes of interpreting a non-impairment clause, the tribunal considered the claimant's reliance on the interpretation of the National Treatment clause in *Occidental v Ecuador* 'inapposite', ibid, paras 312–313.

[50] ibid, para 316.

> in evaluating whether there is discrimination in the sense of the Treaty one should only 'compare like with like'. . . all of the information available to the Tribunal suggests that the three companies are comparable, and subject to the same laws and regulations.[51]

In *Saluka v Czech Republic* the tribunal held '[t]he standard of "reasonableness" has no different meaning in this context than in the context of the "fair and equitable treatment" standard with which it is associated; and the same is true with regard to the standard of "non-discrimination" '.[52] In other cases concerning measures adopted by Argentina in the context of the Argentine crisis of 2001–02, tribunals emphasized the importance of belonging to the same economic sector. In *CMS v Argentina* the tribunal accepted that Argentina's 'argument about discrimination existing only in similarly situated groups or categories of people is correct', but also admitted that it is 'quite difficult to establish whether that similarity exists only in the context of the gas transportation and distribution industry or extends to other utilities as well'.[53] As a result, the tribunal found no violation of discrimination under the non-impairment clause of the Argentina–US BIT and preferred to examine the effect of the measures in question under the FET standard instead.[54] In *Metalpar v Argentina* the tribunal rejected the investors' claim that Argentina breached the prohibition against arbitrary or discriminatory measures finding that the investors did not belong to the same (financial) sector and, thus, were not entitled to the more favourable treatment financial institutions received.[55] Likewise, in *Enron v Argentina* the tribunal emphasized that:

> [t]here are quite naturally important differences between the various sectors that have been affected, so it is not surprising either that different solutions might have been or are being sought for each, but it could not be said that any such sector has been singled out, in particular either to apply to it measures harsher than in respect of others, or conversely to provide a more beneficial remedy to one sector to the detriment of another.[56]

In *El Paso v Argentina*, the investor argued that given that 'the banks are mainly Argentinian and the oil and gas sector companies mainly foreign-owned' and 'the banking sector and the energy sector have not been treated in the same manner', 'there has been de facto discrimination'.[57] The tribunal was not persuaded and held that, while

[51] *Nykomb Synergetics Technology Holding AB v Republic of Latvia*, SCC, Award, 16 December 2003, 34.

[52] *Saluka Investments BV v The Czech Republic*, UNCITRAL, Partial Award, 17 March 2006, para 460. For the examination of likeness in the context of FET in *Saluka v Czech Republic*, see Section 3.1.1.4.

[53] *CMS Gas Transmission Company v the Argentine Republic*, Award, ICSID Case No ARB/01/8, 12 May 2005, para 293.

[54] ibid, para 295.

[55] *Metalpar SA and Buen Aire SA v The Argentine Republic*, ICSID Case No ARB/03/5, Award on the Merits, 6 June 2008, paras 162–164.

[56] *Enron Corporation and Ponderosa Assets, LP v Argentine Republic*, ICSID Case No ARB/01/3, Award, 22 May 2007, para 282.

[57] *El Paso Energy International Company v The Argentine Republic*, ICSID Case No ARB/03/15, Award, 31 October 2011, para 309. See also *Ulysseas, Inc v The Republic of Ecuador*, UNCITRAL, Final Award, 12 June 2012, para 295 ('transmission companies are in a situation different from that of generation companies, so that no discrimination between the two categories may be deemed to exist').

'[i]t is not denied that the banking and the hydrocarbon sectors were not subject to the same measures', 'the measures concerning each of these sectors were reasonable and did not discriminate against either of them'.[58]

3.1.1.4 Fair and Equitable Treatment

While non-discrimination is an essential element of the FET standard,[59] tribunals have not set out in detail the applicable legal test. The relevant cases seem to confirm that a finding of discrimination in the context of FET presupposes that the investor and other foreign or domestic investors which received more favourable treatment are in a comparable, like situation. In *Lemire v Ukaine* the tribunal held that:

> [t]o amount to discrimination, a case must be treated differently *from similar cases* without justification; a measure must be 'discriminatory and expose[s] the claimant to sectional or racial prejudice'; or a measure must 'target[ed] Claimant's investments specifically as foreign investments'.[60]

In *Saluka v Czech Republic* the tribunal delved into the specific details of the big four banks of the country (including size, macroeconomic significance, non-performing loan portfolios, applicable legal framework, prudential supervision, and, importantly, their 'systemic nature') without discussing in detail the relevant legal test for determining likeness.[61]

3.1.1.5 Expropriation

Likeness is also the first question to be examined in the context of discrimination in expropriation of foreign property. The focus in the case law of investment treaty tribunals has been on indirect (or regulatory) expropriation, rather than direct expropriation.[62]

In medieval Europe, the taking of property by the monarch was usually carried out without compensation, unless the property in question belonged to the Church.[63] As the Church enjoyed a uniquely powerful and privileged position in medieval times, it was not considered to be 'like' with the Crown's subjects. This explains why the latter

[58] *El Paso Energy International Company v The Argentine Republic*, ICSID Case No ARB/03/15, Award, 31 October 2011, para 310; see also, ibid, paras 311–315.

[59] See Chapter 2, Section 2.3.2.

[60] *Joseph Charles Lemire v Ukraine*, ICSID Case No ARB/06/18, Decision on Jurisdiction and Liability, 14 January 2010, para 261 (emphasis added).

[61] *Saluka Investments BV v The Czech Republic*, UNCITRAL, Partial Award, 17 March 2006, paras 314–323; see also ibid, para 322: ('[a]ll of them had large non- performing loan portfolios resulting in increased provisions and consequently in insufficient regulatory capital. None of them was able to absorb the losses by calling on shareholder equity. The survival of all of them was sooner or later seriously threatened unless the Czech State was willing to provide financial assistance').

[62] On the distinction between direct and indirect expropriation see Chapter 2, Section 2.3.3.

[63] S Reynolds, *Before Eminent Domain, Towards a History of Expropriation of Land and for the Common Good* (University of North Carolina Press 2010) 31–32 ('I have found no hint about compensation for land taken except what was paid to churches and, thanks to the quite exceptional record of Domes-day Book, to one or two fortunate Normans among the followers of William the Conqueror. I conclude tentatively that, though it is possible that compensation was paid to other laymen but not recorded, the common good may have been held to outweigh individual rights to the extent that compensation may not always have been thought necessary — except for land taken from God and the saints').

frequently did not receive any compensation for expropriated property. Centuries later, in the context of the Cold War, discriminatory takings of foreign property motivated by ideological and/or geopolitical considerations also highlight that the non-discrimination requirement in the context of expropriation is politically charged.[64]

Domestic courts have also examined the issue of discrimination (and, in particular, likeness) in the context of expropriation. The *Indonesian Tobacco* saga is a case in point.[65] Following Indonesia's declaration of independence from the Netherlands in 1945, Indonesia proceeded to a series of nationalizations, directly and exclusively affecting Dutch-owned enterprises. Indonesia did not attempt to conceal that its measure targeted exclusively foreign (Dutch) property. The General Explanation of the Act of Nationalization contained in Ordinance No 2 promulgated in 1958 makes it clear that '[t]he nationalization of Dutch-owned enterprises is intended to further strengthen our national potential as well as to liquidate colonial economic power, in this case the Dutch colonial economy'.[66] Dutch and German courts examined the legality of the Indonesian nationalization measures and reached different conclusions. The Bremen Court of Appeals pronouncing on the non-discrimination requirement of expropriation held that colonial foreign investors and native (Indonesian) investors were not in like circumstances. The Bremen Court of Appeal held that:

> the equality concept means only that equals must be treated equally and that the different treatment of unequals is admissible ... For the statement to be objective, it is sufficient that the attitude of the former colonial people to its former colonial master is of course different from that toward other foreigners. Not only were the places of production predominantly in the hands of the Netherlanders, for the greater part colonial companies, but these companies dominated the worldwide distribution, beyond the production process, through the Dutch markets.[67]

Conversely, the Courts of the former colonial power adopted a different, formal conception of equality. For the Amsterdam Appellate Court, the Indonesian nationalization was 'a manifestly discriminating measure which in a very sharp manner attacks the rights and interests exclusively of nationals of the State of the Netherlands, though a state of war does not exist between Indonesia and that country'.[68] The different approach of the German and Dutch courts is telling and reflects how different values and more precisely different assessments of political and historical phenomena (*in casu* the

[64] See also Chapter 2, Section 2.3.

[65] On the topic see generally Lord McNair's Opinion rendered for De Ondernemersraad voor Indonesia, Lord AD McNair, 'The Seizure of Property and Enterprises in Indonesia' (1959) 6 Netherlands International Law Review 218.

[66] General Explanation of the Act of Nationalisation (31 December 1958), quoted in translation in Da Sokarno and GA Maengkom, 'Act No. 86 of 1958 (Statutes 1958 No. 162) concerning the Nationalization of Dutch-Owned Enterprises In Indonesia' (1959) 6 Netherlands International Law Review 291, 293. According to Lord McNair 'the real motive underlying these measures is to bring pressure upon the Netherlands to transfer sovereignty in respect of West Irian to Indonesia', McNair (n 65) 246.

[67] Quoted in M Domke, 'Indonesian Nationalization Measures before Foreign Courts' (1960) 54 AJIL 305, 315.

[68] ibid, 316.

Dutch colonial rule in Indonesia) led to diametrically opposed interpretations of the same (customary) rule prohibiting discriminatory expropriations.

In the jurisprudence of investment treaty tribunals, the relevant comparison is between the treatment of the investor and other foreign or domestic investors in similar circumstances, rather than entire groups of investors.[69] This is in line with the test for other non-discrimination standards and the nature of discrimination obligations in international investment law as a disparate treatment (or direct) discrimination.[70] The fact that only one foreign investor is involved in a particular project does not shield the State from discrimination claims in the context of expropriation. The tribunal in *ADC v Hungary* held that it 'cannot accept the Respondent's argument that as the only foreign parties involved in the operation of the Airport, the Claimants are not in a position to raise any claims of being treated discriminately'.[71] Rather, 'the comparison of different treatments is made here between that received by the Respondent-appointed operator and that received by foreign investors as a whole'.[72] Conversely, in *Rusoro v Venezuela* the tribunal held if a State expropriates all foreign investments in a particular economic sector, with their state-owned competitors naturally remaining unaffected by (or even benefiting from) the nationalization, this 'is a necessary consequence of the nationalization of a productive sector in which privately owned and State-owned companies coexisted' and 'cannot be considered to amount to discrimination'.[73]

3.1.2 The Normative Argument of this Book

This book rejects the consideration of regulatory purpose in determining likeness. As explained above, under this approach, essentially, 'the policy objective pursued by the measure under scrutiny may be taken into consideration to define the circumstances in which the comparison of the foreign and domestic comparators takes place'.[74] This is reminiscent of the 'aims and effects' test adopted in the international trade law context by General Agreement on Tariffs and Trade (GATT) Panels for determining likeness but subsequently categorically rejected by the World Trade Organization

[69] See below Section 3.2.1. See also *ADC Affiliate Limited and ADC & ADMC Management Limited v Republic of Hungary*, ICSID Case No ARB/03/16, Award, 2 October 2006, para 442 ('It is correct for the Respondent to point out that in order for a discrimination to exist, particularly in an expropriation scenario, there must be different treatments to different parties. However and unfortunately, the Respondent misses the point because the comparison of different treatments is made here between that received by the Respondent-appointed operator and that received by foreign investors as a whole.')

[70] See Chapter 2, Section 2.2.

[71] *ADC Affiliate Limited and ADC & ADMC Management Limited v Republic of Hungary*, ICSID Case No ARB/03/16, Award, 2 October 2006, para 441.

[72] ibid, para 442.

[73] *Rusoro Mining Ltd v Bolivarian Republic of Venezuela*, ICSID Case No ARB(AF)/12/5, Award, 22 August 2016, para 397. See also U Kriebaum, 'Regulatory Takings: Balancing the Interests of the Investor and the State' (2007) 8 JWIT 717, 734, fn 64: '[i]f comparable projects were not stopped, one would have to analyse whether there was a discriminatory expropriation. In that case it would be unlawful. and the state would have to pay damages. It would not be necessary to make the proportionality test. With regard to other potential projects it may be that they have the same negative effect, but are not comparable. Then, they need not be taken into consideration for the discrimination test.'

[74] Diebold (n 6) 840.

(WTO) Panels and the Appellate Body (AB).[75] It is also reflected in modern treaty practice.[76] The latest generation of investment treaties requires an examination of measure's objective in the context of 'likeness'. This is the case for example with the Investment Chapter of the CPTPP[77] and the CPTPP Drafter's note,[78] the Kyrgyzstan–India BIT,[79] the Brazil–India BIT,[80] the African Continental Free Trade Area (AfCFTA) Protocol on Investment,[81] as well as Model BITs, such as India's 2015 Model

[75] AB, *Japan—Alcoholic Beverages* 18; see R Hudec, 'GATT/WTO Constraints on National Regulation: Requiem for an "Aims and Effects" Test' (1998) 32 The International Lawyer 619–649. Despite the rejection of the 'aims-and-effects' test, the jurisprudence of the WTO Appellate Body on Article I and III of the GATT (containing MFN and National Treatment obligations) is not consistent on whether detrimental impact is on its own sufficient to establish discrimination.

[76] Footnote 14 in Article 9.4 of the TTP Agreement provides that '[f]or greater certainty, whether treatment is accorded in "like circumstances" under Article 9.4 (National Treatment) or Article 9.5 (Most-Favoured-Nation Treatment) depends on the totality of the circumstances, including whether the relevant treatment distinguishes between investors or investments on the basis of legitimate public welfare objectives', TPP Agreement, Article 9.4, fn 14. See also DA Gantz, 'Protecting Investment under NAFTA, the Trans-Pacific Partnership and the Comprehensive and Progressive TPP' in JA Huerta-Goldman and DA Gantz (eds), *The Comprehensive and Progressive Trans-Pacific Partnership: Analysis and Commentary* (CUP 2021) 313–326; S Schacherer, *Sustainable Development in EU Foreign Investment Law* (Brill Nijhoff 2021) 318–322. See also USMCA Agreement, Article 14.4(4): 'For greater certainty, whether treatment is accorded in "like circumstances" under this Article [National Treatment] depends on the totality of the circumstances, including whether the relevant treatment distinguishes between investors or investments on the basis of legitimate public welfare objectives'. See also ibid, Article 15.4(4) regarding MFN. Some South-to-South BIT, such as the Reciprocal Investment Promotion and Protection Agreement between the Government of the Kingdom of Morocco and the Government of the Federal Republic of Nigeria 2016 (signed 3 December 2016, not yet into force) (the Morocco–Nigeria BIT) (which has not yet entered into force) in Article 6(3), go a step further:

> [f]or greater certainty, references to 'like circumstances' in paragraph 2 requires an overall examination on a case-by-case basis of all the circumstances of an investment including, but not limited to:
>
> a) its effects on third person and the local community;
> b) its effects on the local, regional or national environment, including the cumulative effects of all investments within a jurisdiction on the environment;
> c) the sector in which the investor is in;
> d) the aim of the measure concerned;
> f) the regulatory process generally applied in relation to the measure concerned;
>
> The examination referred to in this paragraph shall not be limited to or be biased toward anyone factor.

[77] Comprehensive and Progressive Agreement for Trans-Pacific Partnership (adopted 8 March 2018, entered into force 30 December 2018) (CPTPP), Article 9.4, fn 14: '[f]or greater certainty, whether treatment is accorded in "like circumstances" under Article 9.4 (National Treatment) or Article 9.5 (Most-Favoured-Nation Treatment) depends on the totality of the circumstances, including whether the relevant treatment distinguishes between investors or investments on the basis of legitimate public welfare objectives'.

[78] CTPPT Drafter's Note, para 5.

[79] Bilateral Investment Treaty between the Government of the Kyrgyz Republic and the Government of the Republic of India (signed 14 June 2019, not yet entered into force) (Kyrgyzstan–India BIT), Article 4.1, fn 2.

[80] Investment Cooperation and Facilitation Treaty between the Federative Republic of Brazil and the Republic of India (signed 25 January 2020, not yet into force) (Brazil–India BIT), Article 5.2: 'For greater certainty, the treatment accorded "in like circumstances" depends on the totality of the circumstances, including whether the relevant treatment distinguishes between investors or investments on the basis of legitimate public welfare or regulatory objectives.'

[81] Protocol on Investment to the Agreement Establishing the AfCFTA (Draft January 2023) (adopted at the Ministerial level in October 2022 and by the Assembly of Heads of States in February 2023), Article 12(2):

> In assessing 'in like circumstances', an overall examination is required on a case by-case basis, of all the circumstances of an investment, including, among others:
>
> a. its effects on third persons and the local community;
> b. its effects on the local, regional or national environment, the health of the populations, or on the global commons;
> c. the sector in which the investor is active;
> d. the aim of the measure in question;

BIT,[82] Slovakia's 2019 Model BIT,[83] and Canada's 2021 Model BIT.[84] However, Mitchell, Heaton and Henckels rightly criticize taking into account regulatory purpose in determining likeness as 'incoherent' and 'unstainable' on the basis that it conflates 'the concepts of likeness and less favourable treatment'.[85]

This book argues that existence of discriminatory motives or the absence of legitimate (non-discriminatory) objectives behind the measures in question should be examined separately, once likeness and less favourable treatment are established,[86] essentially following the three-stage test which the tribunal used in *Saluka v Czech Republic*.[87] This approach has several advantages. Many (but not all[88]) arbitral awards adopt this approach. Clearly separating the analysis of (i) likeness, (ii) less favourable treatment, and (iii) any links between the less favourable treatment and any protected ground (such as nationality),[89] allows the parties and tribunals to deal with the complex legal concepts and to apply them to the factual matrix in the clearest possible way, thereby enhancing the quality of the parties' pleadings and tribunals' reasoning. As a result, transparency and predictability are improved, by allowing 'States and investors to anticipate more effectively which differentiations are accepted as justified by tribunals'.[90]

e. the regulatory process generally applied in relation to a measure in question; and
f. any other factor directly relating to the investment or investor in relation to the measure in question.

The examination referred to in this Paragraph shall not be limited to or biased towards any one factor.'

[82] Model Text for the Indian Bilateral Investment Treaty, Article 4.1, fn 2: 'For greater certainty, whether treatment is accorded in "like circumstances" depends on the totality of the circumstances, including whether the relevant treatment distinguishes between investors or investments on the basis of legitimate regulatory objectives. These circumstances include, but are not limited to, (a) the goods or services consumed or produced by the investment; (b) the actual and potential impact of the investment on third persons, the local community, or the environment, (c) whether the investment is public, private, or state-owned or controlled, and (d) the practical challenges of regulating the investment.'

[83] Slovakia Model BIT 2019, Article 6(3): 'For greater certainty, a determination of whether an investment or an investor is in like circumstances for the purposes of paragraphs 1 and 2 [National Treatment and MFN] shall be made based on an assessment of the totality of circumstances related to the investor or the investment, including the business sector in which the investor operates, character of the measure, its nature, purpose, duration or and rationale.'

[84] Canada's 2021 Foreign Investment Promotion and Protection Agreement (FIPA) Model, Article 6(4) [MFN]: '[w]hether treatment is accorded in like circumstances depends on the totality of the circumstances, including whether the relevant treatment distinguishes between investors or investments on the basis of legitimate public policy objectives'. ibid, Article 5(4) [National Treatment]: '[w]hether treatment is accorded in like circumstances depends on the totality of the circumstances, including whether the relevant treatment distinguishes between investors or investments on the basis of legitimate public policy objectives'.

[85] Mitchell, Heaton, and Henckels (n 10) 66 and 79. See also, ibid, 88–89.

[86] See Section 3.3.2. See also AK Bjorklund and L Vanhonnaeker, 'National Treatment' in MM Mengue and S Schacherer (eds), *Foreign Investment Under the Comprehensive Economic and Trade Agreement (CETA)* (Springer 2019) 45–70, 66: ('No substantial changes are expected with respect to the interpretation and application of CETA's NT principle. The assessment of a NT claim under CETA will likely entail a three-step analysis to identify whether the investor is in "like circumstances" with respect to domestic investors, whether it suffered nationality-based discriminatory treatment, and whether the discriminatory treatment was justified').

[87] *Saluka Investments BV v The Czech Republic*, UNCITRAL, Partial Award, 17 March 2006, para 313 ('State conduct is discriminatory, if (i) similar cases are (ii) treated differently (iii) and without reasonable justification').

[88] Reinisch and Schreuer (n 41) 669.

[89] See also Mitchell, Heaton, and Henckels (n 10) 160 ('[i]n terms of conceptual approach (relevant consideration versus justification), the more straightforward and intellectually robust approach seems to us to be to employ regulatory purpose as a separate step of justification for an otherwise inconsistent measure, rather than as a factor that is said to eliminate differentiation altogether').

[90] R Dolzer, U Kriebaum, and C Schreuer, *Principles of International Investment Law* (3rd edn, OUP 2022) 259.

Further, in several cases investors will fail to establish likeness and/or less favourable treatment in any event, and their discrimination claims could be dismissed by tribunals exercising judicial economy,[91] without the need to go through a phase of the arbitration which is challenging from an evidentiary perspective, and, therefore, complex and expensive. Finally, it will also facilitate the (limited) review of arbitral awards by ICSID ad hoc annulment committees or (in non-ICSID arbitrations) domestic courts.[92]

On the appropriate methodology to determine likeness, this book suggests adopting a case-by-case and fact-specific approach. As Schreuer suggests, tribunals should start comparing investors which are in close proximity from a business and competition perspective, but, in certain circumstances, for example, the circle could be widened to make sure that any discriminatory treatment is identified.[93] The specific criterion to be used to determine likeness is not always decisive, as all these criteria could be interpreted very narrowly or broadly. Therefore, what is of greater practical importance is the tribunals' approach in interpreting and applying them, rather which criterion is selected. Some tribunals adopted a very broad understanding of likeness, while others opted for a very narrow interpretation. How broadly or narrowly likeness is construed in the context of National Treatment is critical for (ultimately) finding a violation by the State. Further, it demonstrates how investment tribunals see their role and where they strike the balance between protecting investors and preserving governments' regulatory autonomy.

[91] Cf *Eli Lilly and Company v The Government of Canada*, UNCITRAL, ICSID Case No UNCT/14/2, Award, 16 March 2017, para 220; *MCI Power Group LC and New Turbine, Inc v Republic of Ecuador*, ICSID Case No ARB/03/6, Decision on Annulment, 19 October 2009, para 67; *Suez, Sociedad General de Aguas de Barcelona SA and Inter Aguas Servicios Integrales del Agua SA v Argentine Republic*, ICSID Case No ARB/03/17 Award, 9 April 2015, para 57; *Renée Rose Levy and Gremcitel SA v Republic of Peru*, ICSID Case No ARB/11/17, Award, 9 January 2015, para 197; *Spence International Investments et al v Republic of Costa Rica*, Interim Award, 25 October 2016, para 296; *Peter A Allard v The Government of Barbados*, PCA Case No 2012-06, Award, 27 June 2016, paras 139 and 140; see also DM Bigge, 'Judicial Economy in Investor-State Disputes (25 May 2017) available at <https://arbitrationblog.kluwerarbitration.com/2017/05/25/judicial-economy-investor-state-disputes/>; L Johns, C Thrall, and RL Wellhausen, 'Judicial Economy and Moving Bars in International Investment Arbitration' (2020) 15 The Review of International Organizations 923. On judicial economy in other fields of international law see A Sarvarian, 'Procedural Economy at the International Court of Justice' (2019) 18 The Law and Practice of International Courts and Tribunals 74; A Alvarez-Jiménez, 'The WTO Appellate Body's Exercise of Judicial Economy' (2009) 12 JIEL 393.

[92] On the ICSID Annulment process see and C Schreuer, 'From ICSID Annulment to Appeal Half Way Down the Slippery Slope' (2011) 10 The Law and Practice of International Courts and Tribunals 211; W Ben Hamida, 'Two Nebulous ICSID Features: The Notion of Investment and the Scope of Annulment Control' (2007) 24 Journal of International Arbitration 287; JC Thomas and H Kaur Dhillon, 'The Foundations of Investment Treaty Arbitration: The ICSID Convention, Investment Treaties and the Review of Arbitration Awards' (2017) 32 ICSID Review 459; LM Bohmer, 'Finality in ICSID Arbitration Revisited' (2016) 31 ICSID Review 236; see G Kaufmann-Kohler, 'Annulment of ICSID Awards in contract and Treaty Arbitrations: Are There Differences?' in E Gaillard and Y Banifatemi (eds), *Annulment of ICSID Awards* (Juris Publishing 2004) 189–222.

[93] Schreuer (n 47) 196; Kriebaum also agrees with that approach, U Kriebaum, 'Arbitrary/Unreasonable or Discriminatory Measures' in M Bungenberg and others (eds), *International Investment Law* (CH Beck, Hart, Nomos 2013)790–806, 805; see also Reinisch and Schreuer (n 41) 839.

3.2 Less Favourable Treatment

3.2.1 Case Law on Less Favourable Treatment

3.2.1.1. National Treatment

Once the claimant establishes that it is in like circumstances with a domestic investor, it is uncontroversial that the next step of the analysis is to compare their respective 'treatment' by the Host State. According to the ILC, '"[n]ational treatment" means treatment by the granting State of persons or things in a determined relationship with the beneficiary State, not less favourable than treatment of persons or things in the same relationship with itself'.[94]

National Treatment does not oblige the State to strictly adhere to equal treatment, as there is no international legal obstacle treating foreign investors and investments more favourable than domestic investors and investments.[95] One could argue that the analysis of the 'less favourable treatment' component of the legal test lies at the heart of the National Treatment obligation. In the words of the tribunal in *Alpha Projektholding v Ukraine*:

> [i]n order to prove a national treatment violation, it is necessary first and foremost to establish that a government action or inaction has discriminated between domestic and foreign investors, i.e., that it has accorded "less favourable" treatment to foreign as opposed to domestic investors. Such discrimination could arise de jure if there is a government measure such as a law or regulation that explicitly discriminates between domestic and foreign investors, or *de facto* if the measure is not explicitly or inherently discriminatory but discriminates between domestic and foreign investors in the way in which it is applied.[96]

Tribunals construe the meaning of 'treatment' broadly. For example, in *Merrill & Ring v Canada* the tribunal emphasized that 'treatment':

> includes almost any conceivable measure that can be with respect to the beginning, development, management and end of an investor's business activity. The treatment is no different than the aggregate of all the regulatory measures applied to that business.[97]

[94] For a definition of National Treatment see International Law Commission (ILC), Fifth Report on MFN (1974) II(1) Yearbook of the International Law Commission 1, 124.
[95] Reinisch and Schreuer (n 41) 653.
[96] *Alpha Projektholding GmbH v Ukraine*, ICSID Case No ARB/07/16, Award, 8 November 2010, para 426.
[97] *Merrill & Ring Forestry LP v Government of Canada*, UNCITRAL, ICSID Administrated, Award, 31 March 2010, para 79.

Treatment includes both regulatory treatment and factual treatment.[98] It also covers both de jure and de facto treatment.[99] These terms are often conflated. The first distinction (between regulatory and factual treatment) revolves around whether the measure(s) in question 'stem from a legal requirement'.[100] As aptly put by the tribunal in *Lauder v Czech Republic* (interpreting a non-impairment clause), '[f]or a measure to be discriminatory, it does not need to violate domestic law, since domestic law can contain a provision that is discriminatory towards foreign investment, or can lack a provision prohibiting the discrimination of foreign investment'.[101] The second distinction (between de jure and de facto treatment) differentiates between measures explicitly discriminating based on the investors' nationality and measures which, although facially neutral, have a discriminatory effect. However, in any event, the notion of treatment extends only to State measures, and, therefore, attribution is crucial.[102]

Finally, in the jurisprudence of investment treaty tribunals—perhaps with the single exception of *ADF v USA*[103]—the relevant comparison is between the treatment of the investor and other foreign or domestic investors in similar circumstances, rather than entire groups of investors.[104]

[98] This was the approach adopted by the tribunal in *Bayindir v Pakistan* in the context of MFN analysis. *Bayindir Insaat Turizm Ticaret Ve Sanayi AS v Islamic Republic of Pakistan*, ICSID Case No ARB/03/29, Decision on Jurisdiction, para 206: 'The mere fact that Bayindir had always been subject to exactly the same legal and regulatory framework as everybody else in Pakistan does not necessarily mean that it was actually treated in the same way as local (or third countries) investors. In other words, as is evident from the broad wording of Article II(2) of the BIT, the treatment the investor is offered under the MFN clause is not limited to "regulatory treatment"'. This was also confirmed by the ECtHR; see *Zarb Adami v Malta*, Application No 17209/02, 20 June 2006, para 76: 'a discrimination potentially contrary to the Convention may result not only from a legislative measure ... but also from a *de facto* situation.'

[99] See eg *Marvin Roy Feldman Karpa v United Mexican States*, ICSID Case No ARB(AF)/99/1, Award, 16 December 2002, para 169; *Alpha Projektholding GmbH v Ukraine*, ICSID Case No ARB/07/16, Award, 8 November 2010, para 426; *Archer Daniels Midland Company and Tate & Lyle Ingredients Americas, Inc v United Mexican States*, ICSID Case No ARB(AF)/04/5, Award, 21 November 2007, para 193; *Total SA v Argentine Republic*, ICSID Case No ARB/04/01, Decision on Liability, 27 December 2010, para 211; Reinisch and Schreuer (n 41) 658–660. In the context of equality under EU law, the CJEU has repeatedly emphasized that 'the rules regarding equal treatment forbid not only overt discrimination by reason of nationality but also all covert forms of discrimination which, by the application of other criteria of differentiation, lead in fact to the same result', C-155/09, *European Commission v Hellenic Republic* [2011] ECR I-65, para 45; Case C-152/73 *Giovanni Maria Sotgiu v Deutsche Bundespost* [1974] ECR 153, para 11; Case C-103/08, *Arthur Gottwald v Bezirkshauptmannschaft Bregenz* [2009] ECR I-9117, para 27 (with further references).

[100] Reinisch and Schreuer (n 41) 661. See also Chapter 2.

[101] *Ronald S Lauder v Czech Republic*, UNCITRAL, Final Award, 3 September 2001, para 220. On the role of domestic law in investment treaty arbitration see HE Kjos, *Applicable Law in Investor-State Arbitration: The Interplay Between National and International Law* (OUP 2013); J Hepburn, *Domestic Law in International Investment Arbitration* (OUP 2017).

[102] See eg *Mohammad Ammar Al-Bahloul v Republic of Tajikistan*, Partial Award on Jurisdiction and Liability, SCC Case No V064/2008, 2 September 2009, paras 272 and 273; see Reinisch and Schreuer (n 41) 655–656; C De Stefano, *Attribution in International Law and Arbitration* (OUP 2020). See also 2001 ILC Draft articles on Responsibility of Staes for Internationally Wrongful Acts Draft Articles on State Responsibility.

[103] Cf *ADF Group Inc v United States of America*, ICSID Case No ARB (AF)/00/1, Award, 9 January 2003, para 157; for arguments in favour of the approach in *ADF v USA* see Kurtz (n 15) 116–121.

[104] *Pope & Talbot Inc v Government of Canada*, UNCITRAL, Award on the Merits of Phase 2, 10 April 2001, para 42: Article 1102 of the NAFTA guarantees 'the right to treatment equivalent to the "best" treatment accorded to domestic investors or investments in like circumstances'; see also *Archer Daniels Midland Company and Tate & Lyle Ingredients Americas, Inc v United Mexican States*, ICSID Case No ARB(AF)/04/5, Award, 21 November 2007, para 205 ('Claimants and their investment are entitled to the best level of treatment available to any other domestic investor or investment operating in like circumstances'); *Loewen Group, Inc and Raymond L Loewen v United States of America*, ICSID Case No ARB(AF)/98/3, Award, 26 June 2003, para 140 ('[w]hat Article 1102(3) requires is a comparison between the standard of treatment accorded to a claimant and the most favourable standard of treatment accorded to a person in like situation to that claimant'); *Methanex Corporation v the United States of America*,

3.2.1.2 Most Favoured Nation Treatment

After establishing likeness, the second question to consider for determining whether a State complied with its MFN obligation is the analysis of the treatment accorded to the foreign investor. The manner in which tribunals approach the concept of 'treatment' in the context of MFN is similar to the interpretation of 'treatment' for the purposes of National Treatment: 'treatment' is broadly interpreted; it requires some adverse effects on the foreign investor, and includes de facto and de jure treatment, as well as regulatory and factual treatment.[105] This section will focus on the idiosyncratic features of MFN clauses and in particular the meaning of MFN treatment. According to Article 5 of the ILC 1978 Draft Articles on MFN:

> [m]ost-favoured-nation treatment is treatment accorded by the granting State to the beneficiary State, or to persons or things in a determined relationship with that State, not less favourable than treatment extended by the granting State to a third State or to persons or things in the same relationship with that third State.[106]

As explained by Schill, 'MFN clauses oblige the State granting MFN treatment to extend to the beneficiary State the treatment accorded to third States in case this treatment is more favourable than the treatment under the treaty between the granting State and the beneficiary State'.[107]

For centuries MFN clauses have been a commonly used technique of treaty drafting. MFN clauses' long history predates the emergence of modern international investment treaty arbitration,[108] the proliferation of (mostly bilateral) investment treaties (and by

UNCITRAL, Final Award of the Tribunal on Jurisdiction and Merits, 3 August 2005, Part IV, Chapter B, para 21: 'the investor or investment of another party is entitled to the most favourable treatment accorded to some members of the domestic class'); *Mercer International Inc v Government of Canada*, ICSID Case No ARB(AF)/12/3, Award, 6 March 2018, para 7.27 ('where the treatment of both domestic and other foreign comparators is in question, the effect of NAFTA Article 1104 is that the Claimant is entitled to treatment no less favourable than the most favourable of the more favourable treatment afforded to domestic or foreign comparators, in like circumstances'). See also Diebold (n 6) 844.

[105] *Parkerings-Compagniet AS v Republic of Lithuania*, ICSID Case No ARB/05/8 Award, 11 September 2007, para 368 ('[d]iscrimination involves either issues of law, such as legislation affording different treatments in function of citizenship, or issues of fact where a State unduly treats differently investors who are in similar circumstances').

[106] ILC 1978 Draft Articles on MFN, Article 5.

[107] SW Schill, 'Mulitilateralizing Investment Treaties through Most-Favored-Nation Clauses' (2009) 27 Berkeley Journal of International Law 496, 502.

[108] See E Öktem, 'La clausola della nazione piú favorita nelle capitolazioni ottomane: genesi, tipologia, patologia' (2022) 105 Rivista di diritto internazionale 43; W Ben Hamida, 'Clause de la nation plus favorisée et mécanismes de règlement des différends: Que dit l'histoire?' (2007) 134 Clunet 1127; M Risvas, 'Non-discrimination in International Economic Law and Sovereign Equality of States: An Historical Perspective' (2017) 39 Houston Journal of International Law 79; N Ejaz Piracha, *Toward Uniformly Accepted Principles for Interpreting MFN Clauses: Striking a Balance* (Kluwer Law International 2021) Chapter 1; A Wang, *The Interpretation and Application of the Most-Favored-Nation Clause in Investment Arbitration* (Brill Nijhoff 2022) Chapter 1; M Suleimenova, *MFN Standard as Substantive Treatment* (Nomos 2019) Chapter 2; see also RE Clute and RR Wilson, 'The Commonwealth and Favored-Nation Usage' (1958) 52 AJIL 455 and JN Hazard, 'Commercial discrimination and international law' (1958) 52 AJIL 495; J Viner, 'The Most-Favored-Nation Clause in American Commercial Treaties' (1924) 32 Journal of Political Economy 101; EJ Conroy, 'The American Interpretation of the Most Favored Nation Clause' (1926) 12 Cornell Law Quarterly 327.

implication the multilateralization of the international investment law regime[109]). As Paparinskis observes, 'MFN clauses have an impressive historic pedigree. The idea predates Westphalian international law and goes back for almost 1000 years, the recognizable form for more than 500 years, and the MFN wording for more than 350 years'.[110]

As a result, the interpretation of MFN clauses and, in particular, the analysis of 'treatment' have generated importance international law jurisprudence and certain key interpretative questions have been already settled. These questions include the *unconditional* nature of MFN clauses in modern treaty practice,[111] and the *ejusdem generis* principle. The *ejusdem generis* principle is explained in Article 9(1) of the ILC 1978 Draft Articles on MFN:

> [u]nder a most-favoured-nation clause the beneficiary State acquires, for itself or for the benefit of persons or things in a determined relationship with it, only those rights which fall within the limits of the subject-matter of the clause.[112]

In the famous *Ambatielos* arbitration (between Greece and the UK) the Commission was adamant that 'the most-favoured-nation clause can only attract matters belonging to the same category of subject as that to which the clause itself relates'.[113] Investment treaty tribunal consistently endorse the *ejusdem generis* principle, also referring to the *Ambatielos* arbitral award and the ILC 1978 Draft Articles on MFN.[114] However, the

[109] SW Schill, *The Multilateralization of International Investment Law* (CUP 2009).

[110] M Paparinskis, *The International Minimum Standard and Fair and Equitable Treatment* (OUP 2013) 105.

[111] By the middle of the nineteenth century, European states abandoned the principle of reciprocity in favour of trade liberalism and endorsed the use of unconditional MFN. The Cobden Chevalier treaty signed between England and France in 1860, which contained in Article XIX an unconditional MFN clause, is traditionally considered as the beginning of the trade liberalization era. An opposite view, challenging the importance of MFN and focusing on the role of unilateral liberalizing policies, is presented by O Accominotti and M Flandreau, 'Bilateral Treaties and the Most-Favored-Nation Clause: The Myth of Trade Liberalization in the Nineteenth Century' (2008) 60 World Politics 147. However, the US persisted in reciprocity and conditional MFN clauses until the 1930s. The enactment of the Reciprocal Trade Agreements Act (RTAA) of 1934 marks the policy shift as under the RTAA programme twenty-one trade agreements were concluded by the end of the Second World War with various countries, see Weiler (n 7) 351. See also E Ustor, ILC, 'The most-favoured-nation clause in the law of treaties: working paper submitted by Mr. Endre Ustor, Special Rapporteur', A/CN.4/L.127, 19 June 1968, para 10. On the history of conditional and unconditional MFN clauses see B Coutain, 'The Unconditional Most-Favored-Nation Clause and the Maintenance of the Liberal Trade Regime in the Postwar 1870s' (2009) 63 International Organization 139; T Cole, 'The Boundaries of Most Favored Nation Treatment in International Investment Law' 33 Michigan Journal of International Law 537, 543–553. GATT and WTO Panels have emphasized the unconditional nature of the MFN obligation, cf GATT Panel, *US—Section 337*, para 5.16; Panel, *EC—Bananas III (Ecuador)*, para 7.239; GATT Panel, *US—MFN Footwear*, para 6.10; GATT Panel, Belgian Family Allowances, para 3; GATT Panel, *EEC—Animal Feed Proteins*, paras 3.64 and 4.19; Panel, *EC—Tariff Preferences*, paras 7.59 and 7.60; AB, *EC—Tariff Preferences*, para 124. However, as Lang shows inconsistencies and interpretative dilemmas persist, A Lang, *World Trade Law after Neoliberalism: Re-imagining the Global Economic Order* (OUP 2011) 319–320.

[112] ILC, Draft Articles on most-favoured-nation clauses with commentaries (1978) II(2) Yearbook of the International Law Commission 16 (ILC 1978 Draft Articles on MFN), Article 9(1).

[113] *The Ambatielos Claim (Greece v UK)* (6 March 1956) XII 12 RIAA 83, 107.

[114] *Muhammet Cap & Sehil Insaat Endustri ve Ticaret Ltd Sti v Turkmenistan*, ICSID Case No ARB/12/6, Award, 4 May 2021, para 787: 'The ejusdem generis principle refers to the sameness of the subject matter of the MFN clauses and the other substantial provisions in a treaty, not only of the treaties in which the provisions are contained. As established by the tribunal in *Ambatelios* [*sic*], "the most-favoured nation clause can only attract matters belonging to the same category of subject as that to which the clause itself relates". This requirement was also confirmed and provided for by the ILC in its 2015 MFN Report which explained that Article 10 of the ILC Draft Articles provides that an MFN clause can be applied "only if the granting State extends to a third State benefits within the subject matter of the clause." Further, "Articles 9 and 10 also make clear that where the benefit is for persons or things within a determined relationship with the beneficiary State, they must belong to the same category

application of the principle is heavily contested, especially in the context of the debate regarding whether MFN clauses cover jurisdictional matters.

Traditionally, 'treatment' was interpreted broadly for the purposes of applying MFN clauses. In its final (2015) report on MFN, the ILC provided a helpful taxonomy of different MFN clauses, as far as 'treatment' is concerned:

> The first type is where the MFN obligation relates simply to 'treatment' accorded to the investor or the investments. The Austria-Czech and Slovak Republics agreement is an example of this.
>
> The second type of obligation is where the scope of the treatment to be provided has been broadened by referring to 'all' treatment. One example of this is the Argentina-Spain agreement, which specifies that the MFN provision applies '[i]n all matters governed by this Agreement.'
>
> The third type of obligation is where the term 'treatment' is related to specific aspects of the investment process, such as 'management', 'maintenance', 'use', and 'disposal' of the investment to which MFN treatment applies. In some instances agreements provide for MFN treatment in respect of the 'establishment' of investment, thus providing protection for both the pre-investment period as well as the post-investment period.
>
> The fourth type consists of those cases where MFN treatment is related to specific obligations under the treaty, such as the obligation to provide fair and equitable treatment.
>
> The fifth type of obligation is where MFN treatment is to be provided only to those investors or investments that are 'in like circumstances' or 'in similar situations' to investors or investments with which a comparison is being made.
>
> A sixth type consists of those agreements where a territorial limitation appears to have been introduced. For example, the Italy-Jordan agreement of 21 July 1996 provides that the contracting parties agree to provide MFN treatment 'within the bounds of their own territory.'[115]

However, what constitutes 'treatment' for the purposes of interpreting and applying an MFN clause remains highly contested. Three distinct categories can be identified: (1)

and have the same relationship with the beneficiary State as persons or things within a determined relationship with the third State"' [italics omitted] (ILC 2015 MFN Report, paras 15 and 16. See also *Guris Construction and Engineering Inc and others v Arab Republic of Syria*, ICC Case No 21845/ZF/AYZ, Final Award, 31 August 2020, para 278; *Christian Doutremepuich and Antoine Doutremepuich v Republic of Mauritius*, PCA Case No 2018-37, Award on Jurisdiction, 23 August 2019, para 201; *Daimler Financial Services AG v Argentine Republic*, ICSID Case No ARB/05/1, Award, 22 August 2012, para 211; *Sergei Paushok, CJSC Golden East Company and CJSC Vostokneftegaz Company v Government of Mongolia*, Award on Jurisdiction and Liability, 28 April 2011, para 565; *Quasar de Valors SICAV SA and others (formerly Renta 4 SVSA and others) v Russia*, SCC Case No 24/2007, Award on Preliminary Objections, 20 March 2009, para 89 ('The 1956 case of the *Ambatielos Claim* (*23 ILR 306*) is seminal. It examined the ejusdem generis principle: "the most-favoured nation clause can only attract matter belonging to the same category of subject as that to which the clause itself relates"'); *Wintershall Aktiengesellschaft v Argentine Republic*, ICSID Case No ARB/04/14, Award, 8 December 2008, para 103; *Emilio Agustín Maffezini v Kingdom of Spain*, ICSID Case No ARB/97/7, Decision on Jurisdiction, 25 January 2000, para 49.

[115] ILC, 2015 MFN Report, paras 60–65.

more favourable dispute settlement provisions contained in investment treaties concluded between the Host State and third States; (2) more favourable substantive provisions contained in such treaties; and (3) more favourable 'factual' treatment accorded to investors or investments of third States, emanating from legislative, executive, or judicial measures taken by the Host State at the domestic level.[116]

Regarding the first category, there is currently a trend to limit the meaning of 'treatment' in the relation to the MFN standard by excluding from its scope access matters relating to dispute settlement mechanisms. The application of MFN clauses to dispute settlement matters was traditionally a question which has divided both arbitral tribunals[117] but, as explained above, is outside the scope of this book. Naturally, neither

[116] See Article 4(1) of the 2001 ILC Draft articles on Responsibility of Staes for Internationally Wrongful Acts Draft Articles on State Responsibility: '[t]he conduct of any State organ shall be considered an act of that State under international law, whether the organ exercises legislative, executive, judicial or any other functions, whatever position it holds in the organization of the State, and whatever its character as an organ of the central Government or of a territorial unit of the State'. See also *Rumeli Telekom AS and Telsim Mobil Telekomunikasyon Hizmetleri AS v Republic of Kazakhstan*, ICSID Case No ARB/05/16, Award, 29 July 2008, para 338; *CMS Gas Transmission Company v The Republic of Argentina*, ICSID Case No ARB/01/8, Decision of the Tribunal on Objections to Jurisdiction, 17 July 2003, para 108; *Loewen Group, Inc and Raymond L Loewen v United States of America*, ICSID Case No ARB(AF)/98/3, Decision on Hearing of Respondent's Objection to Competence and Jurisdiction, 5 January 2001, para 70; *Eureko BV v Republic of Poland*, Partial Award, 19 June 2005, para 127; *Noble Ventures, Inc v Romania*, ICSID Case No ARB/01/11, Award, 12 October 2005, para 69; *MCI Power Group LC and New Turbine, Inc v Republic of Ecuador*, ICSID Case No ARB/03/6, Award, 31 July 2007, para 225; De Stefano (n 102) 135.

[117] On whether 'treatment' (in the context of MFN) includes access to arbitration cf *Gas Natural SDG, SA v The Argentine Republic*, ICSID Case No ARB/03/10 Decision of the Tribunal on Preliminary Questions on Jurisdiction, 17 June 2005, para 49 ('[u]nless it appears clearly that the state parties to a BIT or the parties to a particular investment agreement settled on a different method for resolution of disputes that may arise, most-favoured-nation provisions in BITs should be understood to be applicable to dispute settlement'); *Garanti Koza LLP v Turkmenistan*, ICSID Case No ARB/11/20, Decision on the Objection to Jurisdiction for Lack of Consent, 3 July 2013, para 63 ('Assuring a prospective investor that neither he nor his investment will be subjected to treatment less favourable than the treatment accorded to investors from third countries and their investments, insofar as the process available to resolve any disputes with the host country that may arise under the BIT is concerned, certainly seems to create a favourable condition for investment by the investor so protected'); *RosInvestCo Ltd v The Russian Federation*, Award on Jurisdiction, SCC V 079/2005, 5 October 2007, paras 130 ('the submission to arbitration forms a highly relevant part of the corresponding protection for the investor by granting him') and 132 ('an arbitration clause, at least in the context of expropriation, is of the same protective value as any substantive protection afforded by applicable provisions'). The award on the merits in *RosInvest v Russia* was annulled by the SVEA Court of Appeal, Case No T 10060-10, 12 September 2013 on the ground that the arbitral tribunal lacked jurisdiction); see also *Siemens AG v The Argentine Republic*, ICSID Case No ARB/02/8, Decision on Jurisdiction, 3 August 2004, para 102 ('the Treaty itself, together with so many other treaties of investment protection, has as a distinctive feature special dispute settlement mechanisms not normally open to investors. Access to these mechanisms is part of the protection offered under the Treaty. It is part of the treatment of foreign investors and investments and of the advantages accessible through a MFN clause'); *Suez, Sociedad General de Aguas de Barcelona SA and Inter Aguas Servicios Integrales del Agua SA v Argentine Republic*, ICSID Case No ARB/03/17, Decision on Jurisdiction, 16 May 2006, para 57; *Hochtief AG v The Argentine Republic*, ICSID Case No ARB/07/31, Decision on Jurisdiction, 24 October 2011, paras 68 and 72; *Emilio Agustín Maffezini v Kingdom of Spain*, ICSID Case No ARB/97/7, Decision on Jurisdiction, 25 January 2000, para 54; *UP (formerly Le Chèque Déjeuner) and CD Holding Internationale v Hungary*, ICSID Case No ARB/13/35, Decision on Preliminary Issues of Jurisdiction, 3 March 2016, paras 192–193 ('"territory" in the MFN clause cannot be construed as imposing a limitation on the operation of the MFN clause to exclude reference to arbitration that takes place internationally ... It is material that the term "treatment" refers to what is to be accorded to the investor, not the investment. An investor's entitlement to resort to arbitration under a BIT must be construed as an integral part of the treatment accorded to him/her/it'); *Plama Consortium Limited v Republic of Bulgaria*, ICSID Case No ARB/03/24, Decision on Jurisdiction, 8 February 2005, para 223 ('an MFN provision in a basic treaty does not incorporate by reference dispute settlement provisions in whole or in part set forth in another treaty unless the MFN provision in the basic treaty leaves no doubt that the Contracting Parties intended to incorporate them'); *Renta 4 SVSA, Ahorro Corporación Emergentes FI, Ahorro Corporación Eurofondo FI, Rovime Inversiones SICAV SA, Quasar de Valors SICAV SA, Orgor de Valores SICAV SA, GBI 9000 SICAV SA v The Russian Federation*, SCC No 24/200, Award on Preliminary Objections, 20 March 2009, para 119 ('"more favourable" may in principle include accessibility to international fora. Ultimately however their view is that the terms of the Spanish BIT restrict MFN treatment to the realm of FET as understood in international law'); *Les*

question arises in National Treatment claims, for the simple reason that domestic investors cannot benefit from the Host State's investment treaties.

For a relatively long period of time the use of MFN clauses to 'import' more favourable substantive provisions contained in other treaties was uncontroversial. In 2006, the tribunal in *Berschader v Rusia* summarized the conventional wisdom on that matter:

> There is a fundamental difference as to how an MFN clause is generally understood to operate in relation to the material benefits afforded by a BIT, on the one hand, and in relation to dispute resolution clauses, on the other hand. While it is universally agreed that the very essence of an MFN provision in a BIT is to afford to investors all material protection provided by subsequent treaties, it is much more uncertain whether such provisions should be understood to extend to dispute resolution clauses. It is so uncertain, in fact, that the issue has given rise to different outcomes in a number of cases and to extensive jurisprudence on the subject.[118]

Tribunals have allowed investors to invoke MFN clauses contained in the treaty under which they were claiming and, via them, rely on clauses which were either absent from, or more favourable compared to those contained in, that treaty. The opposite is not true. Investors cannot use the MFN clause to rely on the absence of a clause in the treaty between the Host State and the third State, if that clause is contained in the basic treaty.[119] Therefore, by using MFN investors were able to rely on different clauses contained in treaties concluded between the Host State and third States in relation to different obligations, including FET[120] and umbrella

Laboratoires Servier, SAS, Biofarma, SAS and Arts et Techniques du Progres SAS v Republic of Poland, UNCITRAL, Award, 14 February 2012, para 511 ('the MFN provisions in Article 4(1) of the France-Poland BIT do not expand arbitral competence in the present proceedings'); *European American Investment Bank AG (Austria) v Slovak Republic*, UNCITRAL, PCA Case No 2010-17, Award on Jurisdiction, 22 October 2012, para 451 ('the term "treatment" is more apposite to cover substantive standards of treatment than to apply to the provision for investor-State arbitration'); *ST-AD GmbH v The Republic of Bulgaria*, UNCITRAL, Award on Jurisdiction, 18 July 2013, para 394 ('a reference to the words "treatment in the territory of the other Contracting Party" cannot be reconciled with an international arbitral procedure, which is not rooted in the territory'); see also *Impregilo SpA v Argentine Republic*, ICSID Case No ARB/07/17, Decision of the Ad Hoc Committee on the Application for Annulment, 24 January 2014, para 140 ('Neither applying an MFN clause to jurisdictional issues nor refusing to apply it to assume jurisdiction may be considered, *per se*, as a manifest excess of powers'); *Ansung Housing Co, Ltd v People's Republic of China*, ICSID Case No ARB/14/25, Award, 9 March 2017, para 138 ('[a] plain reading of this Article does not extend to MFN treatment for a State's consent to arbitrate with investors and, in particular, not to the temporal limitation period for investor-State arbitration in Article 9(7) of the China-Korea BIT"). See also *Dawood Rawat v Republic of Mauritius*, PCA Case No 2016-20, Award on Jurisdiction, 6 April 2018, para 187: '"Matters" cannot be "bettered" by virtue of MFN clauses; "treatment" of matters may, in accordance with the wording of each relevant MFN clause'.

[118] *Vladimir Berschader and Moïse Berschader v The Russian Federation*, SCC Case No 080/2004, Award, 21 April 2006, para 179. See also A Reinisch 'Most Favoured Nation Treatment' in M Bungenberg and others (eds), *International Investment Law* (CH Beck, Hart, Nomos 2013) 807–845, 820.

[119] *CMS Gas Transmission Company v the Argentine Republic*, Award, ICSID Case No ARB/01/8, 12 May 2005, para 377.

[120] See P Dumberry, 'The Importation of the Fair and Equitable Treatment Standard Through MFN Clauses: An Empirical Study of BITs' (2017) 32 ICSID Review 116. I Tudor, *The Fair and Equitable Treatment Standard in the International Law of Foreign Investment* (OUP 2007) 193 ('[t]he strength of the relationship between FET and MFN is fostered by the possibility that the MFN clause offers the Investors that do not have a FET clause in their BIT to benefit from one to which the host State agreed in a different BIT'); Dumberry (ibid) 136 ('[t]here is very

clauses.[121] In any event, the debate on whether MFN clauses could be used to import FET clauses (in case the basic treaty does not contain a FET clause) is not particularly important from a practical perspective, given that 'the vast majority of investment treaties contains FET clauses'[122] with '[a]lmost all modern investment treaties contain a FET clause'.[123] In *EDF v Argentina* the tribunal concluded without much analysis that 'the MFN clause does in fact permit recourse to the —umbrella clauses of third-country treaties',[124] considering that '[t]o ignore the MFN clause in this case would permit more favourable treatment to investors protected under third countries, which is exactly what the MFN Clause is intended to prevent'.[125] The tribunal in *Arif v Moldova* adopted

wide support in case law (as well as among scholars) for the proposition that a MFN clause contained in a BIT without any FET clause can be used by an investor to claim the benefit of FET protection found in other BITs').

[121] On the issue of umbrella clauses cf eg *SGS Société Générale de Surveillance SA v Islamic Republic of Pakistan*, ICSID Case No ARB/01/13, Decision of the Tribunal on Objections to Jurisdiction, 6 August 2003, paras 163–174; *SGS Société Générale de Surveillance SA v Republic of the Philippines*, ICSID Case No ARB/02/6, Decision of the Tribunal on Objections to on Jurisdiction, 29 January 2004, paras 113–129; *Bureau Veritas, Inspection, Valuation, Assessment and Control, BIVAC BV v Republic of Paraguay*, ICSID Case No ARB/07/9, Decision on Jurisdiction, 29 May 2009, paras 138–141; *Eureko BV v Republic of Poland*, Partial Award, 19 August 2005, para 257, *SGS Société Générale de Surveillance SA v Republic of Paraguay*, ICSID Case No ARB/07/29, Decision on Jurisdiction, 12 February 2010, paras 170–185; *Noble Ventures, Inc v Romania*, ICSID Case No ARB/01/11 Award, 12 October 2005, para 53; *Toto Costruzioni Generali SpA v Republic of Lebanon*, ICSID Case No ARB/07/12, Decision on Jurisdiction, 11 September 2009, paras 200–201; *Bosh International, Inc and B&P, LTD Foreign Investments Enterprise v Ukraine*, Award, ICSID Case No ARB/08/11, 25 October 2012, paras 246–247; *Pan American Energy LLC and BP Argentina Exploration Company v Argentine Republic*, ICSID Case No ARB/03/13, 27 July 2006 Decision on Preliminary Objections, paras 112–113; *Gustav F W Hamester GmbH & Co KG v Republic of Ghana*, Award, ICSID Case No ARB/07/24, 18 June 2010, paras 348–349; *El Paso Energy International Company v Argentine Republic*, ICSID Case No ARB/03/15, Award, 31 October 2011, para 532; *Duke Energy Electroquil Partners and Electroquil SA v Republic of Ecuador*, Award, ICSID Case No ARB/04/19, 18 August 2008, paras 321–325; *Kontinental Conseil Ingénierie v Gabonese Republic*, PCA Case No 2015-25, Award, 23 December 2016, paras 172–190; *Consutel Group SpA in liquidazione v People's Democratic Republic of Algeria*, PCA No 2017-33, Award, 3 February 2020. On umbrella clauses see generally E R Gadelshina, 'Hermeneutic Reflections on the Specific Purpose of Umbrella Clauses' (2013) 14 JWIT 804; J Crawford, 'Treaty and Contract in Investment Arbitration' (2008) 24 Arbitration International 351; A Rigo Sureda, 'The Umbrella Clause' in M Kinnear, G R Fischer, J Minguez Almeida, L F Torres, and M Uran Bidegain (eds), *Building International Investment Law: The First 50 Years of ICSID* (Kluwer Law International, Alphen aan den Rijn 2016) 375–388; J Potts, 'Stabilizing the Role of Umbrella Clauses in Bilateral Investment Treaties: Intent, Relience and Internationalization' (2011) 51 Virginia Journal of International Law 1005; S W Schill, 'Enabling Private Ordering, Function, Scope and Effect of Umbrella Clauses in International Investment Treaties' (2009) 18 Minnesota Journal of International Law 1; OECD, 'Interpretation of the Umbrella Clause in Investment Agreements' (October 2006) Working Papers on International Investment Number 2006/3; J Wong, 'Umbrella Clauses in Bilateral Investment Treaties: of Breaches of Contract, Treaty Violations, and the Divide Between Developing and Developed Countries in Foreign Investment Disputes' (2006) 14 George Mason Law Review 135, 139 (arguing that 'an umbrella clause enables a BIT tribunal to exercise jurisdiction over claims concerning such breaches of contract, which are also BIT violations under the clause, and further permits the tribunal to do so notwithstanding an exclusive forum selection clause in the contract'); TW Wälde, 'The "Umbrella" Clause in Investment Arbitration: a comment on original intentions and recent cases' (2006) 6 JWIT 183; A Sinclair, 'The Origins of the Umbrella Clause in the International Law of Investment Protection' (2004) 20 Arbitration International 411. See also more generally J Ho, *State Responsibility for Breaches of Investment Contracts* (CUP 2018); A Florou, *Contractual Renegotiations and International Investment Arbitration: A Relational Contract Theory Interpretation of Investment Treaties* (Brill Nijhoff 2020); Y Chernykh, *Contract Interpretation in Investment Treaty Arbitration: A Theory of the Incidental Issue* (Martinus Nijhoff 2022).

[122] Dumberry (n 120) 119. Patrick Dumberry examined 1964 BITs and found that only 50 of them did not include any FET clause: P Dumberry, 'Shopping for a Better Deal: The Use of MFN Clauses to Get "Better" Fair and Equitable Treatment Protection' (2017) 33 Arbitration International 1, 1.

[123] Dumberry (n 120) 119.

[124] *EDF International SA, SAUR International SA, and León Participaciones Argentinas SA v Argentine Republic*, ICSID Case No ARB/03/23, Award, 11 June 2012, para 929.

[125] ibid, para 932. However, the tribunal was cautious enough to emphasize that it took 'no position on this debate about the interaction of MFN clauses with jurisdictional and procedural provisions', ibid, para 936. See also T Gazzini and A Tanzi, 'Handle with Care: Umbrella Clauses and MFN Treatment in Investment Arbitration' (2013) 14 JWIT 978.

the same approach holding that 'the umbrella clause' was a substantive right (which can be imported through an MFN) clause and not a jurisdictional right (which cannot).[126] In *MTD v Chile* the tribunal discussed the use of MFN clauses to import more favourable treaty provisions contained in other investment treaties;[127] however, as the ad hoc annulment Committee held, the tribunal in *MTD v Chile*:

> appears to confuse the notion of fair and equitable treatment required by the first part of Article 3(1) of the Malaysia-Chile BIT with the most-favoured-nation treatment which is required by the second half. The most-favoured-nation clause in Article 3(1) is not limited to attracting more favourable levels of treatment accorded to investments from third States only where they can be considered to fall within the scope of the fair and equitable treatment standard. Article 3(1) attracts any more favourable treatment extended to third State investments and does so unconditionally. However, the uncertainty in the Tribunal's handling of Article 3(1) was without incidence for its resolution of the case.[128]

Subsequent developments in the case law of investment tribunals and treaty drafting cast doubt on whether it is possible to use MFN clauses to benefit from more favourable clauses contained in investment treaties concluded between the Host State and third States.[129] As a result, States wishing to exclude the possibility of relying on FET clauses contained in other investment treaties via MFN clauses should explicitly state so in the wording of the MFN clause.[130] This is increasingly the case in newer generation investment treaties. For example CETA specifies that '[s]ubstantive obligations in other

[126] *Mr Franck Charles Arif v Republic of Moldova*, ICSID Case No ARB/11/23, Award, 8 April 2013, paras 395 and 396. In *Arif v Moldova* '[b]oth Parties agree that an MFN clause applies to substantive obligations' ibid, para 396. See also Reinisch and Schreuer (n 41) 751–754.

[127] *MTD Equity Sdn Bhd and MTD Chile SA v Republic of Chile*, ICSID Case No ARB/01/7, Award, 25 May 2004, paras 103–104.

[128] *MTD Equity Sdn Bhd and MTD Chile SA v Republic of Chile*, ICSID Case No ARB/01/7, 21 March 2007, Decision on Annulment, para 64.

[129] See *Sergei Paushok, CJSC Golden East Company and CJSC Vostokneftegaz Company v Government of Mongolia*, Award on Jurisdiction and Liability, UNCITRAL, 28 April 2011, paras 562–573; *Teinver SA, Transportes de Cercanías SA and Autobuses Urbanos del Sur SA v The Argentine Republic*, ICSID Case No ARB/09/1, Award, 21 July 2017, paras 882–892; however, as Batifort and Heath (who in general argue against the possibility of importing substantive standards of treatment via MFN) explain, 'these decisions did not expressly challenge the conventional view that, as a matter of principle, MFN clauses are designed to import standards of treatment from third-party treaties', S Batifort and JB Heath, 'The New Debate on the Interpretation of MFN Clauses in Investment Treaties: Putting the Brakes on Multilateralization' (2017) 111 AJIL 873, 897. The categorical rejection of the possibility of 'importing' substantive standards of treatments via MFN was first articulated in *İçkale İnşaat Limited Şirketi v Turkmenistan*, ICSID Case No ARB/10/24, Award, 8 March 2016, paras 326–332. On the use of MFN clauses to import more favourable substantive treaty standards, see SW Schill, 'MFN Clauses as Bilateral Commitments to Multilateralism—A Reply to Simon Batifort and J Benton Heath' (2018) 111 AJIL 914; D McRae, 'Introduction to the Symposium on Simon Batifort and J Benton Heath, 'The New Debate on the Interpretation of MFN Clauses in Investment Treaties: Putting the Brakes on Multilateralization' (2018) 112 AJIL Unbound 38; A Bjorklund, 'The Enduring But Unwelcome Role of Party Intent in Treaty Interpretation' (2018) 112 AJIL Unbound 44; M Paparinskis, 'MFN Clauses and Substantive Treatment: a Law of Treaties perspective of the "Conventional Wisdom"' (2018) 112 AJIL Unbound 49; F Pérez-Aznar, 'The Fictions and Realities of MFN Clauses in International Investment Agreements' (2018) 112 AJIL Unbound 55; M Waibel, 'Putting the MFN Genie Back in the Bottle' (2018) 112 AJIL Unbound 60; Dumberry (n 120).

[130] Dumberry (n 120). P Dumberry, 'The Importation of "Better" Fair and Equitable Treatment Standard Protection Through MFN Clauses: An Analysis of NAFTA Article 1103' (2017) 4 Transnational Dispute Management.

international investment treaties and other trade agreements do not in themselves constitute "treatment", and thus cannot give rise to a breach of this article, absent measures adopted by a Party pursuant to such obligations'.[131] Likewise, the investment protection chapter of the EU–Viet Nam Investment Protection Agreement provides that the MFN obligation 'shall not be construed as obliging a Party to extend to investors of the other Party or covered investments the benefit of any treatment granted pursuant to any bilateral, regional or international agreement that entered into force before the date of entry into force of this Agreement'.[132] The EU–UK Trade and Cooperation Agreement (TCA) also provides that:

> [f]or greater certainty, the existence of substantive provisions in other international agreements concluded by a Party with a third country, or the mere formal transposition of those provisions into domestic law to the extent that it is necessary in order to incorporate them into the domestic legal order, do not in themselves constitute the 'treatment' referred to in paragraphs 1 and 2. Measures of a Party pursuant to those provisions may constitute such treatment and thus give rise to a breach of this Article.[133]

This is also the case with the Protocol on Investment of the AfCFTA.[134] Canada's 2021 Model BIT provides that '[s]ubstantive obligations in other international investment treaties and other trade agreements do not in themselves constitute "treatment", and thus cannot give rise to a breach of this Article, absent measures adopted or maintained by a Party pursuant to those obligations'.[135] The same approach is followed in the 2019 Dutch Model BIT.[136] As a result, States wishing to exclude the possibility of relying on FET clauses contained in other investment treaties via MFN clauses must explicitly state so in the wording of the MFN clause.[137]

Consistent with this trend in treaty drafting arbitral tribunal also begun taking a more cautious approach regarding the application of MFN clauses to more favourable treaty standards contained in other investment treaties concluded between the Host

[131] CETA, Article 8.7(4). According to Daigremont this novel approach is positive and aims at combatting treaty shopping, C Crépet Daigremont, 'Most Favoured Nation Treatment' in MM Mbengue and S Schacherer (eds), *Foreign Investment Under the Comprehensive Economic and Trade Agreement (CETA)* (Springer 2019) 71–94, 88.

[132] Investment Protection Agreement between the European Union and its Member States and the Socialist Republic of Viet Nam (signed 30 June 2019, not yet entered into force), Article 2.4(3).

[133] EU–UK TCA (signed 30 December 2020, entered into force on 1 May 2021 (UKTS 2021 No 8)), Article 130(5).

[134] Protocol on Investment to the Agreement Establishing the AfCFTA (Draft January 2023), Article 14(3).

[135] Canada's 2021 Foreign Investment Promotion and Protection Agreement (FIPA), Article 6(7).

[136] Netherlands model Investment Agreement, 22 March 2019 (2019 Dutch Model BIT), Article 8(3): 'Substantive obligations in other international investment and trade agreements do not in themselves constitute "treatment", and thus cannot give rise to a breach of paragraph 2 of this Article, absent measures adopted or maintained by a Contracting Party pursuant to those obligations.' See also E De Brabandere, 'The 2019 Dutch Model Bilateral Investment Treaty: Navigating the Turbulent Ocean of Investment Treaty Reform' (2021) 36 ICSID Review 319.

[137] Dumberry (n 120). P Dumberry, 'The Importation of "Better" Fair and Equitable Treatment Standard Protection Through MFN Clauses: An Analysis of NAFTA Article 1103' (2017) 4 Transnational Dispute Management.

State and third countries. In *UAB v Latvia*, although the tribunal exercised judicial economy and avoided pronouncing on the issue,[138] it did hold that:

> the specific formulation of the MFN clause making a host State's obligation to grant MFN treatment 'subject to its laws and international agreements' casts doubt whether it can be relied upon to import standards contained in other treaties at all because it may be limited to *de facto* treatment under national law.[139]

In like manner, the *Institute de Droit International* (IDI) adopted in its 2013 session held in Tokyo, a Resolution on investment treaty arbitration. According to Article 12 of this Resolution, 'MFN treatment required by an investment treaty which does not contain an umbrella clause does not apply to an umbrella clause included in a treaty concluded by the host State with a third country'.[140]

At the same time, there are also indications in recent awards that the presumption in favour of the application of MFN to treaty obligations remains strong. For example, in *Guris v Syria* the tribunal held that:

> [t]he natural, ordinary meaning of the terms 'treatment accorded' in Article III(2) [of the Turkey–Syria BIT providing for MFN treatment] encompasses not only treatment that has in fact been accorded but also treatment that is legally required to be accorded. Such a requirement may arise from investment treaties between the host State and third States (as it may also arise under domestic law, given that the terms of Article III(2) are unqualified). This is indeed an uncontroversial proposition in international investment law, as well as general international law.[141]

Likewise, in *Consutel v Algeria* the tribunal relied on *Arif v Moldava* held that MFN clauses can be used to import umbrella clauses.[142]

Finally, only in relatively few cases MFN claims concern de facto treatment on the part of the Host State, that is, treatment in relation to measures taken by the legislative, judicial, or executive branches of the State.[143] The vast majority of MFN cases revolve

[138] *UAB E energija v Republic of Latvia*, ICSID Case No ARB/12/33, Award, 22 December 2017, para 1111.

[139] ibid, para 1112.

[140] Article 12, IDI, Session of Tokyo 'Legal Aspects of Recourse to Arbitration by an Investor Against the Authorities of the Host State under Inter-State Treaties', 13 September 2013, available at <https://www.idi-iil.org/app/uploads/2017/06/2013_tokyo_en.pdf>. See also *Impregilo SpA v Argentine Republic*, ICSID Case No ARB/07/17, Award, 21 June 2011, para 184: 'The substantive protection of the MFN clause is very wide in so far as it relates to all matters regulated by the BIT. Nevertheless, the reference to matters regulated by the BIT sets an outer limit, and it is debatable whether contractual breaches are matters regulated by the BIT.'

[141] *Mr Idris Yamantürk, Mr Tevfik Yamantürk, Mr Müsfik Hamdi Yamantürk, Güriş İnşaat ve Mühendislik Anonim Şirketi (Güris Construction and Engineering Inc) v Syrian Arab Republic*, ICC Case No 21845/ZF/AYZ, Final Award, 31 August 2020, para 252; see also ibid, paras 252–255.

[142] *Consutel Group SpA in liquidazione v People's Democratic Republic of Algeria*, PCA No 2017-33, Award, 3 February 2020, para 359; see also J Chaisse, 'Consutel Group SpA in liquidazione v People's Democratic Republic of Algeria: Umbrella Clauses and Breaches of Contract by Public Entities' (2022) 37 ICSID Review 638, 641–643.

[143] Reinisch and Schreuer (n 41) 687.

around substantive standards of treatment contained in investment treaties concluded between the Host State and third States.[144] One exception is *Parkerings v Lithuania*.[145]

Some but not all MFN clauses refer to both investments and investors; other MFN clauses refer only to investments. Such difference could be without a practical effect.[146] The same conclusion was reached by the tribunal in *Daimler v Argentina*:

> [t]he parallel breadth of these definitions suggests that the (basic) Treaty's grant of MFN treatment to both investors and investments was intended to be complementary and not differential. The MFN guarantees offered to the two categories might even be co-extensive, for it is difficult to imagine a type of MFN treatment enjoyed by an investment that could not correspondingly be claimed by a qualifying investor in connection with that investment.[147]

However, Newcombe and Paradell argue that:

> whether the MFN clause applies to investments, investors or both might be decisive because an investor might argue that it receives less favourable treatment where 'investment', in the basic treaty, is defined more narrowly than 'investment' in the third-part treaty. Thus, if the MFN clause applies to investors, the investor might argue that it is entitled to the more favourable treatment in the third-party treaty—the wider definition of investment.[148]

The conventional view is that MFN clauses cannot be used to broaden the scope of the notion of 'investment', irrespective of whether the MFN clause refers to investors and/or investments.[149] This approach seems to reflect a broader consensus: MFN clauses cannot be used to alter the scope of jurisdiction *ratione personae* of arbitral tribunals by importing definitions of 'investor' or 'investment' from other treaties.[150] This is because, as explained by one arbitral tribunal:

[144] DD Caron and E Shirlow, 'Most-Favored-Nation Treatment: Substantive Protection' in M Kinnear and others (eds), *Building International Investment Law: The First 50 Years of ICSID* (Kluwer Law International 2016) 399–414, 404.

[145] *Parkerings-Compagniet AS v Republic of Lithuania*, ICSID Case No ARB/05/8 Award, 11 September 2007. See also below Section 3.3.1.2.

[146] See *MNSS BV and Recupero Credito Acciaio NV v Montenegro*, ICSID Case No ARB(AF)/12/8, Award, 4 May 2016, paras 359 and 360; see also Wang (n 108) 77.

[147] *Daimler Financial Services AG v Argentine Republic*, ICSID Case No ARB/05/1, Award, 22 August 2012, para 232.

[148] Newcombe and Paradell (n 4) 222.

[149] However, it seems that there is consensus that MFN can 'broaden the scope of the substantive protection granted to the eligible investments of eligible investors; it cannot legitimately be used to broaden the definition of the investors or the investments themselves', *HICEE BV v Slovak Republic*, UNCITRAL, Partial Award, 23 May 2011, para 149 (emphasis in the original); see also *HICEE v Slovakia*, UNCITRAL, Dissenting Opinion of Judge Charles N Brower, 23 May 2011, para 43 ('the MFN clause, cannot be used to alter the scope of the definition of "investments" in the Treaty'); see also *Vannessa Ventures Ltd v Bolivarian Republic of Venezuela*, ICSID Case No ARB(AF)/04/6, Award, 16 January 2013, para 133 ('[t]he benefit of the MFN provision in Article III of the Canada-Venezuela BIT can only be asserted in respect of investments that are within the scope of Article I(f) of the Canada-Venezuela BIT to begin with. The MFN clause cannot be used to expand the category of investments to which the Canada-Venezuela BIT applies').

[150] *PV Investors v Kingdom of Spain*, PCA Case No 2012-14, Preliminary Award on Jurisdiction, 13 October 2014, paras 281–288; *Metal-Tech Ltd v Republic of Uzbekistan*, ICSID Case No ARB/10/3, Award, 4 October 2013,

> [e]ach treaty defines what it considers a protected investment and who is entitled to that protection, and definitions can change from treaty to treaty. In this situation, resort to the specific text of the MFN Clause is unnecessary because it applies only to the treatment accorded to such defined investment, but not to the definition of 'investment' itself.[151]

Finally, unless specifically excluded MFN applies to public procurement matters.[152]

Another issue in relation to the scope of application of MFN clauses concerns their prospective or retrospective effect. In general tribunals accept that the use of MFN clauses cover not only treaties concluded by the Host States and third States after the basic treaty containing the MFN clause entered into force, but also those treaties which were concluded before the entry into force of the basic treaty,[153] although the analysis in some cases is clearer (and more persuasive) than in others.[154]

Finally, MFN treatment could apply to both the pre-establishment and the post-establishment phase. This matter depends on the specific wording of each MFN clause. However, in general, North American treaties, such as NAFTA,[155] the US–Mexico–Canada Agreement (USMCA),[156] and Canadian and US BITs,[157] extend the scope of

para 145 ('[a]s a general matter, the Tribunal notes that, ordinarily, an MFN clause cannot be used to import a more favorable definition of investment contained in another BIT'); *HICEE BV v Slovak Republic*, UNCITRAL, Partial Award, 23 May 2011, para 149. See also *Vladimir Berschader and Moïse Berschader v The Russian Federation*, SCC Case No 080/2004, Award, 21 April 2006, para 188; *Vannessa Ventures Ltd v Bolivarian Republic of Venezuela*, ICSID Case No ARB(AF)/04/6, Award, 16 January 2013, para 133.

[151] *Société Générale in respect of DR Energy Holdings Limited and Empresa Distribuidora de Electricidaddel Este, SA v The Dominican Republic*, Award on Preliminary Objections to Jurisdiction, LCIA Case No UN 7927, 19 September 2008, para 41.

[152] NAFTA, Article 1108(7): 'Articles 1102, 1103 and 1107 do not apply to: (a) procurement by a Party or a state enterprise; or (b) subsidies or grants provided by a Party or a state enterprise, including government supported loans, guarantees and insurance'; see also *ADF Group Inc v United States of America*, ICSID Case No ARB(AF)/00/1, Award, 9 January 2003, paras 165–166.

[153] *Vladimir Berschader and Moïse Berschader v The Russian Federation*, SCC Case No 080/2004, Award, 21 April 2006, para 179; *Bayindir Insaat Turizm Ticaret Ve Sanayi AS v Islamic Republic of Pakistan*, ICSID Case No. ARB/03/29, Award, 27 August 2009, para 155; see also Reinisch and Schreuer (n 41) 713–714; Caron and Shirlow (n 144).

[154] Cf *UP (formerly Le Chèque Déjeuner) and CD Holding Internationale v Hungary*, ICSID Case No ARB/13/35, Decision on Preliminary Issues of Jurisdiction, 3 March 2016, para 175 ('the MFN clause in the France–Hungary BIT had in general contemplation treatment that may be afforded to others in the future that is not afforded to the beneficiaries of the BIT then being concluded') and ibid, para 173 ('unless expressly so provided in the BIT, MFN clauses are not retrospective clauses, included in the BITs for purposes of ensuring that the parties incorporate hereby treatment afforded in BITs previously concluded'). See also Reinisch and Schreuer (n 41) 715.

[155] NAFTA, Article 1103:

> 1. Each Party shall accord to investors of another Party treatment no less favorable than that it accords, in like circumstances, to investors of any other Party or of a non-Party *with respect to the establishment, acquisition, expansion*, management, conduct, operation, and sale or other disposition of investments.
> 2. Each Party shall accord to investments of investors of another Party treatment no less favorable than that it accords, in like circumstances, to investments of investors of any other Party or of a non-Party *with respect to the establishment, acquisition, expansion*, management, conduct, operation, and sale or other disposition of investments.
>
> [Emphasis added.]

[156] USMCA, Article 14.5(1) and (2) reproducing the text contained in Article 1103(1) and (2) of the NAFTA.

[157] See eg Treaty between the United States of America and the Oriental Republic of Uruguay concerning the Encouragement and Reciprocal Protection of Investment (signed 4 November 2005, entered into force 31 October 2006) 2005 (US –Uruguay BIT), Article 5; Agreement between Canada and Mongolia for the Promotion

application of MFN clauses to the pre-establishment phase, while European investment treaties offer MFN treatment only post-establishment.[158]

3.2.1.3 Non-impairment Clauses

Unlike National Treatment and MFN Treatment,[159] tribunals have focused more on other aspects of the relevant legal test in analysing non-impairment clauses (in particular, likeness and public policy reasons),[160] rather than the comparison between the treatment accorded to the foreign investor and other investors.

Like in National Treatment and MFN analysis, the term 'measure' is construed broadly for the purposes of interpreting non-impairment clauses. The ICJ held that, 'in its ordinary sense the word [measure] is wide enough to cover any act, step or proceeding'.[161] Investment tribunals relied on this ICJ dictum (despite the fact that it was made in a different context) in constructing the term 'measures' in the context of non-impairment clauses.[162] The tribunal in *Occidental v Ecuador* seems to suggest that the difference between non-impairment clauses and other treaty standards including National Treatment[163] is that the former requires actual 'impairment' of the foreign investment:

> [t]he claim that these measures are also discriminatory has a meaning under this Article [containing a non-impairment clause] only to the extent that impairment has occurred. Otherwise the claim, as the Respondent has argued, is the same as that concerning other articles of the Treaty that will be examined below.[164]

This is echoed in subsequent decisions. An Energy Charter Treaty (ECT) tribunal distinguished between non-impairment and FET clauses on the basis of whether actual impairment ('harm') was required or not:

> [t]he Tribunal concurs that reasonableness and non-discrimination imply the same obligations on behalf of the host State under the FET and non-impairment standards. This being so, while a FET breach exists irrespective of the harm it may have caused, the non-impairment standard, as its name indicates, implies the existence of

and Protection of Investments (signed 8 September 2016, entered into force 24 February 2017) 2016 (Canada–Mongolia BIT), Article 5. See also 2021 Canada Model BIT, Article 6.

[158] Reinisch and Schreuer (n 41) 695; Wang (n 108) 80–82. See also A Joubin-Bret, 'Admission and Establishment in the Context of Investment Protection' in A Reinisch (ed), *Standards of Investment Protection* (OUP 2008) 9–28.

[159] Discussed above in Sections 3.2.1.1 and 3.2.1.2.

[160] Reinisch and Schreuer (n 41) 836.

[161] *Fisheries Jurisdiction (Spain v Canada)*, Jurisdiction of the Court, Judgment, [1998] ICJ Rep 432, 460, para 66.

[162] *Mr Idris Yamantürk, Mr Tevfik Yamantürk, Mr Müsfik Hamdi Yamantürk, Güriş İnşaat ve Mühendislik Anonim Şirketi (Güris Construction and Engineering Inc) v Syrian Arab Republic*, ICC Case No 21845/ZF/AYZ, Final Award, 31 August 2020, para 243; *Saluka Investments BV v The Czech Republic*, UNCITRAL, Partial Award, 17 March 2006, para 459.

[163] On whether a *de minimis* rules apply in the context of National Treatment, see Section 3.2.1.1.

[164] *Occidental Exploration and Production Company v* Ecuador, LCIA Case No UN 3467, Final Award, 1 July 2004, para 165.

> an impairment, i.e., of harm. If there was no impairment then it serves no purpose to inquire into the reasonable and non-discriminatory nature of a measure.[165]

It is not clear how significant such impairment should be to give rise to a treaty violation. On the one hand, certain tribunals minimize the practical importance of the requirement of actual impairment holding that it does not need to be significant. In *ESPF v Italy* the tribunal held that:

> there is no requirement that the impairment be 'significant' in order for a claim to succeed. Rather, impairment 'in any way' is all that is required. In the majority's view, the ECT protects against any impairment of the operation, management, maintenance, use, enjoyment or disposal of an investment, provided it is caused by unreasonable or discriminatory measures.[166]

In *Saluka v Czech Republic* the tribunal held that '"[i]mpairment" means, according to its ordinary meaning (Article 31 of the Vienna Convention on the Law of Treaties), any negative impact or effect caused by "measures" taken by the Czech Republic'.[167] However, other tribunals agreed with respondent States' submissions 'that a breach of this standard requires the impairment caused by the discriminatory or unreasonable measure to be significant'.[168] The reason given for rejecting a lower threshold for impairment is the need to accord deference to the Host State's regulatory autonomy.[169]

In *Noble Ventures v Romania* (and in the context of assessing compliance with non-discrimination under FET and the prohibition against arbitrary or discriminatory measures), after noting that '[t]he parties have not provided the Tribunal with any information that comparable proceedings have been initiated against investors from other countries or in particular against US investors', the tribunal held that 'that in itself does not exclude the possibility that the proceedings constituted a discriminatory measure because it is possible for a single measure to be discriminatory if proof to that effect is given'.[170]

Finally, as with all international legal obligations, compliance with domestic law does not constitute a justification for their breach.[171] In fact, domestic law could be the

[165] *Muszynianka Spółka z Ograniczona Odpowiedzialnoscia v Slovak Republic*, PCA Case No 2017-08, Award, 7 October 2020, para 646.

[166] *ESPF Beteiligungs GmbH, ESPF Nr.2 Austria Beteiligungs GmbH and InfraClass Energie 5 GmbH & Co KG v Italian Republic*, ICSID Case No ARB/16/5, Award, 14 September 2020, para 700.

[167] *Saluka Investments BV v The Czech Republic*, UNCITRAL, Partial Award, 17 March 2006, para 458.

[168] *Electrabel SA v Republic of Hungary*, ICSID Case No ARB/07/19, Decision on Jurisdiction, Applicable Law and Liability 30 November 2012, para 7.152.

[169] *Sun Reserve Luxco Holdings SRL v Italy*, SCC Case No 132/2016, Final Award, 25 March 2020, para 939: 'not every marginal negative effect suffered by investors will be covered under the Impairment Clause in Article 10(1) ECT. . . . Setting the standard for "impairment" so low shall not afford the due deference to a host State's regulatory authority and shall run counter to the overall high standard for the FET obligation, which forms part of the same legal provision in the ECT, i.e., Article 10(1) ECT.'

[170] *Noble Ventures, Inc v Romania*, Award, ICSID Case No ARB/01/11, 12 October 2005, para 180.

[171] See *Alabama Claims (USA v Great Britain)*, reprinted in 29 RIAA 125, 131 (14 September 1872); *SS Wimbledon (UK, France, Italy and Japan v Germany)*, Judgment, 1923 PCIJ (ser A) No 1, paras 29–30; *Factory at Chorzów (Germany v Poland)*, Judgment, 1928 PCIJ (ser A) No. 17, at 81; *Interpretation of the Convention Between Greece and Bulgaria Respecting Reciprocal Emigration*, Advisory Opinion, 1930 PCIJ (ser B) No 17, para

source of the breach.[172] The breach of a non-impairment clause does not need it to stem out of a single act or measure; it could very well be the cumulative effect of several acts of the Host State.[173]

3.2.1.4 Fair and Equitable Treatment

The 'less favourable treatment' aspect of the non-discrimination component of the FET obligation has not received much attention. In *Air Canada v Venezuela*, Venezuela's failure to approve repeated applications by Air Canada for an Authorization for Foreign Currency Acquisition (AAD), even though 'Venezuela entered into at least ten agreements with other international airlines',[174] was found to be a violation of the non-discrimination aspect of the FET.[175] As Jacob and Schill explain:

> [w]hat emerges is that it is difficult to draw a line between legal and illegal discrepancies. Evidently differential treatment alone is insufficient. This is what the frequent addition of qualifiers such as arbitrariness, gross unfairness or injustice seeks to bring out in this context. The danger of relying solely on these in the determination of an infringement of FET is circularity—i.e. finding unfair conduct by calling it not fair—but it is the combination with divergent treatment that can enable a more meaningful assessment in this context.[176]

A specific aspect of non-discrimination in the context of FET concerns judicial proceedings. Any deviation from the universally recognized principle of equality of treatment between the parties to a judicial process[177] will most likely amount to a breach of

81; *Free Zones of Upper Savoy and the District of Gex (France v Switzerland)*, Judgment, 1932 PCIJ (ser A/B) No 46, para 223; *Treatment of Polish Nationals and Other Persons of Polish Origin or Speech in the Danzig Territory*, Advisory Opinion, 1932 PCIJ (ser A/B) No 44, para 62; *Reparation for Injuries Suffered in the Service of the United Nations, Advisory Opinion* [(1949]) ICJ Rep 174, 180; *Fisheries case (UK v Norway)* [(1951]) ICJ Rep 116, 132; *Nottebohm case (Second Phase) (Liechtenstein v Guatemala)*, Judgment (1955) ICJ Rep 4, 20–21; *Application of the Convention of 1902 Governing the Guardianship of Infants (Netherlands v Sweden)*, Judgment, [1958] ICJ Rep 55, 67; *Applicability of the Obligation to Arbitrate Under Section 21 of the United Nations Headquarters Agreement of 26 June 1947*, Advisory Opinion [(1988]) ICJ Rep 12, para 57; Draft articles on. Responsibility of States for Internationally Wrongful Acts, with commentaries (2001), Articles 3 and 31; VCLT, Article 27. See also *Glamis Gold, Ltd v The United States of America*, UNCITRAL, Final Award, 8 June 2009 ('the unlawfulness of an action according to municipal law will not necessarily entail a violation of international law, the converse also is true: the legality of an act under domestic law does not presuppose its legality under international law').

[172] Dolzer, Kriebaum, and Schreuer (n 2) 250.

[173] *Tethyan Copper Company Pty Limited v Islamic Republic of Pakistan, ICSID Case No ARB/12/1, Decision on Jurisdiction and Liability*, 10 November 2017, para 1365.

[174] *Air Canada v Bolivarian Republic of Venezuela*, ICSID Case No ARB(AF)/17/1, Award, 13 September 2021, para 465.

[175] ibid, para 469 (Venezuela 'discriminated against Claimant and treated it inconsistently, if not arbitrarily, compared to other international airlines with similar pending AAD requests during the same period discriminated against Claimant and treated it inconsistently, if not arbitrarily, compared to other international airlines with similar pending AAD requests during the same period').

[176] M Jacob and SW Schill, 'Standards of Protection: Fair and Equitable Treatment: Content, Practice, Method' in M Bungenberg and others (eds), *International Investment Law* (CH Beck, Hart, Nomos 2015) 700–763, 733.

[177] See *Judgments of the Administrative Tribunal of the ILO upon complaints made against UNESCO* (Advisory Opinion) [1956] ICJ Rep 77, 86; *Maritime International Nominees Establishment v Republic of Guinea*, ICSID Case No ARB/84/4, Decision on Annulment, 14 December 1989, para 5.06. See eg Universal Declaration of Human Rights (General Assembly Resolution A/RES/217A (III), adopted 10 December 1948), Article 10: 'Everyone is entitled in full equality to a fair and public hearing by an independent and impartial tribunal, in the determination of

FET.[178] This was precisely the question in *Loewen v USA*, where the tribunal held that '[a] decision which is in breach of municipal law and is discriminatory against the foreign litigant amounts to manifest injustice according to international law'.[179] Naturally, consistency with domestic law does not preclude a violation of discrimination.[180] Finally, while this statement was made in the context of a claim for denial of justice, there is no reason to limit its application to that particular aspect of the FET.

3.2.1.5 Expropriation

When examining discrimination in the context of direct expropriation the comparison between the treatment received by the investor on the one hand, and other domestic or foreign investors on the other, is rather more straightforward. The property belonging to the claimant would have been formally expropriated while similarly situated property belonging to other investors would have been spared. In the case of indirect or regulatory expropriation, the comparison could be slightly more complicated, as the investor must establish that the effect of the measures adopted by the Host State amounted to expropriation, and this was not the case in relation to the property of other investors in like circumstances.

3.2.2 The Normative Argument of this Book

Viewing non-discrimination obligations contained in investment treaties as belonging to the 'disparate treatment' or 'direct' discrimination paradigm rather than the 'disparate impact' or 'indirect' discrimination paradigm,[181] has important implications for the interpretation of the second element of the legal test for finding violations of the non-discrimination obligations which concerns the concept of 'treatment'.

First, because discrimination obligations in international investment law prohibit discrimination based on nationality (or another protected ground) rather than impact-based discrimination,[182] a comparison between individual investors (not groups) is required.[183] The two methods of comparison, individual or group, are often called in the WTO context 'diagonal test' and 'asymmetrical test' respectively.[184] Although some authors suggest that the issue is controversial,[185] the prevailing view in the case law and

his rights and obligations and of any criminal charge against him'. See generally A Clooney and P Webb, *The Right to a Fair Trial in International Law* (OUP 2021).

[178] Reinisch and Schreuer (n 41) 419; J Paulsson, *Denial of Justice in International Law* (CUP 2005) 192–195.

[179] *Loewen Group, Inc and Raymond L Loewen v United States of America*, ICSID Case No ARB(AF)/98/3, Award, 26 June 2003, para 135; see also SW Schill, 'Fair and Equitable Treatment, the Rule of Law, and Comparative Public Law' in SW Schill (ed), *International Investment Law and Comparative Public Law* (OUP 2010) 151–182, 167.

[180] Paulsson (n 178) 192.

[181] See Chapter 2.

[182] See the analysis in Chapter 2, Section 2.2.

[183] See Chapter 2.

[184] See eg L Ehring, 'De Facto Discrimination in World Trade Law National and Most-Favoured-Nation Treatment—or Equal Treatment?' (2002) 36 Journal of World Trade 921.

[185] Kurtz (n 15) 110–134; Mitchell, Heaton, and Henckels (n 10) 151: 'This issue is sufficiently controversial that we disagree amongst ourselves on the best approach under IIAs.' According to Herdegen, '[i]t is a controversial

in theory is that in international investment law (unlike WTO law) the comparison is between the foreign investor and the domestic investor receiving more favourable treatment.[186] The choice between the two different approaches (the 'asymmetrical' and 'diagonal' test) has profound consequences on States' regulatory autonomy and is highly indicative of the broader system of values endorsed and promoted by the arbitrators. The 'asymmetrical test' gives more regulatory space to States, while the 'diagonal test' is more intrusive.

Second, as in anti-discrimination law and practice in the US and other legal systems, 'treatment' in international investment law is to be interpreted broadly, covering both de jure and de facto discrimination.

Finally, regarding the gravity of the 'less favourable treatment', despite some sporadic suggestions to the contrary in the case law,[187] the most persuasive view is that there is no threshold for finding violation of non-National Treatment obligations.[188] However, less significant breaches of non-discrimination obligations could lead to lower or no damages at the quantum stage.

3.3 Discrimination 'Because of' a Protected Ground: Discriminatory Intent and Public Policy Justifications

The case law of investment treaty tribunals is not settled in relation to two key questions regarding the legal test for establishing violations of National Treatment and other non-discrimination obligations contained in investment treaties. The first question is whether the legal test for discrimination comprises only analysis of 'likeness'[189] and

issue whether the principle of national treatment obliges the host State to treat the foreign investor no less favourably than the national investors in general or whether the national treatment standard requires the best treatment accorded to any national investor', M Herdegen, *Principles of International Economic Law* (2nd edn, OUP 2016) 452.

[186] See also F Ortino, 'From "Non-discrimination" to "Reasonableness": A Paradigm Shift in International Economic Law' (Jean Monnet Working Paper 2005), available at <http://ssrn.com/ abstract=922524>, 22–24; see also F Ortino, 'From "Non-discrimination" to "Reasonableness": A Paradigm Shift in International Economic Law' in F Palermo and others (eds), *Globalization, Technologies and Legal Revolution: Liber Amicorum in Memory of Sergio Ortino* (Nomos Verlagsgesellschaft 2012) 13–60; N DiMascio and J Pauwelyn, 'Nondiscrimination in Trade and Investment Treaties: Worlds Apart or Two Sides of the Same Coin?' (2008) 102 AJIL 48, 77; Diebold (n 6) 844; Mitchell, Heaton, and Henckels (n 10) 151: 'in the view of one of the co-authors (who favours the single-investor approach), it is neither clear—nor articulated—why the purpose of national treatment and MFN treatment obligations requires a pooled approach over a single-investor approach. Nor is it clear why the *measure* should mean that identifying less favourable treatment requires comparing the treatment of the complaining investor whit multiple domestic or other foreign investors (rather than any one treated more favourably). Indeed, in the view of this author, the latter suggestion appears to be a *non-sequitur*'.

[187] *Loewen Group, Inc and Raymond L Loewen v United States of America*, ICSID Case No ARB(AF)/98/3, Award, 26 June 2003, para 139 ('Article 1102 is direct [sic] only to nationality-based discrimination and that it proscribes only demonstrable and significant indications of bias and prejudice on the basis of nationality, of a nature and consequence likely to have affected the outcome of the trial'). See also Reinisch and Schreuer (n 41) 663.

[188] One could argue in favour of the existence of a de minimis rule in relation to other obligations contained in investment treaties, such as the protection of legitimate expectations under FET, see *Voltaic Network GmbH v Czech Republic*, PCA Case No 2014-20, Award, 15 May 2019, para 500; P Ranjan, 'Investor-State Dispute Settlement and Tax Matters: Limitations on State's Sovereign Right to Tax' (2023) 31 Asia Pacific Law Review 219, 219.

[189] Discussed in Section 3.1.

'less favourable treatment'[190] or an inquiry into the purpose of the measure in question is also necessary.

Despite the plethora of arbitral awards dealing with questions of (non-)discrimination, the answer is not yet clear.[191] As Ortino explains:

> [f]urthermore, and fundamentally, when the NT [National Treatment] principle is extended to cover national measures with detrimental impact (on foreign investors), the normative focus of the principle is not on the detrimental impact per se, rather on whether the measure (with detrimental impact) is related to a legitimate regulatory purpose (namely, is justified on public policy grounds). The fact that the national measure has detrimental impact becomes a 'threshold' question, where the justification analysis is the real key test.[192]

The second, distinct but closely related, question is whether discriminatory intent is necessary to establish violations of non-discrimination obligations in international investment law. Again, the relevant jurisprudence (which is discussed in detail in Section 3.3.1) has not provided an unequivocal answer. According to Weiler, '[t]he most significant controversy arising out of this provision [National Treatment], which has not been pled as frequently as the afore-mentioned two standards, concerns whether a claimant must establish that the impugned conduct was the result of a governmental intention to treat investors differently on the basis of the nationality'.[193] These questions are intrinsically linked with questions regarding the allocation of the burden of proof and the appropriate standard of proof, which will be explored separately in the next chapter (in Section 4.1 and Section 4.3 respectively). The argument of this book (set out in Section 3.3.2) is that, after establishing 'likeness' and 'less favourable treatment', the tribunal must examine whether such treatment is connected to a protected ground (such as nationality) or a legitimate policy objective. This flows from understanding non-discrimination in international investment treaty arbitration as a form of disparate treatment or direct discrimination.[194]

190 Discussed in Section 3.2.

191 As Schreuer observes with regard to the prohibition against arbitrary and/or discriminatory measures, '[i]n general, tribunals seem to favour an objective approach that looks at the discriminatory consequences of a particular measure. An intention to discriminate appears to be secondary ... However, there are cases that indicate that discriminatory intent is not entirely irrelevant', Schreuer (n 47) 196–197; A Bjorklund, 'The National Treatment Obligation' in K Yannaca-Small, *Arbitration Under International Investment Agreements: A Guide to the Key Issues* (2nd edn, OUP 2018) 532–561, 552–554.

192 F Ortino, 'Non-Discriminatory Treatment in Investment Disputes' in P-M Dupuy, F Francioni, and E-U Petersmann (eds), *Human Rights in International Investment Arbitration* (OUP 2009) 344–366, 353.

193 Weiler (n 7) 16.

194 See Chapter 2, Section 2.2.

3.3.1 Case Law

3.3.1.1 National Treatment

As Kurtz rightly observes, '[t]he reading of national treatment as a limit on purposeful protectionism has not, however, found uniform endorsement in the jurisprudence to date'.[195] Essentially, '[w]hile there is some uncertainty on where justification fits within the analytical framework—States view it as an aspect of inquiry into likeness, tribunals tend to apply it as a separate step of analysis—it is accepted as a relevant, and at time decisive, consideration'.[196]

Some tribunals clearly distinguish between, and proceed to assess discrimination claims in, three steps relating to (i) likeness, (ii) less favourable treatment, and (iii) the existence of discriminatory intent or the absence of rational justification(s).[197] For example, in *ADM v Mexico* the tribunal held that '[p]ursuant to the ordinary meaning of Article 1102 [of NAFTA], the Arbitral Tribunal shall: (i) identify the relevant subjects for comparison; (ii) consider the treatment each comparator receives; and (iii) consider any factors that may justify any differential treatment'.[198] In *Genin v Estonia*, the tribunal held that it was necessary for the claimants to prove that the less favourable treatment (in that case the revocation of a banking licence) 'was done with the intention to harm the Bank or any of the Claimants in this arbitration, or to treat them in a discriminatory way'.[199] The same idea can be found in *ADM v Mexico* where the tribunal held that '[n]ationality discrimination is established by showing that a foreign investor has *unreasonably* been treated less favourably than domestic investors in like in similar circumstances'.[200]

Other tribunals did not consider necessary to examine whether the measure is motivated by discriminatory intent or justified by valid policy reasons and, instead, they focus solely on 'likeness' and 'less favourable treatment'.[201] Some tribunals accept that policy considerations are relevant for establishing a violation of National Treatment,

[195] Kurtz (n 15) 273.

[196] CL Lim, J Ho, and M Paparinskis, *International Investment Law and Arbitration: Commentary, Awards and other Materials* (2nd edn, CUP 2021) 397.

[197] ibid, 373 ('Tribunals tend to approach claims of national treatment by asking three questions: (1) are the circumstances like, (2) is the treatment different, and (3) is there a reasonable justification for that?'); Reinisch and Schreuer (n 41) 623.

[198] *Archer Daniels Midland Company and Tate & Lyle Ingredients Americas, Inc v United Mexican States*, ICSID Case No ARB(AF)/04/5, Award, 21 November 2007, para 196; *Methanex Corporation v the United States of America*, UNCITRAL, Final Award of the Tribunal on Jurisdiction and Merits, 3 August 2005, Part IV, Chapter B, para 13; *Bayindir Insaat Turizm Ticaret Ve Sanayi AS v Islamic Republic of Pakistan*, ICSID Case No ARB/03/29, Award, 27 August 2009, para 399. See also *Cengiz Insaat Sanayi ve Ticaret AS v Libya*, ICC Case No 21537/ZF/AYZ, Award, 7 November 2018, para 525 (in relation to both prohibition against unreasonable or discriminatory measures and National Treatment).

[199] *Alex Genin, Eastern Credit Limited, Inc and AS Baltoil v The Republic of Estonia*, ICSID Case No ARB/99/2, Award, 25 June 2001, para 369. For a criticism of this approach see Weiler (n 7) 437 ('[t]he need for evidence of discriminatory intent, based upon the nationality of the investor, simply appears in their analyses without the slightest indication of how it got there').

[200] *Archer Daniels Midland Company and Tate & Lyle Ingredients Americas, Inc v United Mexican States*, ICSID Case No ARB(AF)/04/5, Award, 21 November 2007, para 205 (emphasis added).

[201] For a criticism of this approach see Weiler (n 7) 437 ('[t]he need for evidence of discriminatory intent, based upon the nationality of the investor, simply appears in their analyses without the slightest indication of how it got there').

although such considerations must be examined at the stage of determining likeness. Somewhat confusingly other tribunals, while not including consideration of the justification(s) relied on by the State as part of claimant's affirmative case, nonetheless, they accept that the State can avoid a finding of breach of the National Treatment obligation, if less favourable treatment can be justified by reference to a valid regulatory purpose. This is the case (although not always expressed in crystal clear terms) in *Cargill v Poland*,[202] *Olin Holdings v Libya*,[203] *Bilcon v Canada*,[204] *Mercer v Canada*,[205] and *Al Tamini v Oman*.[206] In *Rusoro v Venezuela* the tribunal held that 'difference in treatment, if not properly justified, could indeed have given rise to a breach of the equal treatment principle established in Art. IV.1 of the BIT' (providing for National Treatment).[207] According to the tribunal in *Pawloski v Czech Republic*, '[i]t is also widely accepted that there must be no objective reason which justifies the differential treatment'.[208] In *Champion Trading v Egypt* the tribunal held that '[t]o comply with the non-discrimination provision, the following requirements need to be met: there shall be no treatment less favourable—i.e., no discrimination—between foreign and national investments when they are in like situations'.[209] However, it also added that '[t]he question would remain whether a difference of treatment in like situations could be permissible based on other objective grounds'—a question which the tribunal left unanswered by exercising judicial economy as it had concluded that likeness was not established.[210]

Other tribunals completely ostracize justifications, regulatory purpose, or discriminatory intent from the applicable legal analysis and focus solely on the impact of the measure. The *Occidental v Ecuador* award for example could be 'best described

[202] One the one hand the tribunal did not mention justifications in setting out the applicable legal test, *Cargill, Incorporated v Republic of Poland II*, UNCITRAL, Award, 5 March 2008, para 343: 'Article 11:1 of the Treaty is an objective provision: it requires that (i) there be a foreign investor, (ii) this foreign investor be in like circumstances with a national investor, and (iii) the host State fail to grant the foreign investor as favorable a treatment as that accorded to the domestic investor. If the three conditions are satisfied, there is a breach of the national treatment guarantee.' On the other hand, the tribunal did examine whether 'the difference between the treatment accorded to Cargill and that accorded to domestic sugar producers justified' and concluded that it was not, ibid, and paras 332, 379–385. See also Section 3.1.1.1.

[203] Cf *Olin Holdings Limited v State of Libya*, ICC Case No 20355/MCP, Final Award, 25 May 2018, para 203 ('if the Claimant can prove that it was treated less favourably than a person similarly situated, then there would discriminatory treatment unless the Respondent can prove that such different treatment was justified'); ibid, para 202; see also, ibid, paras 376–377 (referring to the National Treatment analysis when examining a violation of a clause prohibiting unreasonable and/or discriminatory measures).

[204] *William Ralph Clayton, William Richard Clayton, Douglas Clayton, Daniel Clayton and Bilcon of Delaware Inc v Government of Canada*, UNCITRAL, PCA Case No 2009-04, Award on Jurisdiction and Liability, 17 March 2015, paras 717–723.

[205] *Mercer International Inc v Government of Canada*, ICSID Case No ARB(AF)/12/3, Award, 6 March 2018, paras 7.6–7.46.

[206] *Adel A Hamadi Al Tamimi v Sultanate of Oman*, ICSID Case No ARB/11/33, Award, 3 November 2015, para 457.

[207] *Rusoro Mining Ltd v Bolivarian Republic of Venezuela*, ICSID Case No ARB(AF)/12/5, Award, 22 August 2016, para 559; see also *South American Silver Limited v Plurinational State of Bolivia*, PCA Case No 2013-15, Award, 30 August 2018, paras 710–711.

[208] *Pawlowski AG and Project Sever sro v Czech Republic*, ICSID Case No ARB/17/11, Award, 1 November 2021, para 533.

[209] *Champion Trading Company and Ameritrade International, Inc v Arab Republic of Egypt*, ICSID Case No ARB/02/9, Award, 27 October 2006, para 128.

[210] ibid, para 134.

as a "disparate impact" approach to national treatment'.[211] Although Occidental 'has received treatment less favorable than that accorded to national companies' and the tribunal was 'convinced that this has not been done with the intent of discriminating against foreign-owned companies',[212] a breach of the National Treatment obligation was found.[213] Likewise, in *Gavrilovic v Croatia*, '[w]ithout deciding the matter, the Tribunal has proceeded on the basis that considerations of "justification" or "sectional or racial prejudice" are not required to establish a breach of Article 3 [providing for National Treatment and MFN]'.[214] This was also the approach of the tribunal in *UPS v Canada*:

> The Tribunal notes that there are three distinct elements which an investor must establish in order to prove that a Party has acted in a manner inconsistent with its obligations under article 1102. These are:
>
> a) The foreign investor must demonstrate that the Party [Canada] accorded treatment to it [the Claimant or UPS Canada] with respect to the establishment, acquisition, expansion, management, conduct, operation, and sale or other disposition of investments.
> b) The foreign investor or investment must be in like circumstances with local investors or investments; and
> c) The NAFTA Party must treat the foreign investor or investment less favorably than it treats the local investors or investments.[215]

In *Corn Products v Mexico*, Mexico argued that the relevant treatment had nothing to do with the foreign investors' capacity as investors but with broader regulatory objectives, constituting 'a measure taken to address a crisis in the Mexican sugar industry'.[216] The tribunal emphatically rejected this argument by holding that:

> [t]he problem with this argument is that it confuses the nature of the measure taken with the motive for which it was taken. The Tribunal does not doubt either that there was a crisis in the Mexican sugar industry, or that the motive for imposing the HFCS tax was to address that crisis. That does not alter the fact that the nature of the measure which Mexico took was one which treated producers of HFCS in a markedly less favourable way than Mexican producers of sugar. Discrimination does not cease to be

[211] Kurtz (n 15) 274. See also Ortino (n 192) 344–366, 358: '[m]ost of the cases so far decided (in particular under NAFTA Chapter 11) seem to have established a violation of the NT obligation simply by showing that the national measure under review affords less favourable treatment to the foreign investor (who has brought the claim) compared to the treatment afforded to at least one domestic investor in like circumstances'.

[212] *Occidental Exploration and Production Company v* Ecuador, LCIA Case No UN 3467, Final Award, 1 July 2004, para 177.

[213] ibid, paras 167–179.

[214] *Gavrilovic and Gavrilovic doo v Republic of Croatia*, ICSID Case No ARB/12/39, Award, 26 July 2018, para 1206.

[215] *United Parcel Service of America Inc v Government of Canada*, ICSID Case No UNCT/02/1, Award on the Merits, 24 May 2007, para 83.

[216] *Corn Products International Inc v United Mexican States*, ICSID Case No ARB(AF)/04/1, Decision on Responsibility, 15 January 2008, para 141.

> discrimination, nor to attract the international liability stemming therefrom, because it is undertaken to achieve a laudable goal or because the achievement of that goal can be described as necessary.[217]

In *Bayindir v Pakistan* the tribunal held that:

> [i]f the requirement of a similar situation is met, the Tribunal must further inquire whether Bayindir was granted less favourable treatment than other investors. This raises the question whether the test is subjective or objective, i.e. whether an intent to discriminate is required or whether a showing of discrimination of an investor who happens to be a foreigner is sufficient. The Tribunal considers that the second solution is the correct one.[218]

The approach of other tribunals is more ambiguous. In *Thunderbird v Mexico* the tribunal held that '[i]t is not expected from Thunderbird that it show separately that the less favourable treatment was motivated because of nationality. The text of Article 1102 of the NAFTA does not require such showing'.[219] However, in the same paragraph the tribunal stated that '[r]ather, the text contemplates the case where a foreign investor is treated less favourably than a national investor. That case is to be proven by a foreign investor, and, additionally, *the reason why there was a less favourable treatment*'.[220] The tribunal in *Resolute Forest v Canada* attempted to find some degree of coherence in what is an essentially unclear at best, contradictory at worse, jurisprudence:

> [a]s to the ultimate way to distinguish between *nationality*-based discrimination and other differences in treatment that do not relate to nationality, the Tribunal will follow the approach adopted by many other NAFTA Chapter 11 tribunals which have relied on the concept of treatment accorded 'in like circumstances' for this purpose. The tribunals had recourse to a proxy: for instance, the *Pope & Talbot* tribunal looked for 'a reasonable nexus to rational government policies', the *SD Myers* tribunal for 'legitimate public policy measures that are pursued in a reasonable manner', the *Feldman* tribunal for 'a rational justification' or reasonable distinction, the *GAMI* tribunal for 'a plausible connection with a legitimate goal of policy', the *Cargill* tribunal searched for a link between the alleged difference and the 'rationale and objective of the measure in question'. While the tribunals have varied in their formulations, the bottom line is the

[217] ibid, 142. For the context of this dispute, see S Puig, 'Investor-State Tribunals & Constitutional Courts: The Sweeteners Saga' (2013) 5 Mexican Law Review 199.

[218] *Bayindir Insaat Turizm Ticaret Ve Sanayi AS v Islamic Republic of Pakistan*, ICSID Case No ARB/03/29, Award, 27 August 2009, paras 390. Other tribunals, while acknowledging the different approaches, avoid pronouncing on the issue, *Merrill & Ring Forestry LP v Government of Canada*, UNCITRAL, ICSID Administrated, Award, 31 March 2010, para 94; *Grand River Enterprises Six Nations, Ltd, et al v United States of America*, UNCITRAL, Award, 12 January 2011, para 171.

[219] *International Thunderbird Gaming Corporation v United Mexican States*, UNCITRAL, Award, 26 January 2006, para 177 (emphasis removed).

[220] ibid (emphasis added).

same. Using the *Pope & Talbot* formulation as an illustration: a tribunal will conclude the less favorable treatment proven *prima facie* by the Claimant was not provided 'in like circumstances' where the Respondent can provide evidence that the differences in treatment have a 'reasonable nexus to rational government policies' that do not distinguish on their face or *de facto* between foreign and domestic investors or investments. Conversely, if the Respondent cannot provide such evidence, the tribunal will assume that nationality was the reason for the differential treatment (see e.g. *Feldman*).[221]

3.3.1.2 Most Favoured Nation Treatment

As explained above most of the controversy regarding MFN clauses predominantly revolves around whether MFN clauses could be used by investors to rely on more favourable dispute settlement provisions or (more recently) substantive provisions[222] contained in other investment agreements concluded between the Host State and third States. In her monograph on MFN Crépet Daigremont highlights the lack of uniform approach among arbitral tribunals in relation to the role of discriminatory intent.[223] This uncertainty is further exacerbated by the fact that there are relatively fewer cases focusing on MFN and substantive (factual) treatment. One of the few exceptions is *Parkerings v Lithuania*.[224] In that case, the tribunal set out the relevant legal test using a three-pronged test (the last element of which was the absence of legitimate policy justifications):

> [i]n order to determine whether Parkerings was in like circumstances with Pinus Proprius, and thus whether the MFN standard has been violated, the Arbitral Tribunal considers that three conditions should be met:
> (i) Pinus Proprius must be a foreign investor;
> (ii) Pinus Proprius and Parkerings must be in the same economic or business sector;
> (iii) The two investors must be treated differently. The difference of treatment must be due to a measure taken by the State. No policy or purpose behind the said measure must apply to the investment that justifies the different treatments accorded. A contrario, a less favourable treatment is acceptable if a State's legitimate objective justifies such different treatment in relation to the specificity of the investment.[225]

Other tribunals rely on National Treatment case law to interpret MFN provisions or analyse together the two provisions (National Treatment and MFN).[226]

[221] *Resolute Forest Products Inc v Government of Canada*, PCA Case No 2016-13, Award, 25 July 2022, para 575. This is also relevant to the question of standard of review discussed below in Chapter 4, Section 4.2.
[222] See Section 3.2.1.2.
[223] Crépet Daigremont (n 41) 263.
[224] *Parkerings-Compagniet AS v Republic of Lithuania*, ICSID Case No ARB/05/8 Award, 11 September 2007.
[225] ibid, para 371.
[226] *Bayindir Insaat Turizm Ticaret Ve Sanayi AS v Islamic Republic of Pakistan*, ICSID Case No ARB/03/29, Award, 27 August 2009, para 390.

3.3.1.3 Non-impairment Clauses

In the context of the prohibition against arbitrary or discriminatory measures tribunals held that '"non-discrimination" requires a rational justification of any differential treatment of a foreign investor'.[227] In *BG v Argentina* the tribunal set out the three-fold test for establishing violation of non-impairment clauses in the following manner:

> a) identify the relevant entities of the national treatment comparison, to determine whether they are in like circumstances;
> b) consider the relative treatment received by each such entity so as to ascertain the best level of treatment available to any other domestic or foreign investor; and
> c) consider such factors as may be relevant to justify any difference in treatment.[228]

In *Belenergia v Italy* the tribunal placed emphasis on the fact that less favourable treatment was the result of legitimate grounds rather than the investor's nationality:

> Italy's differentiation between smaller plants, on the one hand, and medium and big power plants with nominal capacity in excess of 200kW, on the other, is not discriminatory because it is based on objective and legitimate grounds. *This differentiated treatment is by no means based on the national or foreign origin of producers, but on their capacity, size, economic and commercial dimension. Thus, differentiated treatment based on legitimate grounds leading to special protection of smaller plants is easily justifiable so far as it seeks to guarantee free competition in the energy sector.*
>
> Likewise, differentiated scales applying to minimum prices based on production capacity is objectively justified because production capacity affects the calculation of operational costs, an objective base for the estimation of minimum prices. Moreover, the Claimant has not argued or demonstrated that such an objective differentiated treatment could lead to a subjective differentiated treatment and thus to concealed discrimination.[229]

[227] *Saluka Investments BV v The Czech Republic*, UNCITRAL, Partial Award, 17 March 2006, para 460; *Plama Consortium Limited v Republic of Bulgaria*, ICSID Case No ARB/03/24, Award, 27 August 2008, para 184; *Lidercón, SL v Republic of Peru*, ICSID Case No ARB/17/9, Award, 6 March 2020, paras 168–169. *Enron Corporation and Ponderosa Assets, LP v Argentine Republic*, ICSID Case No ARB/01/3, Award, 22 May 2007, para 282 ('The Tribunal does not find that there has been any capricious, irrational or absurd differentiation in the treatment accorded to the Claimants as compared to other entities or sectors'); *Mohammad Ammar Al-Bahloul v Republic of Tajikistan*, Partial Award on Jurisdiction and Liability, SCC Case No V064/2008, 2 September 2009, para 248; *ECE Projektmanagement International GmbH and Kommanditgesellschaft PANTA Achtundsechzigste Grundstücksgesellschaft mbH & Co v Czech Republic*, PCA Case No 2010-5, Award, 19 September 2013, para 4.825; *SAUR International v Argentine Republic*, ICSID Case No ARB/04/4, Decision on Jurisdiction and Liability, 6 June 2012, para 486; *Venezuela US, SRL v Bolivarian Republic of Venezuela*, PCA Case No 2013-34, Partial Award on Jurisdiction and Liability, 5 February 2021, para 223. See also Kriebaum (n 73) 802.

[228] *BG Group Plc v Republic of Argentina*, UNCITRAL, Award, 24 December 2007, para 356. Other tribunals do not elaborate on the applicable legal test; see also *Zhongshan Fucheng Industrial Investment Co Ltd v The Federal Republic of Nigeria*, Final Award, 26 March 2021, para 129.

[229] *Belenergia SA v Italian Republic*, ICSID Case No ARB/15/40, Award, 28 August 2019, paras 631 and 632 (emphasis added).

In some cases, the application of this three-stage test for discrimination is not in dispute between the parties.[230] Other tribunals examining clauses prohibiting arbitrary or discriminatory treatment focused solely on discriminatory impact[231] or accepted that either intent or impact suffice.[232] The tribunal in *Siemens v Argentina* emphatically held that 'intent is not decisive or essential for a finding of discrimination, and that the impact of the measure on the investment would be the determining factor to ascertain whether it had resulted in nondiscriminatory treatment'.[233]

Finally, in some cases, tribunals seem to conflate the analysis of likeness and public policy justifications,[234] as was also seen in National Treatment cases.[235] However, as explained above, there are good reasons to keep the analysis of these two elements clearly separate.[236]

3.3.1.4 Fair and Equitable Treatment

In *Saluka v Czech Republic*, examining discrimination in the context of FET, and after concluding that the investor's bank, IPB, 'has clearly been treated differently',[237] the tribunal held that the Czech Republic:

> has not offered a reasonable justification for IPB's differential treatment. Consequently, the Czech Republic is found to have given a discriminatory response to the bad debt problem in the Czech banking sector, especially by providing state financial assistance to three of the Big Four banks to the exclusion of IPB, and thereby created an environment impossible for the survival of IPB.[238]

The approach of the tribunal in *Saluka* was widely endorsed.[239] In *Electrabel v Hungary* the tribunal held that:

[230] See eg *South American Silver Limited v Plurinational State of Bolivia*, PCA Case No 2013-15, Award, 30 August 2018, para 710 ('the Parties agree[d] on the standard for discriminatory measures. Consistent with the definition endorsed by both Parties, discrimination involves 'a differential treatment of people or companies in like circumstances, without a rational justification for that differential treatment') (emphasis removed).

[231] *Electrabel SA v Republic of Hungary*, ICSID Case No ARB/07/19, Decision on Jurisdiction, Applicable Law and Liability 30 November 2012, para 7.152 ('discriminatory effects of the measures are sufficient to breach the prohibition. The Tribunal does not consider that that there is a separate requirement to prove discriminatory intent').

[232] *LG&E, Energy Corp, LG&E Capital Corp and LG&E International Inc v Argentine Republic*, ICSID Case No ARB/02/1, Decision on Liability, 3 October 2006, para 146 (in a somewhat contradictory manner due to the reference to *ELSI*): 'In the context of investment treaties, and the obligation thereunder not to discriminate against foreign investors, a measure is considered discriminatory if the intent of the measure is to discriminate or if the measure has a discriminatory effect. As stated in the *ELSI Elettronica Sicula SpA case (United States of America v Italy)*, ICJ Report 1989 RLA 56 at 61–62 (20 July 1989), in order to establish when a measure is discriminatory, there must be (i) an intentional treatment (ii) in favor of a national (iii) against a foreign investor, and (iv) that is not taken under similar circumstances against another national'.

[233] *Siemens AG v Argentine Republic*, ICSID Case No ARB/02/8, Award, 6 February 2007, para 321.

[234] *National Grid plc v The Argentine Republic*, UNCITRAL, Award, 3 November 2008, para 201.

[235] See Section 3.1.1.1.

[236] ibid.

[237] *Saluka Investments BV v The Czech Republic*, UNCITRAL, Partial Award, 17 March 2006, para 326.

[238] ibid, para 347.

[239] See eg *Invesmart BV v Czech Republic*, UNCITRAL, Award, 26 June 2009, para 403; *Joseph Charles Lemire v Ukraine*, ICSID Case No ARB/06/18, Decision on Jurisdiction and Liability, 14 January 2010, para 261.

> a mere showing of differential treatment is not sufficient to establish unlawful discrimination or, in this context, irrationality in breach of the ECT's FET standard. For discriminatory treatment, comparators must be materially similar; and there must then be no reasonable justification for differential treatment.[240]

Likewise, according to the tribunal in *Cavalum v Spain*, '[n]on-discrimination requires a rational justification of any differential treatment' and, thus, '[f]or a measure to be discriminatory two similar situations must be treated differently, without objective justification'.[241] Therefore, succeeding in a discrimination claim under FET requires the absence of a rational justification.[242] *A fortiori*, targeted discrimination, even though it is not strictly speaking on the grounds of nationality, amounts to a FET breach.[243]

In *Air Canada v Venezuela*, the tribunal examined and 'rejected all possible reasons for Respondent's failure to deal with Claimant's AADs' to establish a violation of the non-discrimination aspect of the FET.[244]

Finally, States cannot be held liable if reasonable public policy justifications exist for their actions (or omissions) even in discrimination cases under customary international law. Paparinskis concludes that '[t]he better view therefore is that discrimination is still a part of the international standard, requiring reasonable justification for different treatment of similar cases'.[245] This is also clearly reflected in the legal test used in *Saluka v Czech Republic*.[246]

3.3.1.5 Expropriation

Investment treaty tribunals use the familiar three-pronged test (consisting of an examination of likeness, less favourable treatment, and public policy reasons) also applied in the context of expropriation. For example, in *Quiborax v Bolivia* the tribunal held that '[t]o determine whether the Revocation Decree discriminated against NMM [the investor], the Tribunal will apply the three-pronged test formulated in Saluka, cited by the Respondent: "State conduct is discriminatory, if (i) similar cases are (ii) treated differently (iii) and without reasonable justification" '.[247] However, as the tribunal in *Siag v Egypt* accurately observed, '[a]s to discriminatory intent ... there is some difference

[240] *Electrabel SA v Republic of Hungary*, ICSID Case No ARB/07/19, Award, 25 November 2015, para 175.

[241] *Cavalum SGPS, SA v Kingdom of Spain*, ICSID Case No ARB/15/34, Decision on Jurisdiction, Liability and Directions on Quantum, 31 August 2020, para 416; see also ibid, para 410. See also *Muszynianka Spółka z Ograniczona Odpowiedzialnoscia v Slovak Republic*, PCA Case No 2017-08, Award, 7 October 2020, para 517.

[242] *Manchester Securities Corporation v Republic of Poland*, PCA Case No 2015-18, Award, 7 December 2018, paras 448–484.

[243] *OAO Tatneft v Ukraine*, PCA Case No 2008-8, Award on the Merits, 29 July 2014, para 408: '[e]ven if such measures would not have entailed nationality-based discrimination, the fact that given identifiable interests are targeted indicates a discriminatory treatment as compared to that accorded to other interests in the venture.'

[244] *Air Canada v Bolivarian Republic of Venezuela*, ICSID Case No ARB(AF)/17/1, Award, 13 September 2021, para 468; see also ibid, paras 466–467, and Section 3.2.1.4.

[245] Paparinskis (n 110) 247.

[246] *Saluka Investments BV v The Czech Republic*, UNCITRAL, Partial Award, 17 March 2006, para 313 ('State conduct is discriminatory, if (i) similar cases are (ii) treated differently (iii) and without reasonable justification').

[247] *Quiborax SA and Non Metallic Minerals SA v Plurinational State of Bolivia*, ICSID Case No ARB/06/2, Award, 16 September 2015, para 247; *OI European Group BV v Bolivarian Republic of Venezuela*, ICSID Case No ARB/11/25, Award, 10 March 2015, para 405.

of opinion as to whether such intent is necessary to show discrimination, or whether a discriminatory effect will suffice'.[248]

However, the jurisprudence of the IUSCT highlights that 'it [is] difficult, in the absence of any other evidence, to draw the conclusion that the expropriation of a concern was discriminatory only from the fact that another concern in the same economic branch was not expropriated'.[249] According to the IUSCT, this is because '[r]easons specific to the non-expropriated enterprise, or to the expropriated one, or to both, may justify such a difference of treatment'.[250] As aptly summarised by Pellonpää and Fitzmaurice in the light of the case law of IUSCT:

> [t]hus differential treatment of various persons, or classes of owners of property, does not automatically amount to prohibited discrimination. With similarity to, for example, the principle of non-discrimination as applied in international human rights law, such differentiation is wrongful only if it is unreasonable, or lacks some objective justification. Justification is probably quite easily available in so far as distinctions, made between foreigners as a class on the one hand, and the State and its nationals on the other, are concern- ed, and specific reasons may also justify differential treatment of various classes of foreigners. In similarity to the condition of public purpose, the State's assertion that such reasons exist creates a strong presumption of the correctness of such an assertion. Thus, while both the public purpose and non- discrimination requirements are well established, a certain shift in favour of the State's economic sovereignty appears to be discernible in the way they are interpreted today.[251]

[248] *Waguih Elie George Siag and Clorinda Vecchi v The Arab Republic of Egypt*, ICSID Case No ARB/05/15, Award, 1 June 2009, para 439; see also B Sabahi, 'National Treatment—Is Discriminatory Intent Relevant' in T Weiler (ed), *Investment Treaty Arbitration and International Law, vol 2* (JurisNet 2008) 269–297; and S Tabet, 'Beyond the Smoking Gun—Is Discriminatory Objective Necessary to Find a Breach of National Treatment' in T Weiler (ed), *Investment Treaty Arbitration and International Law, vol 2* (JurisNet 2008) 299–313.

[249] *Amoco International Finance Corporation v The Government of the Islamic Republic of Iran, National Iranian Oil Company, National Petrochemical Company and Kharg Chemical Company Limited*, IUSCT Case No 56, Partial Award (Award No 310-56-3), 14 July 1987, para 142. See also *Aminoil v Kuwait* (1982) 21 ILM 976, 66 ILR 518, 585 ('In 1977 nationalisation was not extended to both of the Companies then operating as concessionaires, viz. Aminoil and the "Arabian Oil Company" (AOC). The latter was spared. The question accordingly arises whether the nationalisation of Aminoil was not thereby tainted with discrimination, and whether this differentiation does not show that the Decree Law had other objects than that of realising a programme of economic development. The Tribunal does not think so. First of all, it has never for a single moment been suggested that it was because of the American nationality of the Company that the Decree Law was applied to Aminoil's Concession. Next, and above all, there were adequate reasons for not nationalising Arabian Oil.')

[250] *Amoco International Finance Corporation v The Government of the Islamic Republic of Iran, National Iranian Oil Company, National Petrochemical Company and Kharg Chemical Company Limited*, IUSCT Case No 56, Partial Award (Award No 310-56-3), 14 July 1987, para 142.

[251] M Pellonpää and M Fitzmaurice, 'Taking of Property in the Practice of the Iran-United States Claims Tribunal' (1988) 19 Netherlands Yearbook of International Law 53, 65.

In *von Pezold v Zimbabwe* the tribunal focused both on 'targeted' discrimination[252] and the absence of valid policy objective motivating the expropriation of the property belonging to the foreign investors.[253]

3.3.2 The Normative Argument of this Book

The previous section (3.3.1) made clear that the case law of investment treaty tribunals is not settled regarding what many tribunals consider the last element of the legal test for establishing breaches of non-discrimination obligations, ie the existence of discriminatory intent or the absence of legitimate policy reasons in relation to measure(s) adopted by States and resulting in less favourable treatment. The case law is not clear regarding evidentiary issues either, but these will be addressed separately in Chapter 4. This section will set out the normative argument of this book arguing that, as a form of disparate treatment or direct discrimination,[254] after 'likeness' and 'less favourable treatment' are established, arbitral tribunals must examine whether less favourable treatment is connected to the foreign investor's nationality or another protected characteristic. In that context, while conceptually distinct, in practice the absence of discriminatory intent is equated with the existence of valid policy reasons underpinning State regulation. This is also in line with the paradigm of 'disparate treatment' discrimination, as explained in Section 2.1 of Chapter 2.

Despite the efforts of various scholars such as Grotius[255] and Ago,[256] subjective fault (including intent) has been ostracized from secondary rules of State responsibility in favour of an objective approach in public international law.[257] Thus, given that the default position is that responsibility for breaches of international law does not require intent, the question is whether specific norms of international law and in particular non-discrimination obligations contained in investment treaties do require such subjective

[252] *Bernhard von Pezold and Others v Republic of Zimbabwe*, ICSID Case No ARB/10/15, Award, 28 July 2015, para 501 ('[a]s regards to the criterion of non-discrimination in the Swiss BIT's expropriation provision, the evidence supports a conclusion that the Claimants were targeted as a result of their skin colour and, hence, the taking was discriminatory in breach of the Swiss BIT').

[253] ibid, para 502 ('the Respondent has failed to establish that there was a legitimate public purpose behind the expropriation. The Tribunal has carefully considered the Respondent's arguments relating, in effect, to the righting of historical wrongs. The Tribunal cannot, however, accept these arguments as support for the expropriation of the Zimbabwean Properties having been carried out for a "public purpose". Once taken, large parts of the properties have not actually been re-distributed to a historically disadvantaged or otherwise landless population, but remain in the de facto possession of the Claimants. With regard to the land that has been re-distributed, there appears to be a clear trend towards politically-motivated allocations of land. Therefore, there is no evidence that the expropriation of the Zimbabwean Properties was in the public interest or served a genuine public purpose').

[254] See Chapter 2, Section 2.2.

[255] H Grotius, *De Jure Belli ac Pacis Libri tres* (1625), Book II, Chapter XVII, sections XX–XXI.

[256] See R Ago, 'Le délit international' (1939) 68 RCADI 419, 450–498.

[257] I Brownlie, 'State Responsibility and the International Court of Justice' in M Fitzmaurice and D Sarooshi (eds), *Issues of State Responsibility Before International Judicial Institutions* (Hart 2004) 11–18, 12. See also O Diggelmann, 'Fault in the Law of State Responsibility—Pragmatism *ad infinitum*?' (2006) 49 German Yearbook of International Law 293; A Gattini, 'Smoking/No Smoking: Some Remarks on the Current Place of Fault in the ILC Draft Articles on State Responsibility' (1999) 10 EJIL 397; S Besson, 'Theorizing International Responsibility Law, an Introduction' in S Besson (ed), *Theories of International Responsibility Law* (CUP 2022) 1–10, 10.

element.[258] This book argues that discrimination in international investment law does not depart from the general public international law rule: responsibility is objective and subjective discriminatory intent is not necessary.[259] However, this book argues that the tribunal need to satisfy itself that less favourable treatment cannot be justified by legitimate policy reasons.[260] While the absence of discriminatory intent and the existence of valid (and, therefore, by definition, non-discriminatory) regulatory justification are conceptual distinct, in practice there is no difference.

As Section 2.2 established, MFN and National Treatment obligations prohibit discrimination on the basis of nationality and non-discrimination under non-impairment clauses, FET, or in the context of expropriation, prohibit discrimination on the basis of any impermissible grounds (including but not limited to nationality). Discriminatory intent is one, but not the only, way to establish a link between the less favourable treatment and the protected ground.[261] How to (and which party must) establish such a link to prevail in a non-discrimination claim is an evidentiary question which is addressed in Chapter 4.

One of the sources of confusion in practice is the unclear relationship between (i) discrimination on the basis of nationality or another protected characteristic, (ii) the existence of discriminatory intent, and (iii) the absence of a valid regulatory purpose regarding a specific State measure giving rise to less favourable treatment. This book argues that, especially from an evidentiary perspective, these three distinct in principle concepts are indistinguishable.[262] *Genin v Estonia* is a good example highlighting this. In that case the measure was found to be consistent with National Treatment as:

[258] See also *EDF International SA, SAUR International SA, and León Participaciones Argentinas SA v Argentine Republic*, ICSID Case No ARB/03/23, Award, 11 June 2012, paras 915–920.

[259] Reinisch and Schreuer (n 41) 843 ('Despite some cases pointing to discriminatory intent, the preponderant view in arbitral practice is that discrimination need not be based on an intention by the host state's authorities to discriminate or on an explicitly discriminatory rule of its domestic law. De facto discrimination is enough. This means that the investor does not bear the burden of proof that the differential treatment was motivated by its foreign nationality.')

[260] For an example where the tribunal was persuaded that the State was motivated legitimate policy reasons, see *Muszynianka Spólka z Ograniczona Odpowiedzialnoscia v Slovak Republic*, PCA Case No 2017-08, Award, 7 October 2020, paras 523–530; cf Partial Dissenting Opinion of Professor Robert G Volterra, 7 October 2020.

[261] See Chapter 2, Section 2.1.

[262] J Larguier, 'La preuve d'un fait négatif' (1953) 51 Revue Trimestrielle de Droit civil 1, 3 ('la preuve d'un fait négatif ne soulève pas de problème spécifique lorsque cette preuve peut se faire par la preuve positive d'une affirmation contraire'). Cf *Standard Chartered Bank (Hong Kong) Limited v Tanzania Electric Supply Company Limited*, ICSID Case No ARB/10/20, Decision on Annulment, 22 August 2018, para 461 ('After considering the position of the Parties, the Committee concludes that the Tribunal properly determined that the burden to prove SCB HK's knowledge was with TANESCO, because it was an element of the positive argument made by it to refute SCB HK's claims. It was not for SCB HK to prove a negative, given that the "the burden lies with the party seeking to prove the allegation"). See also *Ahmadou Sadio Diallo (Republic of Guinea v Democratic Republic of the Congo)* Merits, Judgment [2010] ICJ Reports 639, 661, para 55 ('[i]n particular, where, as in these proceedings, it is alleged that a person has not been afforded, by a public authority, certain procedural guarantees to which he was entitled, it cannot as a general rule be demanded of the Applicant that it prove the negative fact which it is asserting. A public authority is generally able to demonstrate that it has followed the appropriate procedures and applied the guarantees required by law — if such was the case — by producing documentary evidence of the actions that were carried out. However, it cannot be inferred in every case where the Respondent is unable to prove the performance of a procedural obligation that it has disregarded it: that depends to a large extent on the precise nature of the obligation in question; some obligations normally imply that written documents are drawn up, while others do not. The time which has elapsed since the events must also be taken into account').

there is no indication that the Bank of Estonia specifically targeted EIB in a discriminatory way, or treated it less favourably than banks owned by Estonian nationals. Moreover, *Claimants have failed to prove that the withdrawal of EIB's license was done with the intention to harm the Bank or any of the Claimants in this arbitration, or to treat them in a discriminatory way.*[263]

On the basis of this paragraph, it seems that the tribunal allocates the burden of proof to the investor. However, in the next paragraph it is made clear that the tribunal was also persuaded by the legitimacy of the justification relied on by Estonia:

> [i]n this regard, it is relevant that the Tribunal has found no evidence of discriminatory action. In addition, the Tribunal accepts Respondent's explanation that it took the decision to annul EIB's license in the course of exercising its statutory obligations to regulate the Estonian banking sector. The Tribunal further accepts Respondent's explanation that the circumstances of political and economic transition prevailing in Estonia at the time justified heightened scrutiny of the banking sector. Such regulation by a state reflects a clear and legitimate public purpose.[264]

Therefore, 'having regard to the totality of the evidence' the tribunal concluded that the decision of the central bank was non-discriminatory, but justified.[265] As explained by Douglas, analysing *Methanex v USA*, and in particular the non-discrimination aspects of the FET:

> [w]as the dominant purpose behind the two measures attributable to the USA to further the commercial interests of a domestic producer of ethanol by discriminating against a foreign producer of methanol? Such a question can be resolved without delving into the corporate mind of the USA or the intent of its officials. It simply demands an objective assessment of the evidentiary record and a conclusion justified on the balance of probabilities.[266]

Finally, recent trends in treaty drafting support the view that the existence of a valid, public policy objective motivating the measure in question automatically excludes the possibility that such measures are related to the foreign investor's nationality or another protected ground, and, therefore, discriminatory. Article 2.3(3) of the EU–Singapore Investment Protection Agreement provides that:

[263] *Alex Genin, Eastern Credit Limited, Inc and AS Baltoil v The Republic of Estonia*, ICSID Case No ARB/99/2, Award, 25 June 2001, para 369.

[264] ibid, para 370.

[265] ibid, para 371.

[266] Z Douglas, 'Nothing if Not Critical for Investment Treaty Arbitration: Occidental, Eureko and Methanex' (2006) 22 Arbitration International 27, 49–50.

a Party may adopt or enforce measures that accord to covered investors and investments of the other Party less favourable treatment than that accorded to its own investors and their investments, in like situations, subject to the requirement that such measures are not applied in a manner which would constitute a means of arbitrary or unjustifiable discrimination against the covered investors or investments of the other Party in the territory of a Party, or is a disguised restriction on covered investments, where the measures are:

(a) necessary to protect public security, public morals or to maintain public order;
(b) necessary to protect human, animal or plant life or health;
(c) relating to the conservation of exhaustible natural resources if such measures are applied in conjunction with restrictions on domestic investors or investments;
(d) necessary for the protection of national treasures of artistic, historic or archaeological value;
(e) necessary to secure compliance with laws or regulations which are not inconsistent with the provisions of this Chapter including those relating to:
   (i) the prevention of deceptive or fraudulent practices or to deal with the effects of a default on a contract;
   (ii) the protection of the privacy of individuals in relation to the processing and dissemination of personal data and the protection of confidential of individual records and accounts;
   (iii) safety;
(f) aimed at ensuring the effective or equitable imposition or collection of direct taxes in respect of investors or investments of the other Party.[267]

The same applies to the non-discrimination provisions of the Protocol on Investment to the Agreement Establishing the AfCFTA, which clearly indicate that discrimination is intrinsically linked with the absence of legitimate public policy objectives. Article 13 of AfCTA Investment Protocol (Draft January 2023), entitled 'Exceptions to National Treatment' provides:

1. Measures taken by a State Party that are designed and applied to protect or enhance legitimate public policy objectives such as, but not limited to, public morals, public health, prevention of diseases and pests in animals or plants, climate action, essential security interests, safety and the protection of environment shall not be construed as a breach of Article 12 [providing for National Treatment].
2. Preferential treatment granted by State Parties to national investments and investors, in accordance with domestic laws and regulations, in order to achieve national

[267] Investment Protection Agreement between the European Union and its Member States and the Republic of Singapore (signed 15 October 2018, not yet into force) Article 2.3(5) (footnotes omitted).

development objectives or address the internal needs of designated disadvantaged persons, groups, or regions shall not be construed as a breach of Article 12.

3. Each State Party reserves the right to adopt or maintain certain exceptions to the standard of national treatment provided by Article 12 to investments made by investors of another State Party in its territory if those exceptions fall within one of the sectors or geographical regions that represent strategic importance for the Host State in accordance with its laws and regulations.
4. For greater certainty, discriminatory measures taken by a State Party to comply with its obligations under other regional or international agreements shall not be construed as a breach of Article 12.[268]

[268] Protocol on Investment to the Agreement Establishing the AfCFTA, Article 13. See also T Masiko, *Flexible Regional Economic Integration in Africa: Lessons and Implications for the Multilateral Trading System* (Bloomsbury 2022); JT Gathii, *African Regional Trade Agreements as Legal Regimes* (CUP 2011).

4

Procedural and Evidentiary Matters

Burden of Proof, Standard of Review, and Standard of Proof

Chapter 3 set out the applicable legal test for establishing breaches of the different non-discrimination obligations contained in investment treaties (National Treatment, MFN, non-impairment clauses, and non-discrimination under FET, and in the context of expropriation) from a descriptive and normative perspective. This chapter explores three procedural and evidentiary questions regarding the allocation of the burden of proof (Section 4.1), the standard of review (Section 4.2), and the standard of proof (Section 4.3) in relation to these non-discrimination obligations. This chapter also follows the same approach of the previous chapter, clearly separating the description of the case law in relation to these three key questions (in Sections 4.1.1, 4.2.1, and 4.3.1) and the normative suggestions put forward in this book (in Sections 4.1.2, 4.2.2, and 4.3.2).

4.1 Burden of Proof

This section examines the allocation of the burden of proof in relation to each element of the legal test for establishing violations of non-discrimination. Section 4.1.1 analyses the inconsistent jurisprudence of investment tribunals regarding the allocation of the burden of proof in discrimination cases. The most controversial question dividing investment tribunals is whether the claimant (investor) or the respondent (Host State) bears the burden of proving that the investor's less favourable treatment is linked to the investor's nationality or another protected characteristic. Tribunals usually frame the issue with reference to proof of discriminatory intent or legitimate policy objectives on the part of the State.[1] Section 4.1.2 argues that the investor must prove all three main elements of the legal test to establish discrimination on the part of the Host State: likeness, less favourable treatment, and the link between less favourable treatment and investor's nationality or another protected ground. Although this approach is in line with the generally accepted principle[2] *actori incumbit probatio* (Section 4.1.2.1), it also

[1] See Chapter 3.

[2] On the distinction between principles and rules see R Dworkin, *Taking Rights Seriously* (Harvard University Press 1977) 25: 'Rules are applicable in an all-or-nothing fashion. If the facts a rule stipulates are given, then either the rule is "valid, in which case the answer it supplies must be accepted, or it is not, in which case it contributes nothing to the decision"'.

creates serious evidentiary difficulties for investors, as States have better access to the relevant evidence in relation to the adoption and implementation of allegedly discriminatory measures. This book argues that the duty of both parties to cooperate in relation to the production of evidence, as well as the power of arbitral tribunals to draw adverse inferences in case one of the parties fails to do so are instrumental in countering the difficulties arising out of the inherent asymmetry between States and investors as far as access to evidence is concerned in the context of discrimination claims (Section 4.1.2.2).

4.1.1 Case Law on the Allocation of the Burden of Proof

There is no doubt that investors bear the burden of proof in relation to factual aspects regarding the 'likeness' and 'less favourable treatment' parts of the legal test in discrimination cases. This is well established in the relevant case law[3] and is also reflected in recent treaty drafting.[4] However, investment treaty tribunals have failed to adopt a uniform approach regarding the allocation of the burden of proof in discrimination cases regarding the third and last element of the legal test, which revolves around an examination of the link between less favourable treatment and the investors' nationality or other protected grounds.[5] In her analysis of National Treatment jurisprudence, Bjorklund elaborated on the lack of clarity regarding the relevant legal test:

> [e]xactly what is required to establish a prima facie case of a national treatment violation is not clear, and most tribunals have given at most limited attention to burden of proof. Moreover, tribunals have not taken a uniform approach to analysing the existence of a national treatment violation so that discerning a general practice is difficult. Implicit in most cases is that the arguments made by the claimant must give rise to an inference that the difference in treatment was attributable to nationality-based considerations or that the distinction made between apparently similarly situated entities disguises protectionist intent. The main difference in cases seems to be the ease with which an assumption of discriminatory intent can be established.[6]

[3] See eg *Apotex Holdings Inc and Apotex Inc v United States of America*, ICSID Case No ARB(AF)/12/1, Award, 25 August 2014, para 8.21 ('The Tribunal addresses these questions below. In doing so, the Tribunal proceeds on the basis that for the Claimants (Apotex-Holdings for itself and for Apotex–US) to succeed, they are required to prove, on the balance of the evidential record, that the Respondent treated them or their investment less favourably, ie worse than, their comparators who were in like circumstances.') See also *Inversión y Gestión de Bienes, IGB, SL and IGB18 Las Rozas, SL v Kingdom of Spain*, ICSID Case No ARB/12/17, Award (Excerpts), 14 August 2015, para 193: 'Sin embargo, las Demandantes no indicaron cuáles fueron las personas o entidades que recibieron ese trato más favorable, que permitiría calificar de "discriminatorio" el que España les dio a ellas. El Tribunal tampoco encontró prueba alguna de esa alegación de las Demandantes y por ello no puede tener por demostrado que ellas recibieron un trato discriminatorio de las autoridades españolas.'

[4] See eg CPTPP Drafters' Note, para 2: 'When a claimant challenges a measure as inconsistent with Article 9.4 (National Treatment) or Article 9.5 (Most-Favoured-Nation Treatment), the claimant bears the burden to prove that the respondent failed to accord to the claimant or the claimant's covered investment treatment no less favourable than it accords, in like circumstances, (a) to its own investors, or their investments, in its territory (Article 9.4), or (b) to investors of any other Party or of any non-Party, or their investments, in its territory (Article 9.5).'

[5] See Chapter 3, Section 3.3.

[6] A Bjorklund, 'The National Treatment Obligation' in K Yannaca-Small (ed), *Arbitration Under International Investment Agreements: A Guide to the Key Issues* (2nd edn, OUP 2018) 532–561, 555.

Likewise, in her monograph on MFN, Wang concludes that the '[b]urden of proof has not been systematically explored as a concern in the MFN context'.[7]

Certain tribunals allocate the burden of proof to the respondent.[8] Long before arbitral tribunals begun adjudicating disputes on the basis of investment treaties, this position was adopted by the UK in its pleadings in the *Anglo-Iranian Oil Company* case (which concerned the expropriation of foreign property) before the ICJ:

> cases may arise in which a measure of expropriation solely affecting foreign nationals is dictated by such overwhelming considerations of public utility and general welfare that the measure cannot be said to be directed against or discriminatory against foreigners. In such cases the fact that the expropriation affects foreigners only is, in a sense, accidental. The State cannot be expected to refrain from a measure which is of vital importance for the sole reason that the persons affected are foreigners. However, as the arbitral decision [in *Administrator of Posts and Telegraphs of the Republic of Czechoslovakia v Radio Corporation of America*] shows the burden of proof is on the expropriating State to show that these overwhelming considerations exist and the situation is altogether different when the circumstances of the case point cogently to the conclusion that the action taken was embarked upon not in pursuance of a general purpose but with the object of nullifying a transaction which is deemed to be inconvenient or, although more lucrative than was expected at the time when it was entered into, still not as lucrative as the expropriating State would like.[9]

As the ICJ (famously) declined jurisdiction, it did not have an opportunity to pronounce on this matter.[10] However, this seems to be also the approach adopted by tribunals in early investment treaty cases. According to the analysis of DiMascio and Pauwelyn (which dates from 2008), '[i]n most cases the burden of proof was shifted to the defendant as soon as the complainant established differential treatment in the same business or economic sector'.[11] In *Nykomb v Latvia* once the investor established that the companies were in 'like circumstances' and were treated less favourably, the tribunal held that 'in accordance with established international law, the burden of proof lied with the Respondent to prove that no discrimination has taken or is taking place'.[12] For another tribunal (also referring to *Pope & Talbot v Canada*[13] and *Feldman v*

[7] A Wang, *The Interpretation and Application of the Most-Favored-Nation Clause in Investment Arbitration* (Brill Nijhoff 2022) 108.

[8] See eg *Olin Holdings Limited v State of Libya*, ICC Case No 20355/MCP, Final Award, 25 May 2018, para 217: '[t]he Tribunal therefore considers that the Respondent has failed to prove that the difference between the treatment accorded to Olin and the treatment accorded to its national competitors was justified. The Respondent has accordingly failed to discharge its burden of proof in this regard.'

[9] *Anglo-Iranian Oil Co*, Memorial submitted by the Government of the United Kingdom of Great Britain and Northern Ireland 64, 97, para 22.

[10] *Anglo-Iranian Oil Co case (Jurisdiction)*, Judgment of 22 July 1952 [1952] ICJ Rep 93.

[11] N DiMascio and J Pauwelyn, 'Nondiscrimination in Trade and Investment Treaties: Worlds Apart or Two Sides of the Same Coin?' (2008) 102 AJIL 48, 76.

[12] *Nykomb Synergetics Technology Holding AB v Republic of Latvia*, SCC, Award, 16 December 2003, 34.

[13] *Pope & Talbot Inc v Government of Canada*, UNCITRAL, Award on the Merits of Phase 2, 10 April 2001, para 79; see also Chapter 3.

Mexico[14]), finding a breach of National Treatment 'does not require the Claimant to prove that the Respondent's conduct was *motivated* by the Claimant's foreign nationality'.[15] In *Bilcon v Canada* the tribunal held that:

> [c]onsistently with the approach taken in the *Feldman* case, however, the present Tribunal is also of the view that once a *prima facie* case is made out under the three-part *UPS* test, the onus is on the host state to show that a measure is still sustainable within the terms of Article 1102. It is the host state that is in a position to identify and substantiate the case, in terms of its own laws, policies and circumstances, that an apparently discriminatory measure is in fact compliant with the 'national treatment' norm set out in Article 1102 [of NAFTA].[16]

Likewise, in *RosInvest v Russia* the tribunal held that 'in the application of the tax law, in the tax assessments and in the conduct of the YNG auction, Yukos was treated by Respondent quite different to the treatment accorded to its competitors and other comparable tax payers and *no convincing reasons have been shown by Respondent for this differentiation*'.[17] In *Al Tamini v Oman* the tribunal adopted a more equivocal approach holding that:

> [i]f evidence of disparate treatment is produced by a claimant, then it will certainly be for the responding party to justify or negate that evidence of disparate treatment. But the principle does not obviate the need for a claimant to provide at least some relevant evidence to support his or her claim. Mere assertion will not suffice.[18]

Other tribunals strictly adhere to the principle *actori incumbit probatio*,[19] according to which the claimant has to prove all the facts underpinning its legal

[14] *Feldman Karpa v United Mexican States*, ICSID Case No ARB(AF)/99/1, Award, 16 December 2002, para 183, para 183.

[15] *Copper Mesa Mining Corporation v Republic of Ecuador*, PCA Case No 2012-2, Award, 15 March 2016, para 6.71 (emphasis added).

[16] *William Ralph Clayton, William Richard Clayton, Douglas Clayton, Daniel Clayton and Bilcon of Delaware Inc v Government of Canada*, UNCITRAL, PCA Case No 2009-04, Award on Jurisdiction and Liability, 17 March 2015, para 723.

[17] *RosInvestCo UK Ltd v The Russian Federation*, SCC Case No V079/2005, Final Award, 12 September 2010, para 556 (emphasis added).

[18] *Adel A Hamadi Al Tamimi v Sultanate of Oman*, ICSID Case No ARB/11/33Award, 3 November 2015, para 457.

[19] Investment treaty tribunals have consistently endorsed the principle *actor incumbit probatio*, but applied it flexibly, see *SolEs Badajoz GmbH v Kingdom of Spain*, ICSID Case No ARB/15/38, Award, 31 July 2019, para 335. *RREEF Infrastructure (GP) Limited and RREEF Pan-European Infrastructure Two Lux Sàrl v Kingdom of Spain*, ICSID Case No ARB/13/30, Decision on Responsibility and on the Principles of Quantum, 30 November 2018, para 187 ('[e]ach Party bears the burden of proving the facts that it alleges. Thus, in the main, the burden of proof falls on Claimant'); *Vito G Gallo v Government of Canada*, PCA Case No 55798, Award, 15 September 2011, para 277; *Saipem SpA v The People's Republic of Bangladesh*, ICSID Case No ARB/05/07, Award, 30 June 2009, para 113; *Azurix Corp v The Argentine Republic*, ICSID Case No ARB/01/12, Decision on the Application for Annulment of the Argentine Republic, 1 September 2009, para 215: 'Argentina refers to what it claims is "a general principle of law that the party that is in a better position to prove a fact bears the burden of proof" ... The Committee does not accept that such general principle exists in ICSID proceedings: to the contrary, the Committee considers the general principle in ICSID proceedings, and in international adjudication generally, to be that "who asserts must prove", and that in order to do so, the party which asserts must itself obtain and present the necessary evidence in order to prove what it asserts'. See also *International Thunderbird Gaming Corporation v United Mexican States*,

claims.[20] Thus, these tribunals require the investor to bear the burden of proof in relation to *all* factual aspects of the legal test for establishing discrimination.[21] In *UPS v Canada*—where a three-fold test for National Treatment was applied which included consideration of (i) the existence of 'treatment' accorded to the foreign investor, (ii) 'likeness', and (iii) less favourable treatment, but excluded any examination of regulatory purpose[22]—the tribunal held that:

> [f]ailure by the investor to establish one of those three elements will be fatal to its case. This is a legal burden that rests squarely with the Claimant. That burden never shifts to the Party, here Canada.[23]

In *South American Silver v Bolivia* the tribunal allocated the burden of proving the absence of a valid regulatory reason motivating the enactment of the measure to the investor.[24] The tribunal concluded *in casu* that '*the Claimant did not establish* the presence,

UNCITRAL, Award, 26 January 2006, para 95. See also *Gemplus, SA, SLP, SA and Gemplus Industrial, SA de CV v United Mexican States*, ICSID Case No ARB(AF)/04/3 and ARB(AF)/04/4, Award, 16 June 2010, Part XIII, para 13-80. See eg *Spyridon Roussalis v Romania* ICSID Case No ARB/06/1, Award, 7 December 2011, para 436 (emphasis added): 'There is also no evidence that the police sequestration had any actual effect on Claimant's investment. The November 13, 2001 police minute merely records Claimant's declaration that the subscribed capital was deposited at Alpha Bank. *The best evidence of funds on deposit*—copies of Claimant's bank records from Alpha Bank—*was uniquely in Claimant's control.* Claimant presented no such evidence'. Different approaches adopted by investment tribunals can be attributed to the fact that UNCITRAL Rules specifically refer to *actori incumbit probatio*, while other arbitration rules do not as well as differences between ICSID and non-ICSID arbitrations, as in the latter the law of the seat regulates procedural matters. An investment treaty tribunal applying the UNCITRAL Rules and seated in Switzerland held that '[u]nder Swiss international arbitration law, this principle *actori incumbat probatio* is considered part of procedural *ordre public*', *Jan Oostergetel and Theodora Laurentius v Slovak Republic*, UNCITRAL, Final Award, 23 April 2012, para 146. However, the tribunal also clarified that '[w]hile the general principle *actori incumbat probatio* pertains to procedure governed here by Swiss international arbitration law as the law of the seat, the rules establishing presumptions or shifting the burden of proof under certain circumstances, or drawing the inferences from a lack of proof are generally deemed to be part of the *lex causae*' ibid, 147. In *Tenaris v Venezuela II* the ad hoc annulment committee held that *actori incumbit probatio* was not an 'absolute' principle, an 'unshakeable and invariable minimum standard of procedure, as compared, for instance, to the right to be heard and rebut evidence, due process, neutrality and impartiality of tribunals and the equality of parties', *Tenaris SA and Talta—Trading e Marketing Sociedade Unipessoal Lda v Bolivarian Republic of Venezuela II*, ICSID Case No ARB/12/23, Decision on Annulment, 28 December 2018, paras 92 and 93.

[20] The burden of proof refers only to facts and not law as *iura* (or *arbiter*) *novit curia*, *Metal-Tech v The Republic of Uzbekistan*, Award, ICSID Case No ARB/10/3, 4 October 2013, para 287; *Military and Paramilitary Activities in and against Military and Paramilitary Activities in and against Nicaragua (Nicaragua v United States of America) (Merits)* [1986] ICJ Rep 14, 24, para 29. See *Vito G Gallo v Government of Canada*, PCA Case No 2008-03, Award, 15 September 2011, para 277 ('the principle *actori incumbit probatio* is a coin with two sides: the Claimant has to prove its case, and without evidence it will fail; but if the Respondent raises defences, of fraud or otherwise, the burden shifts, and the defences can only succeed if supported by evidence marshalled by the Respondent.'). See also *Case concerning the Application of the Convention of 1902 governing the Guardianship of Infants (Netherlands v Sweden)*, Judgment of 28 November 1958 [1958] ICJ Rep 55, 62: '[The Court] retains its freedom to select the ground upon which it will base its judgment, and is under no obligation to examine all the considerations advanced by the Parties if other considerations appear to it to be sufficient for its purpose.'

[21] See *Resolute Forest Products Inc v Government of Canada*, PCA Case No 2016-13, Award, 25 July 2022, paras 569–575 (with further references to the case law).

[22] *United Parcel Service of America Inc v Government of Canada*, ICSID Case No UNCT/02/1, Award on the Merits, 24 May 2007, para 83; see also Chapter 3, Section 3.3.1.

[23] *United Parcel Service of America Inc v Government of Canada* (n 22) para 84.

[24] *South American Silver Limited v Plurinational State of Bolivia*, PCA Case No 2013-15, Award, 30 August 2018, para 710 ('the Parties agree[d] on the standard for discriminatory measures. Consistent with the definition endorsed by both Parties, discrimination involves "a differential treatment of people or companies in like circumstances, without a rational justification for that differential treatment"') (emphasis removed).

much less the cumulation, of any of the elements derived from the standard mentioned above, that is: (i) the existence of another person or company in like circumstances, (ii) differential treatment, and (iii) *the absence of rational justification for such treatment*.'[25] In *Urbaser v Argentina* the tribunal disagreed with the investor's argument regarding shift the burden of proof by holding that:

> [t]he requirements resulting from Article III(1) [of the Argentina-Spain BIT prohibiting 'unjustified or discriminatory measures'] are at the very basis of Claimants' claims in this respect. The burden of proving the applicable conditions falls on Claimants. The Tribunal does not share Claimants' view that once Respondent has accepted that AGBA was afforded differential treatment, the burden of proof that such treatment was validly justified would shift to Respondent.[26]

In *Cengiz v Libya* the tribunal identified three analytical steps to establish discrimination in investment treaty arbitration: 'first, an appropriate comparator must be identified', '[s]econd, Claimant must prove that Libya has applied to this comparator a treatment more favourable than that accorded to Cengiz or to its investment in Libya', and '[t]hird, there must be a lack of a reasonable or objective justification for the difference of treatment'.[27] The tribunal clarified that '[t]he burden of proving these three elements lies with the Claimant'.[28] In *Unglaube v Costa Rica* the claimant argued that Costa Rica breached the BIT clause prohibiting 'arbitrary or discriminatory' measures. The precise terms for 'arbitrary or discriminatory' measures in Article 2(3) of the applicable Germany–Costa Rica BIT[29] referred to 'trato desigual injustificado' and 'ungleichbehandlung ... nichtgerechtfertigte' in Spanish and German respectively. On the basis of the slightly differently formulation of Article 2(3) in the two languages of the treaty the claimant argued that the tribunal must 'make an objective assessment' of the situation which means that 'the Tribunal should no longer require Claimants to bear the burden of proof. Instead, the Respondent must bear the burden of justifying its actions'.[30] The tribunal disagreed.[31] Although the tribunal held that 'discriminatory

[25] ibid, para 711 (emphasis added).

[26] *Urbaser SA and Consorcio de Aguas Bilbao Bizkaia, Bilbao Biskaia Ur Partzuergoa v The Argentine Republic*, ICSID Case No ARB/07/26, 8 December 2016, para 1087.

[27] *Cengiz Insaat Sanayi ve Ticaret AS v Libya*, ICC Case No 21537/ZF/AYZ, Award, 7 November 2018, para 525.

[28] ibid, para 526.

[29] Treaty between Costa Rica and Germany concerning the Encouragement and Reciprocal Protection of Investments (signed 13 September 1994, entered into force 24 March 1998), Article 2(3).

[30] *Marion Unglaube v Republic of Costa Rica*, ICSID Case No ARB/08/1, Award, 16 May 2012, para 266.

[31] ibid, para 267: 'The Tribunal has carefully considered these arguments of Claimants but is not persuaded by them. As indicated above, the Tribunal does not conclude that the alleged acts or decisions of Respondent, either individually or in combination, establish facts indicating a prima facie violation of Article 2(3) of the Treaty. So far as the Tribunal can discern, Claimants' argument regarding the proper meaning of the key language of Article 2(3) is not supported by the ordinary meaning of the language of the provision, or by interpretive evidence from the history of negotiation of the Treaty or otherwise. In the absence of such evidence, the Tribunal finds that these words, whether in German or Spanish, have been used repeatedly in German and Spanish language treaties; that they have a well-established meaning in international law, and have been correctly translated as equivalent to the phrase 'arbitrary or discriminatory treatment' in English. We thus find that the language of Article 2(3) does not remove the burden of proof from the Claimants. The Tribunal finds that Claimants have not borne the burden of proof on either of these allegations'.

intent' 'may be relevant', it is not required; what was required was the lack of 'explanation or justification' and it was upon the claimant to prove it (at least prima facie).[32] In *Tecmed v Mexico* the discrimination claim was dismissed because:

> *[t]he Claimant has failed to furnish convincing or sufficient evidence to prove*, at least *prima facie*, that the Claimant's investment received, under similar circumstances, less favorable treatment than that afforded to nationals of the State receiving the investment or of a third State, or that said investment was subject to *discriminatory treatment upon the basis of considerations relative to nationality or origin of the investment or the investor.*[33]

In paragraph 391 of the *Lemire v Ukraine* award, the tribunal categorically held that '[t]he burden of proof that the decision was discriminatory or arbitrary (or otherwise violated the FET standard) lies with Claimant'.[34] However, as Lowe explains:

> [t]he reference in paragraph 391 to the burden of proof must be read in conjunction with the *Lemire* Tribunal's observation in paragraph 405 that a finding of arbitrariness or discrimination might be appropriate 'in the absence of a plausible explanation' for decisions of the Ukrainian authorities. The claimant has the burden of proof, but in discharging it he may point to facts that call for an explanation by the respondent.[35]

In *Pawloski v Czech Republic* the tribunal first set out the applicable legal test in the following manner:

> if a claim based on discrimination or breach of the NT and MFN standards is to succeed, the following three-pronged test must be satisfied:
> - First, an appropriate comparator must be identified, i.e., an investor which is in a situation similar to that of Claimants (or an investment which is in a situation similar to Claimants' investment in the Czech Republic);
> - Second, Claimant must prove that the Czech Republic has applied to this comparator a treatment more favourable than that accorded to Pawlowski AG and Projekt Sever, or to their investment in the Czech Republic;

[32] ibid, paras 263–267.

[33] *Técnicas Medioambientales Tecmed, SA v The United Mexican States*, ICSID Case No ARB (AF)/00/2, Award, 29 May 2003, para 181 (emphasis added). See also ibid, para 182 ('With regard to other forms of discrimination apparently originated in the allegedly different treatment accorded by INE to RIMSA's and Claimant's investments, the Arbitral Tribunal holds that the Respondent has furnished satisfactory evidence—not rebutted by the Claimant on this point—of the fact that the circumstances under which RIMSA's investment was made and concerning such investment materially differed from the investment in the Landfill. Thus, it is not possible to establish standards which allow a comparison of the treatment accorded to the investment in RIMSA's landfill and the investment in the Landfill').

[34] *Joseph Charles Lemire v Ukraine*, ICSID Case No ARB/06/18, Decision on Jurisdiction and Liability, 14 January 2010, para 391.

[35] V Lowe, 'Arbitrary and Discriminatory Treatment' in M Kinnear and others (eds), *Building International Investment Law: The First 50 Years of ICSID* (Kluwer Law International 2016) 307–318, 313.

- Third, there must be a lack of a reasonable or objective justification for the difference of treatment.[36]

The tribunal immediately clarified in no unclear terms that '[t]he burden of proving these three elements lies with Claimants'.[37]

The analysis of the relevant case law demonstrated that investment tribunals have failed to adopt a uniform approach in relation to the allocation of the burden of proof in discrimination cases, especially regarding the last element of the legal test, which examines whether the measures(s) in question resulting in less favourable treatment are linked to a protected ground or are adopted to pursue legitimate public policy objectives.

4.1.2 The Normative Argument of the Book: Investors Should Prove that There Were No Justifications for Less Favourable Treatment

A conventional, albeit not universally shared, view is that once the investor proves likeness and less favourable treatment, the burden of proof shifts to the Respondent State to prove that such treatment was justified by legitimate policy goals.[38] The argument put forward in this book is different. This book argues that investors should bear the burden of proving that the less favourable treatment is *connected* to the investors' foreign nationality in National Treatment and MFN claims (or nationality or another protected in discrimination claims based on other non-discrimination obligations). This means that it is the claimant who must prove specific facts which establish that a state measure resulting in less favourable treatment is connected to the foreign investors'

[36] *Pawlowski AG and Project Sever sro v Czech Republic*, ICSID Case No ARB/17/11, Award, 1 November 2021, para 534 (emphasis removed).

[37] ibid, para 535.

[38] See eg A Newcombe and L Paradell, *Law and Practice of Investment Treaties, Standards of Treatment* (Kluwer Law International 2009) 163 ('[t]hus, with respect to a purported breach of national treatment, the claimant must identify the relevant subjects for comparison, demonstrate how it is in comparable circumstances in light of the purposes of the measure at issue and demonstrate that it received less favourable treatment than then applicable comparator. If the claimant makes out a *prima facie* case that the host state has accorded differential treatment to investments in like circumstances, the burden arguably shits to the state to justify the measure based on legitimate non-nationality based public policy considerations'); A Reinisch and C Schreuer, *International Protection of Investments: The Substantive Standards* (CUP 2020) 672 ('[t]he broad consensus appears to be that claimants have to prove that they were discriminated against, while respondent states then bear the burden of proof that a specific discrimination was justified'). According to Schreuer 'the investor does not bear the burden of proof that the differential treatment was motivated by its foreign nationality. The fact of discrimination and the existence of the foreign nationality are enough', C H Schreuer, 'Protection Against Arbitrary or Discriminatory Measures' in CA Rogers and RP Alford (eds), *The Future of Investment Arbitration* (OUP 2009) 183–198, 198. See also B Sabahi, 'National Treatment—Is Discriminatory Intent Relevant' in T Weiler (ed), *Investment Treaty Arbitration and International Law, vol 2* (JurisNet 2008) 269–297, 296 ('when a claimant can show a differential treatment on a prima facie basis, the proof of intent could become irrelevant. But, of course, in a three-step national treatment analysis, at this stage the burden shifts to the government to prove that its measures had a reasonable connection to a rational policy, and this could require showing that the government's motives or intentions were something other than harming foreign investors or investments'). See also U Kriebaum, 'Arbitrary/Unreasonable or Discriminatory Measures' in M Bungenberg and others (eds), *International Investment Law* (CH Beck, Hart, Nomos 2013) 790–806, 806: 'The claimant has the burden of proof for the difference in treatment. Once a difference in treatment is established in a group of comparable investors, the respondent has the burden of proof to establish that the differentiation is justified'.

nationality or another protected ground. In practice, this is inextricably linked to the absence of valid policy reasons that could justify the measures resulting in less favourable treatment. As Section 4.1.2.1 explains, this approach is not only consistent with the understanding of non-discrimination in international investment law as a form of disparate treatment or direct discrimination,[39] but it is also in line with the universally accepted procedural principle *actori incumbit probatio*.

Allocating the burden of proof to investors (rather than to States) strikes an appropriate balance between the competing interests of investors and States, and in particular the right of States to regulate. At the same time, Section 4.1.2.2 argues in favour of placing considerable emphasis on the duty of both parties to cooperate in the production of evidence in the context of arbitral proceedings. This, coupled with the power (and in some instances the duty) of arbitral tribunals to draw adverse inferences from the parties' failure to produce evidence, could alleviate the evidentiary difficulties that the allocation of the burden of proof to claimants creates for investors, especially in the light of the asymmetry of access to information and evidence which exists between sovereign States and private investors. This approach is also in line with the distinction between the burden of proof and evidentiary presumptions. As Walton explains, '[t]he key distinction between presumption and burden of proof (of the type called burden of persuasion in law) is that presumption functions only at the argumentation stage, whereas burden of proof is set at the opening stage, has effects at the argumentation stage and is vitally important in determining when the closing stage has been reached in a given case'.[40]

4.1.2.1 *Actori incumbit probatio*

Economics literature shows that one of the reasons for adopting the *actori incumbit probatio* principle is the asymmetry of information that exists between the parties on the one hand and the court on the other. This asymmetry between the parties and the court, coupled with the finite nature of the resources available to judicial systems, makes the *actori incumbit probatio* the optimal way to organize the procedural framework of litigation,[41] and, at least partly, explains the quasi-universal endorsement of that principle. At the end of the day, while not being indifferent to asymmetry of information problems, different domestic and international courts or tribunals take *actori incumbit probatio* as the starting point in relation to the allocation of the burden of proof. This book argues that this should be case in relation to the legal test for establishing violations of non-discrimination obligations in international investment law.

The ICJ has consistently emphasised that 'in accordance with the well-established principle of *onus probandi incumbit actori*, it is the duty of the party asserting certain

[39] See Chapter 2, Section 2.1 and Section 2.2.

[40] D Walton, *Burden of Proof, Presumption and Argumentation* (CUP 2014) 99; ibid: '[i]n a trial, the burden of persuasion is set at the opening stage and remains fixed until the closing stage'.

[41] CW Sanchirico, 'The Burden of Proof in Civil Litigation: A Simple Model of Mechanism Design' (1997) 17 International Review of Law and Economics 431. Cf D Demougin and C Fluet, 'Rules of Proof, Courts, and Incentives' (2008) 39 RAND Journal of Economics 20.

facts to establish the existence of such facts'.[42] While this principle 'has been consistently upheld by the Court';[43] the ICJ has referred to it in several occasions without engaging in detailed theoretical analysis. The principle was confirmed inter alia in the *Temple of Preah Vihear*,[44] *Nicaragua*,[45] *Avena*,[46] *Pedra Branca*,[47] *Genocide Convention*,[48] and *Maritime Delimitation in the Black Sea*[49] cases, as well as in the case law of the International Tribunal for the Law of the Sea (ITLOS) and the WTO Appellate Body.[50] As the ICJ observed in the *Land and Maritime Boundary between Cameroon and Nigeria*, this means that '[i]t is the applicant which must bear the consequences of an application that gives an inadequate rendering of the facts and grounds on which the claim is based'.[51] It has been suggested that in cases related to the protection of

[42] *Pulp Mills on the River Uruguay (Argentina v Uruguay)*, Judgment, [2010] ICJ Rep 14, 71, para 162; see also Separate Opinion of Judge Greenwood, para 24.

[43] ibid, 71, para 162.

[44] *Case concerning the Temple of Preah Vihear Cambodia v Thailand*, Merits [1962] ICJ Rep 6, 16 ('[t]he burden of proof in respect of these will of course lie on the Party asserting or putting them forward').

[45] *Military and Paramilitary Activities in and against Nicaragua (Nicaragua v United States of America)* Jurisdiction and Admissibility [1984] ICJ Rep 392, 437, para 101 ('the litigant seeking to establish a fact who bears the burden of proving it; and in cases where evidence may not be forthcoming, a submission may in the judgment be rejected as unproved'). See also *Border and Transborder Armed Actions (Nicaragua v Honduras), Jurisdiction and Admissibility*, Judgment, [1988] ICJ Reports 69, 76, para 16: '[t]he Parties have devoted some argument to a question defined by them as that of the burden of proof: whether it is for Nicaragua to show the existence of jurisdiction for the Court to deal with its claims, or for Honduras to establish the absence of such jurisdiction. Each of them has cited, in support of its contention, the Court's dictum that "it is the litigant seeking to establish a fact who bears the burden of proving it"'.

[46] *Avena and Other Mexican Nationals (Mexico v United States of America)*, Judgment, [2004] ICJ Rep 12, 41, para 55 ('[b]oth Parties recognize the well-settled principle in international law that a litigant seeking to establish the existence of a fact bears the burden of proving it').

[47] *Sovereignty over Pedra Branca/Pulau Batu Puteh, Middle Rocks and South Ledge (Malaysia/Singapore)*, Judgment, [2008] ICJ Rep 12, 31, para 45 ('[i]t is a general principle of law, confirmed by the jurisprudence of this Court, that a party which advances a point of fact in support of its claim must establish that fact').

[48] *Application of the Convention on the Prevention and Punishment of the Crime of Genocide (Bosnia and Herzegovina v Serbia and Montenegro)*, Judgment, [2007] ICJ Rep 43, 128, para 204 ('[o]n the burden or onus of proof, it is well established in general that the applicant must establish its case and that a party asserting a fact must establish it').

[49] *Maritime Delimitation in the Black Sea (Romania v Ukraine)*, Judgment, [2009] ICJ Rep 61, 86, para 68 ('the party asserting a fact as a basis of its claim must establish it').

[50] See *'Grand Prince' (Belize v France)*, Prompt Release, Judgment, [2001] ITLOS Rep 17, 38, para 67; AB, *US—Wool Shirts and Blouses*, 14: 'It is a generally accepted canon of evidence in civil law, common law, and, in fact, most jurisdictions, that the burden of proof rests upon the party, whether complaining or defending, who asserts the affirmative of a particular claim or defence. If that party adduces sufficient evidence to raise a presumption that what is claimed is true, the burden then shifts to the other party, who will fail unless it adduces sufficient evidence to rebut the presumption'.

[51] *Land and Maritime Boundary between Cameroon and Nigeria (Cameroon v Nigeria)*, Preliminary Objections, Judgment [1998] ICJ Rep 275, 319, para 101. However, the same facts could constitute the basis of both parties' claims, see eg *Frontier Dispute (Burkina Faso/Mali)*, Judgment, [1986] ICJ Rep 554, 587–588, para 65: 'While it is true that "ultimately ... it is the litigant seeking to establish a fact who bears the burden of proving it" ... it is also for Mali to establish the facts underlying its claims, that is, to demonstrate that the villages were Sudanese at that time'. The principle *actori incumbit probatio* is also codified in national legislation, see eg Code of Civil Procedure (France), Article 9: 'Il incombe à chaque partie de prouver conformément à la loi les faits nécessaires au succès de sa prétention'. Civil Code (France), Article 1353 (ex Article 1315): '[c]elui qui réclame l'exécution d'une obligation doit la prouver'. See also ICC Case No 6653, Award, 26 March 1993 (1993) Clunet (1993) 1040 et seq. In 2017 the French Cour de Cassation (the Civil and Criminal Supreme Court) reversed a decision of the Court of Appeal as contrary to this basic principle, CC Civ, 3rd, Case No 14–14.93, 21 June 2017 ('Qu'en statuant ainsi, alors qu'il appartenait à l'entrepreneur réclamant paiement de démontrer que les travaux avaient été achevés conformément aux prévisions contractuelles, la cour d'appel, qui a inversé la charge de la preuve, a violé le texte susvisé'). The starting point in relation to the allocation of the burden of proof in EU competition law is that the 'burden of proving an infringement of Article 81(1) [101(1)] or of Article 82 [102] of the Treaty [Treaty for the Functioning of the European Union (TFEU)] shall rest on the party or the authority alleging the infringement', Council Regulation (EC) No 1/2003 on the implementation of the rules on competition laid down in Articles 81 and 82 of the Treaty, 16 December 2002, Article 2; see also A Kalintiri, *Evidence Standards in EU Competition Enforcement: The EU*

the environment the precautionary principle[52] justifies the reversal of the burden of proof.[53] Although Judge Weeramatry elaborated on this approach in the 1995 *Nuclear Test* case,[54] the ICJ ultimately rejected this approach and reaffirmed the central importance of the *actori incumbit probatio* principle.[55] The EU legal system also ascribes to the same principle,[56] although EU law also respects the principle of procedural autonomy of each EU Member State.[57]

Approach (Hart 2018), Chapter 3; A Papadelli, *Beweislastverteilung bei der privaten Durchsetzung des Kartellrechts. Eine rechtsvergleichende Studie* (LIT Verlag 2010); F Castillo de la Torre and E Gippini Fournier, *Evidence, Proof and Judicial Review in EU Competition Law* (Edward Elgar 2017).

52 On the precautionary principle generally see C Foster, *Science and the Precautionary Principle in International Courts and Tribunals: Expert Evidence, Burden of Proof and Finality* (CUP 2011); B Sage-Fuller, *The Precautionary Principle in Marine Environmental Law with Special References to High Risk Vessels* (Routledge 2013).

53 JE Viñuales, *Foreign Investment and the Environment in International Law* (CUP 2012) 122–123. See also A Trouwborst, *Precautionary Rights and Duties of States* (Martinus Nijhoff 2006) 219 et seq.

54 *Request for an Examination of the Situation in Accordance with Paragraph 63 of the Court's Judgment of 20 December 1974 in the Nuclear Tests (New Zealand v France)* Order, Dissenting Opinion of Judge Weeramantry [1995] ICJ Rep 317, 348 ('the principle of environmental law under which, where environmental damage of any sort is threatened, the burden of proving that it will not produce the damaging consequences complained of is placed upon the author of that damage. In this view of the matter, the Court would hold that the environmental damage New Zealand complains of is prima facie established in the absence of proof by France that the proposed nuclear tests are environmentally safe. It will be noted in this connection that all the information bearing upon this matter is in the possession of the Respondent. The Applicant has only indirect or secondary information, but has endeavoured to place before the Court such information as it has been able, to the best of its ability, to marshal for the purposes of this application. The second approach is sufficiently well established in international law for the Court to act upon it'). See also *Legality of the Threat or Use of Nuclear Weapons*, Advisory Opinion, Dissenting Opinion of Judge Weeramantry [1996] ICJ Rep 429, 502–503; *Southern Bluefin Tuna (New Zealand v Japan; Australia v Japan)*, Provisional Measures, Order of 27 August 1999, [1999] ITLOS Rep 305, 310–311, para 14: 'The thrust of the notion [of the precautionary principle] is vesting a broad dispensation to policy makers, seeking to provide guidance to administrative and other decisionmakers and shifting the burden of proof to the State in control of the territory from which the harm might emanate or to the responsible actor'; *MOX Plant (Ireland v United Kingdom)*, Provisional Measures Order of 3 December 2001, Separate Opinion of Judge Wolfrum [2001] ITLOS Rep 131, 134: '[t]here is no general agreement as to the consequences which flow from the implementation of this principle other than the fact that the burden of proof concerning the possible impact of a given activity is reversed. A State interested in undertaking or continuing a particular activity has to prove that such activities will not result in any harm, rather than the other side having to prove that it will result in harm.'

55 See also *Pulp Mills on the River Uruguay (Argentina v Uruguay)*, Judgment [2010] ICJ Rep 14, para 71, 164: '[W]hile a precautionary approach may be relevant in the interpretation and application of the provisions of the Statute, it does not follow that it operates as a reversal of the burden of proof'. Nonetheless, it has been argued that 'State practice is changing' in that regard, AA Cançado Trindade, 'Principle 15: Precaution' in JE Viñuales (ed), *The Rio Declaration on Environment and Development: A Commentary* (OUP 2015) 403–428, 409.

56 Although the EU Courts are generally hesitant to explicitly refer to that principle, M Fartunova-Michel, *La preuve dans le droit de l'Union européenne* (Bruylant 2013); see also R Mehdi, 'La preuve devant les juridictions communautaires' in H Ruiz Fabri and J-M Sorel (eds), *La preuve devant les juridictions internationales* (Pédone 2007) 165–181. For an exception, see *Case T-117/89, Paul F Sens v Commission*, 10 May 1990, para 20, in which the Court confirmed 'the principle *actori incumbit probatio*, according to which each party must prove only the positive facts on which it relies; in other words the principle precludes a party from having the burden of proving purely negative facts'. See also A Kalintiri, 'The Allocation of the Legal Burden of Proof in Article 101 TFEU Cases: A "Clear" Rule with Not-So-Clear Implications' (2015) 34 Yearbook of European Law 232. See also G Cumming and M Freudenthal, *Civil Procedure in EU Competition Cases Before the English and Dutch Courts* (Kluwer Law International 2010) 113 ('The option of generally shifting the overall burden of proof does not constitute effective general remedy to the consequence of the structural information asymmetry in competition cases, as do measures to improve access to evidence').

57 See eg *Case C-3/16, Lucio Cesare Aquino v Belgische Staat*, 15 March 2017: '[i]t should be recalled here that, according to settled case-law of the Court, in the absence of EU rules on the matter, it is for the national legal order of each Member State to establish procedural rules for actions intended to safeguard the rights of individuals, in accordance with the principle of procedural autonomy'.

Investment treaty tribunals also adhere to the *actori incumbi probatio* principle.[58] However, tribunals seem to be divided on the whether the burden of proof shifts to the Respondent after the evidence produced by the Claimant in support of its claim reaches a certain threshold or remains with the Claimant throughout the proceedings.[59] As Born persuasively argues, the better view is that the awards adopting the view that the burden of proof shifts should be 'understood as relating to the evidential burden. And, a close reading of the awards in each case suggests that this is precisely what the tribunal in each case was confronted by and addressing'.[60] As Walton, explains one type of burden of proof:

> is the setting of the global burden of proof before the trial begins, which is called the burden of persuasion. It does not change during the argumentation stage, and it is the device used to determine which side has won at the closing stage. The other is the local setting of burden of proof at the argumentation stage, often called the burden of

[58] See eg *Asian Agricultural Products Ltd v Republic of Sri Lanka*, ICSID Case No ARB/87/3, Final Award, 27 June 1990, para 56; *Hussein Nuaman Soufraki v United Arab Emirates*, ICSID Case No ARB/02/7, Award, 7 July 2004, para 58 ('[i]n accordance with accepted international (and general national) practice, a party bears the burden of proof in establishing the facts that he asserts'); see *Chevron Corp and Texaco Petroleum Corp v Republic of Ecuador*, UNCITRAL, PCA Case No 34877, Interim Award, 1 December 2008, para 138; *Waguih Elie George Siag and Clorinda Vecchi v Arab Republic of Egypt*, ICSID Case No ARB/05/15, Award, 1 June 2009, para 315; *RosInvestCo UK Ltd v Russian Federation*, SCC Case No V079/2005, Final Award, 12 September 2010, para 250; *Alpha Projektholding GmbH v Ukraine*, ICSID Case No ARB/07/16, Award, 8 November 2010, para 236; see also FG Sourgens, K Duggal, and IA Laird, *Evidence in International Investment Arbitration* (OUP 2018) 56: 'However, despite these potential problems, the basic rule relating to burden of proof has near unanimity in international law and is recognized in virtually every legal system (international, civil, common, and Roman laws) because reversing the rules of burden of proof would create perverse incentives for the party raising the objection. Indeed, investor-state tribunals have recognized and applied its application at all stages of the arbitration process and for every motion'. See also (n 19).

[59] *Apotex Holdings Inc and Apotex Inc v United States of America*, ICSID Case No ARB(AF)/12/1, Award, 25 August 2014, para 8.8: 'a distinction exists between the legal burden of proof (which never shifts) and the evidential burden of proof (which can shift from one party to another, depending upon the state of the evidence)'; *The Rompetrol Group NV v Romania*, ICSID Case No ARB/06/3, Award, 6 March 2013, para 178: '[o]perating within an international system characterised by principle rather than procedural formality, the Tribunal is not enamoured of arguments setting out to show that a burden of proof can under certain circumstances shift from the party that originally bore it to the other party, and then perhaps in appropriate circumstances shift back again to the original party'; *Jan Oostergetel and Theodora Laurentius v Slovak Republic*, UNCITRAL, Final Award, 23 April 2012, para 148; *United Parcel Service of America Inc v Government of Canada*, ICSID Case No UNCT/02/1, Award on the Merits, 24 May 2007, para 84; *Chevron Corporation (USA) and Texaco Petroleum Company (USA) v The Republic of Ecuador*, UNCITRAL, PCA Case No 34877, Interim Award, 1 December 2008, para 138 ('[a]s a general rule, the holder of a right raising a claim on the basis of that right in legal proceedings bears the burden of proof for all elements required for the claim'); *Pac Rim Cayman LLC v Republic of El Salvador*, ICSID Case No ARB/09/12, Decision on the Respondent's Jurisdictional Objections, 1 June 2012, para 2.13 ('[t]he Tribunal agrees that the burden lies on a claimant who asserts a positive right and on a respondent who asserts a positive answer to the claimant'). Cf *Waguih Elie George Siag and Clorinda Vecchi v The Arab Republic of Egypt*, ICSID Case No ARB/05/15, Award, 1 June 2009, para 317 ('[b]ecause negative evidence is very often more difficult to assert than positive evidence, the reversal of the burden of proof may make it almost impossible for the allegedly fraudulent party to defend itself, thus violating due process standards. It is for this reason that Tribunals have rarely shifted the burden of proof. There are no special circumstances or good reasons for doing so in this case.'); *International Thunderbird Gaming Corporation v United Mexican States*, UNCITRAL, Award, 26 January 2006, para 98 ('The Tribunal shall apply the well-established principle that the party alleging a violation of international law giving rise to international responsibility has the burden of proving its assertion. If said Party adduces evidence that prima facie supports its allegation, the burden of proof may be shifted to the other Party, if the circumstances so justify.'). See also GB Born, 'On Burden and Standard of Proof' in M Kinnear and others (n 35) 43–54.

[60] Born, ibid, 46. As Born highlights, '[c]rucially, allowing the evidential burden to shift does not impact the legal burden of proof or the standard of proof', ibid, 48.

> production (or the evidential burden, or the burden of going forward with evidence) in law. This burden can shift back and forth as the argumentation proceeds.[61]

This book argues that reversing the burden of proof and requiring States (rather than investors) to prove that the measures in question are linked to legitimate policy objectives, let alone the absence of discriminatory intent, will disrupt the balance between the interests of foreign investors and Host States, potentially exposing legitimate regulatory action to investment treaty claims. Given that even if a State prevails in investment treaty arbitration, the cost of successfully defending its actions before an international arbitral tribunal is high in terms of financial and administrative resources as well as reputation. Although if successful, States can claim arbitration costs, this is not automatic and, whether, and to what extent, costs can be recovered depends on several facts including the applicable arbitration rules and the conduct of both parties in the arbitration.[62]

There is no doubt that States are entitled to deference by arbitral tribunals, and, in fact, by any international court or tribunal, when it comes to decision-making in relation to complex policy issues.[63] In *Invesmart v Czech Republic* the tribunal held that '[a] state should not be held to an obligation to act in accordance with international best practice'.[64] In *Levy v Peru* the tribunal emphasized that:

[61] Walton (n 40) 49.

[62] See the Convention on the settlement of investment disputes between States and nationals of other States (adopted 18 March 1965, entered into force 14 October 1966) 575 UNTS 159 (ICSID Convention), Article 61(2) ('In the case of arbitration proceedings the Tribunal shall, except as the parties otherwise agree, assess the expenses incurred by the parties in connection with the proceedings, and shall decide how and by whom those expenses, the fees and expenses of the members of the Tribunal and the charges for the use of the facilities of the Centre shall be paid. Such decision shall form part of the award'); 2022 ICSID Rules, Rules 51(1) and 51(2):

> (1) In allocating the costs of the proceeding, the Tribunal shall consider all relevant circumstances, including:
>
> (a) the outcome of the proceeding or any part of it;
> (b) the conduct of the parties during the proceeding, including the extent to which they acted in an expeditious and cost-effective manner and complied with these Rules and the orders and decisions of the Tribunal;
> (c) the complexity of the issues; and
> (d) the reasonableness of the costs claimed.
>
> (2) If the Tribunal renders an Award pursuant to Rule 41(3), it shall award the prevailing party its reasonable costs, unless the Tribunal determines that there are special circumstances justifying a different allocation of costs.

See also 2010 and 2021 UNCITRAL Arbitration Rules, Article 42(1): 'The costs of the arbitration shall in principle be borne by the unsuccessful party or parties. However, the arbitral tribunal may apportion each of such costs between the parties if it determines that apportionment is reasonable, taking into account the circumstances of the case'; see generally S Puig, 'Contextualizing Cost Shifting in Investment Treaty Arbitration' (2019) 58 Virginia Journal of International Law 261; GA Bermann, 'Costs Allocation in International Arbitration: What Normative Source, If Any?' in S Tung, F Fortese, and C Baltag (eds), *Finances in International Arbitration: Liber Amicorum Patricia Shaughnessy* (Kluwer Law International 2019) 27–34; DF Donovan, 'Allocation of Costs', M Kinnear and others (n 35) 555–566; G Flecke-Giammarco, 'The Allocation of Costs by Arbitral Tribunals in International Commercial Arbitration' in JA Huerta-Goldman, A Romanetti, and FX Stirnimann (eds), *WTO Litigation, Investment Arbitration, and Commercial Arbitration* (Kluwer Law International 2013) 389–420; AW Rovine, 'Allocation of Costs in Recent ICSID Awards' in in DD Caron and others (eds), *Practising Virtue: Inside International Arbitration* (OUP 2015) 658–688; SD Franck, 'Rationalizing Costs in Investment Treaty Arbitration' (2011) 88 Washington University Law Review 769.

[63] See also MN Kinnear, AK Bjorklund, and JFG Hannaford, *Investment Disputes under NAFTA: An Annotated Guide to NAFTA Chapter 11, Supplement No 1, March 2008* (Kluwer Law International 2006) 1102–1126.

[64] *Invesmart BV v Czech Republic*, UNCITRAL, Award, 26 June 2009, para 459.

> it is unacceptable for an Arbitral Tribunal to 'step into the shoes' of any organ and to 'second-guess' its actions. In other words, an Arbitral Tribunal cannot substitute itself for a State organ or convert itself into an appeals body to examine acts or decisions of the relevant authorities.[65]

The need for deference was also highlighted in *SD Myers v Canada*:

> [w]hen interpreting and applying the 'minimum standard', a Chapter 11 tribunal does not have an open-ended mandate to second-guess government decision-making. Governments have to make many potentially controversial choices. In doing so, they may appear to have made mistakes, to have misjudged the facts, proceeded on the basis of a misguided economic or sociological theory, placed too much emphasis on some social values over others and adopted solutions that are ultimately ineffective or counterproductive. The ordinary remedy, if there were one, for errors in modern governments is through internal political and legal processes, including elections.[66]

This idea was subsequently endorsed by other tribunals.[67] In *Quiborax v Bolivia*, the deference was framed in the following terms:

[65] *Renée Rose Levy De Levi v The Republic of Peru*, ICSID Case No ARB/10/17, Award, 26 February 2014, para 161. See also *Glamis Gold, Ltd v The United States of America*, UNCITRAL, Final Award, 8 June 2009, para 762 ('it is not for an international tribunal to delve into the details of and justifications for domestic law'). See also C Henckels, *Proportionality and Deference in Investor-State Arbitration Balancing Investment Protection and Regulatory Autonomy* (CUP 2015); M Wagner, 'Regulatory Space in International Trade Law and International Investment Law' (2014) 36 University of Pennsylvania Journal of International Law 1; A Titi, *The Right to Regulate in International Investment Law* (Nomos 2013); L Boisson de Chazournes and J Rudall, 'Judicial Deference: Why Does It Matter?' (2021) 22 The Law and Practice of International Courts and Tribunals 419; Y Fukunaga, 'Deference and the Authority of International Adjudication' (2021) 22 The Law and Practice of International Courts and Tribunals 425; J Paine, 'Deference and Other Standards of Review in International Adjudication' (2021) 22 The Law and Practice of International Courts and Tribunals 431; A Legg, 'Is There Method in the Margin? The Essence of Judicial Deference and the Margin of Appreciation' (2022) 21 The Law and Practice of International Courts and Tribunals 442; K Sulyok, 'Judicial Deference and Science' (2022) 21 The Law and Practice of International Courts and Tribunals 448; E Shirlow, 'Deference and the Practice of International Law' (2022) 21 The Law and Practice of International Courts and Tribunals 457; JH Fahner, 'The Limited Utility of Deference in International Dispute Settlement' (2022) 21 The Law and Practice of International Courts and Tribunals 467; JH Fahner, *Judicial Deference in International Adjudication: A Comparative Analysis* (Hart 2020); E Benvenisti, 'Explaining Variations in Standards of Review in International Adjudication' in G Kajtár, B Çali, and M Milanovic (eds), *Secondary Rules of Primary Importance in International Law: Attribution, Causality, Evidence, and Standards of Review in the Practice of International Courts and Tribunals* (OUP 2022) 21–41; G Coop and I Seif, 'ECT and States' Right to Regulate' in M Scherer (ed), *International Arbitration in the Energy Sector* (OUP 2018) 221–249; see also J Paine, 'Autonomy to Set the Level of Regulatory Protection in International Investment Law' (2021) 70 ICLQ 697; E Shirlow, 'Deference and Indirect Expropriation Analysis in International Investment Law: Observations on Current Approaches and Frameworks for Future Analysis' (2014) 29 ICSID Review 595; E Shirlow, *Judging at the Interface: Deference to Domestic Authority in International Adjudication* (CUP 2021); Y Fukunaga, 'Margin of Appreciation as an Indicator of Judicial Deference: Is It Applicable to Investment Arbitration?' (2019) 10 JIDS 69; Y Shany, 'Toward a General Margin of Appreciation Doctrine in International Law?' (2005) 16 EJIL 907; WW Burke-White and A von Staden, 'The Need for Public Law Standards of Review in Investor-State Arbitrations' in SW Schill (ed), *International Investment Law and Comparative Public Law* (OUP 2010) 689–720; on the concept of 'economic autonomy' see D Sarooshi, 'Sovereignty, Economic Autonomy, the United States, and the International Trading System: Representations of a Relationship' (2004) 15 EJIL 651.

[66] *SD Myers, Inc v Government of Canada*, UNCITRAL, Partial Award, 13 November 2000, para 261; see also *British Caribbean Bank Ltd v Government of Belize*, PCA Case No 2010–18/BCB-BZ, Award, 19 December 2014, para 236 ('a State is entitled to broad latitude to devise its public policy as it sees fit').

[67] See *Gemplus, SA, SLP, SA and Gemplus Industrial, SA de CV v United Mexican States*, ICSID Case No ARB(AF)/04/3 & ARB(AF)/04/4, Award, 16 June 2010, Part VI, para 6–26.

> [t]he Tribunal wishes to reassure the Government of Bolivia that by no means does it intend to interfere with the policies that Bolivia sets and implements as a sovereign State. The Tribunal agrees with the Respondent that the ICSID arbitration system 'should not be used as a sword of Damocles to hang over [host States'] heads but as a means of ensuring everybody abides by their obligations'.[68]

Showing (but like Caesar's wife, also seen to be showing) deference to States is even more important for tribunal in the current political atmosphere, ie in the light of the backlash against investment treaty arbitration.[69] This backlash is also evident in a series of judgments by the Court of Justice of the EU[70] and the ongoing discussions regarding the reform of the investment treaty system.[71] The need to show deference

[68] *Quiborax SA and Non Metallic Minerals SA v Plurinational State of Bolivia*, ICSID Case No ARB/06/2, Award, 16 September 2015, para 89. See also *Marfin Investment Group Holdings SA and others v Republic of Cyprus*, ICSID Case No ARB/13/27, Award, 26 July 2018, para 900 ('that such deference must not impede its task to verify whether international law was complied with. If there is any evidence that a decision taken by a regulator was abusive, did not afford due process or was a pretense of form designed to conceal improper ends, a tribunal must find a breach of international law').

[69] See M Waibel and others (eds), *The Backlash against Investment Arbitration: Perceptions and Reality* (Kluwer Law International 2010); G Van Harten, *The Trouble with Foreign Investor Protection* (OUP 2020); M Langford and D Behn, 'Managing Backlash: The Evolving Investment Treaty Arbitrator?' (2018) 29 EJIL 551; for a persuasive rebuttal of (some of the) criticisms levelled against investment treaty arbitration see the pioneering empirical work of Susan Franck: SD Franck, *Arbitration Costs: Myths and Realities in Investment Treaty Arbitration* (OUP 2019); S Franck, 'Empirically Evaluating Claims about Investment Treaty Arbitration' (2007) 86 North Carolina Law Review 1; S Franck, 'Empiricism and International Law: Insights for Investment Treaty Dispute Resolution' (2008) 48 Virginia Journal of International Law 767; SD Franck, 'Development and Outcomes of Investment Treaty Arbitration' (2009) 50 Harvard International Law Journal 435; see also D Behn, OK Fauchald, M Langford (eds), *The Legitimacy of Investment Arbitration: Empirical Perspectives* (CUP 2022); L Paradell Trius, 'The legitimacy of investment treaties: Between Exit, Voice and James Crawford's quest for a more democratic international law' in C Chinkin and F Baetens (eds), *Sovereignty, Statehood and State Responsibility: Essays in Honour of James Crawford* (CUP 2015) 90–109. See also JC Hamilton, OE Garcia-Bolivar, and H Otero, 'Latin American Arbitration and Investment Protections' in JC Hamilton, OE Garcia-Bolivar, and H Otero (eds), *Latin American Investment Protections* (Martinus Nijhoff 2012) 1–4, 2; E Gaillard, 'The Denunciation of the ICSID Convention' (2007) 237 NYLJ 1; C Schreuer, 'Denunciation of the ICSID Convention and Consent to Arbitration' in M Waibel and others (eds), *The Backlash against Investment Arbitration: Perceptions and Reality* (Kluwer Law International 2010) 353–368; OM Garibaldi, 'On the Denunciation of the ICSID Convention, Consent to ICSID Jurisdiction, and the Limits of Contract Analogy' in C Binder and others (eds), *International Investment Law for the 21st Century: Essays in Honour of Christoph Schreuer* (OUP 2009) 251–277. Having denounced the ICSID Convention in 2009, Ecuador signed it again in June 2021 <https://icsid.worldbank.org/news-and-events/news-releases/ecuador-signs-icsid-convention>. See also R Brutger and A Strezhnev, 'International Investment Disputes, Media Coverage, and Backlash Against International Law' (2022) 66 Journal of Conflict Resolution 983.

[70] Case C-284/16, *Slovak Republic v Achmea BV*, EU:C:2018:158. The CJEU held that Investor–State Dispute Settlement (ISDS) clauses contained in intra-EU BITs are incompatible with EU law. Following the Achmea decision, 23 EU Member States signed the Agreement for the Termination of Bilateral Investment Treaties between the Member States of the European Union [2020] OJ L169/1. Case C-741/19 *Republic of Moldova v Komstroy*, EU:C:2021:655, para 66 (holding that art 26 (2)(c) of the Energy Charter Treaty (providing for Investor–State arbitration) 'must be interpreted as not being applicable to disputes between a Member State and an investor of another Member State concerning an investment made by the latter in the first Member State'). Case C-109/20 *Republic of Poland v PL Holdings Sàrl*, EU:C:2021:875, para 56 (holding that 'Articles 267 and 344 TFEU [Treaty on the Functioning of the European Union] must be interpreted as precluding national legislation which allows a Member State to conclude an ad hoc arbitration agreement with an investor from another Member State that makes it possible to continue arbitration proceedings initiated on the basis of an arbitration clause whose content is identical to that agreement, where that clause is contained in an international agreement concluded between those two Member States and is invalid on the ground that it is contrary to those articles'). See also O Repoysis and M Risvas, 'International Investment Law and the (International) Rule of Law: The case of the EU Renewable Energy Industry' in R Leal-Arcas (ed), *International Trade, Investment and the Rule of Law* (Eliva Press 2020) 131–156.

[71] See A Roberts and T St John, 'Complex Designers and Emergent Design: Reforming the Investment Treaty System' (2022) 116 AJIL 96; SW Schill and G Vidigal, 'Investment Dispute Settlement à la carte: A Proposal for the Reform of Investor–State Dispute Settlement' in M Elsig, R Polanco, and P van den Bossche (eds), *International*

towards States, and by implication, foster legitimacy in favour of arbitral awards rendered against States is also highlighted by the fact that in several cases enforcement of investment treaty awards is not voluntary but requires (sometimes lengthy and expensive) enforcement proceedings in one or more jurisdictions.[72]

Finally, from a practical perspective, perhaps the most important argument against allocating the burden of proof in relation to the (necessary) link between the protected ground and less favourable treatment in the context of discrimination claims to investors[73] is the asymmetry that exists between investors and States regarding access to relevant evidence and information. Requiring the claimant to prove that measures resulting in less favourable treatment, compared with other (domestic or foreign) investors in like circumstance, were adopted by the State 'because of' the investor's nationality (in National Treatment and MFN claims respectively) or 'because of' the investor's nationality or another protected characteristic, such as race or religion (in non-impairment, FET, and expropriation claims) creates serious, and, in some cases, insurmountable evidentiary difficulties. These difficulties are caused to a great extent by the disproportionately larger, or in some cases even exclusive, control of the State over evidence in relation to its law-making and, more generally, decision-making processes, as well as the fact that these processes are complex and polycentric.[74] As explained above,[75] such concerns led some tribunals to hold that discriminatory intent is not necessary to sustain a discrimination claim[76] or to allocate the burden of proof to the respondent, at least, once a prima facie case was made (as in *Bilcon v Canada*).[77] The tribunal in *Apotex v USA* highlighted that the evidentiary difficulties that the claimant

Economic Dispute Settlement Demise or Transformation? (CUP 2021) 220–263; M Bungenberg and A Reinisch, *From Bilateral Arbitral Tribunals and Investment Courts to a Multilateral Investment Court: Options Regarding the Institutionalization of Investor-State Dispute Settlement* (Springer 2020); A Reinisch, 'Will the EU's Proposal Concerning an Investment Court System for CETA and TTIP Lead to Enforceable Awards?—The Limits of Modifying the ICSID Convention and the Nature of Investment Arbitration' (2016) 19 JIEL 761; see also S Schacherer, 'TPP, CETA and TTIP between innovation and consolidation—resolving Investor-State disputes under mega-regionals' (2016) 7 Journal of International Dispute Settlement 628. Cf W Alschner 'The Impact of Investment Arbitration on Investment Treaty Design: Myth Versus Reality' The (2017) 42 Yale Journal of International Law 1, 5, arguing that the case law of investment treaty tribunals had limited influence on treaty drafting.

[72] See the excellent analysis in E Gaillard and I Mitrev Penushliski, 'State Compliance with Investment Awards' (2020) 35 ICSID Review 540. On the issue of enforcement see also M Risvas, 'Review and Enforcement of Arbitral Awards in International Investment Law and General Public International Law' in C Tams, R Hofmann, and SW Schill (eds), *Investment Law as a Motor of General International Law* (Edward Elgar 2023) 375–400.

[73] See Chapter 3, Section 3.3.

[74] See also *Methanex Corporation v United States of America*, UNCITRAL, Partial Award, 7 August 2002, para 158: '[i]n particular, decrees and regulations may be the product of compromises and the balancing of competing interests by a variety of political actors. As a result, it may be difficult to identify a single or predominant purpose underlying a particular measure. Where a single governmental actor is motivated by an improper purpose, it does not necessarily follow that the motive can be attributed to the entire government. Much if not all will depend on the evidential materials adduced in the particular case.'

[75] See Section 4.1.

[76] See *Marvin Roy Feldman Karpa v United Mexican States*, ICSID Case No ARB(AF)/99/1, Award, 16 December 2002, para 183.

[77] *William Ralph Clayton, William Richard Clayton, Douglas Clayton, Daniel Clayton and Bilcon of Delaware Inc v Government of Canada*, UNCITRAL, PCA Case No 2009-04, Award on Jurisdiction and Liability, 17 March 2015, para 723.

faces (in the context of a discrimination (MFN) case) stem out from 'a procedural aspect inherent in this form of investor-state arbitration':

> [w]hilst Articles 40 and 41(2) of the ICSID Arbitration AF Rules permit an investor-claimant to request documentation from a respondent State, there is no Anglo-Saxon form of automatic discovery of all potentially relevant documentation. Where crucial documents are properly withheld by a respondent State on grounds of strict confidentiality or other like privilege and not ordered for production by a tribunal (on those grounds), how then can the claimant investor discharge the legal burden of proving its positive case under NAFTA Article 1103 in regard to factual matters essentially within the exclusive domain of the respondent State?[78]

Similar evidentiary difficulties regarding intent in the context of discrimination in international trade law led WTO Panels and the Appellate Body to reject the 'aims-and-effects' test,[79] in determining likeness in National Treatment cases, a test which had been used in earlier GATT cases.[80] One of the main reasons for abandoning the 'aims-and-effects' test is that discriminatory treatment is often the result of complex and polycentric regulatory processes. As the WTO Panel explained in *Japan—Alcoholic Beverages*:

> the adoption of the aim-and-effect test would have important repercussions on the burden of proof imposed on the complainant. The Panel noted in this respect that the complainants, according to the aim-and-effect test, have the burden of showing not only the effect of a particular measure, which is in principle discernible, but also its aim, which sometimes can be indiscernible. The Panel also noted that very often there is a multiplicity of aims that are sought through enactment of legislation and it would be a difficult exercise to determine which aim or aims should be determinative for applying the aim-and-effect test. Moreover, access to the complete legislative history, which according to the arguments of the parties defending the aim-and-effect test, is relevant to detect protective aims, could be difficult or even impossible for a complaining party to obtain. Even if the complete legislative history is available, it would be difficult to assess which kinds of legislative history (statements in legislation, in

[78] *Apotex Holdings Inc and Apotex Inc v United States of America*, ICSID Case No ARB(AF)/12/1, Award, 25 August 2014, para 8.66. *In casu*, the tribunal concluded that the claimant 'sufficiently discharged their evidential burden of proof so as to place the evidential burden of rebutting their case upon the Respondent', ibid, para 8.65. These difficulties are well documented in relation to other international norms requiring intent (eg in relation to States' responsibility for acts of genocide). As Bonafé explains, '[i]nternational jurisprudence dealing with other primary norms, of which intent constitutes an integral part, such as, inter alia the international crime of genocide, demonstrates the inherent difficulties in determining intent. As noted by one commentator, "it is almost impossible to equate the mens rea of the state with that of single state organs, since this psychological element is scattered among a plurality of perpetrators"', BI Bonafè, *The Relationship Between State and Individual Responsibility for International Crimes* (Brill 2009) 123. On the difficulties on the part of the investor to establish likeness (as acknowledged by the tribunal) see *Bayindir Insaat Turizm Ticaret Ve Sanayi AS v Islamic Republic of Pakistan*, ICSID Case No ARB/03/29, Award, 27 August 2009, para 419.

[79] See Chapter 3.

[80] See also Chapter 3, Section 3.1.1.

official legislative reports, by individual legislators, or in hearings by interested parties) should be primarily determinative of the aims of the legislation.[81]

Investors acting as claimants in investment treaty arbitration encounter similar difficulties in proving discrimination. Having to prove that a particular measure treating foreign investors less favourably is not adopted because of the investors' foreign nationality or another protected ground such as the foreign investors' race or religion, but, instead, it is reasonably connected with a legitimate policy objective entails serious difficulties for investors. These difficulties can be overcome, or, at least, alleviated, by two principal ways. The first is to place significant emphasis on the duty of both parties to produce evidence in their possession or control, irrespective of the allocation of the burden of proof as well as the consequences of failure to do so (adverse inferences) (Section 4.1.1.2). The second way, as Section 4.3 argues, is a flexible approach in relation to the standard of proof, and in particular the power (and duty) of arbitral tribunals to accept indirect evidence.

Even though the principle *actori incumbit probatio* is derived from Roman law, which is formalistic, it is applied in a flexible manner by international courts and tribunals in the light of asymmetry of information concerns.[82] At the same time, flexibility does not mean that the burden of proof is reversed. As Kurtz explains:

> it is not just any disadvantage suffered by foreign investors (including the claimant) vis-à-vis 'like' domestic investors that should suffice to construct a rebuttable presumption of protectionist purpose on the part of the regulating state. Absent any other key evidential indicators, *the foreign investor would normally need to show that the degree and quality of disparate impact is probative of an intentional policy by the state to advantage its domestic actors at the expense of 'like' foreign investors*.[83]

This view is shared by other arbitration experts. For example, Heiskanen argues that '[t]o the extent that regulatory measures are taken that affect the value of foreign investor's investment, and to the extent that such measures are adopted for a *prima facie* legitimate public purpose, *the burden is on the investor to demonstrate that the measure is* a disguised taking, *discriminatory*, fails to comply with the requirements of due process, or is otherwise irregular'.[84]

[81] Panel, *Japan—Alcoholic Beverages*, para 6.16. This does not mean that, as explained above, the WTO case law on the matter is entirely consistent. See also Chapter 1.

[82] M Kazazi, *Burden of Proof and Related Issues: A Study on Evidence before International Tribunals* (Kluwer Law International 1996) 221.

[83] J Kurtz, *The WTO and International Investment Law: Converging Systems* (CUP 2015) 129 (emphasis added).

[84] V Heiskanen, 'The Doctrine of Indirect Expropriation in Light of the Practice of the Iran-United States Claims Tribunal' (2007) 8 JWIT 215, 228 (emphasis added).

4.1.2.2 The Duty to Cooperate in the Production of Evidence and the Power of Tribunals to Draw Adverse Inferences

Proving that the State measure(s) resulting in difference in treatment (to the detriment of the foreign investor) were adopted 'because of' the investor's nationality or another impermissible ground and, therefore, were not rationally connected to a legitimate policy objective is not easy. However, this can be proven not only by relying on direct evidence but also circumstantial evidence. As in US anti-discrimination law, in disparate treatment cases, '[p]roof of discriminatory motive is critical, although it can in some situations be inferred from the mere fact of differences in treatment'.[85] This was also echoed in one of the first NAFTA discrimination cases in which the tribunal clarified that:

> *[d]ifferences in treatment will presumptively violate Article 1102(2)*, unless they have a reasonable nexus to rational government policies that (1) do not distinguish, on their face or de facto, between foreign-owned and domestic companies, and (2) do not otherwise unduly undermine the investment liberalizing objectives of NAFTA.[86]

One way by which asymmetry of information between the parties can be addressed without reversing the burden of proof is to require the parties to co-operate and furnish all relevant available evidence.[87] That the parties have indeed such duty is widely accepted by different international courts and tribunals, including investment treaty tribunals. In 1928 the US–Mexican Claims Commission was called to adjudicate upon the requisition of two mules and five horses from the ranch of an American citizen (Mr Hatton) in Mexico by General Horacio Lecuro, commander of Mexican Federal Troops. One of the issues before the Commission was whether Mr Hatton was the owner of the ranch in question. The relevant passage is clear in relation to the duty of the parties to produce evidence at their disposal or control:

[85] *Teamsters v United States*, 431 US 324, 335 fn 15 (1977); see also *Hazen Paper Co v Biggins*, 507 US 604, 609 (1993). For a critique of the behavioural theories underpinning intent and whether disparate treatment discrimination should include decisions based on unconscious bias, see L Hamilton Krieger and ST Fisker, 'Behavioral Realism in Employment Discrimination Law: Implicit Bias and Disparate Treatment' (2006) 94 California Law Review 997. See also Chapter 2.

[86] *Pope & Talbot Inc v the Government of Canada*, UNCITRAL, Award on the Merits Phase 2, 10 April 2001, para 78 (emphasis added); see also *Apotex Holdings Inc and Apotex Inc v United States of America*, ICSID Case No ARB(AF)/12/1, Award, 25 August 2014, para 8.55; *Cargill, Incorporated v Republic of Poland II*, UNCITRAL, Award, 5 March 2008, para 332. Cf *Champion Trading Company Ameritrade International, Inc v Arab Republic of Egypt*, ICSID Case No ARB/02/9, Award, 27 October 2006, para 133: 'According to the Claimants, the payments made by the Government did discriminate. An analysis of the intent of the Government of Egypt is irrelevant. Because the Claimants did demonstrate a prima facie difference in treatment, the burden had shifted to the Respondent to demonstrate that a reasonable non-discriminatory policy justification existed that would explain the differences in treatment received by NCC and the other cotton companies.'

[87] On such obligation see G Niyungeko, *La preuve devant les juridictions internationales* (Pédone 2005) 165 et seq. See also CF Amerasinghe, *Evidence in International Litigation* (Martinus Nijhoff 2005) 96:

> [a]n important principle of evidence in international litigation which complements the principle discussed in the previous chapter [the principle *actori incumbit probatio*] is that the parties must co-operate, always with the tribunal and sometimes even with each other, in producing evidence. In general the peaceful settlement of disputes by international tribunals requires to a considerable extent the co-operation of the litigating parties as a basis. The principle flows from the basic principle of affording a fair trial under the influence of another principle of international law requiring good faith.

> [i]t would have been desirable that the United States furnish evidence on this point. To be sure, if Hatton was not the owner of the ranch, Mexico could undoubtedly have been able to show that fact. *There should be little difficulty in obtaining information* respecting this question of title. And while it is not the function of the respondent government to make a case for a claimant government, it is believed that, *in view of the fact that the claimant is in possession of the receipt*, and in view of the further fact that Mexico has adduced nothing to show that the claimant was not the owner of the ranch at the time of the requisition, the Commission should accept without question the claimant's allegation that the property requisitioned from the ranch belonged to him.[88]

Another decision of the US–Mexican Commission went as far as to say that:

> [a]s an international tribunal, the Commission denies the existence in international procedure of rules governing the burden of proof borrowed from municipal procedure. On the contrary, it holds that it is the duty of the respective Agencies to co-operate in searching out and presenting to this tribunal all facts throwing any light on the merits of the claim presented. The Commission denies the 'right' of the respondent merely to wait in silence in cases where it is reasonable that it should speak.[89]

Particular weight was given not only to the nature of the parties (Sovereign States) but also notions of control of, and access to, information evidence.[90] In *Megalidis v Turkey* the Turkish–Greek Mixed Arbitral Tribunal held that Turkey's failure to produce documents (as ordered by the Tribunal) led to the acceptance of the claimant's factual submissions.[91] More recently, the lack of evidence by the respondent to rebut the claimant's case was sufficient for the Ethiopia–Eritrea Claims Commission to draw adverse inferences.[92] While the applicable procedural rules of the Iran–US Claims Tribunal (IUSCT) include the principle *actori incumbit probatio*,[93] the IUSCT also takes into

[88] *Edgar A Hatton (USA) v United Mexican States* (1928) IV RIIA 329, 332 (emphasis added). See also *Grant-Smith Claim (Anglo-Italian Conciliation Commission)* (1952) (1955) 22 ILR 966.

[89] *William A Parker (USA) v United Mexican States* (1926) 4 RIAA 35, 39, para 6; see also ibid, para 7. See also *Lillie S Kling (USA) v United Mexican States* (1930), 4 RIAA 575, 585.

[90] *William A Parker (USA) v United Mexican States* (1926) 4 RIAA 35, 39, para 7 ('the parties before this Commission are sovereign Nations who are in honor bound to make full disclosures of the facts in each case so far as such facts are within their knowledge, or can reasonably be ascertained by them'). See also *Heirs of Jules Brun Case (France v Venezuela)* (French-Venezuelan Commission) (1905) 10 RIAA 24, 41: 'The umpire might hesitate to adopt these findings if it were not true, and had not been always true, the respondent Government could ascertain and produce before this mixed commission the exact facts regarding the positions and movements of its own soldiers, and the position and movements of the insurgent forces at the time in question … Hence against the very proper presumption that the Government of Venezuela will always do its duty by its own nationals and by its neutral friends resident within its domain may very properly be placed the presumption which arises when one is in possession of important truths essential to a judicial inquiry and elects not to produce them.'

[91] *Aristotelis A Megalidis v Turkey*, Award, 26 July 1928 (1932) 4 ILR 395.

[92] See also Eritrea-Ethiopia Claims Commission, *Eritrea's Claims 2, 4, 6, 7, 8, & 22*, Partial Award for the Central Front, 28 April 2004, (2004) 26 RIAA 115, 131, para 71 ('Ethiopia was the Occupying Power of the area that included the cemetery from late May 2000 until late February 2001, and Ethiopia presented no defensive evidence to this claim. Consequently, as with Tserona Town, the Commission finds that Ethiopia is liable for seventy-five percent of the damage caused to the cemetery').

[93] Article 24(1) of the IUSCT Rules, provides that '[e]ach party shall have the burden of proving the facts relied on to support his claim or defence', mirroring Article 24(1) of the 1976 UNCITRAL Arbitration Rules (and Article 27(1) of the 2010 and 2021 UNCTITRAL Arbitration Rules). See also *Iran v United States*, Case No A/I5, Award

consideration information asymmetry.[94] In that vein, '[w]hen a party ... has access to relevant evidence, the Tribunal is authorized to draw adverse inferences from the failure of that party to produce such evidence'.[95] In the *Pulp Mills* case, after confirming once again the basic rule of *actori incumbit probatio*, the ICJ clarified that:

> [i]t is of course to be expected that the Applicant should, in the first instance, submit the relevant evidence to substantiate its claims. This does not, however, mean that the Respondent should not co-operate in the provision of such evidence as may be in its possession that could assist the Court in resolving the dispute submitted to it.[96]

In the *Genocide Convention* case Bosnia argued that failure of Serbia to produce relevant evidence must have as consequence the reversal of the burden of proof.[97] Although the ICJ refused to reverse the burden of proof and draw adverse inferences on that particular occasion, it did so on the basis that it 'has extensive documentation and other evidence available to it' and '[i]t has made very ample use of it'.[98] The WTO Panel in *Argentina—Footwear* described the parties' duty to cooperate in the production of evidence in the following manner:

> [a]nother incidental rule to the burden of proof is the requirement for collaboration of the parties in the presentation of the facts and evidence to the panel and especially the role of the respondent in that process. It is often said that the idea of peaceful

No 529-A15 (1992) 28 Iran–US CTR 139; *Howard Needles Tammen and Bergendoff v Iran*, Award Nos 244–68-2, 8 (1986) 11 Iran–USCTR 336; *Fluor Corp v Iran*, Order, 13 November 1987 (1987) 18 Iran–USCTR 68; *Pointon v Iran*, Award No 516–322-1 (1991) 27 Iran–USCTR 52; *Flexi-Van Leasing, Inc v Iran*, Order, 20 December 1982, Dissenting Opinion of Judge Kashani (1982) 1 Iran–USCTR 46.

[94] *Mohtadi Jahangir and Mohtadi Jila v Iran*, Award No 573–271-3 (1996) 32 Iran–USCTR 124, 151 ('The Tribunal normally would view the responsibility for providing a complete and persuasive explanation of Iranian legislation as falling upon the Respondent. This is because the Respondent is surely better positioned than a claimant to explain the meaning and effect of its own laws. Especially where the legislation is confusing and its scope ambiguous, as in the case of the Lands Grant Act, the Respondent may not confine itself to the mere assertion that a particular legislation does not apply'). See also AZ Marossi, 'Shifting the Burden of Proof in the Practice of the Iran–United States Claims Tribunal' (2011) 28 Journal of International Arbitration 427. See also the 2022 ICSID Arbitration Rules, Rule 36:

'(1) The Tribunal shall determine the admissibility and probative value of the evidence adduced.
(2) Each party has the burden of proving the facts relied on to support its claim or defense.
(3) The Tribunal may call upon a party to produce documents or other evidence if it deems it necessary at any stage of the proceeding.'

[95] *Ultrasystems Incorporated and Islamic Republic of Iran, et al*, Award No 27–84-3, 4 March 1983, (1983) 2 IUSCTR 114, 115, Concurring Opinion of Judge Mosk; quoted in *Prosecutor v Tihomir Blaškić*, Case No I-95–14-PT, Trial Chamber II, Decision on the Objection of the Republic of Croatia to the Issuance of *subpoenae duces tecum*, 18 July 1997, para 55. See also *William J Levitt v Islamic Republic of Iran*, Award No 520–210-3, 29 August 1991, (1991) 27 IUSCTR 145, 163, para 61.

[96] *Pulp Mills on the River Uruguay (Argentina v Uruguay)*, Judgment [2010] ICJ Rep 14, 71, para 163. See also GM Farnelli, 'Consistency in the ICJ Approach to the Standard of Proof: An Appraisal of the Court's Flexibility' (2022) 21 The Law and Practice of International Courts and Tribunals 98.

[97] 'While the Applicant accepts that approach as a general proposition, it contends that in certain respects the onus should be reversed, especially in respect of the attributability of alleged acts of genocide to the Respondent, given the refusal of the Respondent to produce the full text of certain documents', *Application of the Convention on the Prevention and Punishment of the Crime of Genocide (Bosnia and Herzegovina v Serbia and Montenegro)*, Judgment, [2007] ICJ Rep 43, 128, para 204.

[98] ibid, 129, para 206.

> settlement of disputes before international tribunals is largely based on the premise of cooperation of the litigating parties. In this context the most important result of the rule of collaboration appears to be that the adversary is obligated to provide the tribunal with relevant documents which are in its sole possession. This obligation does not arise until the claimant has done its best to secure evidence and has actually produced some *prima facie* evidence in support of its case.[99]

In general WTO Panels and the AB made clear that adverse inferences are also accepted in the practice of the WTO dispute settlement system.[100] The WTO Panel in *Saudi Arabia—IPRs* held that '[a]s a consequence of the applicable evidentiary standard being closer to that of a balance of probabilities, panels may make findings of fact based on inferences and circumstantial evidence'.[101]

The duty of the parties to cooperate in the production of the evidence is also recognized in European human rights law. The ECtHR held that lack of cooperation without a sufficient explanation leads to drawing adverse inferences.[102] As explained in Chapter 2, the ECtHR adopts a more inquisitorial approach in relation to the burden of proof.[103] However, it has also repeatedly held that:

> [w]here the events in issue lie wholly, or in large part, within the exclusive knowledge of the authorities, as in the case of persons within their control in custody, strong presumptions of fact will arise in respect of injuries and death occurring during such

[99] Panel, *Argentina—Textiles and Apparel*, para 6.40.

[100] AB, *Canada—Aircraft*, para 203 ('the Panel had the legal authority and the discretion to draw inferences from the facts before it—including the fact that Canada had refused to provide information sought by the Panel'); AB, *US—Wheat Gluten*, para 172; AB, *US—Anti-Dumping and Countervailing Duties (China)*, para 318 ('the mere fact that a government is the majority shareholder of an entity does not demonstrate that the government exercises meaningful control over the conduct of that entity, much less that the government has bestowed it with governmental authority. In some instances, however, where the evidence shows that the formal indicia of government control are manifold, and there is also evidence that such control has been exercised in a meaningful way, then such evidence may permit an inference that the entity concerned is exercising governmental authority'). See also W Zhou, H Gao, and X Bai, 'Building a Market Economy through WTO-inspired Reform of State-Owned Enterprises in China' (2019) 68 ICLQ 977, 1018–1019; M Matsushita and others, *The World Trade Organization: Law, Practice, and Policy* (3rd edn, OUP 2015)98–99.

[101] Panel, *Saudi Arabia—IPRs*, para 7.39; see also Panel, *Thailand—Cigarettes (Philippines) (Article 21.5—Philippines)*, para 7.778; AB, *US—Wool Shirts and Blouses*, 14.

[102] W Schabas, *The European Convention on Human Rights: A Commentary* (OUP 2015) 812; *Ireland v UK*, Application No 5310/71, 18 January 1978, para 148; *Georgia v Russia (I)* [GC], Application No 13255/07, 3 July 2014, para 104 ('[w]hen, as in the instant case, the respondent Government have exclusive access to information capable of corroborating or refuting the applicant [Government]'s allegations, any lack of co-operation by the Government without a satisfactory explanation may give rise to the drawing of inferences as to the well-foundedness of the applicant [Government]'s allegations'); *Imakayeva v Russia*, Application No 7615/02, 9 November 2006, para 111; *Taniş and others v Turkey*, Application No 65899/01, 2 August 2005, para 160; *Nolan and K v Russia*, Application No 2512/04, 12 February 2009, para 69; *Makhmudov v Russia*, Application No 35082/04, 26 July 2007, para 68; *Fadeyeva v Russia*, Application No 55723/00, 9 June 2005, para 79; *Ahmet Özkan and Others v Turkey*, Application No 21689/93, 6 April 2004, para 426. See also *Nachova and others v Bulgaria* [GC], Application Nos 43577/98 and 43579/98, 6 July 2005, para 147 ('proof may follow from the coexistence of sufficiently strong, clear and concordant inferences or of similar unrebutted presumptions of fact. Moreover, the level of persuasion necessary for reaching a particular conclusion and, in this connection, the distribution of the burden of proof are intrinsically linked to the specificity of the facts, the nature of the allegation made and the Convention right at stake'); *Timishev v Russia*, Application Nos 55762/00 and 55974/00, 13 December 2005, para 39; *D H and others v The Czech Republic* [GC], Application No 57325/00, 13 November 2007, para 178.

[103] See Chapter 2, Section 2.1.

> detention. Indeed, the burden of proof may be regarded as resting on the authorities to provide a satisfactory and convincing explanation.[104]

This is reflected in Article 38 of Rules of Procedure of the Inter-American Commission of Human Rights which provides that '[t]he facts alleged in the petition, the pertinent parts of which have been transmitted to the State in question, shall be presumed to be true if the State has not provided responsive information during the period set by the Commission under the provisions of Article 37 of the Rules of Procedure, as long as other evidence does not lead to a different conclusion'.[105] A 'functionally equivalent provision'[106] is included in the Rules of Procedure of the ECtHR.[107]

Domestic legal systems are not agnostic towards adverse inferences.[108] In French administrative law the principle *actori incumbit probatio* applies in more flexible

[104] *Salman v Turkey* [GC], Application No 21986/93, 27 June 2000, para 100; *Aktaş v Turkey*, Application No 24351/94 24 April 2003, para 291; *Süheyla Aydin v Turkey*, Application No 25660/94, 24 May 2005, para 147. See also *Akkum and others v Turkey*, Application No 21894/93, 24 March 2005, para 210 ('[t]hus, it has found that where an individual is taken into custody in good health but is found to be injured at the time of release, it is incumbent on the State to provide a plausible explanation of how those injuries were caused, failing which an issue will arise under Article 3 of the Convention').

[105] Rules of Procedure of the Inter-American Commission of Human Rights, Article 38.

[106] T Altwicker and A Ellen Hansen, 'Presumptions as Secondary Rules in the Judicial Interpretation of International Human Rights' in G Kajtár, B Çali, and M Milanovic (eds), *Secondary Rules of Primary Importance in International Law: Attribution, Causality, Evidence, and Standards of Review in the Practice of International Courts and Tribunals* (OUP 2023) 167–182, 171.

[107] Rule 44C of the ECtHR Rules of the Court.

[108] See V Ulfbeck and M-L Holle, 'Tort Law and Burden of Proof—Comparative Aspects. A Special Case for Enterprise Liability?' in H Koziol and BC Steininger (eds), *European Tort Law 2008* (Springer 2009) 26–48, 46. The idea that 'proximity' to evidence should play a role in deciding jurisdictional conflicts is recognised in private international law See eg P Lagarde, 'Le principe de proximité dans le droit international privé contemporain' (1986) 196 RCADI 9; C Volpin, 'The Ball is in Your Court: Evidential Burden of Proof and the Proof-Proximity Principle in EU Competition Law' (2014) 51 Common Market Law Review 1159, 1173; Case C-256/00, *Besix SA v Wasserreinigungsbau Alfred Kretzschmar GmbH & Co KG (WABAG) and Planungs-und Forschungsgesellschaft Dipl Ing W Kretzschmar GmbH & KG (Plafog)* [2002] ECR I-1699, para 31 ('The court of the place where the contractual obligation giving rise to the action is to be performed will normally be the most appropriate for deciding the case, in particular on the grounds of proximity and ease of taking evidence'); C-167/00, *Verein für Konsumenteninformation v Karl Heinz Henkel* [2002] ECR I-8111, para 46 ('The courts for the place where the harmful event occurred are usually the most appropriate for deciding the case, in particular on the grounds of proximity and ease of taking evidence'). Article 150 of the Dutch Code of Civil Procedure ('Wetboek van Burgerlijke Rechtsvordering') concerning the allocation of the burden of proof reflects the *actori incumbit probatio* principle, but, at the same time, explicitly provides for a different allocation of the burden of proof if this is required by reasonableness ('redelijkheid') or fairness/equity ('billijkheid'). For a criticism that Article 150 is vague in relation the conditions for reversing the burden of proof, see I Giesen, 'The Reversal of the Burden of Proof in the Principles of European Tort Law: A Comparison with Dutch Tort Law and Civil Procedure Rules' (2010) 6 Utrecht Law Review 22, 26. The Portuguese Civil Code allocates the burden of proof to the party invoking facts in support of its legal claims, including claims for damages, but Article 344(2) explicitly reverses the burden of proof if the other party has intentionally rendered proving a particular fact impossible (but not merely difficult), Civil Code (Portugal), Articles 342, 487 and 344(2). The most serious departure from the *actori incumbit probatio* rule is to be found in Germany in favour of an approach taking into consideration the asymmetry of information between the parties, with other European jurisdictions, such as Austria and Switzerland, follow the German model as well, A Skontzos, 'The Burden and Standard of Proof in Model International Procedural Law: Dealing with the Burden and Standard of Proof in International Disputes' (2018) 23 Uniform Law Review 569, 579–580; E Karner, 'The Function of the Burden of Proof in Tort Law H Koziol and BC Steininger (eds), *European Tort Law 2008* (Springer 2009) 68–78. See also General Code of Procedure (Colombia), Article 167: 'Incumbe a las partes probar el supuesto de hecho de las normas que consagran el efecto jurídico que ellas persiguen. No obstante, según las particularidades del caso, el juez podrá, de oficio o a petición de parte, distribuir, la carga al decretar las pruebas, durante su práctica o en cualquier momento del proceso antes de fallar, exigiendo probar determinado hecho a la parte que se encuentre en una situación más favorable para aportar las evidencias o esclarecer los hechos controvertidos. La parte se considerará en mejor posición para probar en virtud de su cercanía con el material probatorio, por tener en su poder el objeto de prueba, por circunstancias técnicas especiales, por haber intervenido

manner. This can be attributed to the different nature of French administrative law proceedings, which are inquisitorial rather than adversarial,[109] but also demonstrates a greater sensitivity towards the asymmetry of information between claimants and the Administration. In a landmark administrative law case (*Barel*) the French *Conseil d'État* (the Supreme Administrative Court) reviewed the decision of the Administration to refuse to the claimants the right to take the 1953 exam for the prestigious *École Nationale d'Administration* (*ENA*), the National School of Administration. The claimants argued that this decision was due to certain political views attributed to them. The Administration did not comply fully or, in another case, at all to the Court's disclosure order, and, on that basis, taking into account all the relevant circumstances, the Court concluded that the claimants' allegations regarding the Administration's motives had to be accepted as established facts.[110] Discussion of how the burden of proof applies in administrative law is particularly relevant as administrative law is functionally similar to investment treaty arbitration.[111]

Although not frequently, investment treaty tribunals accept that the failure to provide evidence can have evidentiary repercussions, especially when the State does not comply with its document production obligations.[112] In *Metal-Tech v Uzbekistan* the

directamente en los hechos que dieron lugar al litigio, o por estado de indefensión o de incapacidad en la cual se encuentre la contraparte, entre otras circunstancias similares'. For example, in English property law, '[t]he liability of a bailee in negligence, however, differs from that of other defendants in the law of tort in at least one major respect. The burden of proof lies upon the bailee to show that any loss or damage occurred despite the fact that reasonable care was taken. This is a pragmatic response to the fact that the bailee, having controlled the chattel, knows its bailment history better than the bailor', M Bridge, *Personal Property Law* (4th edn, OUP 2015) 64. See also *Joined Cases C-204/00, C-205/00, C-211/00. C-213/00, C-213/00. C-217/00 and C-219/00 Aalborg Portland and others v Commission* [2004] ECR-I-123, 7 June 2004, paras 78 and 79 ('it should be for the party or the authority alleging an infringement of the competition rules to prove the existence thereof and it should be for the undertaking or association of undertakings invoking the benefit of a defence against a finding of an infringement to demonstrate that the conditions for applying such defence are satisfied, so that the authority will then have to resort to other evidence. Although according to those principles the legal burden of proof is borne either by the Commission or by the undertaking or association concerned, the factual evidence on which a party relies may be of such a kind as to require the other party to provide an explanation or justification, failing which it is permissible to conclude that the burden of proof has been discharged').

[109] B Schwartz, *French Administrative Law and the Common-Law World* (The Lawbook Exchange Ltd 2006) 132.

[110] CE, 28 May 1954, *Barel* ('qu'il n'a pas été satisfait à cette dernière demande par les productions faites le 25 mai 1954; qu'il ressort de l'ensemble des circonstances susrelatées de l'affaire que le motif allégué par les auteurs des pourvois doit être regardé comme établi'); L Nevellie Brown and JS Bell, *French Administrative Law* (5th edn, OUP 1998) 100.

[111] See eg Schill (n 65); G Van Harten and M Loughlin, 'Investment Treaty Arbitration as a Species of Global Administrative Law' (2006) 17 EJIL 121; D Kalderimis, 'Investment Treaty Arbitration as Global Administrative Law: What This Might Mean in Practice' in C Brown and K Miles (eds), *Evolution in Investment Treaty Law and Arbitration* (CUP 2011) 145–160.

[112] *Rumeli Telekom AS v Republic of Kazakhstan*, ICSID Case No ARB/05/16, Award, 29 July 2008, para 444 ('If a party, as was the case with Respondent, does not comply with its obligations, for instance by refusing to produce the requested documents and witnesses, the Arbitral Tribunal is authorized to draw adverse conclusions from the party's behavior'); *Caratube International Oil Company LLP and Devincci Salah Hourani v Republic of Kazakhstan*, ICSID Case No ARB/13/13, Award, 27 September 2017, para 319 ('the Tribunal further agrees in principle with the Respondent that while the burden of proof thus is on the Claimants to prove their claims, the Respondent could be held to bear the burden of presenting specific and relevant documents in its possession. In this regard, as noted by the tribunal in the *Rumeli* case, negative inferences may be drawn as a result of a Party's failure to abide with their burden to produce specific, relevant documents.'); cf *African Holding Company of America, Inc et Société Africaine de Construction au Congo SARL v La République Démocratique du Congo*, ICSID Case No ARB/05/21, Partial Award on Jurisdiction, 29 July 2008, para 24–31; *United Parcel Service of America v Government of Canada*, UNCITRAL, Decision of the Tribunal Relating to Canada's Claim of Cabinet Privilege, 8 October 2004, para 15 ('A failure to disclose, found by the Tribunal to be unjustifiable, may lead to the Tribunal drawing adverse

tribunal 'note[d] with concern the Claimant's repeated failure to provide evidence', '[a]lthough the Claimant had several opportunities to do so, and was on notice that the evidence requested would be of importance to the Tribunal's determination'.[113] The tribunal thus concluded that it could not 'establish that the Consultants actually performed any legitimate services for the Claimant at the time of establishment of the Claimant's investment',[114] and ultimately declined jurisdiction. In *Sehil v Turkmenistan*, while the tribunal rejected the investor's request to 'shift the burden to produce evidence to Respondent because they have "limited and incomplete documentation relating to this dispute in their possession" documents',[115] it accepted that:

> it does have the power to draw adverse inferences and decide on its reading of the evidence and arguments concerning the requested inferences. In the present case, both parties accuse the other of failing to produce certain evidence.[116]

The power of arbitral tribunals to draw adverse inferences against the party failing to cooperate and produce evidence in its possession or control is also reflected in arbitration soft law instruments. For example, Article 9.5 of the International Bar Association (IBA) Rules on Taking Evidence in International Arbitration provides that '[i]f a Party fails without satisfactory explanation to produce any Document requested in a Request to Produce to which it has not objected in due time or fails to produce any Document ordered to be produced by the Arbitral Tribunal, the Arbitral Tribunal may infer that such document would be adverse to the interests of that Party'.[117] Likewise, Article 9.6

inferences on the issue in question. Whether it does draw such an inference will depend on the circumstances surrounding that issue'); *Waste Management, Inc v United Mexican States ('Number 2')*, ICSID Case No ARB(AF)/00/3, Procedural Order Concerning Disclosure of Documents, 1 October 2001, para 6 ('The Tribunal would note that under the IBA Rules on the Taking Evidence in International Commercial Arbitration (1999), which provide useful guidance in the matter, the ultimate sanction for non-disclosure in the drawing of an adverse inference against the non-disclosing party (Article 9(4))'). See also *Europe Cement Investment & Trade SA v Turkey*, ICSID Case No ARB(AF)/07/2, Award, 13 August 2009, paras 151–163. In 2017 the Paris Court of Appeal refused to set aside an ICC on the basis that the arbitral tribunal drew adverse inferences. Paris CA, 28 February 2017, 15/06036. See also Paris CA, 21 March 2017, 15/17234. See also ICC Case 16391, Final Award, December 2010, ICC, *ICC Dispute Resolution Bulletin* (ICC Paris 2016) 150, setting out the requirement for drawing adverse inferences, but declining to do so in that case. See also Sourgens, Duggal, and Laird (n 58), Chapter 3. On document production in international arbitration see R Marghitola, *Document Production in International Arbitration* (Kluwer Law International 2015); JDM Lew, 'Document Production and Legal Privilege in International Commercial Arbitration' in in DD Caron and others (eds), *Practising Virtue: Inside International Arbitration* (OUP 2015) 347–356; S Sattar, 'Document Production and the 2010 IBA Rules on the Taking of Evidence in International Arbitration: a Commentary' (2011) 14 International Arbitration Law Review 210. On the IBA Rules on Taking of Evidence see R Khodykin and C Mulcahy, *A Guide to the IBA Rules on the Taking of Evidence in International Arbitration* (OUP 2019).

[113] *Metal-Tech Ltd v the Republic of Uzbekistan*, ICSID Case No ARB/10/3, Award of 4 October 2013, para 207.

[114] ibid.

[115] *Muhammet Cap & Sehil Insaat Endustri ve Ticaret Ltd Sti v Turkmenistan*, ICSID Case No ARB/12/6, Award, 4 May 2021, para 722.

[116] ibid, para 744.

[117] IBA Rules on the Taking of Evidence in International Arbitration, Article 9.5. See also 2018 Rules on the Efficient Conduct of Proceedings in International Arbitration (Prague Rules), Article 10 ('If a party does not comply with the arbitral tribunal's order(s) or instruction(s), without justifiable grounds, the arbitral tribunal may draw, where it considers appropriate, an adverse inference with regard to such party's respective case or issue'). 1996 UNCITRAL Notes on Organizing Arbitral Proceedings, para 51 ('The parties might be reminded that, if the requested party duly invited to produce documentary evidence fails to do so within the established period of

stipulates that '[i]f a Party fails without satisfactory explanation to make available any other relevant evidence, including testimony, sought by one Party to which the Party to whom the request was addressed has not objected in due time or fails to make available any evidence, including testimony, ordered by the Arbitral Tribunal to be produced, the Arbitral Tribunal may infer that such evidence would be adverse to the interests of that Party'.[118] This approach finds support in arbitration scholarship.[119]

In the context of discriminatory claims in investment treaty arbitration this means that the power of arbitral tribunals to draw adverse inferences in practice assists investors in establishing that the Host State breaches its international obligations under the applicable investment treaty. Investors, as claimants, must prove that the measures in question resulting in less favourable treatment (compared to the treatment of other foreign or domestic investors in similar circumstances) were adopted because of the investor's nationality or other protected ground, and, thus, were not reasonably connected with a legitimate policy objective. Nonetheless, the lack of any rebutting evidence by the respondent State—especially in the light of its exclusive control over evidence from the law-making or decision-making processes—must be taken into consideration by the arbitral tribunals and, when appropriate, lead to drawing adverse inferences.[120] At the same time, the power of tribunals to draw adverse inferences should be exercised with caution, avoiding jeopardizing the procedural rights of the other party.[121]

The duty of both parties to produce all relevant evidence in their possession or control plays a significant role in the document production phase of the arbitration. Despite

time, without showing sufficient cause for such failure, the arbitral tribunal is free to draw its conclusions from the failure and may make the award on the evidence before it'). However, there is no such reference in the 2016 UNCITRAL Notes on Organizing Arbitral Proceedings, para 75 ('if a party is requested to submit evidence to support its case but fails to do so within the time limit without showing sufficient cause for such failure, the arbitral tribunal may make the award solely on the evidence before it').

[118] IBA Rules on the Taking of Evidence in International Arbitration, Article 9.6.

[119] See generally MJ Solis, 'Adverse Inferences in Investor–State Arbitration' (2018) 34 Arbitration International 79; GR Amaral, 'Burden of Proof and Adverse Inferences in International Arbitration: Proposal for an Inference Chart' (2018) 35 Journal of International Arbitration 1; M Polkinghorne and CB Rosenberg, 'The Adverse Inference in ICSID Practice' (2015) 30 ICSID Review 741, 743–744; S Greenberg and F Lautenschlager, 'Adverse Inferences in International Arbitral Practice' (2011) 22(2) ICC International Court Arbitration Bulletin 43; GB Born, *International Commercial Arbitration* (Kluwer Law International 2009) 1919; JK Sharpe, 'Drawing Adverse Inferences from Non-Production of Evidence' (2006) 22 Arbitration International 549; CN Brower and JD Brueschke, *The Iran–United States Claims Tribunal* (Martinus Nijhoff 1998) 195. See also the French case law on the matter, Paris CA, Case No 16/11182, 28 May 2019 (overturned by the French Supreme Court (*Cour de Cassation*) Case No 19–19769, 29 September 2021 but in relation to the principle that corruption can be proven by circumstantial evidence which must be 'sufficiently serious, precise and consistent'). See also Paris CA, Case No 15/17442 and 15/2379016 May 2017; Paris CA, Case No 18/07347 and 18/02568, 17 November 2020; Paris CA, Case No 19/1753, 17 September 2021.

[120] See also A D Mitchell, D Heaton, and C Henckels, *Non-Discrimination and the Role of Regulatory Purpose in International Trade and Investment Law* (Edward Elgar 2016) 170: 'a defending party's assertion that a measure does *not* have a particular regulatory purpose should not be given greater weight because it is made by the state that has promulgated the measure. Bare denial without evidence to demonstrate *other* regulatory purposes, is unlikely to be persuasive, especially where denials are made in response to evidence-based assertions from a complaint. Close examination of factors including the measure's text, structure, context, design, application and its impact will be critical where a defending party argue that its measure does not have a particular purpose.'

[121] See *Mohammad Ammar Al-Bahloul v Republic of Tajikistan*, Partial Award on Jurisdiction and Liability, SCC Case No V064/2008, 2 September 2009, para 115 ('[w]hile the Tribunal can understand that currently Claimant may have no or very limited access to documents in Tajikistan, this does not allow the Tribunal to make far reaching assumptions to the detriment of Respondent').

the different approaches of common law and civil law jurisdictions and legal cultures in relation to document production,[122] including a document production phase in the procedural timetable is extremely common in international investment treaty arbitration.[123] Crucially, Article 43 of ICSID Convention provides that:

> [e]xcept as the parties otherwise agree, the Tribunal may, if it deems it necessary at any stage of the proceedings,
> (a) call upon the parties to produce documents or other evidence, and
> (b) visit the scene connected with the dispute, and conduct such inquiries there as it may deem appropriate.[124]

Likewise, Rule 34 of the ICSID Arbitration Rules (entitled 'Evidence: General Principles') provides that:

> (1) The Tribunal shall determine the admissibility and probative value of the evidence adduced.
> (2) Each party has the burden of proving the facts relied on to support its claim or defense.
> (3) The Tribunal may call upon a party to produce documents or other evidence if it deems it necessary at any stage of the proceeding.[125]

[122] Such differences are reflected in the content of the IBA Rules on Taking Evidence in International Arbitration (IBA Rules on Evidence) and the Rules on the Efficient Conduct of Proceedings in International Arbitration (Prague Rules). Cf IBA Rules on Evidence, Article 3.2 ('Within the time ordered by the Arbitral Tribunal, any Party may submit to the Arbitral Tribunal and to the other Parties a Request to Produce') and Prague Rules, Article 4.2 ('Generally, the Arbitral Tribunal shall avoid extensive production of documents, including any form of e-discovery'). See also Prague Rules, Article 4.3: 'However, if a party believes that it would need to request certain documents from the other party, it should indicate this to the arbitral tribunal at the case management conference and explain the reasons why the document production may be needed in this particular case. If the arbitral tribunal is satisfied that the document production may be needed, it should decide on a procedure for document production and make an appropriate provision for it in the procedural timetable.' See also KAN Duggal and R Rangachari, 'A Challenger Approaches: An Assessment of the Prague Rules on the Efficient Conduct of Proceedings in International Arbitration' (2020) 37 Journal of International Arbitration 27; M Henry and E Silva Romero, 'La Preuve dans l'Arbitrage: Prague Rules v. IBA Rules' (2020) 1 Revue de l'Arbitrage 71; DG Henriques, 'The Prague Rules: Competitor, Alternative or Addition to the IBA Rules on the Taking of Evidence in International Arbitration' (2018) 36 ASA Bulletin 351.

[123] See Marghitola (n 112); Lew (n 112); L Shore, 'Document Production, Witness Statements, and Cross-Examination: The Enduring Tensions in International Arbitration' in SL Brekoulakis, JDM Lew, and LA Mistelis (eds), *The Evolution and Future of International Arbitration* (Kluwer Law International 2016) 39–45. See also *Bayindir Insaat Turizm Ticaret Ve Sanayi AS v Islamic Republic of Pakistan*, ICSID Case No. ARB/03/29, Award, 27 August 2009, para 417.

[124] ICSID Convention, Article 43.

[125] ICSID Arbitration Rules (2022) Rule 36. See also ICSID Arbitration Rules (2006), Rule 34(3): 'The parties shall cooperate with the Tribunal in the production of the evidence and in the other measures provided for in paragraph (2). The Tribunal shall take formal note of the failure of a party to comply with its obligations under this paragraph and of any reasons given for such failure.' See also *Churchill Mining and Planet Mining Pty Ltd v Republic of Indonesia*, ICSID Case No ARB/12/14 and 12/40, Award, 6 December 2016, para 248: 'As the Tribunal interprets this provision, it (i) enshrines a general obligation to cooperate, (ii) and therefore does not aim at particular failures to comply with particularized disclosure requirements, (iii) provides for the opportunity, under certain circumstances to excuse non-compliance, such as the invocation of privilege, and (iv) does not necessarily imply specific consequences in cases of non-compliance, such as the drawing of adverse.' On the parties' duty to conduct arbitral proceedings in good faith, see *Methanex Corporation v United States of America*, UNCITRAL, Final Award of the Tribunal on Jurisdiction and Merits, 3 August 2005, Part II, Chapter I, para 54:

Finally, the power (and in some instances the duty) of investment treaty arbitral tribunals to draw adverse inferences is a meaningful way in which they can enforce compliance, given that they 'lack a coercive power to "demand" or "order" the production of evidence'.[126]

4.2 Standard of Review

Most discrimination cases in international investment treaty arbitration revolve around state measures which do not explicitly differentiate between investors on the basis of nationality or another protected ground. This is hardly surprising, as States are (usually) mindful of their treaty commitments which prohibit discrimination. This book argues that discrimination in investment treaty arbitration, being a form of disparate treatment (or direct) discrimination, requires claimants to prove that that less favourable treatment accorded to them is connected with their nationality in National Treatment and MFN claims or their nationality or another protected ground, such as race or religion, in claims based on other non-discrimination obligations under FET, non-impairment clauses or in the context of expropriation. However, a question of pivotal practical importance is what kind of connection is required? In answering this question, the standard of review to be used by tribunals when assessing the nexus between a state measure on the one hand, and the State measures' objectives on the other emerges as one of the key factors determining States' compliance with their treaty obligations of non-discrimination. Section 4.2.1 sets out the different approaches adopted in the case law, while Section 4.2.2 argues that the 'reasonable connection' test should be adopted as the appropriate standard of review.

4.2.1 Case Law

As it is the case with the jurisprudence of investment treaty tribunals regarding other aspects of discrimination analysis, there is lack of a *jurisprudence constante* regarding

> [i]n the Tribunal's view, the Disputing Parties each owed in this arbitration a general legal duty to the other and to the Tribunal to conduct themselves in good faith during these arbitration proceedings and to respect the equality of arms between them, the principles of 'equal treatment' and procedural fairness being also required by Article 15(1) of the UNCITRAL Rules. As a general principle, therefore, just as it would be wrong for the USA ex hypothesi to misuse its intelligence assets to spy on Methanex (and its witnesses) and to introduce into evidence the resulting materials into this arbitration, so too would it be wrong for Methanex to introduce evidential materials obtained by Methanex unlawfully.

[126] C Brown, 'Procedure in Investment Treaty Arbitration and the Relevance of Comparative Public Law' in Schill (n 65) 659–688, 682. In 2022 the US Supreme Court in *ZF Automotive US, Inc, et al v Luxshare*, Ltd, No 21–401 and *AlixPartners, LLP, et al v Fund for Protection of Investors' Rights in Foreign States*, No 21–518 held that international (commercial and investment treaty) arbitral tribunals do not fall within the scope of Section 1782(a) USC which provides that '[t]he district court of the district in which a person resides or is found may order him to give his testimony or statement or to produce a document or other thing for use in a proceeding in a foreign or international tribunal, including criminal investigations conducted before formal accusation.'

the appropriate standard of review in discrimination claims. Indeed, 'most tribunals have not articulated reasons for, and adopted varying approaches to establishing, a certain nexus between a measure and its objective'.[127] In other words, 'although most tribunals appear to agree that the standard is not breached if there is a reasonable justification for the differentiated treatment, whether a particular regulatory policy qualifies as such also defies precise definitions'.[128] As Dolzer, Kriebuam, and Schreuer explain, 'the case law is not uniform on whether the pursuit of some rational policy by the government to justify the differential treatment is sufficient or whether the State must use the least interfering means with investor rights if there are several alternative ways to achieve its policy goal'.[129]

At least three distinct approaches can be identified in the case law.[130] One approach regarding the required nexus between the measures and legitimate objective(s) is to explore whether there is a 'reasonable' or 'rational' connection between the two.[131] In *Feldman v Mexico* the tribunal held that 'the concept of discrimination has been defined to imply *unreasonable* distinctions between foreign and domestic investors in like circumstances'.[132] The tribunals in *Pope & Talbot v Canada*, *Apotex v USA*, and *Bilcon v Canada* also adopted the reasonable nexus standard.[133] In *Parkerings v Lithuania* the tribunal combined the 'reasonable' nexus approach with a proportionality analysis:

> to violate international law, discrimination must be unreasonable or lacking proportionality, for instance, it must be inapposite or excessive to achieve an otherwise legitimate objective of the State.[134]

Other tribunals require a 'plausible', rather than 'reasonable', connection, which is less exacting, and, by implication, more deferential to the State. The tribunal's analysis in *GAMI v Mexico* is illuminating regarding the appropriate degree of deference to the State:

[127] Mitchell, Heaton, and Henckels (n 120) 142.

[128] S Sacco and MC Fernández-Fonseca, 'National Treatment in Investment Arbitration' in JA Huerta-Goldman, A Romanetti, and FX Stirnimann (eds), *WTO Litigation, Investment Arbitration, and Commercial Arbitration* (Kluwer Law International 2013) 239–262, 261.

[129] R Dolzer, U Kriebaum, and C Schreuer, *Principles of International Investment Law* (3rd edn, OUP 2022) 259.

[130] Mitchell, Heaton, and Henckels (n 120) 159–167.

[131] ibid, 142–145.

[132] *Marvin Roy Feldman Karpa v United Mexican States*, ICSID Case No ARB(AF)/99/1, Award, 16 December 2002, para 170 (emphasis in the original).

[133] *Pope & Talbot Inc v Government of Canada*, UNCITRAL, Award on the Merits of Phase 2, 10 April 2001, paras 78, 81, 87, and 93; *Apotex Holdings Inc and Apotex Inc v United States of America*, ICSID Case No ARB(AF)/12/1, Award, 25 August 2014, para 8.55; *William Ralph Clayton, William Richard Clayton, Douglas Clayton, Daniel Clayton and Bilcon of Delaware Inc v Government of Canada*, UNCITRAL, PCA Case No 2009–04, Award on Jurisdiction and Liability, 17 March 2015, paras 720–724. See also C McLachlan, L Shore, and M Weiniger, *International Investment Arbitration: Substantive Principles* (2nd edn, OUP 2017) 342, para 7.295 ('[i]f the application of the above elements points to a less favourable treatment in comparison with a local investor in like circumstances, the tribunal must still consider whether those differences can be justified by reference to rational government policies'); Foster (n 52) 232.

[134] *Parkerings-Compagniet AS v Republic of Lithuania*, ICSID Case No ARB/05/8 Award, 11 September 2007, para 368. On the role of using a proportionality analysis in the context of determining the nexus between the enactment of the measure and the measure itself, see Mitchell, Heaton, and Henckels (n 120) 149–150; see also Henckels (n 65) 164–168 and Foster (n 52) 231–234.

> The Arbitral Tribunal has not been persuaded that GAM's circumstances were demonstrably so 'like' those of nonexpropriated mill owners that it was wrong to treat GAM differently. Mexico determined that nearly half of the mills in the country should be expropriated in the public interest. The reason was not that they were prosperous and the Government was greedy. To the contrary: Mexico perceived that mills operating in conditions of effective insolvency needed public participation in the interest of the national economy in a broad sense. The Government may have been misguided. That is a matter of policy and politics. The Government may have been clumsy in its analysis of the relevant criteria for the cutoff line between candidates and non-candidates for expropriation. Its understanding of corporate finance may have been deficient. But ineffectiveness is not discrimination. *The arbitrators are satisfied that a reason exists for the measure which was not itself discriminatory. That measure was plausibly connected with a legitimate goal of policy (ensuring that the sugar industry was in the hands of solvent enterprises)* and was applied neither in a discriminatory manner nor as a disguised barrier to equal opportunity.[135]

The tribunal made clear that if the Government's 'measure was *plausibly connected* with a legitimate goal of policy' and was applied in a non-discriminatory manner a discrimination claim must fail.[136]

Finally, the most demanding test from the perspective of States is the 'least restrictive means' test, which the tribunal adopted in *SD Myers v Canada*, influenced by WTO law:

> where a state can achieve its chosen level of environmental protection through a variety of equally effective and reasonable means, it is obliged to adopt the alternative that is most consistent with open trade. This corollary also is consistent with the language and the case law arising out of the WTO family of agreements.[137]

In any case, and irrespective of which approach is adopted, the general rule is that 'tribunals did not second-guess the legitimacy and importance of the regulatory objective provided that it was plausible and not discriminatory'.[138] Attempting to downplay the difference between the two approaches the tribunal in *Resolute Forest v Canada* held that '[w]hile the tribunals have varied in their formulations, the bottom

[135] *GAMI Investments, Inc v Government of the United Mexican States*, UNCITRAL, Final Award, 15 November 2004, para 114 (emphasis added); see also *Sergei Paushok, CJSC Golden East Company and CJSC Vostokneftegaz Company v Government of Mongolia*, Award on Jurisdiction and Liability, 28 April 2011, paras 310–311.

[136] *GAMI Investments, Inc v Government of the United Mexican States*, UNCITRAL, Final Award, 15 November 2004, para 114 (emphasis added).

[137] *SD Myers, Inc v Government of Canada*, UNCITRAL, Partial Award, 13 November 2000, para 221; see also ibid, paras 195 and 215. See also Mitchell, Heaton, and Henckels (n 120) 145–149. On the application of the 'least-restrictive means' test in the WTO context, see T Voon, 'Exploring the Meaning of Trade-Restrictiveness in the WTO' (2015) 14 World Trade Review 451; AO Sykes, 'The Least Restrictive Means' (2003) 70 The University of Chicago Law Review 403. On the interplay between non-discrimination and non-restrictions see NF Diebold, 'Standards on Non-discrimination in International Economic Law' (2011) 60 ICLQ 831, 852–854.

[138] Mitchell, Heaton, and Henckels (n 120) 166.

line is the same';[139] at the same time, the tribunal endorsed the rational connection test.[140]

4.2.2 The Normative Argument of the Book: 'Reasonable Connection' as the Appropriate Standard of Review

This section explores the normative question of the required nexus between (i) the lack of legitimate regulatory purpose behind the enactment of the measure, and (ii) the measure itself. While, as the previous section explained, certain tribunals opted for a proportionality analysis[141] or a plausible connection test in the context of examining the measure's adverse impact on foreign investors and the measures' (legitimate) regulatory objective, this book argues that the appropriate standard is that of 'reasonable connection'.

With some exceptions, the most notable of which is *Occidental v Ecuador II*,[142] the principle of proportionality is not widely endorsed and applied by investment tribunals outside the context of expropriation. This is in contract with other fields of international law and, in particular, WTO law,[143] and human rights law[144]. Further, requiring the existence of a 'reasonable connection' between the measure's objectives and the measure

[139] *Resolute Forest Products Inc v Government of Canada*, PCA Case No 2016-13, Award, 25 July 2022, para 575.

[140] ibid, para 576 ('the point of the analysis is to allow the Tribunal to ascertain whether a less favorable treatment accorded to an investor/investment from another Party was provided by reason of the Claimant's nationality (or not). And that is why previous tribunals have focused on "nexus", "connection", or links between the differential treatment and the objectives that are rational or legitimate (and not on the policies in and of themselves)').

[141] On proportionality in international investment treaty arbitration see G Bücheler, *Proportionality in Investor-State Arbitration* (OUP 2015); C Foster, *Global Regulatory Standards in Environmental and Health Disputes: Regulatory Coherence, Due Regard, and Due Diligence* (OUP 2021), Chapter 8; B Kingsbury and SW Schill, 'Public Law Concepts to Balance Investors' Rights with State Regulatory Actions in the Public Interest—the Concept of Proportionality' in Schill (n 65) 75–104; Henckels (n 65); A Stone Sweet, 'Investor-State Arbitration: Proportionality's New Frontier' (2010) 4(1) Law & Ethics of Human Rights 48; V Vadi, *Proportionality, Reasonableness and Standards of Review in International Investment Law and Arbitration* (Edward Elgar 2018); EM Leonhardsen, 'Looking for Legitimacy: Exploring Proportionality Analysis in Investment Treaty Arbitration' (2012) 3 JIDS 95; C Martinez Lopez and L Martinez, 'Proportionality in Investment Treaty Arbitration And Beyond: An "Irresistible Attraction"?' (2015) 2 BCDR International Arbitration. Review 261, 261.

[142] *Occidental Petroleum Corporation and Occidental Exploration and Production Company v The Republic of Ecuador*, ICSID Case No ARB/06/11, Award, 5 October 2012, para 450 ('the overriding principle of proportionality requires that any such administrative goal must be balanced against the Claimants' own interests and against the true nature and effect of the conduct being censured'). See also *Técnicas Medioambientales Tecmed, SA v United Mexican States*, ICSID Case No ARB (AF)/00/2, Award, 29 May 2003, para 122; *Azurix Corp v The Argentine Republic*, ICSID Case No ARB/01/12, Award, 14 July 2006, para 311; CT Kotuby Jr and LA Subota, *General Principles of Law and International Due Process: Principles and Norms Applicable* (OUP 2017) 114–119.

[143] See AB, *Korea—Various Measures on Beef*, para 164; see also P Van en Bossche, 'Looking for Proportionality in WTO Law' (2008) 35 Legal Issues of Economic Integration 283; M Andenas and S Zleptnig, 'Proportionality: WTO Law: In Comparative Perspective' (2007) 42 Texas International Law Journal 371; AD Mitchell, 'Proportionality and Remedies in WTO Disputes' (2006) 17 EJIL 985; A Desmedt, 'Proportionality in WTO Law' (2001) 4 JIEL 441.

[144] See eg *James and Others v UK* [GC], Application No 8793/79, 21 February 1986, paras 50 and 77; *Lingens v Austria* [GC], Application No 9815/82, 8 July 1986, para 37; Cf S Tsakyrakis, 'Proportionality: An Assault on Human Rights?' (2009) 7 International Journal of Constitutional Law 468; M Khosla, 'Proportionality: An Assault on Human Rights?: A Reply' (2010) 8 International Journal of Constitutional Law 298; S Tsakyrakis, 'Proportionality: An Assault on Human Rights?: A Rejoinder to Madhav Khosla' (2010) 8 International Journal of Constitutional Law 307; M Klatt and M Meister, 'Proportionality—A Benefit to Human Rights? Remarks on the I·CON Controversy' (2012) 10 International Journal of Constitutional Law 687; FJ Urbina, *A Critique of Proportionality and Balancing* (CUP 2017).

itself is consistent with the appropriate degree of deference that States should enjoy in regulatory matters.[145] At the same time, merely requiring that the measure in question is plausibly, rather than reasonably, connected with a legitimate, non-discriminatory, public policy objective creates the risk that violations of non-discrimination obligations in international investment law remain unchallenged or are unsuccessfully challenged before arbitral tribunals.

By contrast, the concept of reasonableness, despite its inherently open-ended nature,[146] has been, and continues to be, the subject of judicial interpretation and application as well as theoretical analysis in many jurisdictions, and will likely be workable in the context of investment treaty arbitration as well. Finally, while this book does not advocate transplanting WTO law into international investment law,[147] an additional argument in favour of the reasonable connection approach is that this is in line with

[145] See Section 4.1.2; as Foster explains:

> investment tribunals' articulations of applicable regulatory coherence tests can accommodate domestic level decision-making rather than encouraging an international legal override of the exercise of domestic authority. The social dynamics associated with the working out of relative domestic and international legal authority in environment- related investment treaty arbitration jurisprudence appear, most of the time, to produce formulae that should enable States' and populations' regulatory needs to be met while also affording an appropriate measure of investment protection. By facilitating acceptance of decision-making at the national level these tests allow room for the operation of democratic processes that may assist with traditional procedural justifications for authority at the domestic and international level.

Foster (n 52) 244.

[146] See eg FG Sourgens, 'Reason and Reasonableness: The Necessary Diversity of the Common law' (2014) 67 Maine Law Review 73.

[147] On this debate see eg J Kurtz, 'The Use and Abuse of WTO Law in Investor-State Arbitration: Competition and its Discontents' (2009) 20 EJIL 749; R Howse and E Chalamish, 'The Use and Abuse of WTO Law in Investor-State Arbitration: A Reply to *Jürgen Kurtz*' (2010) 20 EJIL 1087; G Sacerdoti, 'Trade and Investment Law: Institutional Differences and Substantive Similarities' (2014) 9 Jerusalem Review of Legal Studies 1; D McRae, 'The World Trade Organization and International Investment Law: Converging Systems—Can the Case for Convergence be Made?' (2014) 9 Jerusalem Review of Legal Studies 13; T Broude, 'Toward an Economic Approach to the Consolidation of International Trade Regulation and International Investment Law' (2104) 9 Jerusalem Review of Legal Studies 24; J Kurtz, 'Charting the Future of the Twin Pillars of International Economic Law' (2014) 9 Jerusalem Review of Legal Studies 36; See A R Ziegler, 'Investment Law in Conflict with WTO Law' in M Bungenberg and others (eds), *International Investment Law* (CH Beck, Hart, Nomos 2013) 1784–1801; Mitchell, Heaton, and Henckels (n 120) 68–69, 135–136, and 146–147. One of the key structural differences between the WTO and international investment treaty regimes (also regarding non-discrimination obligations) is the absence from the latter of a 'general exceptions' clauses (like Article XX of the GATT) in most investment treaties. Naturally, this question is separate from whether investment arbitration can be used to secure compliance with WTO law, which will not be dealt with in this thesis, G Verhoosel, 'The Use of Investor-State Arbitration under Bilateral Investment Treaties to Seek Relief for Breaches of WTO Law' (2003) 6 JIEL 493. International trade law and international investment law have followed largely divergent paths in terms of substantive rules but also dispute settlement structures, BE Allen and T Soave, 'Jurisdictional Overlap in WTO Dispute Settlement and Investment Arbitration' (2014) 30 Arbitration International 1. Nonetheless, the Softwood lumber, the corn syrup and the feed-in tariffs for renewable energy disputes serve as an illustration of such overlaps: cf Panel, *Mexico—Taxes on Soft Drinks*; AB, *Mexico—Taxes on Soft Drinks*; Panel, *Mexico—Corn Syrup*; AB, *Mexico—Corn Syrup (Article 21.5—US)*; Panel, *Mexico—Corn Syrup (Article 21.5—US)*; *Cargill, Incorporated v Republic of Poland II*, UNCITRAL, Award, 5 March 2008; *Corn Products International Inc v United Mexican States*, ICSID Case No ARB(AF)/04/1, Decision on Responsibility, 15 January 2008; *Archer Daniels Midland Company and Tate & Lyle Ingredients Americas, Inc v United Mexican States*, ICSID Case No ARB(AF)/04/5, Award, 21 November 2007; Panel, *Canada—Renewable Energy/Canada—Feed-in Tariff Program*; AB, *Canada—Renewable Energy/Canada—Feed-in Tariff Program*; *Mesa Power Group, LLC v Government of Canada*, UNCITRAL, PCA Case No 2012-17, Award, 24 March 2016. On a rare (and unsuccessful) attempt to rely on the WTO General Agreement on Trade in Services through an MFN clause see, *Menzies Middle East and Africa SA and Aviation Handling Services International Ltd v Republic of Senegal*, ICSID Case No ARB/15/21, Award, 5 August 2016. For a comparison of the two regimes see D Sarooshi, 'Investment Treaty Arbitration and the World Trade Organization: What Role for Systemic Values in the Resolution of International Economic

WTO practice. In WTO law, Article XX of the GATT could potentially justify violations of WTO law provided that inter alia there is no 'arbitrary or unjustifiable discrimination between countries where the same conditions prevail'.[148] The legal test was set out by the AB in *EC—Seals*:

> in the present case, the causes of the 'discrimination' found to exist under Article I:1 of the GATT 1994 [containing an MFN obligation] are the same as those to be examined under the chapeau. We also note that this is not disputed by the participants. We therefore turn to examine whether such discrimination is 'arbitrary or unjustifiable' within the meaning of the chapeau. As noted above, one of the most important factors in the assessment of arbitrary or unjustifiable discrimination is the question of whether the discrimination can be reconciled with, or is *rationally related to*, the policy objective with respect to which the measure has been provisionally justified under one of the subparagraphs of Article XX.[149]

Likewise, several WTO Panels repeatedly held that 'the test for "arbitrary or unjustifiable discrimination" in Article 2.3. of the SPS Agreement rests on whether the regulatory distinction 'bears a rational connection to the stated objective of the measures'.[150] In *India—Agricultural Products*, the Panel held 'the meaning of "arbitrary or unjustifiable discrimination" within the context of Article 2.3 of the SPS Agreement involves a consideration of the "cause" or "rationale" put forward to explain the discrimination in question, and whether there is a "rational connection" between the reasons given for the discriminatory treatment and the objective of the measure'.[151]

Disputes?' (2014) 49 Texas International Law Journal 445; M Lubambo de Melo, 'Protection of Domestic Investors under the WTO and International Investment Regimes' (2020) 19 World Trade Review 589.

[148] General Agreement on Tariffs and Trade 1947 (adopted 30 October 1947, entered into force 1 January 1948) 55 UNTS 187; General Agreement on Tariffs and Trade 1994 (adopted 15 April 1994, entered into force 1 January 1995) 1867 UNTS 187 (GATT), Article XX.

[149] AB, *EC—Seal Products*, para 5.318 (emphasis added); for a sophisticated criticism of the AB's approach see L Bartels, 'The Chapeau of the General Exceptions in the WTO GATT and GATS Agreements: A Reconstruction' (2015) 109 AJIL 95.

[150] Panel, *US—Animals*, para 7.589; Panel, *India—Agricultural Products*, para 7.429; Panel, *US—Poultry (China)*, para 7.261; see also D Prévost, 'National Treatment in the SPS Agreement: A sui generis obligation' in A Kamperman Sanders (ed), *The Principle of National Treatment in International Economic Law: Trade, Investment and Intellectual Property* (Edward Elgar 2014) 125–155, 131; NF Diebold, *Non-Discrimination in International Trade in Services: 'Likeness' in WTO/GATS* (CUP 2010) 143.

[151] Panel, *India—Agricultural Products*, para 7.429. The same applies to the WTO jurisprudence on Article 5.5 SPS. The non-discrimination obligation under Article 5.5 SPS is also an autonomous standard, complementary to other obligations under the SPS Agreement such the risk assessment requirement, see Panel, *Australia—Salmon*, para 8.126. Article 5.5 SPS is a specific application of the non-discrimination principle set in Article 2.3 SPS, A Seibert-Fohr, 'Article 2 SPS' in R Wolfrum, P-T Stoll, and A Seibert-Fohr (eds), *WTO—Technical Barriers and SPS Measures* (Brill 2007) 392–411, 408. A violation of Article 5.5 SPS leads to a violation of the more general obligation under Article 2.3 SPS (but not vice versa). See AB, *Australia—Salmon*, para 178; Panel, *Australia—Salmon*, para 8.109; AB, *EC—Hormones*, para 212. While in *Australia—Salmon* the AB focused on objective considerations and not on the subjective intent of the measure, in *EC—Hormones* the genuine health concerns rather than protectionist intent AB, *Australia—Salmon*, para 76; AB, *EC—Hormones*, para 240, reversing the Panels' finding, Panel, *EC—Hormones (US)*, paras 8.203, 8.216, 8.241 and Panel, *EC—Hormones (Canada)*, para 8.206, 8.219, 8.244; M Ming Du, 'Autonomy in Setting Appropriate Level of Protection under the WTO Law: Rhetoric or Reality?' (2010) 13 JIEL 1077, 1086–1087; J Pauwelyn, 'The WTO Agreement on Sanitary and Phytosanitary (SPS) Measures as Applied in the First Three SPS Disputes, *EC—Hormones, Australia—Salmon and Japan—Varietals*' (1999) 2 JIEL

Mitchell, Heaton, and Henckels in their monograph advocate a complex approach which outlaws important discriminatory purposes but allow minor ones:

> [i]f significant discriminatory regulatory purposes are permitted on the basis that a state can establish *one* non-discriminatory, legitimate regulatory purpose, the object of promoting international investment free from discriminatory interference will largely be defeated. Making the existence of a protectionist or discriminatory regulatory purpose permissible only to the extent that it is *de minimis* or totally insignificant compared with other purposes avoids this outcome. This should be ascertained by examining whether *all* features of the measure are reasonably necessary to achieve the asserted legitimate purpose; if they pursue other, illegitimate purposes only to a very small extent (relative to other purposes pursued), the measures is not likely to be discriminatory.[152]

There are two potential problems with this approach. First it does not avoid the risk of granting broad discretion to arbitral tribunals to distinguish between what qualifies as important or unimportant objectives, which entails highly subjective and, therefore controversial, value-judgments. The open-ended and value-laden nature of the concept of equality,[153] makes this exercise even more difficult in the context of adjudicating discrimination claims. Second, this approach does not offer sufficient incentives to States to avoid discrimination altogether, which is what non-discrimination clauses in investment treaties aim to do; rather it incentivizes States to conceal their discriminatory motives by adopting a highly sophisticated and complex regulatory framework.

Finally, DiMascio and Pauwelyn argue that instead of adopting one approach in all case, investment tribunals should adhere to a variable geometry model, whereby:

> the nexus required within the national treatment test itself should vary depending on the 'relative importance' of the non protectionist objective proffered by the defendant. The required nexus could be 'related to', 'substantially related to' or, in certain circumstances, 'necessary to achieve' the nonprotectionist objective.[154]

However, such variable geometry not only would lead to legal uncertainty, unnecessarily complicating the legal analysis, but also, as Mitchell, Heaton, and Henckels correctly point out, impudently increases tribunals' discretion.[155]

641, 653–655; L Gruszczynski, *Regulating Health and Environmental Risks under WTO Law: A Critical Analysis of the SPS Agreement* (OUP 2010) 239–240; J Scott, *The WTO Agreement on Sanitary and Phytosanitary Measures: A Commentary* (OUP 2007) 154.

[152] Mitchell, Heaton, and Henckels (n 120) 166 (emphasis in the original).

[153] See Chapter 1.

[154] DiMascio and Pauwelyn (n 11) 87.

[155] Mitchell, Heaton, and Henckels (n 120) 164: '[m]aking the nexus requirement dependent on tribunal members' own perception as to the value of certain regulatory objectives is both unworkable and undesirable'.

4.3 Standard of Proof

Having examined questions regarding the burden of proof (in Sections 4.1.1 and 4.1.2) and questions regarding the standard of review (in Sections 4.2.1 and 4.2.2) from a descriptive and normative perspective, this section focuses on the standard of proof in the context of discrimination claims in international investment treaty arbitration. This book argues that in the light of the serious evidentiary difficulties that investors face because they bear the burden of proof in discrimination claims, the standard of proof should not be exacting but flexible.

4.3.1 Case Law on the Standard of Proof

The lack of consistency in the jurisprudence regarding non-discrimination obligations contained in investment treaties[156] can be (at least partly) attributed to the conflation between (i) the substantive test for discrimination and (ii) evidentiary issues such as the type of evidence required to establish, discrimination. However, the elements of the substantive legal test and evidentiary issues relating to proving facts relevant to that test should be clearly distinguished. The analysis of the tribunal in *Rompetrol v Romania* in relation to the distinction between the burden and standard of proof is illuminating (and merits to be quoted in full):

> the distinction between the two can be stated quite simply: the burden of proof defines which party has to prove what, in order for its case to prevail; the standard of proof defines how much evidence is needed to establish either an individual issue or the party's case as a whole. As soon as the distinction is stated in that way, it becomes evident that the burden of proof is absolute, whereas the standard of proof is relative. By this the Tribunal means (again, in simple terms) that if, according to basic principle, it is for the one party, or for the other, to establish a particular factual assertion, that will remain the position throughout the forensic process, starting from when the assertion is first put forward and all the way through to the end. Operating within an international system characterised by principle rather than procedural formality, the Tribunal is not enamoured of arguments setting out to show that a burden of proof can under certain circumstances shift from the party that originally bore it to the other party, and then perhaps in appropriate circumstances shift back again to the original party. To the mind of the Tribunal, arguments of that kind confuse, unhelpfully, the separate questions of who has to prove a particular assertion and whether that assertion has in fact been proved on the evidence. Conversely, by stating the standard of proof as relative, the Tribunal means that whether a proposition has in fact been proved by the party which bears the burden of proving it depends not just on its own evidence but on the

[156] See above Chapter 3, Section 3.1.

> overall assessment of the accumulated evidence put forward by one or both parties, for the proposition or against it. A trivial example is that, if a factual allegation is put forward by one side and conceded by the other, it no longer requires to be 'proved'.[157]

In other words, the need to demonstrate that the measure was adopted because of the investor's nationality (or another impermissible ground) is conceptually and legally distinct from the type of evidence—direct or circumstantial—which is required to prove this. In *Feldman v Mexico* the tribunal insightfully distinguished between nationality-based discrimination and the need the measure to be enacted 'explicitly' on the basis of nationality:

> [i]t is clear that the concept of national treatment as embodied in NAFTA and similar agreements is designed to prevent discrimination on the basis of nationality, or 'by reason of nationality.' . . . However, it is not self-evident, as the Respondent argues, that any departure from national treatment must be explicitly shown to be a result of the investor's nationality . . . *For practical as well as legal reasons, the Tribunal is prepared to assume that the differential treatment is a result of the Claimant's nationality, at least in the absence of any evidence to the contrary.*[158]

Investment tribunals have not dealt with the problem in a systematic and coherent way. From the relevant fragments of the jurisprudence a picture of hesitation and uncertainty emerges. In *Lemire v Ukraine* the tribunal emphasised that the tribunal should look at the totality of the evidence: 'evidence in the aggregate might establish conclusive evidence of a manipulation of the tender process, even if none of these circumstances did so by itself'.[159] When examining 'remarks of individual members of the Mexican Congress about the purpose of the legislation',[160] another tribunal hesitantly noted that:

[157] *The Rompetrol Group NV v Romania*, ICSID Case No ARB/06/3, Award, 6 March 2013, para 178. See also B S Vasani, T L Foden, and H Zayyan, 'Burden and Standard of Proof at the Jurisdictional Stage' in K Yannaca-Small, *Arbitration Under International Investment Agreements: A Guide to the Key Issues* (2nd edn, OUP 2018) 312–331. See also *Apotex Holdings Inc and Apotex Inc v United States of America*, ICSID Case No ARB(AF)/12/1, Award, 25 August 2014, para 8.8: '[t]he Tribunal considers such a distinction exists between the legal burden of proof (which never shifts) and the evidential burden of proof (which can shift from one party to another, depending upon the state of the evidence)'. See also *Mercer International Inc v Government of Canada*, ICSID Case No ARB(AF)/12/3, Award, 6 March 2018, para 7.16: 'whilst the legal burden of proof rests always on the Claimant to prove its claims under NAFTA Articles 1102 and 1103, the question whether the evidential burden shifts to the Respondent remains relevant, including the question whether any positive defence put forward by the Respondent is established'.

[158] *Marvin Roy Feldman Karpa v United Mexican States*, ICSID Case No ARB(AF)/99/1, Award, 16 December 2002, para 181 (emphasis removed and added). Dolzer, Kriebaum, and Schreuer interpret *Feldman v Mexico* as supporting the proposition that it is 'not necessary to show discrimination based on nationality', Dolzer, Kriebaum, and Schreuer (n 129) 258. However, the more nuanced approach of the tribunal in *Feldman v Mexico* does not support this view. This paragraph was also quoted in *William Ralph Clayton, William Richard Clayton, Douglas Clayton, Daniel Clayton and Bilcon of Delaware Inc v Government of Canada*, UNCITRAL, PCA Case No 2009-04, Award on Jurisdiction and Liability, 17 March 2015, para 719. See also *International Thunderbird Gaming Corporation v The United Mexican States*, UNCITRAL, Separate Opinion of Professor Thomas Wälde, 1 December 2005, para 102; *United Parcel Service of America Inc v Government of Canada*, UNCITRAL, Separate Statement of Dean Ronald A Cass, 24 May 2007, para 102 (discussing 'rebuttable presumption that there was an intention to discriminate').

[159] *Joseph Charles Lemire v Ukraine*, ICSID Case No ARB/06/18, Decision on Jurisdiction and Liability, 14 January 2010, para 405.

[160] *Corn Products International Inc v United Mexican States*, ICSID Case No ARB(AF)/04/1, Decision on Responsibility, 15 January 2008, para 137.

> [w]e have doubts about the extent to which such comments can legitimately be treated as evidence of the intent of the Legislature as a whole, let alone of the State itself, in imposing a measure of this kind, although we do not need finally to decide that point.[161]

In *Mondev v USA* the claimant relied on 'certain remarks by officials of Boston and BRA which ... indicated a certain anti-Canadian animus',[162] but, as they were made before NAFTA entered into force, the tribunal remained unimpressed.[163] In *Glamis Gold v USA* the tribunal examined (in the context of a FET claim under Article 1105 of the NAFTA) different types of evidence to establish whether or not the investor's gold mining project (the 'Imperial Project') was specifically targeted by the State.[164] The tribunal began its analysis by noting that while 'the Imperial Project was indeed on the minds of the legislators drafting' the relevant bill,[165] 'determining whether this circumstance should be taken as proof of targeting of the Imperial Project is a complicated task'.[166] The tribunal highlight the relevant complexities in the following manner:

> [t]he Tribunal acknowledges that discerning legislative intent is always a difficult endeavor, however. If one legislator speaks, it is hard to know whether he or she speaks for the legislature as a whole, or just for him or herself. It is even more difficult to ascertain whether an individual speaks for the legislature when that individual is not a member of the legislature. In addition, even if an individual did single out the Imperial Project, it could be in the nature of describing a symbol that has come to represent the harm that the legislature is striving to remedy. Symbols often can serve as a rallying call for expedited action; if, however, this symbolic project is merely a very visible member of a larger class of projects that are viewed as harmful by the legislature, and which also are addressed by the subsequent litigation, it cannot be said that this project alone was 'targeted.'[167]

Subsequently, the tribunal turned to the drafting history of the bill and concluded that the bill was of general application, on its face applying both to existing and future mines.[168] On the basis of 'one quote from an internal State of California memo', the tribunal identified a 'general concern that the California state legislators had regarding

[161] ibid. Another tribunal emphasized that '[b]y calling attention to this congressional debate, the Tribunal does not intend to attribute responsibility to Ecuador for the statements of individual congressmen. However, in the overall assessment of the facts and the evidence on record, these statements shed light on the manner in which at least some members of Congress understood the context leading to the enactment of Law 42', *Burlington Resources Inc v Republic of Ecuador*, ICSID Case No ARB/08/5, Decision on Liability, 14 December 2012, para 305. 'This does not mean, however, that a discriminatory tax amounts per se to an expropriation. To reach the level of an expropriation, the discriminatory tax must still meet the test of substantial deprivation', ibid, para 402.

[162] *Mondev International Ltd v United States of America*, ICSID Case No ARB(AF)/99/2, Award, 11 October 2002, para 64.

[163] ibid, para 65.

[164] *Glamis Gold, Ltd v The United States of America*, UNCITRAL, Final Award, 8 June 2009, paras 791–797.

[165] ibid, para 791.

[166] ibid.

[167] ibid, para 792.

[168] ibid, para 794.

the potential damage to sacred sites caused by present and future open pit mines in general, and the Imperial Project specifically, and the hope that this legislation, at a minimum, would repair some of that damage.'[169] Therefore, the tribunal held that the claimant did not discharge its burden of proving that the relevant bill targeted 'solely' its mining project.[170] In *Crystallex v Venezuela* 'repeated and rather derogatory references to "transnationals" and "transnational companies"' by President Chavez were found to be inadequate to 'support the conclusion that the expropriation was carried out in a discriminatory manner'.[171] In *Baghat v Egypt* the tribunal held that '[t]he reference to newspaper reports upon which Claimant relies to prove that the actions of Respondent were politically motivated is not enough to prove Respondent's improper conduct'.[172] In *Eureko v Poland* the tribunal held that measures which 'have been proclaimed by successive Ministers of the State Treasury as being pursued in order to keep PZU under majority Polish control and to exclude foreign control such as that of Eureko', amounted to a blunt violation of the non-discrimination element of FET and expropriation.[173] In *LETCO v Liberia* (an ICSID arbitration pursuant to a concession agreement, the breach of which by Liberia was found to amount to expropriation) the tribunal was persuaded this was a genuine case of discrimination because:

> evidence was given to the Tribunal that areas of the concession taken way from LETCO were granted to other foreign-owned companies; according to Mr Alain de Marti, who was LETCO's general manager in Liberia for the entire period of the concession, these foreign companies were run by people who were 'good friends' of the Liberian authorities.[174]

Finally, the relevant case law suggests that timing is relevant. In *CMS v Argentina* the tribunal decided to assess the measures taken by Argentina in the context of the 2001–2002 Crisis (and which differentiated between various business sectors) under the FET standard rather than the clause prohibiting arbitrary or discriminatory measures.[175] However, the tribunal also noted that 'the fact is that to the extent that the measures persisted beyond the crisis, the differentiation between various categories or groups of businesses becomes more difficult to explain' and '[t]he longer the differentiation is kept the more evident the issue becomes, thus eventually again reinforcing the related finding about the breach of fair and equitable treatment'.[176] In sum, as Kurtz observes,

[169] ibid, para 795.

[170] ibid, paras 796–797.

[171] *Crystallex International Corporation v Bolivarian Republic of Venezuela*, ICSID Case No ARB(AF)/11/2, Award, 4 April 2016, para 715.

[172] *Mohamed Abdel Raouf Bahgat v Arab Republic of Egypt I*, PCA Case No 2012–07, Final Award, 23 December 2019, para 249.

[173] *Eureko BV v Republic of Poland*, Partial Award, 19 August 2005, para 242; see also ibid, paras 191–229 and 233.

[174] *Liberian Eastern Timber Corporation v Republic of Liberia*, ICSID Case No ARB/83/2, Award, 31 March 1986, (1987) 2 ICSID Reports 346, 366.

[175] *CMS Gas Transmission Company v the Argentine Republic*, Award, ICSID Case No ARB/01/8, 12 May 2005, para 294.

[176] ibid.

'[d]espite the growing sophistication at play in uncovering state purpose, there are two persistent flaws in some of the arbitration case to date. The first is a distinct tendency towards deference in setting the burden of persuasion ... A second flaw centres on the preparedness to accept the mere presence of an external legal norm as evidence of the bona fides state in question'.[177]

4.3.2 The Normative Argument of the Book: Discrimination Can be Proven Based on Circumstantial Evidence

The central thesis of this book is that to prevail in discrimination claims foreign investors must prove that the 'less favourable treatment' accorded to them by the Host State is 'because of' their foreign nationality (in National Treatment and MFN claims) or their nationality or another impermissible ground for differentiation (in discrimination claims on the basis of the prohibition of arbitrary and/or discriminatory measures, FET or in the context of expropriation). This book argues that this is in practice equated with a *rational* connection between the measure(s) in question and non-discriminatory, ie legitimate justifications[178] and, as explained above, this is upon the investor to prove.[179] In doing so, investors face significant evidentiary difficulties, primarily because (i) the decision-making process within States is complex and polycentric, and (ii) States enjoy asymmetric access over the relevant evidence compared to the foreign investor.[180] To alleviate investors' evidentiary burden, this book argues that investors can discharge such burden by not only requesting tribunal to draw adverse inferences in case States fail to produce evidence at their possession or control (as already explained in Section 4.1.2.1) but also by relying on indirect, circumstantial evidence. Circumstantial evidence is not only widely accepted in international practice and sanctioned by investment treaty tribunals, but also strikes the right balance between States' and investors' interests.

The ICJ has clarified on more than one occasions that:

> it would be wrong to regard this rule, based on the maxim *onus probandi incumbit actori*, as an absolute one, to be applied in all circumstances. The determination of the burden of proof is in reality dependent on the subject-matter and the nature of each dispute brought before the Court; it varies according to the type of facts which it is necessary to establish for the purposes of the decision of the case.[181]

[177] Kurtz (n 83) 131–132.
[178] See Section 4.2.2.
[179] See Section 4.1.
[180] See Section 4.1.
[181] *Ahmadou Sadio Diallo (Republic of Guinea v Democratic Republic of the Congo)* Merits, Judgment [2010] ICJ Reports 639, 660, para 54; *Application of the Convention on the Prevention and Punishment of the Crime of Genocide (Croatia v Serbia)*, Judgment, [2015] ICJ Rep 3, 73, paras 170–174; *Armed Activities on the Territory of the Congo (Democratic Republic of the Congo v Uganda)* 9 February 2022, paras 115–119.

For example, in *Diallo* the ICJ held that:

> [i]n particular, where, as in these proceedings, it is alleged that a person has not been afforded, by a public authority, certain procedural guarantees to which he was entitled, it cannot as a general rule be demanded of the Applicant that it prove the negative fact which it is asserting. A public authority is generally able to demonstrate that it has followed the appropriate procedures and applied the guarantees required by law—if such was the case—by producing documentary evidence of the actions that were carried out. However, it cannot be inferred in every case where the Respondent is unable to prove the performance of a procedural obligation that it has disregarded it: that depends to a large extent on the precise nature of the obligation in question; some obligations normally imply that written documents are drawn up, while others do not. The time which has elapsed since the events must also be taken into account.[182]

Corruption cases constitute another example in which a less strict approach and a lower standard of proof are suggested. As Tussupov concludes, 'the observations of arbitral tribunals have been gradually evolving from the categorical choice of "clear and convincing evidence" standard to the recognition of "circumstantial evidence" and finally to the application of the "balance of probabilities" for the allegations of fraud and corruption', thus identifying 'clear footprints of a changing trend on the approach to the determination of the applicable standard of proof for such allegations'.[183]

Different international courts and tribunals recognise that information asymmetry between the parties is a relevant consideration in evaluating the probative value of evidence. In its first case (the *Corfu Channel* case) the ICJ held that:

> [t]he fact of this *exclusive territorial control exercised by a State within its frontiers has a bearing upon the methods of proof available* to establish the knowledge of that State as to such events. *By reason of this exclusive control*, the other State, *the victim of a breach of international law, is often unable to furnish direct proof of facts giving rise to*

[182] *Ahmadou Sadio Diallo (Republic of Guinea v Democratic Republic of the Congo)* (n 182) para 55.

[183] A Tussupov, *Corruption and Fraud in Investment Arbitration: Procedural and Substantive Challenges* (Springer 2022) 162. See also ICC Case No 12290, 2005 (2010) 137 JDI Clunet 1406, 1410: 'En vertu d'un principe général, la charge de la preuve incombe à la partie invoquant le caractère illicite du contrat. Cependant, ce caractère illicite est souvent difficile à prouver, les parties masquant l'object réel du contrat derrière des stipulations contractuelles anodines. Les Tribunaux—ou les arbitres—peuvent, en principe, utiliser tous moyens de preuve autorisés par la loi, étant entendu qu'ils ne sont pas liés par la formulation du contrat. Pour cette raison, les arbitres n'one d'autre choix que de se repose sur des indications extracontractuelles. Il n'est en effet pas nécessaire que la nature illicite du contrat se déduise des termes de celui-ci. L'exigence en matière de preuve est dès lors réduite et peut se limiter à une présomption reposant sur des indices.' (Internal references omitted.) Cf ICC Case No 14470, Final Award, 2008, (2011) JDI 1229, 1234: 'Le Tribunal arbitral est conscient des difficultés qu'il y a à rapporter la preuve de la corruption, opération par définition occulte, mais il estime que les arguments avancés par la défenderesse sont insuffisants pour en établir la réalité.' See also *Application of the Convention on the Prevention and Punishment of the Crime of Genocide*, Provisional Measures, Order of 13 September 1993, Separate Opinion of Judge Lauterpacht [1993] ICJ Rep 407, 430, para 67: 'As to the first of these questions, it seems impossible to avoid the conclusion that the Respondent State was involved in the actions taken by the Serbs in Bosnia-Herzegovina... At the very least, the effect of the evidence is to shift the burden of proof completely to the Respondent. It has made no attempt to meet this burden, even to the limited extent that would have been open to it within the framework of the proceedings for interim measures'.

> *responsibility*. Such a State should be allowed *a more liberal recourse to inferences of fact and circumstantial evidence. This indirect evidence is admitted in all systems of law, and its use is recognised by international decisions.*[184]

For Judge Owada, 'this dictum of the Corfu Channel case contains some valid points which could be susceptible of general application to an international court'.[185] Judge Owada emphasized that in case of asymmetry of information between the claimant and the respondent the Court's approach in relation to evidentiary and procedural issues must take into account equitable considerations.[186] In general, it is more likely than not that direct evidence of improper motives would be unavailable and, therefore, recourse to, and reliance on, circumstantial evidence is necessary.[187] The arbitral tribunal in the *Lena Goldfields Ltd v USSR* arbitration was faced with an extreme case of asymmetry, as the Government of the USSR, after the constitution of the arbitral refused to participate in the proceedings. The tribunal recognized the evidentiary difficulties and adjusted its approach.[188]

[184] *Corfu Channel case (United Kingdom v Albania)*, Judgment [1949] ICJ Rep 4, 18 (emphasis added). Circumstantial evidence is accepted in investment arbitration, *Methanex Corporation v United States of America*, UNCITRAL, Partial Award, 7 August 2002, para 149. See also M P Scharf and D Margaux, 'The International Court of Justice's Treatment of Circumstantial Evidence and Adverse Inferences' (2012) 13 Chicago Journal of International Law 123, 143. For a similar idea in EU case law, see Case C-390/07, *Commission v United Kingdom*, 10 December 2009, para 44: 'where the Commission has adduced sufficient evidence of certain matters in the territory of the defendant Member State, it is incumbent on the latter to challenge in substance and in detail the information produced and the consequences flowing therefrom'; Case C-494/01, *Commission v Ireland*, 26 April 2005 para 44; Case C-365/97, *Commission v Italy*, 9 November 1999, paras 84 and 86.

[185] *Oil Platforms (Islamic Republic of Iran v United States of America)*, Dissenting Opinion of Judge Owada, [2003] ICJ Rep 161, 322, para 51.

[186] ibid, para 47 ('Accepting as given this inherent asymmetry that comes into the process of discharging the burden of proof, it nevertheless seems to me important that the Court, as a court of justice whose primary function is the proper administration of justice, should see to it that this problem relating to evidence be dealt with in such a way that utmost justice is brought to bear on the final finding of the Court and that the application of the rules of evidence should be administered in a fair and equitable manner to the parties, so that the Court may get at the whole truth as the basis for its final conclusion'). In one of the rare occasions of review of an arbitral award the ICJ held 'the appraisal of the probative value of documents and evidence appertained to the discretionary power of the arbitrator is not open to question', *Case Concerning the Arbitral Award Made by the King of Spain on December 23, 1906 (Honduras v Nicaragua)* [1960] ICJ Rep 192, 215, 216.

[187] See *South West Africa case (Ethiopia v South Africa, Liberia v South Africa) (Second Phase), Separate Opinion of Judge Van Wyk* [1966] ICJ Rep 6, 152: 'An improper purpose or motive may be proved in a number of ways, such as by direct statements of the person concerned. However, a more frequent source of proof is circumstantial evidence, including the nature of the act itself. If an act is so unreasonable that no reasonable person placed in the position of the holder of the power would have performed it, one may deduce that such act was motivated by some improper motive or consideration. Of course, such a conclusion can only be arrived at after considering all relevant facts including the purported purposes and effects of the act in question.' A similar question often arises in the context of interpreting the intent of the Parliament in UK constitutional law, see P Craig, *UK, EU and Global Administrative Law: Foundations and Challenges* (CUP 2015) 125–153; R Dworkin, *Law's Empire* (Fontana 1986) 313–354; J Waldron, *Law and Disagreement* (OUP 1999) 199–246. R Ekins, 'The Intention of Parliament' (2010) Public Law 709; R Ekins, *The Nature of Legislative Intent* (OUP 2016); A Dolcetti, 'The Central Case Method in *The Nature of Legislative Intent*' (2019) 64 American Journal of Jurisprudence 41.

[188] *Lena Goldfields Ltd v USSR*, 2 September 1930, para 15, reproduced in A Nussbaum, 'Arbitration Between the Lena Goldfields Ltd. and the Soviet Government (1950) 36 Cornell Law Review 31, 44: '[t]his information, by reason of the premises, the Court was not able to obtain direct from the Government, and in order to ascertain the truth upon the issues before it, the Court was thus compelled to admit the best evidence available of various facts and documents, upon which Lena was unable to produce primary evidence by reason of the documents or witnesses being in Russia and not available at the trial. The Court finds as a fact upon the evidence that this was rendered necessary by the difficulty in which the company found itself of getting either documents or persons out of Russia for the purposes of the trial'. See also VV Veeder, 'The Lena Goldfields Arbitration: The Historical Roots of Three Ideas' (1998) 47 ICLQ 747.

Investment tribunals do recognise the polycentric nature of the State's decision-make processes.[189] In *SD Myers v Canada* the tribunal highlighted the relevant difficulties by observing that '[t]he intent of government is a complex and multifaceted matter. Government decisions are shaped by different politicians and officials with differing philosophies and perspectives. Each of the many persons involved in framing government policy may approach a problem from a variety of different policy objectives and may sometimes take into account partisan political factors or career concerns'.[190]

At the same time, adopting a flexible approach in relation to evidence does not necessarily mean that no standards apply. For example, the ICJ was sceptical of multiple press reports regarding facts drawn from a single source[191]—and rightly so. At the same time, the ICJ highlighted the importance of unchallenged evidence and evidence tested through witness cross-examination (which is frequently used in investment treaty arbitration):

> [t]he Court will also give weight to evidence that has not, even before this litigation, been challenged by impartial persons for the correctness of what it contains. The Court moreover notes that evidence obtained by examination of persons directly involved, and who were subsequently cross-examined by judges skilled in examination and experienced in assessing large amounts of factual information, some of it of a technical nature, merits special attention. The Court thus will give appropriate consideration to the Report of the Porter Commission, which gathered evidence in this manner. The Court further notes that, since its publication, there has been no challenge to the credibility of this Report, which has been accepted by both Parties.[192]

For the ICJ the key to determine genocidal intent in the *Bosnia Genocide* case was the existence of a 'pattern of conduct'.[193] In principle, the stance of state officials directly

[189] On the asymmetry of power between investors and States in the context of investment treaty arbitration see generally T Wälde, 'Procedural Challenges in Investment Arbitration under the Shadow of the Dual Role of the State: Asymmetries and Tribunal's Duty to Ensure, Pro-actively the Equality of Arms' (2010) 26 Arbitration International 3.

[190] *SD Myers, Inc v Government of Canada*, UNCITRAL, Partial Award, 13 November 2000, para 161. The tribunal added that it 'can only characterize CANADA's motivation or intent fairly by examining the record of the evidence as a whole', ibid. The same difficulties apply in disparate treatment cases in the US when the employer (as it happens frequently) is a company rather an individual, see R Thompson Ford, 'Bias in the Air: Rethinking Employment Discrimination Law' (2014) 66 Stanford Law Review 1381, 1396: 'But to say that an employer (which is often a corporation and therefore itself incapable of intending anything) "intentionally discriminated" is not so much to say that someone acted based on a prohibited subjective (but objectively knowable?) state of mind but rather to aver to a set of objective circumstances and the lack of other (extenuating) circumstances'. See also Chapter 2.

[191] *Military and Paramilitary Activities in and against Nicaragua (Nicaragua v United States of America)*, Merits, [1986] ICJ Rep 14, 41, para 63 ('The Court has however to show particular caution in this area. Widespread reports of a fact may prove on closer examination to derive from a single source, and such reports. however numerous, will in such case have no greater value as evidence than the original source.') This approach was endorsed in subsequent cases, see *Oil Platforms (Islamic Republic of Iran v United States of America)*, Judgment [2003] ICJ Rep 161, 190, para 60 and *Armed Activities on the Territory of the Congo (Democratic Republic of the Congo v Uganda)*, Judgment, [2005] ICJ Rep 168, 201, para 61.

[192] *Armed Activities on the Territory of the Congo (Democratic Republic of the Congo v Uganda)*, Judgment, [2005] ICJ Rep 168, 201, para 61.

[193] *Application of the Convention on the Prevention and Punishment of the Crime of Genocide (Bosnia and Herzegovina v Serbia and Montenegro)* (Judgment) [2007] ICJ Rep 43, 198, para 373 ('The dolus specialis, the specific intent to destroy the group in whole or in part, has to be convincingly shown by reference to particular

involved in the design, promulgation or (mis-)application of the measure in question is crucial from an evidentiary perspective. How broad this category of persons should be is difficult to determine *in abstracto*; it must be assessed on a case-by-case basis in light of the factual matrix of each dispute.[194] Suggesting that the stance of all actors, whose acts are attributable to the State, is relevant risks casting the net too wide, in particular when they are not interfering with foreign investments. Baetens aptly epitomizes the relevant difficulties:

> if a measure is adopted without any explicit discriminatory reference to foreign investors and without a clear discriminatory effect on foreigners, but in the course of adopting this measure, one minister has uttered a biased remark, is this sufficient to establish a violation of the non-discrimination standard? If the answer is that the bias of some outweighs the unbiased position of others, how should this be quantified? And how much bias would be needed to 'tip the balance'? Would 10 per cent bias obliterate 90 per cent legitimate objectives? Merely asking these questions makes clear that this is an impossible exercise for an arbitral tribunal.[195]

On the other hand, statements revealing protectionist intent made by certain very high-ranking officials will (almost) always be relevant or even decisive. One could look by analogy to, or merely draw inspiration from, Article 7(2)(a) of the Vienna Convention on the Law of Treaties ('VCLT')[196] or the jurisprudence of the ICJ.[197] Investment tribunals have accepted that there are no strict rules of evidence and acknowledged that in

circumstances, unless a general plan to that end can be convincingly demonstrated to exist; and for a pattern of conduct to be accepted as evidence of its existence, it would have to be such that it could only point to the existence of such intent'); see also ibid, 376: 'the Applicant has not established the existence of that intent on the part of the Respondent, either on the basis of a concerted plan, or on the basis that the events reviewed above reveal a consistent pattern of conduct which could only point to the existence of such intent'.

[194] *Vigotop Limited v Hungary*, ICSID Case No ARB/11/22, Award, 1 October 2014, para 633 ('during the course of the Project and its negotiation, certain anti-Semitic remarks were published about the Project or its Sponsors. In Claimant's view, Respondent did not take any actions against the persons responsible for these anti-Semitic incidents and therefore violated its duty not to act in a discriminatory way. Although the Tribunal does not have jurisdiction beyond the expropriation determination, the Cyprus-Hungary BIT itself does impose anti-discrimination obligations on the State (duty not to impair the operation, management, use, enjoyment, or disposal of the investment by discriminatory measures in Article 3(1); duty not to deprive investors of their investment unless the measures are not discriminatory in Article 4(1)(b)). The Tribunal also recalls that the tribunal in FFIC v. Mexico held that discrimination may also, to a certain extent, be relevant to the determination of whether an expropriation occurred. The Tribunal takes these concerns of discrimination very seriously. Remarks such as those published are always a concern. However, the Tribunal has not found any such remarks that are clearly attributable to the State').

[195] F Baetens, 'Discrimination on the basis of Nationality: Determining Likeness in Human Rights and Investment Law' in Schill (n 65) 279–315, 306.

[196] Vienna Convention on the Law of Treaties (adopted 23 May 1969, entered into force 27 January 1980) 1155 UNTS 331, Article 7(2)(a) ('Heads of State, Heads of Government and Ministers for Foreign Affairs, for the purpose of performing all acts relating to the conclusion of a treaty').

[197] *Armed Activities on the Territory of the Congo (New Application: 2002) (Democratic Republic of the Congo v Rwanda) (Jurisdiction and Admissibility, Judgment)* [2006] ICJ Rep 6, 25, para 47; *Arrest Warrant of 11 April 2000 (Democratic Republic of the Congo v Belgium)* (Judgment) [2002] ICJ Rep 3, 22, para 53. Particularly regarding unfavourable facts to the State, see also *Armed Activities on the Territory of the Congo (Democratic Republic of the Congo v Uganda)*, Judgment, [2005] ICJ Rep 168, 206, para 78 ('The Court finds that most evidence of events in this period is indirect and less reliable than that which emerges from statements made under oath before the Porter

certain cases *prima facie* evidence will be all that the claimant is required to produce.[198] As Kurtz explains:

> [o]n occasion, protectionist statements may only be made by one or two individual legislators and simply reflect opportunist attempts to harness interest group support. Instead, *all* pertinent evidence should be examined as part of an overall inquiry into trying to identify what political forces are ultimately responsible for the measure in question. We have seen arbitral tribunals—with different emphases and integrity—traverse a range of *indicia* to construct a ruling on purpose. These have included the structure and effect of the measure, its timing (and particularly that of an ex post justification), and the presence of any less restrictive alternative to the measure in question.[199]

The WTO jurisprudence, albeit inconsistent,[200] offers valuable insights on how protectionism (as opposed to valid regulatory considerations) could be identified. In *Chile—Alcoholic Beverages*, a National Treatment case under the GATT, the WTO Appellate Body held that:

> [t]he subjective intentions inhabiting the minds of individual legislators or regulators do not bear upon the inquiry, if only because they are not accessible to treaty interpreters. It does not follow, however, that the statutory purposes or objectives—that is, the purpose or objectives of a Member's legislature and government as a whole—to the extent that they are given objective expression in the statute itself, are not pertinent.[201]

As a result, an 'examination of the design, architecture and structure of a tax measure precisely to permit identification of a measure's objectives or purposes as revealed or objectified in the measure itself' is necessary.[202] Therefore, 'a measure's purposes,

Commission. The Court has already noted that statements "emanating from high-ranking official political figures, sometimes indeed of the highest rank, are of particular probative value when they acknowledge facts or conduct unfavourable to the State represented by the person who made them" (*Military and Paramilitary Activities in and against Nicaragua (Nicaragua v. United States of America), Merits, Judgment, I.C.J. Reports 1986*, p. 41, para. 64). The Court believes the same to be the case when such statements against interest are made by senior military officers given the objective circumstances in which those statements were taken. Accordingly, the Court finds it relevant that before the Porter Commission, Brigadier General Kazini, who was commander of the Ugandan forces in the DRC, referred to "the capture of Beni, that was on 7 August 1998" "); *Military and Paramilitary Activities in and against Nicaragua (Nicaragua v United States of America)* (Merits) [1986] ICJ Rep 14, 41, para 64.

198 *Asian Agricultural Products LTD (AAPL) v Republic of Sri Lanka*, ICSID Case No ARB/87/3, Final Award, 27 June 1990, para 56; *Middle East Cement Shipping and Handling Co SA v Arab Republic of Egypt*, ICSID Case No ARB/99/6, Award, 12 April 2002, para 94.

199 J Kurtz, 'The Merits and Limits of Comparativism: National Treatment in International Investment Law and the WTO' in Schill (n 65) 243–278, 275 (emphasis in the original). See also Kurtz (n 83) 125–131.

200 See Chapter 3, Section 3.1.

201 AB, *Chile—Alcoholic Beverages*, para 62.

202 Ibid, para 71; see also Diebold (n 137) 849; W Zhou, 'The Role of Regulatory Purpose under Article III:2 and 4—Toward Consistency between Negotiating History and WTO Jurisprudence' (2012) 11 WTR 81; H Horn and PC Mavroidis, 'Still Hazy after All These Years: The Interpretation of National Treatment in the GATT/WTO Case-law on Tax Discrimination' (2004) 15 EJIL 39.

objectively manifested in the design, architecture and structure of the measure, are intensely pertinent to the task of evaluating whether or not that measure is applied so as to afford protection to domestic production'.[203] The same understanding of discrimination is adopted by the WTO Panels and the Appellate Body in relation to discrimination under the TBT and SPS Agreements.[204] In the context of non-discrimination under the TBT Agreement what is key is 'whether the detrimental impact on imports stems exclusively from a legitimate regulatory distinction':[205]

> Naturally, the inquiry into text, structure and disparate impact should always be placed in context, in order to determine whether the harm suffered by the foreign investor resulted from a deliberately protectionist policy. This will, firstly and fundamentally, require an adjudicator to situate his or her assessment of the measure against its overall legislative history.[206]

Hirsch, writing in an exclusively trade law (WTO) context makes a similar argument in favour of examining regulators' subjective considerations, by:

[203] AB, *Chile—Alcoholic Beverages*, para 71. Naturally, '[w]hether the design, architecture, structure, and overall application of the measure do reveal a protective nature of the measure in question can only be determined "on a case by case basis, taking account of all relevant facts." Of course, in difficult factual circumstances a Panel will have to make a judgement call as to whether this is the case, and reasonable people may disagree with a decision that is characterized by a significant margin of appreciation', Matsushita and others (n 100) 204. This is due to the conceptual link between non-discrimination treaty provisions with the idea of equality, which, as explained in Chapter 1 is value-dependent.

[204] Agreement on Technical Barriers to Trade (TBT) (adopted 15 April 1994, entered into force 1 January 1995) Marrakesh Agreement Establishing the World Trade Organization, Annex 1A, 1868 UNTS 120; Agreement on the Application of Sanitary and Phytosanitary Measures (SPS) (adopted 15 April 1994, entered into force 1 January 1995) Marrakesh Agreement Establishing the World Trade Organization Annex 1A, 1867 UNTS 493.

[205] This is also the case with the WTO TBT jurisprudence, see AB, *US—Tuna II (Mexico) (Article 21.5—US)/ US—Tuna II (Mexico) (Article 21.5—Mexico II)*, para 6.9: 'The Appellate Body has identified a two-step analysis for examining whether the technical regulation at issue accords less favourable treatment to imported products under Article 2.1 of the TBT Agreement: (i) whether it modifies the conditions of competition to the detriment of such imported products vis-à-vis like products of domestic origin and/or like products originating in any other country; and (ii) whether the detrimental impact on imports stems exclusively from a legitimate regulatory distinction. Where the detrimental impact caused by a technical regulation is found to stem exclusively from a legitimate regulatory distinction, "such a technical regulation does not accord less favourable treatment to imported products and is therefore consistent with Article 2.1 of the TBT Agreement." ', AB, *US—Tuna II (Mexico)*, paras 212–213; AB, *US—Clove Cigarettes*, para 182: 'the existence of a detrimental impact on competitive opportunities for the group of imported vis-à-vis the group of domestic like products is not dispositive of less favourable treatment under Article 2.1. Instead, a panel must further analyze whether the detrimental impact on imports stems exclusively from a legitimate regulatory distinction rather than reflecting discrimination against the group of imported products. In making this determination, a panel must carefully scrutinize the particular circumstances of the case, that is, the design, architecture, revealing structure, operation, and application of the technical regulation at issue, and, in particular, whether that technical regulation is even-handed, in order to determine whether it discriminates against the group of imported products'; AB, *US—COOL*, para 271: '[i]f a panel determines that a measure has such an impact on imported products, however, this will not be dispositive of a violation of Article 2.1. This is because not every instance of a detrimental impact amounts to the less favourable treatment of imports that is prohibited under that provision. Rather, some technical regulations that have a de facto detrimental impact on imports may not be inconsistent with Article 2.1 when such impact stems exclusively from a legitimate regulatory distinction'; G Marceau, 'The New TBT Jurisprudence in US—Clove Cigarettes, WTO US—Tuna II, and US—Cool' (2013) 8 Asian Journal of WTO and International Health Law and Policy 1, 8–13.

[206] Kurtz (n 83) 130.

> highlight[ing] the role of socio-cognitive and social factors in discriminatory behavior against foreign products, primarily key regulators' intentions, ingroup favoritism norms, and related cognitive biases. Although detecting such subjective factors presents WTO tribunals with certain difficulties, ignoring or underestimating them does not reflect the real life of trade discrimination and is not in line with the human tendency (including among adjudicators) to 'mindread' other people. International tribunals in other fields often cope with such tasks, for example, with regard to findings regarding 'good faith' or treaty interpretation according to the parties' intention. Thus, where WTO tribunals are presented with credible evidence regarding key role regulators' intentions (discerned from both objective and subjective items of evidence) or relevant norms prevailing in their social groups, it is desirable that they openly and seriously take into account such evidence and grant it appropriate probative weight.[207]

Evidentiary difficulties are often cited as a reason (or explanation) for the adoption of an impact-based approach in assessing discrimination in international investment law.[208] However, as Mitchell, Heaton, and Henckels persuasively explain 'adjudicators *can* determine purpose in many contexts' and '[a]scertaining regulatory purpose is a process of legal characterisation of a measure, a task'.[209] Weiler aptly frames the relevant practical (evidentiary) question in the following manner:

> Yet another way to think about the spuriousness of the 'treatment on the basis of nationality' *problématique* is to unpack it from the perspective of a practitioner. Should it be necessary to prove that the impugned measure was imposed on the basis of nationality? If the answer is yes, how should one go about identifying such evidence?[210]

To conclude, Kurtz powerfully sets out why and how protectionist statements by key actors are relevant for determining whether a particular measure is discriminatory:

> of this sort and, indeed, question the ability of arbitrators to properly evaluate the probative nature of such evidence. Some commentators have nonetheless cast doubt on the relevance of subjective evidence for instance, claims that examination of 'hard-to-prove subjective state intent', such as where 'one minister has uttered a biased remark', would be an 'impossible exercise for an arbitral tribunal'. Yet to my mind, there are strong and compelling reasons to draw on such evidence, where it exists. A test requiring evidence of protectionist purpose ultimately positions national treatment as a discipline on political failure, being the excessive influence accorded to protectionist

[207] M Hirsch, 'Regulators' Mindsets, Ingroup Favoritism, and National Treatment Obligation in World Trade Organization Law' (2022) 23 German Law Journal 298, 313.

[208] D Collins, *An Introduction to International Investment Law* (CUP 2023) 117 ('[o]ne of the reasons for precluding the need to find intent is that it is often very difficult to prove the legislative aim behind a particular measure').

[209] Mitchell, Heaton, and Henckels (n 120) 158–157 (emphasis in the original).

[210] T Weiler, *The Interpretation of International Investment Law, Equality, Discrimination and Minimum in Historical Context* (Martinus Nijhoff 2013) 444.

> forces—usually domestic industry that competes with foreign investors—in the political process of the host state. An adjudicator will then be charged with identifying what political forces are responsible for the adoption of the law or practice in question. This will require careful assessment of the legislative process as a whole to isolate those causal political forces. Explicitly protectionist statements necessarily form part of the legislative record and deserve close attention—naturally together with all other evidence—in coming to a view on the controlling purpose of the state in promulgating and enforcing the relevant law or regulation.[211]

This book answered this question in the affirmative, arguing that discrimination in international investment law falls within the disparate treatment (or direct) discrimination paradigm and argued that the relevant evidence is hard, but not impossible, to be obtained and produced in the context of arbitral proceedings, providing that the standard of proof is pragmatic and flexible.

211 Kurtz (n 83) 126–127.

5
Conclusions

The analysis of the case law of investment treaty arbitral tribunals on non-discrimination obligations contained in investment treaties (National Treatment, MFN, non-impairment clauses, as well as the non-discrimination components of the FET and expropriation[1]) demonstrated that there is no *jurisprudence constante* in relation to key legal questions, ranging from the content of the applicable legal test and the meaning of each step of the legal test to procedural questions regarding the burden and standard of proof, as well as the standard of review.

This uncertainty concerns first and foremost the content of the relevant legal test to establish discrimination in investment treaty arbitration. There is consensus that likeness and less favourable treatment are *sine qua non* conditions of any successful discrimination claim; however, it is unclear whether the analysis stops with the consideration of these two elements or includes an examination of discriminatory intent or, more broadly, any relevant policy objectives on the part of the State enacting the measure(s) giving rise to less favourable treatment.

Even when tribunals agree on the applicable legal test, they disagree on the construction of the key components of that test. There is no consensus on how to determine likeness between investors and investments. Different tribunals adopt different criteria looking at the competitive relationship between investors, the regulatory framework to which they are subject, or the economic section in which they are operating.[2] At the same time, tribunal also diverge on how strictly or broadly likeness should be understood.[3] Similar uncertainty exists in relation to the interpretation of 'less favourable treatment'. Counterintuitively, the growth of investment treaty arbitral jurisprudence has produced less clarity, with relatively uncontroversial propositions until recently becoming increasingly controversial. Tribunals cannot agree on the meaning of discriminatory intent or legitimate policy considerations motivating the measures which the investors claim to be discriminatory.[4]

The case law does not offer clear answers in relation to the relevant procedural and evidentiary questions, which are equally important both from a doctrinal and practical

[1] It is for the first time that a monograph examined separately the different non-discrimination obligations contained in investment treaties. The case law regarding National Treatment is examined in Sections 3.1.1.1, 3.2.1.1, and 3.3.1.1. MFN clauses are examined in Sections 3.2.1.1, 3.1.1.2, and 3.3.1.2. Non-impairment clauses are discussed in Section 3.1.1.3, 3.2.1.3, and 3.3.1.3. The case law on non-discrimination under FET is examined in Sections 3.1.1.4, 3.2.1.4, and 3.3.1.4. Finally, non-discrimination in the context of expropriation is analysed in Sections 3.1.1.5, 3.2.1.5, and 3.3.1.5.

[2] See Section 3.1.1.

[3] ibid.

[4] See Section 3.3.1.

perspective. While tribunals agree that investors bear the burden of proof for proving the relevant facts supporting the conclusion that they are in like circumstances with other foreign or domestic investors receiving more favourable treatment, it is unclear whether they also must prove the existence of discriminatory intent on the part of the State or the absence of any valid regulatory purposes.[5] Further, among the tribunals that consider necessary to examine the relevant state policy objectives, there is no uniform approach regarding the standard of review. The two main approaches are a proportionality analysis (requiring that that measure adopted to pursue a legitimate policy objective must be proportionate to that objective) and a rational connection analysis (requiring that the measure adopted must bear a rational connection with the non-discriminatory, legitimate policy goal, without necessarily being the most proportionate means to achieve this goal).[6] Finally, there is no comprehensive and consistent answer regarding the standard of proof required to substantiate the different elements of the legal test for discrimination claims.[7]

In the light of these uncertainties, this book looked—for the first time beyond the realm of international economic law—to (i) the philosophical concept of equality (which underpins, and is reflected in, all legal non-discrimination obligations)[8] and (ii) non-discrimination practice in the field of domestic and international human rights, and in particular US anti-discrimination law which has been the source of inspiration for anti-discrimination practice in the EU and other jurisdictions.[9] Drawing from this analysis, this book puts forward normative arguments in relation to the interpretation of non-discrimination obligations in international investment treaty arbitration: one concerns the substantive elements of the non-discrimination legal test; the other concerns procedural issues (including the burden and standard of proof).

This book argued that non-discrimination obligations in international investment treaty arbitration fall within the 'disparate treatment' paradigm. The analysis of non-discrimination legislation and case law in the US, EU, and international human rights law demonstrated that two main paradigms of discrimination exists: 'disparate treatment' discrimination[10] and 'disparate impact' discrimination.[11] Disparate treatment discrimination involves the comparison of individuals rather than groups, requires a connection between less favourable treatment and the protected ground, and prohibits less favourable treatment of individuals 'because of their race, color, religion, sex, or national origin. Proof of discriminatory motive is critical, although it can in some situations be inferred from the mere fact of differences in treatment'.[12] In EU and UK anti-discrimination law, discriminatory intent is not necessary and whether there is a

[5] See Section 4.1.1.
[6] See Section 4.2.1.
[7] See Section 4.3.1.
[8] See Section 1.1.
[9] See Chapter 2.
[10] See Section 2.1.
[11] See Section 2.2.
[12] *Teamsters v United States*, 431 US 324, 335 fn 15 (1977); see also *Hazen Paper Co v Biggins*, 507 US 604, 609 (1993).

connection between the protected ground and less favourable treatment is examined from an objective (rather than subjective) perspective. From a procedural perspective, in disparate treatment cases the claimant bears the burden of proof (including in relation to the motives behind the measure(s) in question), although adverse inferences can be drawn from the failure of the Respondent to produce the relevant evidence in its possession or control. By contrast, in disparate impact discrimination the comparison is between groups and the claimant does not need to give any consideration to the motives behind the measure resulting in less favourable treatment.

This conceptualization has important implications for the interpretation of such clauses by arbitral tribunals both in relation to the substantive legal test for establishing violations of non-discrimination as well as procedural and evidentiary matters. There are three key arguments put forward in this book flowing from understanding non-discrimination in international investment law as a form of disparate treatment discrimination.

The first key argument of this book concerns the substantive test for establishing breaches of non-discrimination obligations under investment treaties. For discrimination claims to succeed the tribunal must be satisfied that (i) the investor is in like circumstances with other foreign or domestic investors (depending on the particular non-discrimination clause being invoked) which (ii) received more favourable treatment, and (iii) such treatment is connected to the foreign investors' nationality (or another protected ground such as race or religion) and does not have a reasonable nexus with a legitimate, non-discriminatory state policy objective. Proof of discriminatory intent is (logically and legally) mutually exclusive with the existence of valid regulatory purposes motivating the state measures in question.[13]

The two other arguments put forward in this book relate to procedural and evidentiary matters, concerning the allocation of the burden of proof and ways of alleviating the evidentiary difficulties that claimants face in proving discrimination precisely as a result of the fact that they bear the burden of proof. As in disparate treatment discrimination, the comparison takes place between individual investors, not group of investors, and the burden of proof in relation to likeness, less favourable treatment and the nexus between less favourable treatment and the foreign investors' protected characteristics remains with the claimant and never shifts to the respondent. This allocation of the burden of proof entails serious evidentiary difficulties that for foreign investors, in the light of the State's control over documents and information regarding state regulatory and decision-making processes, and especially in cases where foreign investors have left (or have been forced to leave) the Host State. To counter such difficulties, this book argues that irrespective of the allocation of the burden of proof to investors, both parties must co-operate and produce all relevant evidence in their possession or control, especially during the document production phase of the arbitration.[14] As domestic and international courts accept, discrimination claims can succeed not only on the basis

[13] See Section 3.3.2.
[14] See Section 4.1.2.2.

of direct evidence, but also circumstantial, indirect evidence.[15] This is especially important in relation to the existence of protectionist motives or the absence of legitimate regulatory objectives behind state measures resulting in less favourable treatment.

If international investment treaty arbitration is concerned not only with attracting foreign investments (a claim that it has not yet been empirically proven[16]), but also with the promotion of the Rule of Law and Good Governance,[17] the prohibition against discrimination is instrumental. An essential aspect of the Rule of Law both at the domestic and at the international sphere is legal certainty and predictability. The aspiration of this book was to contribute towards greater coherence in what is a complex and, to date, largely inconsistent corpus of arbitral awards dealing with the interpretation of different, yet similarly formulated, non-discrimination obligations contained in international investment treaties.

Building on important work on non-discrimination in international investment treaty arbitration,[18] this book attempted to offer a comprehensive analytical and normative framework of what is perhaps one of the most complex (one would even say chaotic) areas of international investment law, covering both substantive as well as procedural and evidentiary questions. The reader will be the judge of whether this book accomplished this ambitious task. Even if unsuccessful in that regard, the author hopes that this book may still assist arbitrators, investors, States, scholars and everyone interested in the world of investment treaty arbitration to (re)frame the consequential questions.

[15] See Section 4.3.2.

[16] E Neumayer and L Spess, 'Do Bilateral Investment Treaties increase Foreign Direct Investment to Developing Countries?' in KP Sauvant and LE Sachs (eds), *The Effect of Treaties on Foreign Direct Investment: Bilateral Investment Treaties, Double Taxation Treaties, and Investment Flows* (OUP 2009) 225–252; P Egger and M Pfaffermayr, 'The Impact of Bilateral Investment Treaties on Foreign Direct Investment' (2004) 32 Journal of Comparative Economics 788. Another study found that BITs concluded that BITs concluded by the US had a positive effect on investment, but BITs from other OECD countries did not, JW Salacuse and NP Sullivan, 'Do BITs really work? An Evaluation of Bilateral Investment Treaties and Their Grand Bargain' (2005) 46 Harvard International Law Journal 67. Other authors conclude that, although in general BITs increase foreign direct investment (FDI), States appearing before ICSID tribunals experience substantial loses in FDI, T Allee and C Peinhardt, 'Contingent Credibility: The Impact of Investment Treaty Violations on Foreign Direct Investment' (2011) 65 International Organization 401, 429. See also LN Skovgaard Poulsen, *Bounded Rationality and Economic Diplomacy: The Politics of Investment Treaties in Developing Countries* (CUP 2015).

[17] See also A Reinisch and SW Schill (eds), *Investment Protection Standards and the Rule of Law* (OUP 2023); V Zivkovic, 'Pursuing and Reimagining the International Rule of Law through International Investment Law' (2020) 12 Hague Journal on the Rule of Law 1; V Zivkovic, *International Rule of Law Through International Investment Law: Strengths, Challenges and Opportunities* (Elsevier 2018); M Sattorova, *The Impact of Investment Treaty Law on Host States: Enabling Good Governance?* (Hart 2018). On the rule of more generally, see P Craig, 'Formal and Substantive Conceptions of the Rule of Law: An Analytical Framework' (1997) 21 Public Law 467; BZ Tamanaha, On the Rule of Law: History, Politics, Theory (CUP 2004). See also the empirical analysis of Schultz and Dupont, concluding that '[s]ince the mid-to-late 1990s, investment arbitration has seemed more oriented towards serving the function for which most international courts and tribunals are created—that is, to strengthen the international rule of law', T Schultz and C Dupont, 'Investment Arbitration: Promoting the Rule of Law or Over-empowering Investors? A Quantitative Empirical Study' (2014) 25 EJIL 1147, 1168.

[18] See eg N DiMascio and J Pauwelyn, 'Nondiscrimination in Trade and Investment Treaties: Worlds Apart or Two Sides of the Same Coin?' (2008) 102 AJIL 48; F Baetens, 'Discrimination on the Basis of Nationality: Determining Likeness in Human Rights and Investment Law' in SW Schill (ed), *International Investment Law and Comparative Public Law* (OUP 2010) 279–315; F Ortino 'Non-Discriminatory Treatment in Investment Disputes' in P-M Dupuy, E-U Petersmann, and F Francioni (eds), *Human Rights in International Investment Law and Arbitration* (OUP 2009) 344–366; AD Mitchell, D Heaton, and C Henckels, *Non-Discrimination and the Role of Regulatory Purpose in International Trade and Investment Law* (Edward Elgar 2016); J Kurtz, *The WTO and International Investment Law: Converging Systems* (CUP 2015); A Bjorklund, 'The National Treatment Obligation' in K Yannaca-Small, *Arbitration Under International Investment Agreements: A Guide to the Key Issues* (2nd edn, OUP 2018) 532–561; A Reinisch and C Schreuer, *International Protection of Investments: The Substantive Standards* (CUP 2020), Chapters 4, 5, and 6.

Bibliography

A

MS Abdel Wahab, 'Itisaluna and Others v Iraq: The OIC Agreement Conundrum: Consent to ICSID Arbitration and the MFN Clauses Saga' (2021) 36 ICSID Review 1.

O Accominotti and M Flandreau, 'Bilateral Treaties and the Most-Favored-Nation Clause: The Myth of Trade Liberalization in the Nineteenth Century' (2008) 60 World Politics 147.

ET Achiume, 'Digital Racial Borders' (2021) 115 AJIL Unbound 333.

R Ago, 'Le délit international' (1939) 68 RCADI 419.

E Aisbett and J Bonnitcha, 'A Pareto-Improving Compensation Rule for Investment Treaties' (2021) 24 JIEL 181.

L Alexander, 'What Makes Wrongful Discrimination Wrong? Biases, Preferences, Stereotypes, and Proxies' (1992) 141(3) University of Pennsylvania Law Review 149.

T Allee and C Peinhardt, 'Contingent Credibility: The Impact of Investment Treaty Violations on Foreign Direct Investment' (2011) 65 International Organization 401.

BE Allen and T Soave, 'Jurisdictional Overlap in WTO Dispute Settlement and Investment Arbitration' (2014) 30 Arbitration International 1.

W Alschner, 'The Impact of Investment Arbitration on Investment Treaty Design: Myth Versus Reality' (2017) 42 Yale Journal of International Law 1.

W Alschner, *Investment Arbitration and State-Driven Reform: New Treaties, Old Outcomes* (OUP 2022).

P Alston, 'Resisting the Merger and Acquisition of Human Rights by Trade Law: A Reply to Petersmann' (2002) 13 EJIL 815.

T Altwicker and A Ellen Hansen, 'Presumptions as Secondary Rules in the Judicial Interpretation of International Human Rights' in G Kajtár, B Çali, and M Milanovic (eds), *Secondary Rules of Primary Importance in International Law: Attribution, Causality, Evidence, and Standards of Review in the Practice of International Courts and Tribunals* (OUP 2023) 167–182.

JE Alvarez, *The Public International Law Regime Governing International Investment* (Brill 2011).

JE Alvarez, *Boundaries of Investment Arbitration: The Use of Trade and European Human Rights Law in Investor-State Disputes* (JurisNet 2018).

A Alvarez-Jiménez, 'The WTO Appellate Body's Exercise of Judicial Economy' (2009) 12 JIEL 393.

GR Amaral, 'Burden of Proof and Adverse Inferences in International Arbitration: Proposal for an Inference Chart' (2018) 35 Journal of International Arbitration 1.

CF Amerasinghe, *Evidence in International Litigation* (Martinus Nijhoff 2005).

M Andenas and S Zleptnig, 'Proportionality: WTO Law: In Comparative Perspective' (2007) 42 Texas International Law Journal 371.

Aristole, *Nichomachean Ethics*.

Aristotle, *Politics*.

OM Arnardóttir, *Equality and Non-Discrimination under the European Convention on Human Rights* (Martinus Nijhoff 2002).

S Atrey, *Intersectional Discrimination* (OUP 2018).

S Atrey, 'Structural Racism and Race Discrimination' (2021) 74 Current Legal Problems 1.

B

F Baetens, 'Discrimination on the Basis of Nationality: Determining Likeness in Human Rights and Investment Law' in SW Schill (ed), *International Investment Law and Comparative Public Law* (OUP 2010) 279–315.

EN Baklanoff, *Expropriation of U.S. Investments in Cuba, Mexico, and Chile* (Praeger 1975).

Y Banifatemi, 'The Emerging Jurisprudence on the Most-Favoured-Nation Treatment in Investment Arbitration' in A Bjorklund, I Laird, and S Ripinsky (eds), *Investment Treaty Law: Current Issues III* (BIICL 2009) 241–273.

L Bartels and C Häberli, 'Binding Tariff Preferences for Developing Countries under article II GATT' (2010) 13 JIEL 969.

J Basdevant, 'L'affaire des pêcheries des côtes septentrionales de l'Atlantique entre *Etats-Unis d'Amerique et Grande-Bretagne*' (1912) RGDIP 421.

S Batifort and JB Heath, 'The New Debate on the Interpretation of MFN Clauses in Investment Treaties: Putting the Brakes on Multilateralization' (2017) 111 AJIL 873.

I Bego, *Gender Equality Policy in the European Union: A Fast Track to Parity for the New Member States* (Palgrave Macmillan 2015).

D Behn, OK Fauchald, and M Langford (eds), *The Legitimacy of Investment Arbitration: Empirical Perspectives* (CUP 2022).

W Ben Hamida, 'Clause de la nation plus favorisée et mécanismes de règlement des différends: Que dit l'histoire?' (2007) 134 Clunet 1127.

W Ben Hamida, 'Two Nebulous ICSID Features: The Notion of Investment and the Scope of Annulment Control' (2007) 24 Journal of International Arbitration 287.

F Benoît-Rohmer, 'Lessons from the Recent Case Law of the EU Court of Justice on the Principle of Non-discrimination' in LS Rossi and F Casolari (eds), *The Principle of Equality in EU Law* (Springer 2017) 151–166.

JR Bent, 'The Telltale Sign of Discrimination: Probabilities, Information Asymmetries, and the Systemic Disparate Treatment Theory' (2011) 44 University of Michigan Journal of Law Reform 807.

E Benvenisti, 'Explaining Variations in Standards of Review in International Adjudication' in G Kajtár, B Çali, and M Milanovic (eds), *Secondary Rules of Primary Importance in International Law: Attribution, Causality, Evidence, and Standards of Review in the Practice of International Courts and Tribunals* (OUP 2022) 21–41.

S Besson, *The Morality of Conflict: Reasonable Disagreement and the Law* (Hart 2005) 156.

S Besson, 'Theorizing International Responsibility Law: An Introduction' in S Besson (ed), *Theories of International Responsibility Law* (CUP 2022) 1–24.

R Bhala, 'The Myth About Stare Decisis and International Trade Law (Part One of a Trilogy)' (1999) 14 American University International Law Review 845.

R Bhala, 'The Precedent Setters: De Facto Stare Decisis in WTO Adjudication (Part Two of a Trilogy)' (1999–2000) 9 Journal of Transnational Law and Policy 1.

R Bhala, 'The Power of the Past: Towards De Jure Stare Decisis in WTO Adjudication (Part Three of a Trilogy)' (2001) 33 George Washington International Law Review 873.

A Bjorklund, 'The Enduring but Unwelcome Role of Party Intent in Treaty Interpretation' (2018) 112 AJIL Unbound 44.

A Bjorklund, 'The National Treatment Obligation' in K Yannaca-Small, *Arbitration Under International Investment Agreements: A Guide to the Key Issues* (2nd edn, OUP 2018).

AK Bjorklund and L Vanhonnaeker, 'National Treatment' in MM Mengue and S Schacherer (eds), *Foreign Investment Under the Comprehensive Economic and Trade Agreement (CETA)* (Springer 2019) 45–70.

K Bleimaier, 'The Legal Status of the Free City of Danzig 1920–1939: Lessons to be Derived from the Experiences of a Non-State Entity in the International Community' (1989) 2 Hague Yearbook of International Law 69.

LM Bohmer, 'Finality in ICSID Arbitration Revisited' (2016) 31 ICSID Review 236.

L Boisson de Chazournes and J Rudall, 'Judicial Deference: Why Does It Matter?' (2021) 22 The Law and Practice of International Courts and Tribunals 419.

BI Bonafè, *The Relationship Between State and Individual Responsibility for International Crimes* (Brill 2009).

J Bonnitcha and S Brewin, 'Compensation under Investment Treaties' (November 2020) 8 IISD, available at <https://www.iisd.org/system/files/publications/compensation-treaties-best-practices-en.pdf>.

GB Born, *International Commercial Arbitration* (Kluwer Law International 2009).

C Briddick, 'When Does Migration Law Discriminate Against Women?' (2021) 115 AJIL Unbound 356.

C Briddick and C Costello, 'Introduction to the Symposium on Undoing Discriminatory Borders' (2021) 115 AJIL Unbound 328.

M Bridge, *Personal Property Law* (4th edn, OUP 2015).

LJ Brierly, 'Règles générales du droit de la paix' (1936) 58 RCADI 1.

M Brillat, *Le principe de non discrimination à l'épreuve des droits européens* (LGDJ 2015).

MS Brodin, 'The Demise of Circumstantial Proof in Employment Discrimination Litigation: St. Mary's Honor Center v. Hicks, Pretext, and the "Personality" Excuse' (1997) 18 Berkeley Journal Employment and Labor Law 183.

T Broude, 'Toward an Economic Approach to the Consolidation of International Trade Regulation and International Investment Law' (2104) 9 Jerusalem Review of Legal Studies 24.

CN Brower and JD Brueschke, *The Iran–United States Claims Tribunal* (Martinus Nijhoff 1998).

C Brown, 'Procedure in Investment Treaty Arbitration and the Relevance of Comparative Public Law' in SW Schill (ed), *International Investment Law and Comparative Public Law* (OUP 2009) 659–688.

I Brownlie, *The System of the Law of Nations: State Responsibility* (OUP 1983).

I Brownlie, 'State Responsibility and the International Court of Justice' in M Fitzmaurice and D Sarooshi (eds), *Issues of State Responsibility Before International Judicial Institutions* (Hart 2004) 11–18.

G Bücheler, *Proportionality in Investor-State Arbitration* (OUP 2015).

LC Buchheit and JS Pam, 'The Pari Passu Clause in Sovereign Debt Instruments' (2003) 53 Emory Law Journal 869.

M Bungenberg and A Reinisch, *From Bilateral Arbitral Tribunals and Investment Courts to a Multilateral Investment Court: Options Regarding the Institutionalization of Investor-State Dispute Settlement* (Springer 2020).

WW Burke-White and A von Staden, 'The Need for Public Law Standards of Review in Investor-State Arbitrations' in SW Schill (ed), *International Investment Law and Comparative Public Law* (OUP 2010) 689–720.

S Burri, 'EU Anti-discrimination Law: Historical Development and Main Concepts' in Y Li and J Goldschmidt (eds), *Taking Employment Discrimination Seriously: Chinese and European Perspectives* (Martinus Nijhoff 2009) 209–238.

C

DA Calloway, 'St. Mary's Honor Center v. Hicks: Questioning the Basic Assumption' (1994) 26 Connecticut Law Review 997.

C Campbell and D Smith, 'Distinguishing Between Direct and Indirect Discrimination' (2023) 86 MLR 307.

AA Cançado Trindade, 'Principle 15: Precaution' in JE Viñuales (ed), *The Rio Declaration on Environment and Development: A Commentary* (OUP 2015).

DD Caron and E Shirlow, 'Most-Favored-Nation Treatment: Substantive Protection' in M Kinnear and others (eds), *Building International Investment Law: The First 50 Years of ICSID* (Kluwer Law International 2016) 399–414.

E Castellarin, 'Le principe de non-discrimination' in W Ben Hamida and F Coulée (eds), *Convergences et contradictions du droit des investissements et des droits de l'homme: une approche contentieuse* (Pedone 2017) 171–196.
C Castoriadis (translated by A Arato), 'From Marx to Aristotle, from Aristotle to Us' (1978) 45 Social Research 667.
J Chaisse, 'Consutel Group SpA in liquidazione v People's Democratic Republic of Algeria: Umbrella Clauses and Breaches of Contract by Public Entities' (2022) 37 ICSID Review 638, 641–643.
C Charpy, 'The *Conseil d'Etat* Abandons Its *Cohn Bendit* Case-Law; *Conseil d'Etat*, 30 October 2009, *Mme Perreux*' (2010) 6 European Constitutional Law Review 123.
TH Cheng and R Trisotto, 'Urbaser SA and others v Argentine Republic and Teinver SA and others v Argentine Republic, A Workaround to the Most-Favoured-Nation Clause Dispute' (2014) 29 ICSID Review 289.
Y Chernykh, *Contract Interpretation in Investment Treaty Arbitration: A Theory of the Incidental Issue* (Martinus Nijhoff 2022).
Y Chernykh, 'The Gust of Wind: The Unknown Role of Sir Elihu Lauterpacht in the Drafting of the Abs-Shawcross Draft Convention' in SW Schill, CJ Tams, and R Hofmann (eds), *International Investment Law and History* (Edward Elgar 2018) 241–285.
D Chin and J Golinsky, 'Employment Discrimination: Moving Beyond McDonnell Douglas: A Simplified Method for Assessing Evidence in Discrimination Cases' (1998) 64 Brooklyn Law Review 659.
CÓ Cinnéide, 'Why Challenging Discrimination at Borders is Challenging (and Often Futile)' (2021) 115 AJIL Unbound 362.
A Clooney and P Webb, *The Right to a Fair Trial in International Law* (OUP 2021).
RE Clute and RR Wilson, 'The Commonwealth and Favored-Nation Usage' (1958) 52 AJIL 455.
T Cohen and D Schneiderman, 'The Political Economy of Chinese Bilateral Investment Treaty Policy' (2017) 5 Chinese Journal of Comparative Law 110.
T Cole, 'The Boundaries of Most Favored Nation Treatment in International Investment Law' 33 Michigan Journal of International Law (2012) 537.
D Collins, *An Introduction to International Investment Law* (CUP 2023).
D Collins, 'National Treatment in Emerging Market Investment Treaties' in A Kamperman Sanders (ed), *The Principle of National Treatment in International Economic Law: Trade, Investment and Intellectual Property* (Edward Elgar 2014) 161–182.
J Commission, 'Precedent in Investment Treaty Arbitration—A Citation Analysis of a Developing Jurisprudence' (2007) 2 Journal of International Arbitration 129.
M Connolly, 'The "Associative" Discrimination Fiction: Part 2' (2021) 72 Northern Ireland Legal Quarterly 29.
M Connolly, *Equality, Discrimination, and the Law* (Routledge 2022).
M Connolly, *The Judiciary, Discrimination Law and Statutory Interpretation: Easy Cases Making Bad Law* (Routledge 2018).
M Connolly, 'The Myth of Associative Discrimination and the Court of Justice's Great Vanishing: Part 2' (2021) 72 Northern Ireland Legal Quarterly 510.
EJ Conroy, 'The American Interpretation of the Most Favored Nation Clause' (1926) 12 Cornell Law Quarterly 327.
G Coop and I Seif, 'ECT and States' Right to Regulate' in M Scherer (ed), *International Arbitration in the Energy Sector* (OUP 2018) 221–249.
WR Corbett, 'The "Fall" of Summers, the Rise of "Pretext Plus," and the Escalating Subordination of Federal Employment Discrimination Law to Employment at Will: Lessons from McKennon and Hicks' (1996) 30 Georgia Law Review 305.
J Cornides, 'Three Case Studies on "Anti-Discrimination"' (2012) 23 EJIL 517.
C Costello and M Foster, 'Race Discrimination Effaced at the International Court of Justice' (2021) 115 AJIL Unbound 339.
T Cottier, 'Towards a Five Storey House' in C Joerges and E-U Petersmann, *Constitutionalism, Multilevel Trade Governance and International Economic Law* (Hart 2011).

T Cottier and M Oesch, 'Direct and Indirect Discrimination in WTO and EU Law' in SE Gaines and others (eds), *Liberalising Trade in the EU and the WTO: A Legal Comparison* (CUP 2012) 141–175.

T Cottier, J Pauwelyn, and E Bürgi (eds), *Human Rights and International Trade* (OUP 2005); A Lang, 'Re-thinking Trade and Human Rights' (2007) 15 Tulane Journal of International and Comparative Law 335.

B Coutain, 'The Unconditional Most-Favored-Nation Clause and the Maintenance of the Liberal Trade Regime in the Postwar 1870s' (2009) 63 International Organization 139.

JF Coyle, 'The Treaty of Friendship, Commerce and Navigation in the Modem Era' (2012) 51 Colombia Journal of Transnational Law 302.

P Craig, 'Formal and Substantive Conceptions of the Rule of Law: An Analytical Framework' (1997) 21 Public Law 467.

P Craig, *UK, EU and Global Administrative Law: Foundations and Challenges* (CUP 2015).

P Craig and G de Búrca, *The Evolution of EU Law* (2nd edn, OUP 2011).

C Craven, 'Between Law and History: The Berlin Conference of 1884–1885 and the Logic of Free Trade' (2015) 3 London Review of International Law 31.

JR Crawford, *Browlie's Principles of Public International Law* (8th edn, OUP 2012).

JR Crawford, *The Creation of States in International Law* (2nd edn, OUP 2006).

JR Crawford, 'Treaty and Contract in Investment Arbitration' (2008) 24 Arbitration International 351.

C Crépet Daigremont, *La Clause de la Nation la Plus Favorisée* (Pedone 2015).

C Crépet Daigremont, 'Most Favoured Nation Treatment' in MM Mbengue and S Schacherer (eds), *Foreign Investment Under the Comprehensive Economic and Trade Agreement (CETA)* (Springer 2019) 71–94.

M Csernus, 'Is There Life After Death?: The Persuasive Value of Annulled Investment Awards' (2022) 23 Journal of International Dispute Settlement 393.

G Cumming and M Freudenthal, *Civil Procedure in EU Competition Cases Before the English and Dutch Courts* (Kluwer Law International 2010).

D

WJ Davey and KE Maskus, '*Thailand-Cigarettes (Philippines)*: A More Serious Role for the 'Less Favourable Treatment' Standard of Article III:4' (2013) 12 World Trade Review 163.

M Davis, 'A Government of Judges: An Historical Re-View' (1987) 35 American Journal of Comparative Law 559.

AM Daza-Clark, *International Investment Law and Water Resources Management: An Appraisal of Indirect Expropriation* (Brill Nijhoff 2017).

E De Brabandere, 'The 2019 Dutch Model Bilateral Investment Treaty: Navigating the Turbulent Ocean of Investment Treaty Reform' (2021) 36 ICSID Review 319.

E De Brabandere, 'Fair and Equitable Treatment and (Full) Protection and Security in African Investment Treaties Between Generality and Contextual Specificity' (2017) 18 JWIT 530.

E De Brabandere, *Investment Treaty Arbitration as Public International Law: Procedural Aspects and Implications* (CUP 2014).

G De Búrca, 'The Trajectories of European and American Antidiscrimination Law' (2012) 60 American Journal of Comparative Law 1.

C De Stefano, *Attribution in International Law and Arbitration* (OUP 2020).

B De Witte, 'New Institutions for Promoting Equality in Europe: Legal Transfers, National Bricolage and European Governance' (2012) 60 American Journal of Comparative Law 49.

D Demougin and C Fluet, 'Rules of Proof, Courts, and Incentives' (2008) 39 RAND Journal of Economics 20.

DA Desierto, *Public Policy in International Economic Law: The ICESCR in Trade, Finance and Investment* (OUP 2015).

DA Desierto, 'Shifting Sands in the International Economic System: "Arbitrage" In International Economic Law and International Human Rights' (2018) 49 Georgetown Journal of International Law 1019.

A Desmedt, 'Proportionality in WTO Law' (2001) 4 JIEL 441.

NF Diebold, 'Standards on Non-discrimination in International Economic Law' (2011) 60 ICLQ 831.

NF Diebold, *Non-Discrimination in International Trade in Services: 'Likeness' in WTO/GATS* (CUP 2010).

O Diggelmann, 'Fault in the Law of State Responsibility—Pragmatism *ad infinitum*?' (2006) 49 German Yearbook of International Law 293.

N DiMascio and J Pauwelyn, 'Nondiscrimination in Trade and Investment Treaties: Worlds Apart or Two Sides of the Same Coin?' (2008) 102 AJIL 48.

A Dolcett, 'The Central Case Method in *The Nature of Legislative Intent*' (2019) 64 American Journal of Jurisprudence 41.

R Dolzer, U Kriebaum, and C Schreuer, *Principles of International Investment Law* (3rd edn, OUP 2022).

M Domke, 'Indonesian Nationalization Measures before Foreign Courts' (1960) 54 AJIL 305.

JJ Donohue III and P Siegelman, 'The Changing Nature of Employment Discrimination Litigation' (1991) 43 Stanford Law Review 983.

DF Donovan, 'Allocation of Costs', in M Kinnear and others (eds), *Building International Investment Law: The First 50 Years of ICSID* (Kluwer Law International 2016) 555–566.

Z Douglas, 'The MFN Clause in Investment Arbitration: Treaty Interpretation Off the Rails' (2011) 2 Journal of International Dispute Settlement 97.

Z Douglas, 'Nothing if Not Critical for Investment Treaty Arbitration: Occidental, Eureko and Methanex' (2006) 22 Arbitration International 27.

KAN Duggal and R Rangachari, 'A Challenger Approaches: An Assessment of the Prague Rules on the Efficient Conduct of Proceedings in International Arbitration' (2020) 37 Journal of International Arbitration 27.

P Dumberry, *The Fair and Equitable Treatment Standard: A Guide to NAFTA Case Law on Article 1105* (Kluwer Law International 2013).

P Dumberry, 'The Importation of the Fair and Equitable Treatment Standard Through MFN Clauses: An Empirical Study of BITs' (2017) 32 ICSID Review 116.

P Dumberry, 'The Importation of "Better" Fair and Equitable Treatment Standard Protection Through MFN Clauses: An Analysis of NAFTA Article 1103' (2017) 4 Transnational Dispute Management.

P Dumberry, 'Shopping For a Better Deal: The Use of MFN Clauses to Get "Better" Fair and Equitable Treatment Protection' (2017) 33 Arbitration International 1.

P-M Dupuy, E-U Petersmann, and F Francioni (eds), *Human Rights in International Investment Law and Arbitration* (OUP 2009).

R Dworkin, *Taking Rights Seriously* (Havard University Press 1977).

R Dworkin, *Law's Empire* (Fontana 1986) 313–354.

R Dworkin, *Sovereign Virtue, the Theory and Practice of Equality* (Harvard University Press 2000).

E

P Egger and M Pfaffermayr, 'The Impact of Bilateral Investment Treaties on Foreign Direct Investment' (2004) 32 Journal of Comparative Economics 788.

L Ehring, 'De Facto Discrimination in World Trade Law National and Most-Favoured-Nation Treatment—or Equal Treatment?' (2002) 36 Journal of World Trade 921.

N Ejaz Piracha, *Toward Uniformly Accepted Principles for Interpreting MFN Clauses: Striking a Balance* (Kluwer Law International 2021).

R Ekins, 'The Intention of Parliament' (2010) 39 Public Law 709.

R Ekins, *The Nature of Legislative Intent* (OUP 2016).

E Ellis and P Watson, *EU Anti-discrimination Law* (2nd edn, OUP 2012).

F

AP Fachiri, 'Expropriation and International Law' (1925) 6 BYIL 159.
JH Fahner, 'The Limited Utility of Deference in International Dispute Settlement' (2022) 21 The Law and Practice of International Courts and Tribunals 467.
JH Fahner, *Judicial Deference in International Adjudication: A Comparative Analysis* (Hart 2020).
A Farahat, 'Discrimination Inside: Non-Discrimination as a Tool of Migrant Integration' (2021) 115 AJIL Unbound 350.
GM Farnelli, 'Consistency in the ICJ Approach to the Standard of Proof: An Appraisal of the Court's Flexibility' (2022) 21 The Law and Practice of International Courts and Tribunals 98.
M Fartunova-Michel, *La preuve dans le droit de l'Union européenne* (Bruylant 2013).
AA Fatouros, 'An International Code to Protect Private Investment-Proposals and Perspectives (1961) 14 The University of Toronto Law Journal 77.
BJ Flagg, '"Was Blind, but Now I See": White Race Consciousness and the Requirement of Discriminatory Intent' (1993) 91 Michigan Law Review 953.
G Flecke-Giammarco, 'The Allocation of Costs by Arbitral Tribunals in International Commercial Arbitration' in JA Huerta-Goldman, A Romanetti, and FX Stirnimann (eds), *WTO Litigation, Investment Arbitration, and Commercial Arbitration* (Kluwer Law International 2013) 389–420.
J Flett, 'WTO Space for National Regulation: Requiem for a Diagonal Vector Test' (2013) 16 JIEL 37.
A Florou, *Contractual Renegotiations and International Investment Arbitration: A Relational Contract Theory Interpretation of Investment Treaties* (Brill 2020).
LY Fortier and SL Drymer, 'Indirect Expropriation in the Law of International Investment: I Know It When I See It, or *Caveat Investor*' (2004) 19 ICSID Review 293.
C Foster, *Science and the Precautionary Principle in International Courts and Tribunals: Expert Evidence, Burden of Proof and Finality* (CUP 2011).
C Foster, *Global Regulatory Standards in Environmental and Health Disputes: Regulatory Coherence, Due Regard, and Due Diligence* (OUP 2021).
SD Franck, *Arbitration Costs: Myths and Realities in Investment Treaty Arbitration* (OUP 2019).
SD Franck, 'Rationalizing Costs in Investment Treaty Arbitration' (2011) 88 Washington University Law Review 769.
SD Franck, 'Empiricism and International Law: Insights for Investment Treaty Dispute Resolution' (2008) 48 Virginia Journal of International Law 767.
SD Franck, 'Empirically Evaluating Claims about Investment Treaty Arbitration' (2007) 86 North Carolina Law Review 1.
SD Franck, 'Development and Outcomes of Investment Treaty Arbitration' (2009) 50 Harvard International Law Journal 435.
S Fredman, *Discrimination Law* (2nd edn, OUP 2011).
S Fredman, 'The Reason Why: Unravelling Indirect Discrimination' (2016) 45 Industrial Law Journal 231.
SD Franck, 'Occidental Exploration & Production Co. v. Republic of Ecuador. Final Award. London Court of International Arbitration Administered Case No. UN 3467' (2005) 99 AJIL 675.
S Friedman, *Expropriation in International Law* (Stevens & Sons Ltd, London 1953).
Y Fukunaga, 'Margin of Appreciation as an Indicator of Judicial Deference: Is It Applicable to Investment Arbitration?' (2019) 10 JIDS 69.

G

ER Gadelshina, 'Hermeneutic Reflections on the Specific Purpose of Umbrella Clauses' (2013) 14 JWIT 804.
E Gaillard, 'The Denunciation of the ICSID Convention' (2007) 237 NYLJ 1.

E Gaillard and I Mitrev Penushliski, 'State Compliance with Investment Awards' (2020) 35 ICSID Review 540.

DA Gantz, 'Protecting Investment under NAFTA, the Trans-Pacific Partnership and the Comprehensive and Progressive TPP' in JA Huerta-Goldman and DA Gantz (eds), *The Comprehensive and Progressive Trans-Pacific Partnership: Analysis and Commentary* (CUP 2021) 313–326.

OM Garibaldi, 'On the Denunciation of the ICSID Convention, Consent to ICSID Jurisdiction, and the Limits of Contract Analogy' in C Binder and others (eds), *International Investment Law for the 21st Century: Essays in Honour of Christoph Schreuer* (OUP 2009) 251–277.

JT Gathii, *African Regional Trade Agreements as Legal Regimes* (CUP 2011).

A Gattini, 'Smoking/No Smoking: Some Remarks on the Current Place of Fault in the ILC Draft Articles on State Responsibility' (1999) 10 EJIL 397.

T Gazzini and A Tanzi, 'Handle with Care: Umbrella Clauses and MFN Treatment in Investment Arbitration' (2013) 14 JWIT 978.

PM Gerhart and AS Kella, 'Power and Preferences: Developing Countries and the Role of the WTO Appellate Body' 30 North Carolina Journal of International Law and Commercial Regulation (2004) 515.

I Giesen, 'The Reversal of the Burden of Proof in the Principles of European Tort Law: A Comparison with Dutch Tort Law and Civil Procedure Rules' (2010) 6 Utrecht Law Review 22.

AE Gildemeister, 'Burlington Resources, Inc v Republic of Ecuador, How Much is Too Much: When is Taxation Tantamount to Expropriation?' (2014) 29 ICSID Review 315.

A Gourgourinis, 'Reviewing the Administration of Domestic Regulation in WTO and Investment Protection Law: The International Minimum Standard of Treatment of Aliens as "One Standard to Rule Them All"?' (2011) 8 Transnational Dispute Management 1.

H Grant Cohen, 'Nations and Markets' (2020) 23 JIEL 793.

S Greenberg and F Lautenschlager, 'Adverse Inferences in International Arbitral Practice' (2011) 22(2) ICC International Court Arbitration Bulletin 43.

G Grossman, H Horn, and PC Mavroidis, ALI, 'Principles of the World Trade Law: National Treatment', available at <http://papers.ssrn.com/sol3/papers.cfm?abstract_id=2094286>.

H Grotius, *De Jure Belli ac Pacis Libri tres*.

L Gruszczynski, *Regulating Health and Environmental Risks under WTO Law: A Critical Analysis of the SPS Agreement* (OUP 2010).

S Guest, 'The role of Moral Equality in Legal Argument' in F Du Bois (ed), *The Practice of Integrity, Reflections on Ronald Dworkin and South African Law* (Juta and Co Ltd 2005) 18–43.

H

JC Hamilton, OE Garcia-Bolivar, and H Otero, 'Latin American Arbitration and Investment Protections' in JC Hamilton, OE Garcia-Bolivar, and H Otero (eds), *Latin American Investment Protections* (Martinus Nijhoff 2012) 1–4.

L Hamilton Krieger and ST Fisker, 'Behavioral Realism in Employment Discrimination Law: Implicit Bias and Disparate Treatment' (2006) 94 California Law Review 997.

HLA Hart, *The Concept of Law* (Clarendon Press 1961).

FA Hayek, *The Constitution of Liberty* (Routledge 2006).

JN Hazard, 'Commercial Discrimination and International Law' (1958) 52 AJIL 495.

V Heiskanen, 'Arbitrary and Unreasonable Measures' in A Reinisch (ed), *Standards of Investment Protection* (OUP 2008) 87–110.

V Heiskanen, 'The Doctrine of Indirect Expropriation in Light of the Practice of the Iran-United States Claims Tribunal' (2007) 8 JWIT 215.

C Henckels, *Proportionality and Deference in Investor-State Arbitration Balancing Investment Protection and Regulatory Autonomy* (CUP 2015).

DG Henriques, 'The Prague Rules: Competitor, Alternative or Addition to the IBA Rules on the Taking of Evidence in International Arbitration' (2018) 36 ASA Bulletin 351.

M Henry and E Silva Romero, 'La Preuve dans l'Arbitrage: Prague Rules v. IBA Rules' (2020) 1 Revue de l'Arbitrage 71.

J Hepburn, *Domestic Law in International Investment Arbitration* (OUP 2017).
J Hepburn and others, 'Investment Law before Arbitration' (2020) 23 JEIL 929.
M Herdegen, *Principles of International Economic Law* (2nd edn, OUP 2016).
JH Hertz, 'Expropriation of Foreign Property' (1941) 35 AJIL 243.
V Heiskanen, 'The Regulatory Philosophy of International Trade Law' (2004) 38 JWT 1.
R Higgins, 'Policy Considerations and the International Judicial Process' (1968) 17 ICLQ 58.
R Higgins, 'The Taking of Property by the State: Recent Developments in International Law' (1982) 176 RCADI 259.
M Hirsch, 'Regulators' Mindsets, Ingroup Favoritism, and National Treatment Obligation in World Trade Organization Law' (2022) 23 German Law Journal 298.
J Ho, *State Responsibility for Breaches of Investment Contracts* (CUP 2018).
BM Hoekman and PC Mavroidis, 'To AB or Not to AB? Dispute Settlement in WTO Reform' (2020) 23 JIEL 1.
AK Hoffmann, 'Indirect Expropriation' in A Reinisch (ed), *Standards of Investment Protection* (OUP 2008) 151–170.
H Horn and PC Mavroidis, 'Still Hazy after All These Years: The Interpretation of National Treatment in the GATT/WTO Case-law on Tax Discrimination' (2004) 15 EJIL 39.
R Howse, 'Human Rights in the WTO: Whose Rights, What Humanity? Comment on Petersmann' (2002) 13 EJIL 651.
R Howse and E Chalamish, 'The Use and Abuse of WTO Law in Investor-State Arbitration: A Reply to *Jürgen Kurtz*' (2010) 20 EJIL 1087.
R Hudec, 'GATT/WTO Constraints on National Regulation: Requiem for an "Aims and Effects" Test' (1998) 32 The International Lawyer 619.
C Hull, *Economic Barriers to Peace* (Woodrow Wilson Foundation 1937).
AZ Huq, 'What Is Discriminatory Intent' (2018) 103 Cornell Law Review 1211.
K Hyder (Hasan), *Equality of Treatment and Trade Discrimination in International Law* (Springer 1968).

I

IDI, Session of Tokyo, 'Legal Aspects of Recourse to Arbitration by an Investor Against the Authorities of the Host State under Inter-State Treaties', 13 September 2013, available at <http://www.idi-iil.org/idiE/resolutionsE/2013_tokyo_en.pdf>.
ILC, Draft Articles on Most-Favoured-Nation Clauses with Commentaries (1978) II(2) Yearbook of the International Law Commission 16.
ILC, Draft Articles on Responsibility of States for Internationally Wrongful Acts with Commentaries (2001) II Yearbook of the International Law Commission 31.
ILC, Final Report of the Study Group on the Most-Favoured Nation Clause (2015) II(2) Yearbook of Internnational Commission.
ILC, First Report on the Most-Favoured-Nation Clause (1969) 2 Yearbook of the International Law Commission 157.
GM Ingram, *Expropriation of U.S. Property in South America: Nationalization of Oil and Copper Companies in Peru, Bolivia and Chile* (Praeger 1974).

J

M Jackson, 'The Definition of Apartheid in Customary International Law and the International Convention on the Elimination of All Forms of Racial Discrimination' (2022) 71 ICLQ 831.
M Jacob and SW Schill, 'Standards of Protection: Fair and Equitable Treatment: Content, Practice, Method' in M Bungenberg and others (eds), *International Investment Law* (CH Beck, Hart, Nomos 2015) 700–763.

N Jansen Calamita, 'The British Bank Nationalizations: An International Law Perspective' (2009) 58 ICLQ 119.

R Jennings and A Watts, *Oppenheim's International Law, Volume 1 Peace* (9th edn, OUP 1992).

L Johns, C Thrall, and RL Wellhausen, 'Judicial Economy and Moving Bars in International Investment Arbitration' (2020) 15 The Review of International Organizations 923.

A Joubin-Bret, 'Admission and Establishment in the Context of Investment Protection' in A Reinisch (ed), *Standards of Investment Protection* (OUP 2008) 9.

K

HA Kadouf and UA Oseni, 'The Discrimination Conundrum in the Appointment of Arbitrators in International Arbitration' (2012) 29 Journal of International Arbitration 519.

D Kalderimis, 'Investment Treaty Arbitration as Global Administrative Law: What This Might Man in Practice' in C Brown and K Miles (eds), *Evolution in Investment Treaty Law and Arbitration* (CUP 2011) 145–160.

A Kalintiri, *Evidence Standards in EU Competition Enforcement: The EU Approach* (Hart 2018).

A Kalintiri, 'The Allocation of the Legal Burden of Proof in Article 101 TFEU Cases: A "Clear" Rule with Not-So-Clear Implications' (2015) 34 Yearbook of European Law 232.

J Kammerhofer, *International Investment Law and Legal Theory: Expropriation and the Fragmentation of Sources* (CUP 2021).

E Karner, 'The Function of the Burden of Proof in Tort Law H Koziol and BC Steininger (eds), *European Tort Law 2008* (Springer 2009) 68–78.

MJ Katz, 'Gross Disunity' (2010) 114 Penn State Law Review 857.

G Kaufmann-Kohler, 'Arbitral Precedent: Dream, Necessity or Excuse?: The 2006 Freshfields Lecture' (2007) 23 Arbitration International 357.

G Kaufmann-Kohler, 'Annulment of ICSID Awards in contract and Treaty Arbitrations: Are There Differences?' in E Gaillard and Y Banifatemi (eds), *Annulment of ICSID Awards* (Juris Publishing 2004) 189–222.

M Kazazi, *Burden of Proof and Related Issues: A Study on Evidence before International Tribunals* (Kluwer Law International 1996).

H Kelsen, 'La gurantie juridictionelle de la Constitution' (1928) 45 Revue du droit public 197.

H Kelsen (translated by M Knight), *Pure Theory of Law* (University of California Press 1967).

D Kennedy, 'Theses about International Law Discourse' (1980) 23 German Yearbook of International Law 353.

E Kessie, 'The legal status of Special and Differential Treatment Provisions under the WTO Agreements' in G Bermann and PC Mavroidis (eds), *WTO Law and Developing Countries* (CUP 2007).

D Khachvani, 'Compensation for Unlawful Expropriation: Targeting the Illegality' (2017) 32 ICSID Review 385.

T Khaitan, *A Theory of Discrimination Law* (OUP 2015).

T Khaitan and S Steel, 'Wrongs, Group Disadvantage and the Legitimacy of Indirect Discrimination Law' in H Collins and T Khaitan, *Foundations of Indirect Discrimination Law* (Hart 2018) 197–221.

R Khodykin and C Mulcahy, *A Guide to the IBA Rules on the Taking of Evidence in International Arbitration* (OUP 2019).

M Khosla, 'Proportionality: An Assault on Human Rights?: A Reply' (2010) 8 International Journal of Constitutional Law 298.

B Kingsbury and SW Schill, 'Public Law Concepts to Balance Investors' Rights with State Regulatory Actions in the Public Interest—the Concept of Proportionality' in SW Schill (ed), *International Investment Law and Comparative Public Law* (OUP 2010) 75–104.

MN Kinnear, AK Bjorklund, and JFG Hannaford, *Investment Disputes under NAFTA: An Annotated Guide to NAFTA Chapter 11, Supplement No 1, March 2008* (Kluwer Law International 2006) 1102–1126.

HE Kjos, *Applicable Law in Investor-State Arbitration: The Interplay Between National and International Law* (OUP 2013).

R Kläger, *'Fair and Equitble Treatment' in International Investment Law* (CUP 2011).

M Klatt and M Meister, 'Proportionality—A Benefit to Human Rights? Remarks on the I·CON Controversy' (2012) 10 International Journal of Constitutional Law 687.

M Koskenniemi, *From Apology to Utopia: The Structure of the International Legal Argument* (CUP 2005).

CT Kotuby Jr and LA Subota, *General Principles of Law and International Due Process: Principles and Norms Applicable* (OUP 2017).

U Kriebaum, 'Arbitrary/Unreasonable or Discriminatory Measures' in M Bungenberg and others (eds), *International Investment Law* (CH Beck, Hart, Nomos 2015) 790–806.

U Kriebaum, 'Regulatory Takings: Balancing the Interests of the Investor and the State' (2007) 8 JWIT 717.

J Kurtz, 'The Use and Abuse of WTO Law in Investor-State Arbitration: Competition and its Discontents' (2009) 20 EJIL 749.

J Kurtz, 'The Merits and Limits of Comparativism: National Treatment in International Investment Law and the WTO' in SW Schill (ed), *International Investment Law and Comparative Public Law* (OUP 2010) 243–278.

J Kurtz, *The WTO and International Investment Law: Converging Systems* (CUP 2015).

J Kurtz, 'Charting the Future of the Twin Pillars of International Economic Law' (2014) 9 Jerusalem Review of Legal Studies 36.

L

P Lagarde, 'Le principe de proximité dans le droit international privé contemporain' (1986) 196 RCADI 9.

E Lambert, *Le Gouvernement des Juges et la lute contre la Législation Sociale aux Etats-Unis* (Marcel Giard 1921).

M Lando, 'Identification as the Process to Determine the Content of Customary International Law' (2022) 42(4) Oxford Journal of Legal Studies 1040.

ATF Lang, 'Reflecting on "Linkage": Cognitive and Institutional Change in the International Trading System' (2007) 70 MLR 523.

A Lang, *World Trade Law after Neoliberalism: Re-imagining the Global Economic Order* (OUP 2011) .

R Lang, *Complex Equality and the Court of Justice of the European Union; Reconciling Diversity and Harmonisation* (Brill Nijhoff 2018).

M Langford and D Behn, 'Managing Backlash: The Evolving Investment Treaty Arbitrator?' (2018) 29 EJIL 551.

J Larguier, 'La preuve d'un fait négatif' (1953) 51 Revue trimestrielle de droit civil 1.

H Lauterpacht, *The Development of International Law by the International Court* (Stevens and Sons 1958).

N Lavranos and A Mazlom, 'The Investment Treaty Implications of Covid-19 Responses by States' (2021) 6 European Investment Law and Arbitration Review Online 1.

A Legg, 'Is There Method in the Margin? The Essence of Judicial Deference and the Margin of Appreciation' (2022) 21 The Law and Practice of International Courts and Tribunals 442.

B Legum and I Petculescu, 'GATT Article XX and International Investment Law' in R Echandi and P Sauvé (eds), *Prospects in International Investment Law and Policy* (CUP 2013).

EM Leonhardsen, 'Looking for Legitimacy: Exploring Proportionality Analysis in Investment Treaty Arbitration' (2012) 3 JIDS 95.

S Lester, B Mercurio, and A Davies, *World Trade Law: Text, Materials and Commentary* (3rd edn, Hart 2018).

JDM Lew, 'Document Production and Legal Privilege in International Commercial Arbitration' in DD Caron and others (eds), *Practising Virtue: Inside International Arbitration* (OUP 2015) 347–356.

Y Li and C Bian, 'China's Stance on Investor-State Dispute Settlement: Evolution, Challenges, and Reform Options' (2020) 67 Netherlands International Law Review 503.

RB Lillich, 'International Law and the Chilean Nationalizations: The Valuation of the Copper Companies' (1973) 7 International Lawyer 124.

CL Lim, J Ho, and M Paparinskis, *International Investment Law and Arbitration: Commentary, Awards and other Materials* (2nd edn, CUP 2021).

JR Lindgren and others, *The Law of Sex Discrimination* (4th edn, Wadsworth 2011).

K Linos, 'Path Dependence in Discrimination Law: Employment Cases in the United States and the European Union' (2010) 35 Yale Journal of International Law 115.

DR Livingston, 'The Civil Rights Act Of 1991 and EEOC Enforcement' (1993) 23 Stetson Law Review 53.

D Locke, 'The Trivializability of Universalizability' (1968) 77 The Philosophical Review 25.

V Lowe, 'Arbitrary and Discriminatory Treatment' in M Kinnear and others (eds), *Building International Investment Law: The First 50 Years of ICSID* (Kluwer Law International 2016) 307–318.

M Lubambo de Melo, 'Protection of Domestic Investors under the WTO and International Investment Regimes' (2020) 19 WTR 589.

M

K Magraw, 'Investor-State Disputes and the Rise of Recourse to State Party Pleadings As Subsequent Agreements or Subsequent Practice under the Vienna Convention on the Law of Treaties' (2015) 30 ICSID Review 142.

DC Malamud, 'The Last Minuet: Disparate Treatment After Hicks' (1995) 93 Michigan Law Review 2229.

F Mantilla-Serrano, 'International Arbitration and Insolvency Proceedings' (1995) 11 Arbitration International 51.

I Marboe, *Calculation of Compensation and Damages in International Investment Law* (2nd edn, OUP 2017).

G Marceau, 'The New TBT Jurisprudence in *US—Clove* Cigarettes, WTO *US—Tuna II*, and *US—Cool*' (2013) 8 Asian Journal of WTO and International Health Law and Policy 1.

R Marghitola, *Document Production in International Arbitration* (Kluwer Law International 2015).

AZ Marossi, 'Shifting the Burden of Proof in the Practice of the Iran–United States Claims Tribunal' (2011) 28 Journal of International Arbitration 427.

C Martinez Lopez and L Martinez, 'Proportionality in Investment Treaty Arbitration and Beyond: An "Irresistible Attraction"?' (2015) 2 BCDR International Arbitration. Review 261.

T Masiko, *Flexible Regional Economic Integration in Africa: Lessons and Implications for the Multilateral Trading System* (Bloomsbury 2022).

M Matsushita and others, *The World Trade Organization: Law, Practice, and Policy* (3rd edn, OUP 2015).

J Maupin, 'MFN-Based Jurisdiction in Investor–State Arbitration: Is There Any Hope for a Consistent Approach?' (2011) 14 Journal of International Economic Law 157.

C McCrudden, 'A Common Law of Human Rights?: Transnational Judicial Conversations on Constitutional Rights' (2000) 20 Oxford Journal of Legal Studies 499.

MS McDougal, 'International Law, Power and Policy' (1953) 82 RCADI 133.

MS McDougal, 'Law as a Process of Decision: A Policy-Oriented Approach to Legal Study' (1956) 1 Natural Law Forum 53.

MS McDougal, HD Lasswell, and L-C Chen, 'The Protection of Aliens from Discrimination and World Public Order: Responsibility of States Conjoined with Human Rights' (1976) 70 AJIL 432.

C McLachlan, L Shore, and M Weiniger, *International Investment Arbitration: Substantive Principles* (2nd edn, OUP 2017).

AD McNair, 'The Seizure of Property and Enterprises in Indonesia' (1959) 6 Netherlands International Law Review 218.

D McRae, 'Introduction to the Symposium on Simon Batifort and J. Benton Heath, "The New Debate on the Interpretation of MFN Clauses in Investment Treaties: Putting the Brakes on Multilateralization"' (2018) 112 AJIL Unbound 38.

D McRae, 'The World Trade Organization and International Investment Law: Converging Systems—Can the Case for Convergence be Made?' (2014) 9 Jerusalem Review of Legal Studies 13.

E McWhinney, *Judicial Settlement of International Disputes.* Jurisdiction, *Justiciability and Law-Making on the Contemporary International Court* (Martinus Nijhoff 1991).

R Mehdi, 'La preuve devant les juridictions communautaires' in H Ruiz Fabri and J-M Sorel (eds), *La preuve devant les juridictions internationales* (Pédone 2007) 165–181.

P Merkouris, J Kammerhofer, and N Arajärvi (eds), *The Theory, Practice, and Interpretation of Customary International Law* (CUP 2022).

M Milanovic, *Extraterritorial Application of Human Rights Treaties: Law, Principles, Policy* (OUP 2011).

K Miles, *The Origins of International Investment Law: Empire, Environment and the Safeguarding of Capital* (CUP 2013).

M Ming Du, 'The Rise of the National Regulatory Autonomy in the GATT/WTO Regime' (2011) 14 JIEL 639.

M Ming Du, 'Autonomy in Setting Appropriate Level of Protection under the WTO Law: Rhetoric or Reality?' (2010) 13 JIEL 1077.

AD Mitchell, 'A Legal Principle of Special and Differential Treatment for WTO Disputes' (2006) 5 World Trade Review 445.

AD Mitchell, 'Proportionality and Remedies in WTO Disputes' (2006) 17 EJIL 985.

AD Mitchell, D Heaton, and C Henckels, *Non-Discrimination and the Role of Regulatory Purpose in International Trade and Investment Law* (Edward Elgar 2016).

M Mitsi, The Decision-making Process of Investor-State Arbitration Tribunals (Kluwer Law International 2019).

BC Mizer, 'Toward a Motivating Factor Test for Individual Disparate Treatment Claims' (2001) 100 Michigan Law Review 234.

JB Moore, *Digest of International* Law, *Vol 2* (Government Printing Office 1906).

TH Moran, *Multinational Corporations and the Politics of Dependence: Copper in Chile* (Princeton University Press 1974).

M Möschel, 'The Strasbourg Court and Indirect Race Discrimination: Going Beyond the Education Domain' (2017) 80 Modern Law Review 110.

P Muchlinski, *Multinational Enterprises and the Law* (3rd edn, OUP 2021).

N

E Neumayer and L Spess, 'Do Bilateral Investment Treaties increase Foreign Direct Investment to Developing Countries?' in KP Sauvant and LE Sachs (eds), *The Effect of Treaties on Foreign Direct Investment: Bilateral Investment* Treaties, *Double Taxation* Treaties, *and Investment Flows* (OUP 2009) 225–252.

L Nevellie Brown and JS Bell, *French Administrative Law* (5th edn, OUP 1998).

A Newcombe and L Paradell, *Law and Practice of Investment Treaties* (Kluwer Law International 2009).

A Newcombe, 'General Exceptions in International Investment Agreements in MC Cordonier Segger', M Gehring and A Newcombe (eds), *Sustainable Development in World Investment Law* (Kluwer Law International 2011).

C Nikolaidis, 'Unravelling the Knot of Equality and Privacy in the European Court of Human Rights and the US Supreme Court: From Isonomia to Isotimia' (2018) 18 Human Rights Law Review 719.

C Nikolaidis, *The Right to Equality in European Human Rights Law* (Routledge 2015).

G Niyungeko, *La preuve devant les juridictions internationales* (Pédone 2005).

D Npoanlari Dagbanja, *The Investment Treaty Regime and Public Interest Regulation in Africa* (OUP 2022).

A Nussbaum, 'Arbitration Between the Lena Goldfields Ltd. and the Soviet Government (1950) 36 Cornell Law Review 31.

O

OECD, 'Interpretation of the Umbrella Clause in Investment Agreements' (October 2006) Working Papers on International Investment Number 2006/3.

OECD, *National Treatment for Foreign-Controlled Enterprises* (OECD Publications 1993).

E Öktem, 'La clausola della nazione più favorita nelle capitolazioni ottomane: genesi, tipologia, patologia' (2022) 105 Rivista di diritto internazionale 43.

L Oppenheim, *International Law: A Treatise* (Volume I: Peace, Longmans, Greens & Co, London 1905).

L Orgad, 'When Is Immigration Selection Discriminatory?' (2021) 115 AJIL Unbound 345.

F Ortino, 'Non-Discriminatory Treatment in Investment Disputes' in P-M Dupuy, E-U Petersmann, and F Francioni (eds), *Human Rights in International Investment Law and Arbitration* (OUP 2009) 344–366.

F Ortino, 'From "Non-discrimination" to "Reasonableness": A Paradigm Shift in International Economic Law' (Jean Monnet Working Paper 2005), available at <http://ssrn.com/ abstract= 922524>.

F Ortino, 'From "Non-discrimination" to "Reasonableness": A Paradigm Shift in International Economic Law' in F Palermo, G Poggeschi, G Rautz, and J Woelk (eds), *Globalization, Technologies and Legal Revolution: Liber Amicorum in Memory of Sergio Ortino* (Nomos Verlagsgesellschaft 2012) 13–60.

F Ortino, *The Origin and Evolution of Investment Treaty Standards: Stability, Value, and Reasonableness* (OUP 2019).

P

FI Paddeu and K Parlett, 'COVID-19 and Investment Treaty Claims' Kluwer Arbitration Blog (30 March 2020), available at <http://arbitrationblog.kluwerarbitration.com/2020/03/30/covid-19-and-investment-treaty-claims/>.

J Paine, 'Autonomy to Set the Level of Regulatory Protection in International Investment Law' (2021) 70 ICLQ 697.

J Paine, 'Deference and Other Standards of Review in International Adjudication' (2021) 22 The Law and Practice of International Courts and Tribunals 431.

F Palombino, *Fair and Equitable Treatment and the Fabric of General Principles* (Asser Press 2018).

A Papadelli, *Beweislastverteilung bei der privaten Durchsetzung des Kartellrechts. Eine rechtsvergleichende Studie* (LIT Verlag 2010).

M Paparinskis, *The International Minimum Standard and Fair and Equitable Treatment* (OUP 2013).

M Paparinskis, 'MFN Clauses and International Dispute Settlement: Moving beyond Maffezini and Plama?' (2011) 26 ICSID Review 14.

M Paparinskis, 'MFN Clauses and Substantive Treatment: A Law of Treaties Perspective of the "Conventional Wisdom"' (2018) 112 AJIL Unbound 49.

L Paradell Trius, 'The Legitimacy of Investment Treaties: Between Exit, Voice and James Crawford's Quest for a More Democratic International Law' in C Chinkin and F Baetens (eds), *Sovereignty, Statehood and State Responsibility: Essays in Honour of James Crawford* (CUP 2015) 90–109.

K Parlett, 'The PCIJ's Opinion in *Jurisdiction of the Courts of Danzig*. Individual Rights under Treaties' (2008) 10 Journal of History of International Law 119.

J Paulsson, *Denial of Justice in International Law* (CUP 2005).

J Paulsson, 'Indirect Expropriation in Investment treaty Arbitrations' in J Paulsson and Z Douglas (eds), *Arbitrating Foreign Investment Disputes* (Kluwer Law International 2004) 145–158.

J Paulsson, 'The Role of Precedent in Investment Treaty Arbitration' in K Yannaca-Small (ed), *Arbitration Under International Investment Agreements: A Guide to the Key Issues* (2nd edn, OUP 2018) 81–100.

J Pauwelyn, 'WTO Dispute Settlement Post 2019: What to Expect? (2019) 22 JIEL 297.
J Pauwelyn, 'The WTO Agreement on Sanitary and Phytosanitary (SPS) Measures as Applied in the First Three SPS Disputes, *EC—Hormones, Australia—Salmon* and *Japan—Varietals*' (1999) 2 JIEL 641.
M Pearson, 'Religious Discrimination and the "Hierarchy of Rights": Non-existent, Appropriate or Problematic?' (2016) 16 International Journal of Discrimination and the Law 37.
M Pellonpää and M Fitzmaurice, 'Taking of Property in the Practice of the Iran-United States Claims Tribunal' (1988) 19 Netherlands Yearbook of International Law 53.
F Pérez-Aznar, 'The Fictions and Realities of MFN Clauses in International Investment Agreements' (2018) 112 AJIL Unbound 55.
E-U Petersmann, 'The WTO Constitution and Human Rights' (2000) 3 JIEL 19.
E-U Petersmann, 'Human Rights, International Economic Law and Constitutional Justice: A Rejoinder' (2008) 19 EJIL 955.
E-U Petersmann, *Transforming World Trade and Investment Law for Sustainable Development* (OUP 2022).
M Pinchis, 'The Ancestry of "Equitable Treatment" in Trade Lessons from the League of Nations during the Inter-War Period' (2014) 15 JWIT 13.
M Polkinghorne and CB Rosenberg, 'The Adverse Inference in ICSID Practice' (2015) 30 ICSID Review 741.
MC Porterfield, 'State Practice and the (Purported) Obligation under Customary International Law to Provide Compensation for Regulatory Expropriations' (2011) 37 North Carolina Journal of International Law 159.
J Potts, 'Stabilizing the Role of Umbrella Clauses in Bilateral Investment Treaties: Intent, Relience and Internationalization' (2011) 51 Virginia Journal of International Law 1005.
D Prévost, 'National Treatment in the SPS Agreement: A sui generis obligation' in A Kamperman Sanders (ed), *The Principle of National Treatment in International Economic Law: Trade, Investment and Intellectual Property* (Edward Elgar 2014) 125–155.
RA Primus, 'Equal Protection and Disparate Impact: Round Three' (2003) 117 Harvard Law Review 494.
S Puig, 'Investor-State Tribunals & Constitutional Courts: The Sweeteners Saga' (2013) 5 Mexican Law Review 199.
S Puig, 'Social Capital in the Arbitration Market' (2014) 25 EJIL 387.
S Puig and A Strezhnev, 'The David Effect and ISDS' (2017) 28 EJIL 731.
S Puig, 'Contextualizing Cost Shifting in Investment Treaty Arbitration' (2019) 58 Virginia Journal of International Law 261.

Q

Y Qin, 'Defining Nondiscrimination under the law of the World Trade Organization' (2005) 23 Boston University International Law Journal 215.
G Quinn and E Flynn, 'Transatlantic Borrowings: The Past and Future of EU Non-Discrimination Law and Policy on the Ground of Disability' (2012) 60 American Journal of Comparative Law 23.

R

Y Radi, 'The Application of the Most-Favoured-Nation Clause to the Dispute Settlement Provisions of Bilateral Investment Treaties: Domesticating the "Trojan Horse'" (2007)18 EJIL 757.
R Radović, 'Between Rights and Remedies: The Access to Investment Treaty Arbitration as a Substantive Right of Foreign Investors' (2019) 10 Journal of International Dispute Settlement 42.
P Ranjan, 'Investor-State Dispute Settlement and Tax Matters: Limitations on State's Sovereign Right to Tax' (2023) 31 Asia Pacific Law Review 219.
J Rawls, *Theory of Justice* (revised edn, Harvard University Press 1999).

P Raynaud, 'Le juge, la loi, le droit: de Platon à Aristote' in O Cayla and M-F Renoux-Zagamé (eds), *L'office de juge: part de souveraineté ou puissance nulle* (Bruylant, LGDJ 2001).

A Reinisch, 'Most Favoured Nation Treatment' in in M Bungenberg and others (eds), *International Investment Law* (CH Beck, Hart, Nomos 2015) 807–845.

A Reinisch, 'Expropriation' in P Muchlinski, F Ortino, and C Schreuer (eds), *The Oxford Handbook of International Investment Law* (OUP 2008) 407–458.

A Reinisch, 'National Treatment' in M Bungenberg and others (eds), *International Investment Law* (CH Beck, Hart, Nomos 2015) 846–869.

A Reinsich, 'Will the EU's Proposal Concerning an Investment Court System for CETA and TTIP Lead to Enforceable Awards?—The Limits of Modifying the ICSID Convention and the Nature of Investment Arbitration' (2016) 19 JIEL 761.

A Reinisch and C Schreuer, *International Protection of Investments: The Substantive Standards* (CUP 2020).

A Reinisch and SW Schill (eds), *Investment Protection Standards and the Rule of Law* (OUP 2023).

MW Reisman, 'The View from the New Haven School of International Law' (1992) 86 ASIL Proceedings 118.

MW Reisman and RD Sloane, 'Indirect Expropriation and its Valuation in the BIT Generation' (2004) 74 BYIL 115.

O Repousis, and M Risvas, 'International Investment Law and the (International) Rule of Law: The Case of the EU Renewable Energy Industry' in R Leal-Arcas (ed), *International Trade, Investment and the Rule of Law* (Chisinau 2010) 131–156.

A Rigo Sureda, 'The Umbrella Clause' in M Kinnear and others (eds), *Building International Investment Law: The First 50 Years of ICSID* (Kluwer Law International 2016) 375–388.

M Risvas, 'Non-discrimination in International Economic Law and Sovereign Equality of States: An Historical Perspective' (2017) 39 Houston Journal of International Law 79.

M Risvas, 'Non-discrimination and the Protection of Foreign Investments in the Context of an Armed Conflict' in K Fach Gómez, A Gourgourinis, and C Titi (eds), *International Investment Law and the Law of Armed Conflict (European Yearbook of International Economic Law: Special Issue)* (Springer 2019) 199–215.

M Risvas, 'International Law as the Basis for Extending Arbitration Agreements concluded by States or State Entities to Non-Signatories' (2022) 71 ICLQ 183.

M Risvas, 'Review and Enforcement of Arbitral Awards in International Investment Law and General Public International Law' in C Tams, R Hofmann, and S Schill (eds), *Investment Law as a Motor of General International Law* (Edward Elgar 2023) 375–400.

A Roberts, 'Power and Persuasion in Investment Treaty Interpretation: The Dual Role of States' (2010) 104(2) AJIL 179.

A Roberts and T St John, 'Complex Designers and Emergent Design: Reforming the Investment Treaty System' (2022) 116 AJIL 96.

E Roucounas, *A Landscape of Contemporary Theories of International Law* (Brill Nijhoff 2019).

AW Rovine, 'Allocation of Costs in Recent ICSID Awards' in DD Caron and others (eds), *Practising Virtue: Inside International Arbitration* (OUP 2015) 658–688.

N Rubins, T-N Papanastastiou, and NS Kinsella, *International Investment, Political Risk, and Dispute Resolution: A Practitioner's Guide* (2nd OUP 2020).

S

B Sabahi, *Compensation and Restitution in Investor–State Arbitration: Principles and Practice* (OUP 2011).

B Sabahi, 'National Treatment—Is Discriminatory Intent Relevant' in T Weiler (ed), *Investment Treaty Arbitration and International* Law, *Vol 2* (JurisNet 2008) 269–297.

B Sabahi, N Rubins, and D Wallace, Jr, *Investor-State Arbitration* (2nd edn, OUP 2019).

L Sabanogullari, *General Exceptions Clauses in International Investment Law: The Recalibration of Investment Agreements via WTO-Based Flexibilities* (Nomos 2018).

D Sabbagh, 'La discrimination sur le lieu de travail: éléments pour une comparaison transatlantique' (2019) 102 Droit et Société 321.

S Sacco and MC Fernández-Fonseca, 'National Treatment in Investment Arbitration' in JA Huerta-Goldman, A Romanetti, and FX Stirnimann (eds), *WTO Litigation, Investment Arbitration, and Commercial Arbitration* (Kluwer Law International 2013) 239–262.

G Sacerdoti, 'Trade and Investment Law: Institutional Differences and Substantive Similarities' (2014) 9 Jerusalem Review of Legal Studies 1.

B Sage-Fuller, *The Precautionary Principle in Marine Environmental Law with Special References to High Risk Vessels* (Routledge 2013).

JW Salacuse, *The Law of Investment Treaties* (OUP 2010).

JW Salacuse and NP Sullivan, 'Do BITs Really Work? An Evaluation of Bilateral Investment Treaties and Their Grand Bargain' (2005) 46 Harvard International Law Journal 67.

CW Sanchirico, 'The Burden of Proof in Civil Litigation: A Simple Model of Mechanism Design' (1997) 17 International Review of Law and Economics 431.

D Sarooshi, 'The Move from Institutions: The Case of the World Trade Organization' (2006) 100 ASIL Proceeding 298.

D Sarooshi, 'Sovereignty, Economic Autonomy, the United States, and the International Trading System: Representations of a Relationship' (2004) 15 EJIL 651.

D Sarooshi and M Risvas, 'Foundational Concept—State Responsibility' in K Nadakavukaren Schefer and T Cottier (eds), *Elgar Encyclopedia of International Economic Law* (forthcoming).

D Sarooshi, 'Investment Treaty Arbitration and the World Trade Organization: What Role for Systemic Values in the Resolution of International Economic Disputes?' (2014) 49 Texas International Law Journal 445.

A Sarvarian, 'Procedural Economy at the International Court of Justice' (2019) 18 The Law and Practice of International Courts and Tribunals 74.

S Sattar, 'Document Production and the 2010 IBA Rules on the Taking of Evidence in International Arbitration: a Commentary' (2011) 14 International Arbitration Law Review 210.

M Sattorova, *The Impact of Investment Treaty Law on Host States: Enabling Good Governance?* (Hart 2018).

W Schabas, *The European Convention on Human Rights: A Commentary* (OUP 2015).

S Schacherer, *Sustainable Development in EU Foreign Investment Law* (Brill Nijhoff 2021).

S Schacherer, 'TPP, CETA and TTIP between innovation and consolidation - resolving Investor-State disputes under mega-regionals' (2016) 7 Journal of International Dispute Settlement 628.

MP Scharf and D Margaux, 'The International Court of Justice's Treatment of Circumstantial Evidence and Adverse Inferences' (2012) 13 Chicago Journal of International Law 123.

SW Schill, 'Tearing down the Great Wall: The New Generation Investment Treaties of the People's Republic of China' (2007) 15 Cardozo Journal of International and Comparative Law 73.

SW Schill, 'Mulitilateralizing Investment Treaties through Most-Favored-Nation Clauses' (2009) 27 Berkeley Journal of International Law 502.

SW Schill, 'Enabling Private Ordering, Function, Scope and Effect of Umbrella Clauses in International Investment Treaties' (2009) 18 Minnesota Journal of International Law 1.

SW Schill, *The Multilateralization of International Investment Law* (CUP 2009).

SW Schill (ed), *International Investment Law and Comparative Public Law* (OUP 2010).

SW Schill, 'System-Building in Investment Treaty Arbitration and Lawmaking' (2011) 12 German Law Journal 108.

SW Schill, 'W(h)ither Fragmentation? On the Literature and Sociology of International Investment Law' (2011) 22 EJIL 875.

SW Schill, 'Allocating Adjudicatory Authority: Most-Favoured-Nation Clauses as a Basis of Jurisdiction—A Reply to Zachary Douglas' (2011) 2 Journal of International Dispute Settlement 353.

SW Schill, 'MFN Clauses as Bilateral Commitments to Multilateralism—A Reply to Simon Batifort and J Benton Heath' (2018) 111 AJIL 914.

SW Schill and G Vidigal, 'Investment Dispute Settlement à la carte: A Proposal for the Reform of Investor–State Dispute Settlement' in M Elsig, R Polanco, and P van den Bossche (eds), *International Economic Dispute Settlement Demise or Transformation?* (CUP 2021) 220–263.

D Schneiderman, *Constitutionalizing Economic Globalization: Investment Rules and Democracy's Promise* (CUP 2008).

D Schneiderman, *Investment Law's Alibis:* Colonialism, Imperialism, *Debt and Development* (CUP 2022).

CH Schreuer, 'Protection Against Arbitrary or Discriminatory Measures' in CA Rogers and RP Alford (eds), *The Future of Investment Arbitration* (OUP 2009) 183–198.

C Schreuer, 'Denunciation of the ICSID Convention and Consent to Arbitration' in M Waibel and others (eds), *The Backlash against Investment Arbitration: Perceptions and Reality* (Kluwer Law International 2010) 353–368.

C Schreuer, 'From ICSID Annulment to Appeal Half Way Down the Slippery Slope' (2011) 10 The Law and Practice of International Courts and Tribunals 211.

C Schreuer and M Weiniger, 'A Doctrine of Precedent?' in P Muchlinski, F Ortino, and C Schreuer (eds), *The Oxford Handbook of International Investment Law* (OUP 2008) 1188–1206.

T Schultz and C Dupont, 'Investment Arbitration: Promoting the Rule of Law or Over-empowering Investors? A Quantitative Empirical Study' (2014) 25 EJIL 1147.

MA Schuman, 'The Politics of Presumption: St. Mary's Honor Center v. Hicks and the Burdens of Proof in Employment Discrimination Cases' (1993) 9 St John's Journal of Legal Commentary 67.

B Schwartz, *French Administrative Law and the Common-Law World* (The Lawbook Exchange Ltd 2006).

G Schwarzenberger, 'Most Favoured Nation in British State Practice' (1945) 22 BYIL 96.

G Schwarzenberger, 'The Abs-Shawcross Draft Convention on Investments Abroad: A Critical Commentary' (1961) 14 Current Legal Problems 213.

J Scott, *The WTO Agreement on Sanitary and Phytosanitary Measures: A Commentary* (OUP 2007).

A Seibert-Fohr, 'Article 2 SPS' in R Wolfrum, P-T Stoll, and A Seibert-Fohr (eds), *WTO—Technical Barriers and SPS Measures* (Brill 2007) 392–411.

I Seidl-Hohenveldern, 'Notes and Comments: Chilean Copper Nationalization Cases Before German Courts' (1975) 69 AJIL 110.

M Selmi, 'Proving Intentional Discrimination: The Reality of Supreme Court Rhetoric' (1997) 86 Georgetown Law Journal 279.

M Selmi, 'Was the Disparate Impact Theory a Mistake?' (2006) 53 UCLA Law Review 701.

M Selucká, M Grochová, and J Komendová, 'Czech Republic' in M Mercat-Bruns, DB Oppenheimer, and C Sartorius (eds), *Comparative Perspectives on the Enforcement and Effectiveness of Antidiscrimination Law* (Springer 2018) 153–173.

A Sen, *Inequality Reexamined* (OUP 1995).

W Shan and N Gallagher, *Chinese Investment Treaties: Policies and Practice* (OUP 2009).

W Shan, N Gallagher, and S Zhang, 'National Treatment for Foreign Investment in China: A Changing Landscape' (2012) 27 ICSID Review 120.

Y Shany, 'Toward a General Margin of Appreciation Doctrine in International Law?' (2005) 16 EJIL 907.

Y Shany, 'No Longer a Weak Department of Power? Reflections on the Emergence of a New International Judiciary' (2009) 20 EJIL 73.

U Sharma, 'The Invisible Stigmatisation of Female Practitioners in International Arbitration' (2021) 17 International Journal of Law in Context 371.

T Sharmin and E Laryea, 'Australian COVID-19 Measures and its International Investment Obligations' (2022) 21 Journal of International Trade Law and Policy 182.

JK Sharpe, 'Drawing Adverse Inferences from Non-Production of Evidence' (2006) 22 Arbitration International 549.

E Shirlow, 'Deference and Indirect Expropriation Analysis in International Investment Law: Observations on Current Approaches and Frameworks for Future Analysis' (2014) 29 ICSID Review 595.

E Shirlow, *Judging at the Interface: Deference to Domestic Authority in International Adjudication* (CUP 2021).

E Shirlow, 'Deference and the Practice of International Law' (2022) 21 The Law and Practice of International Courts and Tribunals 457.

E Shirlow and M Waibel, 'A Sliding Scale Approach to *Travaux* in Treaty Interpretation: The Case of Investment Treaties' BYIL (forthcoming).

L Shore, 'Document Production, Witness Statements, and Cross-Examination: The Enduring Tensions in International Arbitration' in SL Brekoulakis, JDM Lew, and LA Mistelis (eds), *The Evolution and Future of International Arbitration* (Kluwer Law International 2016) 39–45.

A Sinclair, 'The Origins of the Umbrella Clause in the International Law of Investment Protection' (2004) 20 Arbitration International 411.

A Skontzos, 'The Burden and Standard of Proof in Model International Procedural Law: Dealing with the Burden and Standard of Proof in International Disputes' (2018) 23 Uniform Law Review 569.

LV Skovgaard Poulsen, *Bounded Rationality and Economic Diplomacy: The Politics of Investment Treaties in Developing Countries* (CUP 2015).

A Smith, *An Inquiry into the Nature and Causes of The Wealth of the* Nations, *Vol 2* (Clarendon Press 1869).

RC Snyder, 'The Most Favored Nation Clause and Recent Trade Practices' (1940) 55 Political Science Quarterly 77.

I Solanke, *Discrimination as Stigma: A Theory of Anti-discrimination Law* (Hart 2017).

MJ Solis, 'Adverse Inferences in Investor–State Arbitration' (2018) 34 Arbitration International 79.

FG Sourgens, 'Reason and Reasonableness: The Necessary Diversity of the Common Law' (2014) 67 Maine Law Review 73.

FG Sourgens, K Duggal, and IA Laird, *Evidence in International Investment Arbitration* (OUP 2018).

S Spears, 'The Quest for Policy Space in a New Generation of International Investment Agreements' (2010) 13 JIEL 1037.

JE Spero and JA Hart, *The Politics of International Economic Relations* (Wadsworth Publishing 2010).

O Spiermann, *International Legal Argument in the Permanent Court of International Justice* (CUP Cambridge 2005).

T St John, *The Rise of Investor-State Arbitration: Politics, Law, and Unintended Consequences* (OUP 2018).

S Steininger, 'What's Human Rights Got To Do With It? An Empirical Analysis of Human Rights References in Investment Arbitration' (2018) 31 Leiden Journal of International Law 33.

G Stephens-Chu, 'Discrimination Claims by Foreign Investors in the Aftermath of the COVID-19 Pandemic' in Y Levashova and P Accaoui Lorfing (eds), *Balancing the Protection of Foreign Investors and States Responses in the Post-Pandemic World* (Kluwer Law International 2022) 171–189.

A Stone Sweet, 'Investor-State Arbitration: Proportionality's New Frontier' (2010) 4(1) Law & Ethics of Human Rights 48.

JC Suk, 'From Antidiscrimination to Equality: Stereotypes and the Life Cycle in the United States and Europe' (2012) 60 American Journal of Comparative Law 75.

M Suleimenova, *MFN Standard as Substantive Treatment* (Nomos 2019).

K Sulyok, 'Judicial Deference and Science' (2022) 21 The Law and Practice of International Courts and Tribunals 448.

C Sunstein, D Schkade, and LM Ellman, *Are Judges Political?: An Empirical Analysis of the Federal Judiciary* (Brookings Institution 2006).

O Suttle, *Distributive Justice and World Trade Law: A Political Theory of International Trade Regulation* (CUP 2018).

AO Sykes, 'The Economic Structure of International Investment Agreements with Implications for treaty Interpretation and Design' (2019) 113 AJIL 482.

AO Sykes, 'The Least Restrictive Means' (2003) 70 The University of Chicago Law Review 403.

T

S Tabet, 'Beyond the Smoking Gun—Is Discriminatory Objective Necessary to Find a Breach of National Treatment' in T Weiler (ed), *Investment Treaty Arbitration and International* Law, *Vol 2* (JurisNet 2008) 299–313.

BZ Tamanaha, *On the Rule of Law: History, Politics, Theory* (CUP 2004).

D Tarullo, 'Logic, Myth, and the International Economic Order' (1985) 26 Harvard International Law Journal 533.

G Ténékidès, 'L'action des Nations unies contre la discrimination raciale' (1980) 168 RCADI 269.

JC Thomas and H Kaur Dhillon, 'The Foundations of Investment Treaty Arbitration: The ICSID Convention, Investment Treaties and the Review of Arbitration Awards' (2017) 32 ICSID Review 459.

R Thompson Ford, 'Bias in the Air: Rethinking Employment Discrimination Law' (2014) 66 Stanford Law Review 1381.

A Titi, *The Right to Regulate in International Investment Law* (Nomos 2013).

C Titi, 'Full Protection and Security, Arbitrary or Discriminatory Treatment and the Invisible EU Model BIT' (2014) 15 JWIT 534.

I Tourkochoriti, 'Jenkins v. Kingsgate and the Migration of the US Disparate Impact Doctrine in EU Law' in F Nicola and B Davies (eds), *EU Law Stories: Contextual and Critical Histories of European Jurisprudence* (CUP 2017) 418–445.

LE Trakman, 'Geopolitics, China, and Investor-State Arbitration' in L Toohey, CB Picker, and J Greenacre (eds), *China in the International Economic Order: New Directions and Changing Paradigms* (CUP 2015) 268–292.

A Trebilock, 'Approaches to Discrimination Claims: A Comparison of the Administrative Tribunals of the Asian Development Bank and the Inter-American Development Bank Group' (2022) 12 Asian Journal of International Law 216.

A Trouwborst, *Precautionary Rights and Duties of States* (Martinus Nijhoff 2006).

S Tsakyrakis, 'Proportionality: An Assault on Human Rights?' (2009) 7 International Journal of Constitutional Law 468.

S Tsakyrakis, 'Proportionality: An Assault on Human Rights?: A Rejoinder to Madhav Khosla' (2010) 8 International Journal of Constitutional Law 307.

I Tudor, *The Fair and Equitable Treatment Standard in the International Law of Foreign Investment* (OUP 2007).

A Tussupov, *Corruption and Fraud in Investment Arbitration: Procedural and Substantive Challenges* (Springer 2022).

N Tzouvala, *Capitalism as Civilisation: A History of International Law* (CUP 2020).

U

I Uchkunova and O Temnikov, 'Toss Out the Baby and Put the Water to Bed: On MFN Clauses and the Significance of Treaty Interpretation' (2015) 30 ICSID Review 414.

V Ulfbeck and M-L Holle, 'Tort Law and Burden of Proof—Comparative Aspects. A Special Case for Enterprise Liability?' in H Koziol and BC Steininger (eds), *European Tort Law 2008* (Springer 2009) 26–48.

UNCTAD, Series on issues in international investment agreements, *National Treatment* (UN 1999).

UNCTAD, *Bilateral Investment Treaties 1995–2006: Trends in Investment Rulemaking* (UN 2007).

UNCTAD, *Fair and Equitable Treatment: UNCTAD Series on Issues in International Investment Agreements II* (UN 2012).

UNCTAD, *Expropriation: UNCTAD Series on Issues in International Investment Agreements II* (UN 2012).

FJ Urbina, *A Critique of Proportionality and Balancing* (CUP 2017).

E Ustor, ILC, 'The Most-Favoured-Nation Clause in the Law of Treaties: Working Paper Submitted by Mr. Endre Ustor, Special Rapporteur', A/CN.4/L.127, 19 June 1968.

V

V Vadi, *Proportionality, Reasonableness and Standards of Review in International Investment Law and Arbitration* (Edward Elgar 2018).

A van Aaken and J Kurtz, 'Prudence or Discrimination? Emergency Measures, the Global Financial Crisis and International Economic Law' (2009) 12 JIEL 859.

P Van en Bossche, 'Looking for Proportionality in WTO Law' (2008) 35 Legal Issues of Economic Integration 283.

G Van Harten, *Investment Treaty Arbitration and Public Law* (OUP 2006) 93.

G Van Harten, *The Trouble with Foreign Investor Protection* (OUP 2020).

G Van Harten and M Loughlin, 'Investment Treaty Arbitration as a Species of Global Administrative Law' (2006) 17 EJIL 121.

KJ Vandevelde, *The First Bilateral Investment Treaties U.S. Postwar Friendship, Commerce, and Navigation Treaties* (OUP 2017).

S Vasciannie, 'The Fair and Equitable Treatment Standard in International Investment Law and Practice' (1999) 70 BYIL 99.

VV Veeder, 'The Lena Goldfields Arbitration: The Historical Roots of Three Ideas' (1998) 47 ICLQ 747.

I Venzke, *How Interpretation makes International Law: On Semantic Change and Normative Twists* (OUP 2012).

G Verhoosel, 'The Use of Investor-State Arbitration under Bilateral Investment Treaties to Seek Relief for Breaches of WTO Law' (2003) 6 JIEL 493.

FO Vicuña, 'Reports of [Maffezini's] Demise have been Greatly Exaggerated' (2012) 3 Journal of International Dispute Settlement 299.

FO Vicuña, 'Some International Law Problems Posed by the Nationalization of the Copper Industry by Chile' (1973) 67 AJIL 711.

EW Vierdag, *The Concept of Discrimination in International Law, with Special References to Human Rights* (Martinus Nijhoff 1973).

J Viner, 'The Most-Favored-Nation Clause in American Commercial Treaties' (1924) 32 Journal of Political Economy 101.

JE Viñuales, *Foreign Investment and the Environment in International Law* (CUP 2012).

C Volpin, 'The Ball is in Your Court: Evidential Burden of Proof and the Proof-Proximity Principle in EU Competition Law' (2014) 51 Common Market Law Review 1159.

A von Bogdandy and I Venzke, 'Beyond Dispute: International Judicial Institutions as Lawmakers' (2011) 12 German Law Journal 971.

A von Bogdandy and I Venzke, 'In Whose Name? An Investigation of International Courts' Public Authority and Its Democratic Justification' (2012) 23 EJIL 7.

T Voon, 'Exploring the Meaning of Trade-Restrictiveness in the WTO' (2015) 14 World Trade Review 451.

W

D Walton, *Burden of Proof, Presumption and Argumentation* (CUP 2014).

M Waibel, *Sovereign Defaults before International Courts and Tribunals* (CUP 2011).

M Waibel and others (eds), *The Backlash against Investment Arbitration: Perceptions and Reality* (Kluwer Law International 2010).

M Waibel, 'Putting the MFN Genie Back in the Bottle' (2018) 112 AJIL Unbound 60.

M Wagner, 'Regulatory Space in International Trade Law and International Investment Law' (2014) 36 University of Pennsylvania Journal of International Law 1.

TW Wälde, 'The "Umbrella" Clause in Investment Arbitration: A Comment on Original Intentions and Recent Cases' (2006) 6 JWIT 183.

TW Wälde, 'Procedural Challenges in Investment Arbitration under the Shadow of the Dual Role of the State: Asymmetries and Tribunal's Duty to Ensure, Pro-actively the Equality of Arms' (2010) 26 Arbitration International 3.

TW Wälde and B Sabahi, 'Compensation, Damages, and Valuation' in P Muchlinski, F Ortino, and C Schreuer (eds), *The Oxford Handbook of International Investment Law* (OUP 2008) 1052–1119.

J Waldron, 'The Substance of Equality' (1991) 89 Michigan Law Review 1350.

J Waldron, *Law and Disagreement* (OUP 1999).

H Walker Jr, 'Modern Treaties of Friendship, Commerce and Navigation' (1958) 42 Minnesota Law Review 1491.

G Wang, *International Investment Law: A Chinese Perspective* (Routledge 2014).

A Wang, *The Interpretation and Application of the Most-Favored-Nation Clause in Investment Arbitration* (Brill Nijhoff 2022).

P Webb, *International Judicial Integration and Fragmentation* (OUP 2013).

T Weiler, 'Saving Oscar Chin: Non-Discrimination in International Investment Law' in T Weiler (ed), *International Investment Law and Arbitration: Leading Cases from the ICSID, NAFTA, Bilateral Treaties and Customary International Law* (Cameron May 2005) 557–595.

T Weiler, *The Interpretation of International Investment* Law, Equality, *Discrimination and Minimum in Historical Context* (Martinus Nijhoff 2013).

P Westen, 'The Empty Idea of Equality' (1982) 95 Harvard Law Review 537.

G White, *Nationalisation of Foreign Property* (Stevens and Sons Ltd 1961).

J Wong, 'Umbrella Clauses in Bilateral Investment Treaties: of Breaches of Contract, Treaty Violations, and the Divide Between Developing and Developed Countries in Foreign Investment Disputes' (2006) 14 George Mason Law Review 135.

Y

JW Yackee, 'Expelling the "Sinister Vilgrain": Nationalization, Diplomacy, and Sugar in the People's Republic of Congo, 1970–1978' (2021) 44 French Historical Studies 119.

JW Yackee, 'Investor-State Dispute Settlement at the Dawn of International Investment Law: France, Mauritania, and the Nationalization of the MIFERMA Iron Ore Operations' (2019) 59 American Journal of Legal History 71.

JW Yackee, 'The First Investor-State Arbitration' (2016) 17 JWIT 40.

Z

F Zarbiyev, 'On the Judge Centredness of the International Legal Self' (2021) 32 EJIL 1139.

Q Zhang and A Mitchell, 'Data Localization and the National Treatment Obligation in International Investment Treaties' (2022) 21 WTR 391.

W Zhou, 'The Role of Regulatory Purpose under Article III:2 and 4—Toward Consistency between Negotiating History and WTO Jurisprudence' (2012) 11 WTR 81.

W Zhou, H Gao, and X Bai, 'Building a Market Economy through WTO-inspired Reform of State-Owned Enterprises in China' (2019) 68 ICLQ 977.

AR Ziegler, 'Investment Law in Conflict with WTO Law' in M Bungenberg and others (eds), *International Investment Law* (CH Beck, Hart, Nomos 2015) 1784–1801.

MJ Zimmer, 'A Chain of Inferences Proving Discrimination' (2008) 79 University of Colorado Law Review 1243.

V Zivkovic, 'Fair and Equitable Treatment between the International and National Rule of Law' (2019) 20 JWIT 513.

V Zivkovic, 'Pursuing and Reimagining the International Rule of Law through International Investment Law' (2020) 12 Hague Journal on the Rule of Law 1.

V Zivkovic, *International Rule of Law through International Investment Law: Strengths, Challenges and Opportunities* (Elsevier 2018).

J Zrilič, 'Are We in for a New Wave of Investment Arbitrations?: Russia's Measures Against Foreign Investors and Investment Treaty Implications' VerfBlog (21 March 2022), available at <https://verfassungsblog.de/are-we-in-for-a-new-wave-of-investment-arbitrations/>.

Index

For the benefit of digital users, indexed terms that span two pages (e.g., 52–53) may, on occasion, appear on only one of those pages.